SSSP

Springer
Series in
Social
Psychology

Advisory Editor:
Robert F. Kidd

Springer Series in Social Psychology

Advisory Editor: Robert F. Kidd

SSSP

James R. Averill

Anger and Aggression
An Essay on Emotion

Springer-Verlag New York Heidelberg Berlin

James R. Averill
Department of Psychology
Tobin Hall
University of Massachusetts—Amherst
Amherst, Massachusetts 01003 U.S.A.

Robert F. Kidd, *Advisory Editor*
Department of Psychology
Boston University
Boston, Massachusetts 02215 U.S.A.

Library of Congress Cataloging in Publication Data
Averill, James R.
  Anger and aggression.
  (Springer series in social psychology)
  Bibliography: p.
  Includes index.
  1. Anger.   2. Aggressiveness (Psychology)
I. Title.   II. Series.
BF575.A5A93   1982   152.4   82-10549

With 3 Figures.

Typeset by Publisher's Service, Bozeman, Montana.
Printed and bound by R. R. Donnelley & Sons Company, Harrisonburg, Virginia.
Printed in the United States of America.

9 8 7 6 5 4 3 2 1

ISBN 0-387-90719-X   Springer-Verlag   New York   Heidelberg   Berlin
ISBN 3-540-90719-X   Springer-Verlag   Berlin   Heidelberg   New York

To Judy, and Laurie and Andrea

Preface

In recent years, a great deal has been written on the topic of aggression; another book on the same topic might seem superfluous at this time. However, the present volume is not just—or even primarily—about aggression. It is, rather, a book on anger. Anger and aggression are closely related phenomena, and it is not possible to discuss one without the other. Yet, not all anger is aggressive, nor can all aggression be attributed to anger. Therefore, somewhat different considerations apply to each. Even more importantly, the type of theoretical generalizations one can make differs depending upon whether the primary focus is on anger or aggression. The present volume is subtitled "an essay on emotion." This indicates that the generalizations to be drawn have more to do with emotional responses (e.g., grief, love, envy, etc.) than with various forms of aggression (e.g., riots, war, crimes of violence, etc.). Stated somewhat differently, anger is here being used as a paradigm case for the study of emotion, not for the study of aggression.

While emphasizing the implications of the present study for theories of emotion, I do not want to understate the importance of anger as a phenomenon of interest in its own right. Much violence is committed in the name of anger, or excused after the fact by an appeal to anger. The inability to express anger also has been implicated in a wide range of psychological disorders. However, before we can hope to understand and ultimately control such undesirable vicissitudes of anger, we must know more about the reasons for and consequences of anger as it occurs normally. To contribute to such knowledge is one purpose of this work.

If we are to understand a phenomenon such as anger, we cannot afford to be parochial, limiting ourselves to artificial disciplinary boundaries or to a favored methodology. Rather, we must bring to bear on the issue data from whatever sources are relevant. In the case of anger, the sources are many. The first complete work on anger was written nearly 2,000 years ago by the Roman philosopher, Seneca. In the centuries that have followed, there has been a steady stream of commentaries, debates, and ethical teachings on the nature of anger. These often provide considerable insight into the social norms and functions of anger. Also instructive in this respect are legal studies dealing with the adjudication of crimes of passion, i.e., homicides committed out of anger. Of course, it would be difficult to understand anger within our own society without cross-cultural comparisons; hence, anthropological studies of anger-like syndromes in other societies must be taken into consideration. In recent years, a great deal of information has been collected on the physiological bases and evolutionary significance of various forms of aggression. This information, too, needs to be integrated into a comprehensive analysis of anger. The psychological clinic provides yet another source of data, i.e., on the psychodynamics of anger and aggression gone awry. And, finally, experimental social psychologists have conducted many hundreds of studies over the last several decades elucidating some of the mechanisms that help mediate anger and aggression in normal populations.

The above sources of information (historical, legal, cross-cultural, biological, clinical, and psychological) complement one another, and all are drawn upon in the present volume in an attempt to understand the phenomenon of anger. But in spite of the wealth of data already available, there is still an embarrassing lack of information about some of the most elementary aspects of anger. How often do people become angry? at whom? for what reasons? and to what effect? Obviously, any adequate analysis of anger cannot proceed without answers to questions such as these.

In order to provide a more adequate empirical foundation for theory construction, about half the volume is devoted to the presentation of original data on the everyday experience of anger. These data, based on a series of written interviews (detailed questionnaires), describe the typical experience of anger, both from the angry person's and the target's point of view. Comparisons are also made between anger and a closely related experience, annoyance; between short-term and long-term anger; and between anger as experienced by men and women. Together, these studies provide a great deal of normative data on anger as it occurs in everyday affairs.

With regard to theory, the present analysis might best be described as "social-constructivist." To adumbrate briefly, anger is conceived of as a socially constituted syndrome—a transitory social role, so to speak. Such a conception does not deny the importance of biological factors; it does, however, focus attention on the functions that anger might serve within broader social systems. Thus, anger is not viewed here as a remnant of our phylogenetic past, that serves primarily to disrupt and disturb social relations. Such a view might be comforting to our self-image, but it does little to advance our understanding; nor does it conform well to the everyday experience of anger as reported by most people.

No one is ever the sole author of a book like this. In collecting the data for the studies reported in the book, and in writing the book itself, I have benefited from the assistance of numerous students and colleagues. I owe special thanks to Patricia Jeney, who assisted with the construction of the questionnaires and the collection of the data for the initial studies; to Doug Frost, who was responsible for most of the data analyses and who co-authored Chapter 13, the chapter on sex differences; to Bram Fridhandler, whose Master's thesis forms the basis for Chapter 12, the chapter on the temporal dimensions of anger; and to Barbara Sabol, who helped in ways too numerous to mention. The entire manuscript was read by Jeff Goldstein and Bob Kidd. Without their comments, the book would be more tedious and less informative than it is. The fact that I did not follow all of their suggestions (more out of ennui than out of disagreement) accounts for some of the shortcomings that remain. I also want to thank the staff at Springer-Verlag for both their friendliness and professionalism in seeing the book through publication. Finally, the research reported in the book was made possible, in part, by grants from the National Institute of Mental Health (MH22299) and the National Science Foundation (BNS-7904786).

Amherst, Massachusetts   James R. Averill

Contents

Part I

Perspectives on Anger and Aggression

Chapter 1

The Nature of Emotion

That anger is an emotion no one would deny. But what is an emotion? Few other questions in the history of psychology have proven as troublesome as this one. Surfeited by too much reading on the topic, William James (1890) commented that he would "as lief read verbal descriptions of the shapes of the rocks on a New Hampshire farm" as toil again through the "classic works" on emotion. Nowhere, James complained, do such works give "a central point of view, or a deductive or generative principle" (p. 448). Anyone familiar with the rocky soil of New England and with the classic works to which James referred can readily sympathize with the feeling of frustration which he expressed. James's own deductive principle—that bodily changes follow directly the perception of an exciting event and that an emotion is the feeling of those changes as they occur—has continued to stimulate psychological thought, but is quite inadequate as a general theory of emotion. In the 100 years since James first wrote on the topic of emotion, various other principles have been proposed, but none has proven to be enduring or widely accepted.

Part of the problem is that psychologists, in their search for simplifying principles, have tended to ignore the very phenomena they wish to explain—anger, fear, grief, jealousy, love, envy, hope, joy, and the myriad of other emotions experienced in everyday life. Surely there must be a middle ground between the intuitive and quasi-literary descriptions characteristic of the classic works on emotion and oversimplified "deductive or generative" principles. The present volume attempts to explore that middle ground. Our focus will be on anger and, because of its close association with anger, on aggression. The hope is that by examining a single emotion in considerable detail, we will be able to gain a better understanding of emotional processes in general.

The approach taken in this volume is largely inductive. However, data collection and analysis never proceed without prior conceptualizations. The purpose of this introductory chapter is therefore to provide an overview of the theory (*point of view* might be a better term) that helped guide, and that was in turn guided by, the research reported in subsequent chapters. In the course of this overview, we will be taking up a wide range of topics of concern to any theory of emotion. These topics include, among other things, the place of emotion in the hierarchy of behavioral systems; the appraisal of emotional objects; the attribution of emotion to the self and others; the role of feedback (self-monitoring) in the experience of emotion; emotional feelings as rule-governed phenomena; language and emotion; the relationship between subjective experience and overt behavior; and the distinction between expressive reactions and instrumental responses.

These topics are not always discussed under separate headings. Rather, like the threads of a tapestry, they weave in and out of the chapter in a complex fashion. As far as organization is concerned, the first half of the chapter is devoted primarily to background considerations leading to a definition of emotion from a social-constructivist point of view. The second half of the chapter embroiders on this definition while critically examining a number of traditional issues in the psychology of emotion. To be more precise, emotions are here defined as socially constituted syndromes (transitory social roles) which include a person's appraisal of the situation, and which are interpreted as passions (things that happen to us) rather than as actions (things we do). As syndromes, emotions include both subjective (experiential) and objective (behavioral) elements. Any specific emotion, such as anger, refers to the way such elements are organized and the functions which they serve in relation to broader systems of behavior.

Most traditional theories have attempted to identify emotions with specific subsets of elements (e.g., felling states, physiological changes, expressive reactions) or else have postulated elements of a special kind (e.g., intervening drive variables) to which emotional concepts might refer. And when principles of organization have been sought, they have been sought primarily at a biological level of analysis. That is, emotions have been viewed as remnants of our phylogenetic past, with little functional significance in the modern world. By contrast, a constructivist view emphasizes the social origins and current functions of emotional syndromes.

In the next section I will explain more fully what I mean by "emotional syndromes," "systems of behavior," and "principles of organization." We will then be in a better position to develop a definition of emotion from a constructivist point of view.

The Place of Emotions in Systems of Behavior

Human behavior is seldom simple. This is perhaps more true of the emotions than of most other kinds of behavior typically studied by psychologists. Any theory of emotion that does not taken into account this complexity is bound to be inadequate. But how can justice be done to the complexity of behavior without violating the need for simplicity on a conceptual or theoretical level? A systems approach offers one answer to this question. Our first task, therefore, is to situate the emotions within the hierarchy of behavioral systems.

The term *system* can be applied to a wide range of phenomena—from molecules to orbiting planets to entire galaxies; from cells to organisms to species; from reflexes to behavioral syndromes (such as emotions) to personalities; from groups to institutions to societies. As this brief list illustrates, systems can be distinguished in terms of (a) levels of organization (e.g., molecules vs. galaxies) and (b) levels of analysis (e.g., physical vs. social).

Levels of Organization

The *level of organization* of a system refers to how complex the system is or how inclusive its boundaries are. Systems at different levels of organization can be arranged in a hierarchy, so that a system at one level (e.g., a galaxy) may include systems at a lower level (e.g., solar systems). To avoid terminological confusion, the term *system* is typically applied to the level of organization that serves as a convenient reference point. Systems at lower levels of organization may then be referred to as *subsystems* and, descending further in the hierarchy, as *elements*. Thus, Jupiter and its moons are an element in our solar system, and our solar system is but one of many subsystems that constitute our galaxy. Of course, for certain analyses Jupiter and its moons might be taken as a point of reference and treated as a system in its own right, in which case a single moon would be conceptualized as a subsystem, and so forth.

As explained below, the reference level that we will use for the analysis of emotion is that of the species (biological systems), the individual (psychological systems), and the society (sociocultural systems). The emotions may then be defined as subsystems of behavior or, to use a less relative term, as behavioral syndromes. As subsystems, or syndromes, the emotions can be further analyzed into elements, including physiological and expressive reactions, feelings, cognitions, and instrumental responses.

Levels of Analysis

Whereas the level of organization refers to the scope of a system, the *level of analysis* refers to the principles by which a system is organized. For the analysis of human behavior, it is generally sufficient to recognize three general levels of analysis—biological, psychological, and sociocultural. Systems at the biological level have their origins in the evolution of the species, that is, their principles of organization are genetic. The organizing principles of psychological systems are a product of individual experience or learning. In the case of sociocultural systems, the organizing principles are institutional and their origins are in the history of the society.

It will be noted that the term *level* has a somewhat different meaning when used with reference to levels of organization and levels of analysis. With regard to levels of organization, the meaning is quite clear: The higher the level, the more encompassing the organizational principles. By contrast, a sociocultural level of analysis is not necessarily more encompassing or broader in scope than is, say, a biological level of analysis, or vice versa. In speaking of levels of analysis, a different kind of hierarchy is often implied, but improperly so, I believe. I am referring to the commonplace assumption that a biological level of analysis is somehow more fundamental than an analysis at the psychological level, and that a psychological level of analysis is more fundamental than an analysis at the sociocultural level. That, however, is not the way the term *level of analysis* is being used in the present context. Indeed, if it were not for the weight of tradition, it would perhaps be better to do away with the term level of analysis altogether, and speak instead only of *principles of organization.*

The Relationships Between Levels of Organization and Levels of Analysis

Any behavioral system, subsystem, or element can be organized according to principles (or a combination of principles) that are sociocultural, psychological, or biological in origin. These relationships are diagrammed in Figure 1-1.

Using Figure 1-1 as a reference, we can speak of sociocultural systems, psychological systems, and biological systems of behavior, and correspondingly of subsystems and elements. However, since any system is influenced by principles at all three levels of analysis, a sociocultural system per se is an abstraction from reality; so too, of course, is a psychological or biological system.

Emotions Defined

Earlier, emotions were defined as subsystems of behavior, taking as a reference point biological, psychological, and sociocultural systems as a higher level of organization. Such a definition is not very useful, for it is much too inclusive—it could apply to practically any organized set of responses. Moreover, when focusing on the emotions per se, we could just as well speak of emotional systems (rather than of subsystems). In fact, for ease of discourse, it is often easier to do away with the systems terminology altogether (as long as we keep the basic ideas in mind). In subsequent discussion, therefore, I will frequently refer to the emotions as behavioral syndromes or as transitory social roles. More specifically, emotions may be defined as *socially constituted syndromes (transitory social roles)* which include an individual's *appraisal of the situation* and which are *interpreted as passions, rather than as actions* (Averill,

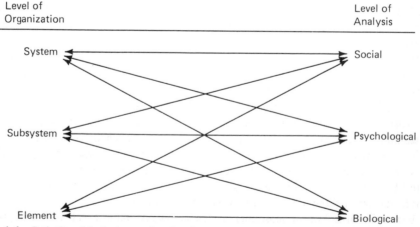

Fig. 1-1. Relationship between levels of organization and levels of analysis.

1980a, 1980b). In this section, we will explicate the three key (italicized) elements of this definition.

Emotions as Socially Constituted Syndromes (Transitory Social Roles)

The concepts of syndrome and social role both refer to subsystems of behavior at approximately the same level of organization. However, the two concepts have somewhat different connotations, and hence one can be used to elaborate on the other.

A syndrome is a set or population of responses that covary in a systematic fashion. A syndrome is thus not a unitary or invariant response. In fact, no single response element can be considered essential to most syndromes; moreover, the same response may often be incorporated into more than one syndrome. This fact needs to be emphasized, since it is central to the present definition of emotions as syndromes. The postulation of some "essential characteristic" has been a common feature of many theories of emotion. An emotion, many have argued, is really a pattern of physiological arousal, a neurological circuit, a feeling, or even a kind of cognitive appraisal. By contrast, the assumption underlying the definition of emotions as syndromes is that *no single response, or subset of responses, is a necessary or sufficient condition for the attribution of emotion*. The significance of this assumption will become evident in the subsequent discussion.

Since the concept of a syndrome is so frequently used in reference to disease states, its use in connection with emotional behavior may be somewhat misleading. In defining emotions as syndromes, I do not wish to reinforce the hoary notion that emotions are "diseases of the mind." Nor do I wish to imply that a biological or physiological level of analysis is the most appropriate for the study of emotional behavior. On the contrary, to the extent that any one level of analysis is more appropriate than another, I believe that the emotions can best be viewed as social constructions, that is, as *socially constituted* syndromes.

In order to bring out the implications of this last assumption, we can also conceptualize emotional syndromes as transitory social roles. The relationship between the syndrome concept and the role concept can be clarified in the following manner. Consider for a moment a typical disease syndrome. The symptomatology that a patient displays when ill is determined, in part, by the "sick role" he or she adopts (Parsons, 1951; Segall, 1976). This is true even in the cases where the source of the illness can be traced rather directly to some physiological cause, such as injury or infection. In the case of brain damage and other organically based mental disorders, the role expectations of the subject may actually outweigh physiological factors in determining the way the syndrome is manifested. And when we consider "functional" or neurotic disorders, such as a hysterical conversion reaction, organic factors are by definition absent or minimal. Syndromes of the latter type are constituted by the role being played; or, stated somewhat differently, the syndrome is a manifestation of the sick role as interpreted by the patient.

Extending this line of reasoning to the emotions, we can say that any given emotional syndrome represents the enactment of a transitory social role. Consider the following description by LaBarre (1947) of the behavior of a Kiowa woman at her brother's funeral:

> She wept in a frenzy, tore her hair, scratched her cheeks, and even tried to jump into the grave (being conveniently restrained from this by remoter relatives). I happened to know that she had not seen her brother for some time, and there was no particular love lost between them: she was merely carrying on the way a decent woman should among the Kiowa. Away from the grave, she was immediately chatting vivaciously about some other topic. Weeping is used differently among the Kiowas. (p. 55)[1]

From this description it would appear that the woman was only playing the role of a grief-stricken sister. But that is apparent only to an outsider; to the woman herself, any suggestion that she was merely playing a role would probably be met with incomprehension, if not outright antagonism. From her own perspective, and that of her culture, she was responding appropriately and, we may presume, with sincerity.

Let us take another example, one from our own cultural sphere. Linton (1936) has described the syndrome of romantic love in the following manner:

> All societies recognize that there are occasional violent emotional attachments between persons of opposite sex, but our present American culture is practically the only one which has attempted to capitalize on these and make them the basis for marriage. Most groups regard them as unfortunate and point out the victims of such attachments as horrible examples. Their rarity in most societies suggests that they are psychological abnormalities to which our own culture has attached an extraordinary value just as other cultures have attached extreme values to other abnormalities. The hero of the modern American movie is always a romantic lover just as the hero of the old Arab epic is always an epileptic. *A cynic might suspect that in any ordinary population the percentage of individuals with a capacity for romantic love of the Hollywood type was about as large as that of persons able to throw genuine epileptic fits. However, given a little social encouragement, either one can be adequately imitated without the performer admitting even to him/herself that the performance is not genuine.* (p. 175, italics added)[2]

One does not have to be a cynic to agree with the general drift of Linton's argument. All societies must have rules (norms) that stipulate, among other things, who is an eligible mate, the proper forms of courtship, when and how sexual intercourse can be performed, what obligations and rights the couple has toward one another and toward any children that might be conceived, and so forth. Through observation and direct experience (e.g., adolescent play), as well as through formal and informal didactic means (e.g., direct instructions, songs, literature, myths) couples learn how and when to apply the rules, so that their behavior follows an appropriate "script" (cf. Gagnon, 1974; Simon, 1974). In order to complete the script, each

---

[1] Reprinted by permission of Duke University Press, Durham, N.C. Copyright © 1947, Duke University Press.
[2] Reprinted by permission of Prentice-Hall, Inc., Englewood Cliffs, N.J. Copyright © 1936, renewed 1964, Prentice-Hall, Inc.

participant must play his or her role according to the relevant subset of rules. In the case of falling in love, which is only one variety of script relevant to mating, these roles are temporary—the young couple typically recovers. However, if the love script has followed its conventional course within our own society, it will result in marriage and a more permanent set of roles—that of husband and wife.

At this point, it might be objected that a role analysis is inappropriate to *real* emotions, for example, to "true" love. To say that a person is "playing a role" is meaningful only if there are other occasions when the person is *not* playing a role. By eliminating the contrast between true emotion and merely playing a role, have we not stretched the role concept beyond usefulness?

This objection raises some very complex issues, not only with respect to the concept of a social role but also with respect to the meaning of scientific concepts in general. Without going into a great deal of detail at this point, a few observations can nevertheless be made.

When, in ordinary discourse, I distinguish true emotion from mere role playing, I am making a relative contrast. That is, I am contrasting what I sincerely believe and feel with what I only feign to believe. However, if I shift my vantage point away from the ordinary, then what I sincerely believe and feel can often be viewed as, in some sense, feigned. The person suffering from hysterical blindness, for example, is not the same as a malingerer. The hysteric is sincere. He is playing the role of the blind man so convincingly that he is able to fool even himself.

In the case of a hysteric, of course, we do have a clear contrast; namely, with a person who is blind because of some physiological disorder. In other words, the contrast has shifted from one of sincere (hysterical blindness) versus feigned (malingering) to one of true blindness (a physiological disorder) versus hysterical blindness (a kind of role playing). In the case of ordinary emotional syndromes, there is no contrast comparable to that between a hysterical reaction and the corresponding physiological disorder. Yet by analogy one of the meanings of emotions as transitory social roles is evident from this example. As will be discussed more fully in Chapter 2, emotions are not "hard wired" into the person (either through prior experience or genetic determination), and they are not explicable in strictly mechanistic (e.g., physiological) terms.

But we can go even further, for not all behavior (in contrast to physiological reactions or disorders) can be usefully conceptualized in terms of social roles. I do many things each day that are idiosyncratic to myself or that are determined largely by the nonsocial aspects of the situation. In order to count as a social role, the behavior in question must fulfill at least three conditions: first, the behavior must be meaningful in terms of social expectations or rules of conduct; second, the person must attempt (on some level, not necessarily consciously) to conform his or her behavior to those expectations; and third, other persons in similar circumstances must be capable of performing the relevant (role) aspects of the behavior.[3]

---

[3] This condition requires some qualification. A social role may sometimes be created for a single individual, but that is unusual. More typically, what appears to be an idiosyncratic role is really a variation on a common theme. Outside of ritual contexts, most roles allow a good deal of improvisation, so that they may be enacted in different ways by different individuals. This is the case with most emotional roles.

Emotions Include an Individual's Appraisal of the Situation

Until recently, it was common to treat emotions as intervening "drive" variables, placing them in the same logical category as hunger and thirst. There is, however, an obvious difference between a typical emotion, such as fear, and a typical drive state, such as hunger. Hunger increases as a function of food deprivation, but fear occurs only if a person appraises a situation as dangerous or fearful. This distinction may seem trivially obvious. Nevertheless, its implications are far-reaching and often overlooked. For example, the distinction helps to shift the focus of theoretical concern away from the traditional analysis of emotional responses (and underlying physiological mechanisms) to an analysis of emotional appraisals (and underlying cognitive mechanisms). From the latter perspective, emotions are less like deficit (drive) states than they are like judgments about the world in which we live.

Let us consider for a moment some features of judgments in general and of emotional judgments (appraisals) in particular. A judgment cannot exist without content; that is, I can only make a judgment about something. That which a judgment is about is often called its *intentional object*. The latter may or may not correspond to an actually existing object. Thus, I can make judgments about unicorns, which exist only intentionally, or I can make judgments about horses, which exist both actually and intentionally. But even an actually existing horse is never judged in a completely realistic fashion, for all judgments necessarily involve some meaning imposed on, or abstracted from, events.

Emotions also have intentional objects. A person cannot be angry without being angry *at* something; fearful without being fearful *of* something; in love without being in love *with* somebody, and so forth. The intentionality of emotional objects is even more apparent than in the case of ordinary ("rational") judgments. Take love as an example. Love can transform even the most homely and uninteresting person into someone very special. The object of love is (among other things) the transformed person, not the actually existing person. After the ardor of passion has cooled, the lover may rightfully wonder what he or she formerly saw in the beloved. Similar considerations apply to anger, which can transform a friend or stranger into an enemy; of joy, which can make the entire world appear brighter; and so forth.

According to Solomon (1976), "An emotion is a basic judgment about our selves and our place in our world, the projection of the values and ideals, structures and mythologies, according to which we experience our lives" (pp. 186-187). This notion, that emotions are judgments, is not the common one, but it has an ancient and respected tradition. As we shall see in Chapter 4, the Greek and Roman Stoics regarded anger (as well as most other emotions) as basically false judgments.

Solomon (and the Stoics) go too far, I believe, when they define emotions as judgments. In the definition of emotion offered above, it is stipulated only that emotional syndromes *include* a person's appraisal of the situation. This terminology was deliberately chosen to emphasize the fact that the appraised (intentional) object of an emotion is an element of the entire syndrome (as opposed to a causal antecedent). And, as was discussed in the previous section, no single element, or subset of elements, is a necessary or sufficient condition for an emotional syndrome. This is as true of appraised objects as it is of physiological responses, expressive reactions, overt behavior, and the like. For example, a person may judge a situation as dangerous, and even try to escape, without being afraid; and conversely, a person may be afraid of harmless things (e.g., household spiders or garden snakes) even though he or she knows perfectly well that no danger exists. In other words, the object of an emotion may sometimes be absent; at other times, the object may be inappropriate, unreasonable, or in some sense false. Nevertheless, if a sufficient number of other elements of an emotion (fear, let us say) are present, then it may still be legitimate to characterize the entire syndrome as fear.

But even if we grant the above qualification,[4] it must still be admitted that the appraised object is probably the most consistent and surest guide to the identification of an emotional episode. Each kind of emotion has its own characteristic objects, reflecting a particular set of appraisals. The importance of this fact for distinguishing one kind of emotional syndrome from another is easily illustrated by the following thought experiment. Try to distinguish among anger, jealousy, and envy. Exactly the same physiological reactions, overt behavior, and so on can occur in each emotion. What distinguishes them is primarily their objects. The object of anger typically involves some appraised wrong; the object of jealousy, a potential loss to another; and the object of envy, the good fortune of another.

At this point, we should specify more precisely what constitutes the object of an emotion. The object of fear, for example, involves an appraised danger. This is the *instigation*. The object of fear also includes the state of affairs (e.g., a wild animal, high place, menacing stranger) that presents the danger. We may call this aspect the *target* of the emotion. But there is still a third aspect. Courage may have the same instigation (an appraised danger) and target (a wild animal) as does fear. The

---

[4] Not all theorists would grant the contention that the appraised object is not a necessary aspect of an emotional syndrome. For example, Kenny (1963) has maintained that "the most important difference between a sensation and an emotion is that emotions, unlike sensations, are *essentially* directed to objects" (p. 60, italics added). Thus, I may become angry at my wife for something she has done; I cannot, however, have a headache at my wife, no matter what she has done. This is not due to any psychological limitations on my part. Rather, it reflects a logical difference between concepts that refer to emotions and sensations. There are, however, several difficulties with the essentialist position as it applies to emotional objects. First, the objects of emotions are typically multifaceted (as described below), and it is not evident whether all relevant aspects of an object are necessary for the proper attribution of emotion, or whether only some need be present on any given occasion. Second, naturally occurring events do not always follow the rules of logic in a strict sense. The statement "Either it is raining now, or it is not" is true by virtue of the *law of the excluded middle*. But on a cloudy, drizzly day, one might well question the applicability of the law of the excluded middle. Similarly, even if the concept of anger logically requires that there be an object (in some sense), it does not follow that all naturally occurring episodes of anger have objects that can be unequivocally specified. For more on emotions and their objects, see Gosling (1965) and Wilson (1972).

difference lies in the *objectives* of the two emotions. In fear the objective is to flee the danger; in courage, it is to stand one's ground in spite of the danger.[5]

Not all emotional objects involve all three of these aspects, that is, an instigation, a target, and an objective. Joy, for example, typically has no objective; its aim does not reach beyond its expression. Also, emotional objects may differ in how closely they are tied to particular targets. Love cannot be easily transferred from one target to another; anger, by contrast, focuses more on the instigation and/or objective than on the target. This point deserves brief elaboration. It would be proper if I were to love Jane and not Mary, even though both are identical twins and look and act in much the same way. However, it would not be proper if I were to become angry at Mary and not at Jane if both committed a similar act of injustice. In other words, the object of anger is more abstract and universal than is the object of love. As we shall see in Chapter 11, this is also one way in which anger differs from annoyance—the object of the latter is more immediate, concrete, and less tied to universal principles. This fact has rather obvious implications for the analysis of anger, both in terms of its social functions and in terms of underlying cognitive mechanisms.

In subsequent chapters, especially Chapter 8, a great deal of attention will be devoted to elucidating the objects of anger. In these introductory comments only one additional distinction needs to be noted briefly. That is the distinction between the object and the cause of an emotion. As already noted, the object of an emotion is part of the syndrome, a meaning imposed on events. The causes of an emotion are those organismic and environmental events that lead a person to make one kind of appraisal rather than another, and to respond in one way rather than another. Examples would include occurrences in the history of the individual (e.g., childhood traumas), the individual's present state of physiological arousal, and extraneous stimuli present in the situation, as well as the immediate eliciting conditions ("objectively" defined). One of the major differences between the objects and causes of emotion is that the former are dependent on social norms—they help constitute the emotional syndrome as a social role. In the case of pride, for instance, it is normatively appropriate that I should be proud of my own accomplishments, or of the

---

[5] The objective of an emotion, it must be emphasized, is an integral part of the appraised object, and not simply a characteristic of the response to the object. Earlier (Averill, Opton, & Lazarus, 1969) I used the rather awkward phrase *response-determined stimulus properties* to refer to the fact that the stimulus array conveys information with regard to potential responses, and hence that the latter help determine the way an object is perceived. This is an old idea (cf. Dewey, 1896; von Uexküll, 1928). Gibson (1979) has used the term *affordance* to express a similar notion. Of course, affordances (by whatever name) depend not only on the nature of the stimulus but also on the individual's ability and/or motivation to respond. Looked at from the side of the individual, one may thus peak of the objective, aim, motive, or goal of the response, rather than of the affordances of the stimulus. None of these terms is entirely appropriate for our purposes, but there is no need for additional neologisms. The context, together with these few introductory remarks, should make the meaning clear.

accomplishments of others with whom I can identify (relatives, countrymen, even ancestors). I cannot, however, be proud of my failures, or of the aurora borealis. The causes of an emotion are not under such normative restrictions. That I am in a state of heightened physiological arousal may contribute to my sense of pride on a given occasion, but it does not help define my response as pride. In Chapter 6, we will consider in detail some of the nonnormative or contributory causes of anger.

Emotions Are Interpreted as Passions Rather Than as Actions

Thus far, we have discussed two of the three features of emotion stipulated in the definition offered earlier. By themselves these two conditions are not sufficient to distinguish emotions from at least some other behavioral phenomena. A third condition must therefore be added, namely, emotions are interpreted as passions rather than as actions.

An action is something that a person does deliberately. A passion, in the generic sense of the term, is something that a person suffers. In this sense, a disease is a passion. (The terms *passion*, *patient*, *pathology*, and *passivity* all stem from the same root.) In most classical discussions (i.e., from the time of the ancient Greeks to about the mid-18th century) the emotions also were typically referred to as passions. Today, the terminology has changed, but the connotation of passivity remains central to the concept of emotion. Thus, a person is "gripped" by fear, "falls" in love, is "torn" by jealousy, "bursts" with pride, is "dragged down" by grief, and so forth.

As the above expressions suggest, the emotions are interpreted not as self-initiated responses (i.e., as actions) but rather as responses that somehow happen to the self (i.e., as passions). But how can a person suffer or be overcome by his or her own behavior? To answer this question, we must make a brief digression and say a few words about the *self*.

Figure 1-2 presents a schematic diagram of the self. In the upper left-hand corner is a representation of what we may call the total self-system. This represents all the psychologically relevant aspects of the individual as an organism. In a sense, the total self-system might be compared to a master computer program which transforms environmental inputs, performs complex operations on the information received, and organizes response outputs. Some aspects of this self-system are prewired into the person (i.e., are genetically determined); other aspects are a product of socialization.

The person continuously monitors and evaluates his or her own operations. The aspect of this monitoring that involves conscious experience may be called the phenomenal self. It is depicted in the bottom right-hand corner of Figure 1-2. The phenomenal self (or ego, as it is sometimes called) is itself an intentional object of thought. As Sartre (1957) has stated; "The ego is not the owner of consciousness; it is the object of consciousness" (p. 97). Or, put somewhat differently, the phenomenal self (ego) is an interpretation of one's own experiences.

The phenomenal self can be subdivided into two main categories that correspond to what we have been calling actions and passions. As Figure 1-2 illustrates, these are broad categories that include a wide range of behavior. Some states, such as

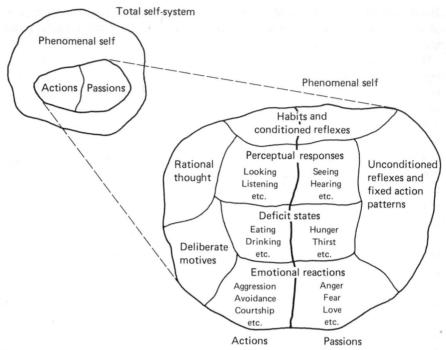

Fig. 1-2. A schematic representation of the self, illustrating the distinction between actions and passions. (Source: Averill, 1980 b)

rational thought and deliberately motivated behaviors, are actions by definition. Other states, such as unconditioned reflexes and fixed action patterns ("instincts") are passions by definition. Most behaviors, however, can be interpreted as either actions or passions, depending on the circumstances or on the aspect of the response being emphasized. Perceptual responses illustrate this point. If I am facing an object with my eyes open, I normally cannot help but see the object. In this sense, seeing is something that happens to me—it is a passion in the broadest sense. By contrast, looking is an action that I perform. The difference between looking and seeing is evident in the adverbs that may be used to describe them. Thus, I may look carefully, but not see carefully; look attentively, but not see attentively; look disdainfully, but not see disdainfully; and so forth. The difference is also evidenced by the fact that persons may be held responsible for what they look at, but not for what they see.

Similar considerations apply to deficit states. Hunger is a passion, whereas eating is an action. A person can eat sloppily, rapidly, politely, and so on. Hunger, by contrast, is something a person has (or is), not something a person does. Thus, a person may be urged to exercise self-control with regard to eating, but not with regard to hunger.

Turning to emotional reactions proper, we find an analogous distinction. When we speak of emotions as passions, we refer to anger, fear, love, and so forth. But when we want to emphasize the role of the self in initiating the response, we use a different set of terms and speak of instrumental aggression, avoidance, courtship, and so on. The principle is by now familiar, namely, passions are something that happen to people, not something people do.

The concept of passion is obviously broad, encompassing not only emotions proper, but also certain aspects of perceptual experiences, deficit states, reflexes and the like. The emotions may be distinguished from these other "passions" in terms of the two criteria discussed earlier, namely, emotions are socially constituted syndromes (transitory social roles) and they include a person's appraisal of the situation. Of course, among the various forms of passion, the dividing line is not sharp, and hence it is not surprising that attempts have frequently been made to analyze emotions in terms of perception (Leeper, 1970), reflexes (Cannon, 1929), and deficit states (Brown & Farber, 1951). Our concern here, however, is not to differentiate emotions from other passions, but rather to identify some of the reasons for interpreting (and experiencing) the emotions as passions.[6]

There are many different grounds for interpreting a response as a passion, and hence as emotional. For example, responses that are irrational, impulsive, intense, persistent, or unusual, and/or that involve a high degree of commitment, may also be interpreted as emotional. But irrationality, impulsivity, and the like are only surface characteristics of a response. Although theoretically suggestive, they explain little. Why is a response irrational or impulsive? When we pursue the question, we are necessarily led to a consideration of origins, causes, and underlying mechanisms, or what might be called the *primary* grounds for interpreting a response as a passion. These are of five general types.

1. *Biological imperatives.* Emotions have often been regarded as biologically basic ("instinctive") responses, mediated by the autonomic nervous system and dependent on the phylogenetically older portions of the brain (e.g., the hypothalamus and limbic system). This way of thinking reflects value judgments as much as empirical facts (Averill, 1974); nevertheless, it is the case that some elements of many—if not most—emotional syndromes are at least partially under genetic control. For example, it was undoubtedly adaptive for our hominid ancestors to feel queasy when in high places, to attack the source of pain, to be distraught upon separation from other members of the group, and so forth. By themselves, such reactions do not constitute emotional syndromes. However, to the extent that biologically based elements are activated during emotion, the behavior is likely to be interpreted (and experienced) as a passion rather than as an action. We shall have much more to say about this issue in Chapter 2, where we discuss the biological bases of anger and aggression.

2. *Social imperatives.* It is commonplace among biologists, even biologists who postulate innate aggressive tendencies (e.g., Lorenz, 1962), to argue that one of the primary characteristics of the human species is the ability to acquire new and

---

[6] The notion of interpretation is being used here in a very broad sense. In a later section on the experience and expression of emotion its meaning will be made more precise.

unique forms of behavior. Humans may not be blank slates upon which experience can write unencumbered, but they are very open to experience. Such openness is a mixed blessing. On the one hand, it allows humans to adapt to a wide range of environments; on the other hand, it would be incapacitating if allowed to endure or to be too encompassing. Therefore, what nature has not provided, society does—in the form of socially constituted response tendencies that are in many respects analogous to the biological instincts found in lower animals. Such response tendences are taken for granted—even demanded—by members of the society, and the behavior that results is not premeditated nor easily subjected to voluntary control. In Chapter 3 we will describe a number of aggressive syndromes that are typically interpreted as uncontrollable or passionate, and yet are clearly a product of social imperatives.

3. *Psychological imperatives*. In addition to biological and social evolution, each human being is a product of his or her own past history. Early patterns of reinforcement (whether by design or fortuitous), traumatic conditioning, modeling, and so on, all may leave their residue on adult behavior, for example, in the form of vaguely but deeply felt likes and dislikes, tendences to respond in particular ways, or even physiological reactions that persist even though the corresponding overt behavior has long since been extinguished (a phenomenon that Gantt, 1953, termed schizokinesis). Of course, learning does not cease in infancy and early childhood. As adults, behavior comes under the control of many discriminative stimuli, the influence of which may not be recognized by the person. The resulting behavior may then be interpreted as impulsive or emotional. This and related phenomena will be discussed in Chapter 6.

4. *Systemic conflict*. Each of the preceding three grounds may result in a more or less straightforward impulse to respond. Sometimes conditions occur in which two impulses conflict, or an impulse conflicts with the demands of reality. The conflict may then be resolved through a compromise reaction. Moreover, if the compromise presents some threat to the integrity of the individual, as is frequently the case, the compromise reaction may be "disclaimed" (Schafer, 1976), for example, by interpreting it as a passion rather than as an action. The psychodynamics of hysterical reactions illustrates this process well. By engaging in a subterfuge, the hysteric may express unacceptable impulses while denying responsibility for his behavior. Some standard emotional reactions may be analyzed in a similar manner, except that the source of the conflict, and the rationale for its resolution are to be found within the sociocultural system; that is, the conflict and its resolution are common to the society and not idiosyncratic to the individual, as in the case of hysterical reactions. In Chapter 4 we will explore through historical teachings some of the conflicts that underlie anger; and in Chapter 5 we will examine the attribution of responsibility (or, more accurately, the abnegation of responsibility) for acts committed out of anger, as exemplified by the legal treatment of crimes of passion.

5. *Cognitive disorganization*. As dscussed with respect to Figure 1-2, when a response is interpreted as either an action or a passion, it is related to the self in a particular way (i.e., as either self-initiated or as happening to the self). However, the self in this sense is an intentional object, a meaning imposed on the

ongoing stream of behavior (or consciousness). Like any other intentional object, the self presumes an underlying set of cognitive structures or "programs" for the processing of information. If these structures are disrupted (through trauma, drugs, meditation, or the like), the distinction between actions and passions loses its bases, and the individual is engulfed in an undifferentiated flood of experience. Such an experience is typically interpreted as a passion, since it is something that just seems to happen to the person.

Of course, cognitive disorganization is not an all-or-none affair. Menninger (1954) has distinguished four stages along the route from normal adjustment to a threatening situation to an ultimate state of psychological disintegration. The first stage is characterized by an exaggeration of normal ego functions, but in a manner that appears uncomfortable, unpleasant, or "nervous." The second stage involves a partial detachment from and distortion of the world of reality (e.g., by dissociation, displacement, and substitution). As Menninger describes the third stage, the "already stretched, compromised, injured, wearied, over-taxed ego may simply have to yield" to the persistent or increased threat. As a result, more or less disorganized outbursts may occur, including assaultive violence, panic attacks, demoralization, and schizoid reactions. Such episodic explosions may be sufficient to relieve the tension, and the "rupture" of the ego may quickly "heal." However, if the rupture is too great or the threat continues, a fourth stage of disorganization may ensue. At this stage, the person may feel desolate, estranged, and hopeless as a result of a severance of linkages with reality; at the same time, he may seek to bolster his ego with omnipotent fantasies of destroying the whole world. But even this fourth state, which represents psychosis (a term that Menninger would like to abandon), is not the ultimate catastrophe. The ego sometimes disintegrates entirely. The result, according to Menninger, is a furious, violent mania, which nearly always ends in complete exhaustion and death.

Kinds of Emotion

The class of emotions is complex. In the English language, for example, there are over 500 terms that refer more or less directly to emotional states (Averill, 1975). One of the traditional problems addressed by emotional theorists has been the subclassification of these states. This not the place to review the various schemes, both dimensional (e.g., Osgood, 1966; Russell, 1980) and categorical (e.g., Izard, 1971, 1977), that have been proposed at one time or another. Nevertheless, if we are going to use anger as a paradigm for the study of emotion, it is important to have some idea of how anger relates to other kinds of emotional syndromes.

The foregoing primary grounds for interpreting (or experiencing) a response as a passion can be used to distinguish among three broad classes of emotional syndromes (Averill, 1980a). These classes will be described briefly and their relevance to anger and aggression indicated.

The class of *impulsive* emotions represents straightforward desires and aversions which are so automatic and compelling that they are not regarded as stemming from the self-as-agent. Examples are grief, joy, hope, sexual desire, and many common fears. Such desires and aversions may stem from biological, social, and/or psychological imperatives (grounds 1-3), and almost always from a combination of all three. Aggressive reactions to a painful stimulus or to simple frustration can also be impulsive in this sense.

The class of *conflictive* emotions is based on the fourth ground for interpreting a response as a passion, namely, systemic conflict. Emotions of this type are like conversion reactions. They are social hysterias, so to speak, that result from conflicting demands placed on the individual by society. Any conflictive emotion will, of course, have impulsive elements, but the underlying social and psychological dynamics are typically more complex than in the case of impulsive emotions. As we shall see in subsequent chapters (especially Chapters 4 and 5), anger epitomizes many of the features of a conflictive emotion.

A third class of emotions, namely, *transcendental* emotional states, is a product of cognitive disorganization (ground 5). Whereas both impulsive and conflictive emotions presuppose a well-integrated sense of self, transcendental emotional states involve a disruption of ego boundaries. The self is, in a sense, transcended; as a result, behavior tends to be disorganized and lacking in purpose, and the entire experience may be described as "ineffable." Anxiety and mystical experiences are examples of transcendental emotional states, since both involve some degree of cognitive disorganization (or "deautomatization," to use Deikman's, 1966, more positive-sounding term). The disorganized and seemingly purposeless rage reactions that sometimes accompany extreme stress can also be placed within this category, as indicated by Menninger's (1954) description of the various stages of cognitive disorganization presented earlier.

It must be emphasized that no actually occurring emotional syndrome fits neatly into any one of the three subclasses of emotion. For example, depending on the person and the circumstances, anger may involve—to varying degrees—impulsive, conflictive, and transcendental elements. Also, since the classification is based on underlying dynamics, the kind of emotion cannot be inferred directly from overt behavior. We have noted, for instance, how aggression may accompany all three kinds of emotion. With these qualifications in mind, the distinction among impulsive, conflictive, and transcendental emotional states has both theoretical and heuristic value. Not only does the distinction have deep historical roots, but many contemporary theories of emotion can also be divided roughly along these same lines. Thus, instinct theories typically draw their examples from the class of impulsive emotions; psychoanalytic and related "depth" theories focus on the conflictive emotions; and theories within the existentialist tradition tend to emphasize transcendental emotional states.

This brief discussion of various kinds of emotions concludes our definition of emotion from a constructivist point of view. In the second half of the chapter, we will expand upon the definition and reexamine a number of traditional issues in the theory of emotion. These issues include, among other things, the relationship between subjective experience (the "feeling" of emotion) and overt behavior; between two kinds of overt behavior, namely, expressive reactions and instrumental responses; and between anger and aggression. But before broaching these issues, it might be helpful to recapitulate briefly some of the major points that have been discussed thus far.

Like any complex human behavior, the emotions can be analyzed at social, psychological, and/or biological levels of analysis. At each level, it is also possible to distinguish broader systems of behavior, of which the emotions are a part. Thus, we can analyze the emotions in relation to social systems, psychological systems, and biological systems. The emotions themselves (as subsystems of behavior) are composed of elements—physiological changes, expressive reactions, instrumental responses, and subjective feelings. These elements can also be analyzed at social, psychological, and/or biological levels of analysis.

Most traditional theories of emotion have emphasized a biological level of analysis. The present ("constructivist") approach, by contrast, emphasizes the social. Specifically, the emotions are here viewed as socially constituted syndromes, the meaning and function of which are determined primarily by the social system(s) of which they are a part.

The basic unit of analysis at the social level is the role. Hence, emotions may also be viewed as transitory social roles. Emotions can be distinguished from other transitory social roles, in part, on the basis of the cognitive appraisals involved. Each emotion is based on a particular set of appraisals or evaluative judgments, and each has its own corresponding set of intentional objects. The intentional object of an emotion is a cognitive construction consisting of the instigation, the target, and the objective of the response. The intentional object is as much a part of an emotional role as are physiological changes, overt behavior, and other component reactions.

Emotions can be distinguished from other social roles not only by their intentional objects, but also by the fact that emotions are interpreted as passions rather than as actions. There are a variety of grounds for interpreting a response as a passion. Some of these are primary in that they refer to origins, causes, and underlying mechanisms; others are secondary in that they refer to the manifest properties or characteristics of the response. The primary grounds can be used to distinguish among three broad classes of emotion, namely, impulsive, conflictive, and transcendental emotional states. These classes are idealizations, and hence no actual emotion fits neatly into any one class. With this qualification in mind, it may be said that anger is representative of the class of conflictive emotions.

The Experience and Expression of Emotion

An emotion is not just the sum of its parts. For example, none of the grounds described above for interpreting a response as a passion is sufficient by itself (or in combination with other such grounds) for the attribution of emotion, whether to oneself or to another. The attribution of emotion also depends on the nature of the appraised object and on the meaning of the emotional role (i.e., how the emotional role relates to broader systems of behavior, primarily at the social level of analysis). In the present section, we will attempt to show how the various aspects of emotion fit together to form an integrated whole.

We will proceed by considering, first, the nature of emotional feelings. A critic might argue that a definition of emotion in terms of social roles is applicable to the outward expression of emotion but not to feelings. In response to this potential criticism, we will attempt to show how emotional feelings are socially constituted in much the same manner as are emotional responses.

A second potential criticism, not unrelated to the foregoing, is based on the traditional distinction between expressive reactions and instrumental responses. Expressive reactions, it is often maintained, are truly reflective of emotion; whereas instrumental responses, being deliberate and goal directed, are more prone to social influence and individual dissimulation. I shall argue, however, that the distinction between expressive reactions and instrumental responses is only relative, that both kinds of behavior are integral parts of emotional syndromes.[7]

Finally, we will consider how feelings and reponses vary as a function of a person's involvement in an emotional role. At very low levels of involvement, there often is a disjunction between feelings and responses, and behavior may be largely instrumental. But that does not invalidate the interpretation of such behavior as emotional. And as involvement increases, all aspects of an emotional syndrome—feelings, expressive reactions, physiological changes, instrumental responses—become closely woven into a pattern dictated by the emotional role.

Emotional Feelings

Let us return for a moment to William James's theory of emotion. As noted in the introduction to this chapter, James argued that the experience of emotion is due to a person's perception of his or her own behavior, and in particular, to proprioceptive feedback from visceral and other bodily changes. There is no need here to review the many criticisms and defenses that have been made of this famous "deductive or generative principle" over the past century (see Mandler, 1979). Ample research has demonstrated that although feedback from bodily changes may add a certain quale to experience, emotional responses are much too varied and (as far as the viscera are concerned) too nonspecific to account for the experience of emotion. This has led Schachter (1971) and others to propose that bodily feedback must itself be interpreted in terms of whatever stimuli may be present in the situation. Thus, the same state of arousal might be experienced as anger, fear, love, joy, or grief, depending on situational cues. There is a difficulty with this suggestion, however. As pointed out in the previous discussion of emotional appraisals, the object of an emotion is a meaning imposed on the environment. Situational cues do not come prelabeled as angry, fearful, and so on, any more than do bodily responses. Both the situational cues and the bodily responses accrue meaning as part of an emotional syndrome. Where does that meaning come from, and how does it get translated into the subjective experience of emotion?

---

[7]Most of the observations that will be made with regard to expressive reactions (crying, blushing, frowning, etc.) also apply to physiological changes. For the sake of brevity we will not discuss the latter here.

In order to answer this question we must consider three closely related issues: (a) the monitoring of behavior; (b) feeling rules; and (c) emotional meanings. The first issue has to do with what is experienced; the second with the ways in which experience is informed or structured; and the third with the meaning of experience in relation to broader systems of behavior.

The monitoring of behavior. Humans and infrahuman animals continually monitor their behavior (including internal bodily changes) in relationship to situational cues. Such monitoring, accomplished through innumerable feedback loops, provides the stuff of conscious experience—the raw sensations, so to speak. Following Harré and Secord (1972), we may call this process first-order monitoring. Among humans, the conscious aspects of first-order monitoring correspond roughly to what phenomenological psychologists have called "prereflective" experience. James's theory of emotion has generally been regarded as referring to the prereflective experience of emotion. However, such a reading of James is not entirely accurate; for in another context James (1890) also argued that no one "ever had a simple sensation by itself." Raw sensations are, he argued, an abstraction, the "results of discriminative attention, pushed to a very high degree" (Vol. 1, p. 224). Unfortunately, James did not follow through on the implications of this insight when it came to an analysis of emotional experiences.

The experience of emotion is a product not of first-order monitoring, but of second-order monitoring. In second-order monitoring, awareness is reflected back upon itself, interpreting (imposing meaning on) the original experience. The capacity for reflective experience evolved concomitantly with the capacity for symbolization, and hence is closely related to language. But more of that shortly.

The distinction between first-order monitoring (prereflective experience) and second-order monitoring (reflective experience) is perhaps most easily illustrated in the case of aesthetic emotions. Consider a music critic at a symphony. She may become absorbed in the experience. But subsequently, when writing about the experience, she must analyze the performance, relate it to other performances of the same work that she has heard before, and so on. In the latter case, the critic is reflecting upon the original experience. The reflection in this example is retrospective; but that is not a necessary feature of reflective experience. Typically, a music critic analyzes a performance while listening to it, that is, she reflects upon (monitors) her experience as it occurs.

This distinction between prereflective and reflective experience having been drawn for analytical purpose, an important qualification must now be added. Completely prereflective experience is a myth, at least on the human level. All experience is filtered, organized, and given meaning by the rules and categories of reflective thought. For example, a music critic listening to a new performance can never completely disregard her past learning and ways of thinking, no matter how hard she tries to discard the role of critic. And by the same token, a socialized human being can never experience events without also interpreting that experience in some way.

Feeling rules. A music critic who evaluates a new performance follows certain rules. Those rules are not easy to specify (although books on musical appreciation often make an attempt). A better example of how experience is informed by rules is the case of language. When I listen to another person speak, I interpret what is said according to the rules of grammar (and, of course, knowledge of the vocabulary). If I do not know the relevant rules, as when I hear an unfamiliar language being spoken, the experience is not meaningful. The emotions, too, have a grammar, a set of rules that help make the experience meaningful. Much of the remainder of this volume concerns the rules—social norms, for the most part—that help constitute the experience of anger.[8] In these introductory comments we will simply mention briefly the four broad classes of rules that help inform emotional experiences in general.

First, there are *rules of appraisal*. These help determine the intentional object of an emotion. If one violates a rule of appraisal (e.g., by becoming angry at another's good intentions), not only may the response be condemned, but the experience may even be denied legitimacy as "true" anger. Conversely, "unconscious" or "repressed" feelings (e.g., of anger) may be ascribed to a person if there is reason to believe that he has appraised the situation in an appropriate way and yet is responding in an affectively neutral manner.

Second, there are *rules of behavior*, which are also rules of feeling. William James was partly right. Feedback from our behavior (including physiological changes and expressive reactions) contributes to the experience of emotion. However, such feedback is never experienced as raw sensations. It is always informed, and the same rules that helped shape the behavior also guide the interpretation of any feedback from that behavior.

Third, there are *rules of attribution*. These rules help determine how a response is related to the self (e.g., as an action or as a passion). Earlier, we discussed some of the primary grounds for interpreting a response as a passion. We also noted various secondary grounds or surface characteristics that help guide such an interpretation. For example, responses that are considered nonrational, unusual, intense, impulsive, or highly committed—regardless of the underlying mechanism—may also be interpreted as passions. But the situation is more complex than that earlier discussion might have indicated. The person who, in a sudden flash of insight, perceives the solution to an important problem is unlikely to interpret the event as emotional. On the other hand, the sudden intrusion of some bizarre or unwanted thought might well be interpreted as a sign of emotion, thus divorcing it from the self-as-agent.

What is the difference? In both cases the ideation is preemptive and, in a strict sense, nonrational. However, when we wish to assume credit for a response, it will be attributed to the self-as-agent; on the other hand, if we wish to deny responsibility, one way to do this is by interpreting the response as a passion rather than as an action. Of course, it is not only undesirable responses that are interpreted as passions. On some occasions, a response may be divorced from the self-as-agent because it is considered so central to a person's being that it cannot be attributed to rational,

---

[8] As used here, rules are primarily social norms. Not all behavior that is regulated is regulated by rules in this sense. There are, for example, biological constraints that help regulate some emotional reactions. Moreover, many of the rules (norms) that help constitute emotional syndromes are open ended. That is, they allow a great deal of negotiation or improvisation as an episode proceeds.

deliberate thought. Take the case of commitment. A highly committed response may also be interpreted as passionate. Why should this be so? Commitment implies a "decision" to respond in a particular way because of some general principle, or because such a response reflects one's image of his "true" self (Scruton, 1980).[9] The person who is committed cannot help responding the way he does—at least, not if he wishes to remain true to his convictions or to himself.

As these examples illustrate, rules of attribution are not only subtle and complex; they are also closely tied to issues of social desirability and to a person's conception of himself.

Finally, there are *rules of prognostication*. Each emotion has a characteristic time course. Some emotional episodes typically last only moments (e.g., startle), others may last for months or even years (e.g., grief). This aspect of emotional syndromes has often been overlooked by theorists, especially those who tend to equate emotions with short-term states of physiological arousal or other specific bodily changes (e.g., expressive reactions). In Chapter 12 we will examine in some detail the temporal characteristics of anger. For the moment, suffice it to note that the experience of emotion is dependent not only on immediate proprioceptive feedback, but also on the anticipation of future events. Indeed, the rules of prognostication may sometimes even extend beyond the limits of a single emotional episode. Consider the case of the young man who asks himself, "Is this truly love I feel?" He is not puzzled so much by the butterflies in his stomach as he is unsure about what future course of action to take (e.g., with respect to marriage).

Feeling rules of the above kinds—having to do with the appraisal of objects, the organization of behavior, attributions to the self, and prognostication—are largely social in origin. A person has not only the right, but in some cases even the obligation, to feel a certain way in appropriate circumstances. And like other social rules, the rules of feeling are not inviolable. They can be broken or followed only half-heartedly. When that occurs, the person may be asked to justify his feelings (or lack of feelings), and if he cannot, may suffer disapprobation. In fact, much of education—particularly moral education—consists of learning the rules of feeling, that is, how to feel the right way toward the right objects in the right circumstances.

For a more detailed analysis of the social nature of feeling rules, the reader can consult an excellent paper by Hochschild (1979). There is not space here to pursue the topic further. Rather, we must turn briefly to a consideration of how rules of feeling acquire content or meaning with respect to specific emotions.

Emotional meanings. We have said that the (reflective) experience of emotion involves an interpretation of one's own behavior in relation to situational cues, and we have described in an abstract way the kinds of rules that help guide the interpretation. But behavior cannot simply be interpreted, it must be interpreted *as* something (e.g., as anger or fear). That something is the meaning of the emotion.

---

[9] For example, one would not say of a rabbit fleeing from a fox that it was committed to a particular course of action, no matter how intense or persistent the response.

A concrete example may help to clarify the nature of emotional meanings. In the 12th century, Andreas Capellanus (ca. 1185/1941) wrote *The Art of Courtly Love*. The book was written as a practical guide for young courtiers on how to start, maintain, and/or end a love affair. The rules that each partner were to follow are spelled out in great detail so that, for example, a man of the middle class might know how to approach a woman of the higher nobility. It is clear from the advice offered by Andreas Cappelanus that the rules of courtly love embodied the general norms and values of his society. This has led one commentator to observe that *The Art of Courtly Love* is "one of those capital works which reflect the thought of a great epoch, which explain the secret of a civilization" (Bossuat, 1926, cited by Parry, 1941).

Generalizing from this example, we can say that most emotions reflect—to a greater or lesser extent—the thought of an epoch, the secret of a civilization. It follows that to understand the meaning of an emotion is to understand the relevant aspects of the sociocultural system of which the emotion is a part (subsystem).

Of course, understanding in this sense is largely intuitive and admits of degrees. Few people have the insight or the skill of Andreas Capellanus, so that they can articulate as he did many of the rules (social norms) that govern the feeling and expression of a particular emotion. But even the insight of Andreas Capellanus was limited to a kind of practical knowledge. He displayed little insight into the latent functions that courtly love served in medieval society (on the latter, see Beigel, 1951, and de Rougemont, 1940). However, a theoretical understanding of the functional significance of an emotion is not necessary for, and may even be inimical to, the actual experience of that emotion.

Much of the practical knowledge related to the emotions (as to other psychological phenomena) is embedded in our ordinary language. For example, a person who knows how to use the concept of love correctly also knows the rules (norms) that govern the experience and expression of love. Whether he can apply those rules to his own behavior is another matter. Like everything else, the emotions require practice.

In Chapter 3 we will discuss in detail the relationship between language and emotion. At this point, only a few general observations are in order. Freud suggested that dreams are the royal road to the unconscious. Be that as it may, language is the royal road to conscious experience. This fact has been recognized by many thinkers of diverse persuasion. "Language is as old as consciousness, language is practical consciousness, as it exists for other men, and for that reason is really beginning to exist for me personally as well; for language, like consciousness, only arises from the need, the necessity, of intercourse with other men" (Marx & Engels, 1845-1846/ 1939, p. 19). "The subtlety and strength of consciousness are always in proportion to the capacity for communication. . . In short, the development of speech and the development of consciousness (not of reason, but of reason becoming self-conscious) go hand in hand" (Nietzsche, 1882/1960, p. 296). And to take a more contemporary example: "Without the help of a verbal community all behavior would be unconscious. Consciousness is a social product. It is not only *not* the special field of autonomous man, it is not within the range of a solitary man" (Skinner, 1971, p. 192).

If these observations have any validity, one would expect a close relationship between the "labeling" of an emotional state (e.g., as anger, fear, or love) and the experience of emotion. Such a relationship has, in fact, frequently been demonstrated, especially by Schachter (1971) and his colleagues. However, much of the current theorizing on the relationship between language and the experience of emotion remains on a rather superficial level, and most research has not gone beyond the demonstration stage. As already mentioned, a person who knows the meaning of an emotional concept also knows the appropriate rules (regarding appraisal, etc.) as they apply to that particular emotion. If the person can be convinced—for example, by subtle manipulation of situational cues—that one aspect of his behavior (e.g., physiological arousal) is appropriately labeled as love, say, or anger, then he must necessarily apply the relevant rules to other aspects of his experience and behavior —or else run the risk of inconsistency and self-contradiction.

Of course, since the various rules form an interlocking network, many checks and balances exist that help prevent the incorrect labeling of an emotion during the course of everyday affairs. The person who says "I am angry with you" or "I love you" is not simply labeling a state of physiological arousal; he is entering into a complex relationship with another person. The meaning of the relationship, not only for the individuals involved but also for the larger society, is embodied in the feeling rules (social norms) for that emotion.

We can now tie these various observations together. The experience of emotion is reflective, an interpretation of events. Any interpretation involves at least three aspects: (a) the state of affairs that is being interpreted; (b) the rules that guide the interpretation; and (c) that which the state of affairs is interpreted *as*. In the case of emotional experiences, the state of affairs consists of the actual and potential behavior of the individual, proprioceptive feedback from any bodily changes that might be occurring, the perception of situational cues, and so forth. The rules that guide the interpretation pertain to the appraisal of emotional objects, the organization of responses, self-attributions, and expectancies with regard to the future course of events. Finally, that which the experience is interpreted as (i.e., the meaning of the experience) is determined by the way a particular emotion relates to other aspects of the sociocultural system. This meaning is epitomized in the language we use to label and to communicate about an emotional state.

These three aspects of an emotional experience are, of course, abstractions. Any actual experience is necessarily informed by the relevant feeling rules; and the latter, in turn, are meaningful primarily to the extent that they embody the social norms that help constitute the emotion in question. It should also go without saying that many of the same considerations that apply to the experience of emotion apply *mutatis mutandis* to the expression of emotion. For example, the rules of appraisal, behavior, attribution, and prognostication guide the way we behave as well as how we feel; and the meaning of an emotion—its relationship to broader systems of behavior—is as relevant to behavior as to feelings. If such were not the case, we would have little ground for judging whether or not our behavior was consonant with our feelings.

Nevertheless, the expression of emotion does pose some problems in its own right. Just as some theorists have maintained that emotions *really* refer to feelings as opposed to overt behavior, others have tended to identify emotions with certain kinds or subclasses of behavior. Expressive reactions (e.g., facial grimaces, tone of voice, postural adjustments) have figured prominently in such theorizing (see Izard, 1977; Tomkins, 1981a). Instrumental responses, by contrast, have often been considered of secondary importance to theories of emotion, presumably because such responses are under the voluntary control of the individual. However, instrumental responses are important for a constructivist theory of emotion, and hence the distinction between these two kinds of behavior deserves brief comment.

On the Distinction Between Expressive Reactions and Instrumental Responses

This is a useful distinction for many purposes, but its theoretical significance should not be overdrawn. All behavior has both expressive and instrumental aspects. For example, I cannot say anything without varying the tone of my voice. Both what I say and how I say it can convey meaningful—and cometimes contradictory—information. But this does not mean that one kind of information is more "emotional" than the other. As we shall see in Chapter 10, people tend to place about equal weight on both the expressive and instrumental aspects of behavior when judging another person's anger. (Situational cues, particularly the precipitating incident, also play an important role in such judgments.)

Some responses (e.g., crying) are more expressive than others (e.g., writing a letter); and of the former, some are biologically based (genetically determined), while others are the product of socialization or of individual learning. Ever since Darwin's (1872/1965) classic work, *The Expression of the Emotions in Man and Animals*, biologically based expressive reactions have figured prominently in theories of emotion. In Chapter 3 we will consider how such "biological expressors" become incorporated into emotional syndromes. In these introductory remarks I only wish to emphasize that instrumental responses are as integral to emotional syndromes as are expressive reactions. This fact is fundamental to a constructivist view of emotion such as that being developed here. It is not, however, limited to any one theoretical orientation.

From a behaviorist point of view, Skinner (1953) has warned against the tendency to identify the emotions not only with subjective states, but also with physiological changes or expressive reactions. He argues that

> the names of the so-called emotions serve to classify behavior with respect to various circumstances which affect its probability. The safest practice is to hold to the adjectival form. Just as the hungry organism can be accounted for without too much difficulty, although "hunger" is another matter, so by describing behavior as fearful, affectionate, timid, and so on, we are not led to look for *things* called emotions. (p. 162)[10]

To take a specific example, the probability of instrumental aggressive responses may increase when there is an interference with behavior, depending on whether or not similar responses were reinforced in the past. Colloquially, we may describe

---

[10] Reprinted by permission of Macmillan Publishing, New York, New York. Copyright © 1953 by Macmillan Publishing Co.; renewed 1981 by B. F. Skinner.

such responses as angry, but this should not lead us to assume that they are caused by an internal state, anger. Their cause, and hence the explanation for angry behavior, according to Skinner, is to be found in the present circumstances and the past reinforcement of the individual.

Of course, Skinner recognizes that when a person becomes angry, he may not only engage in instrumental responses (aggression) designed to overcome the frustrating conditions, but he may also show a wide range of physiological and expressive reactions. Indeed, instrumental behavior may be completely inhibited, so that only physiological and expressive reactions occur. Such "reflex responses" may have important consequences (e.g., leading to psychosomatic symptoms if circumstances are not altered), but they are not the primary characteristics of an emotional syndrome. For example, they do not ordinarily allow a distinction among closely related emotions, although they may "add characteristic details to the final picture of the effect of a given emotional circumstance" (1953, p. 166).

It is, of course, not surprising that Skinner would place major emphasis on eliciting conditions and instrumental responses as the primary criteria for identifying emotional states. Therefore, let us turn to a theorist of quite a different persuasion. Schafer (1976) has argued that much of psychoanalytic theory could be better expressed in terms of an "action language" rather than in the mechanistic and structural terms often used by Freud. An action, according to Schafer, is any human behavior that is goal directed or that is done for a reason. Thinking and overt instrumental responses are actions in this sense, but simple sensations, physiological changes, and expressive reactions typically are not. Some actions, which we might call deliberate or intentional, are recognized by the actor as such. There are other kinds of actions, however, for which the individual may disclaim responsibility. Hysterical reactions—a traditional concern of psychoanalysis—are one form of disclaimed action. The hysteric who suffers the paralysis of a limb without any organic damage to the nervous system is engaging in an action for which he cannot admit responsibility, even to himself. The task of psychoanalysis is to uncover the goals of such disclaimed action and to make the behavior unnecessary, either by eliminating the goal or by substituting more adaptive responses.

Emotions are also disclaimed actions, according to Schafer. They are modes of acting the goals of which are not fully recognized. In order to emphasize the latter point, Schafer recommends that when we speak of emotion we use only verbs (e.g., to love, to hate, to fear) or adverbs (e.g., lovingly, hatefully, fearfully). The use of nouns (e.g., love, hate, fear) fosters the tendency to think of emotions as things we have rather than as actions we do. Applying this analysis to anger, Schafer observes:

> The mode of acting angrily includes tensing muscle, clenching teeth, biting fiercely, hitting, soiling, thinking of attack, and subjectively defining it as vengeance or defense or even pleasure, and so on and so forth. Acting angrily, even if only by fantasying, tends to be accompanied by certain kinds of appropriately speeded-up physiological processes; these, however, though they support the designation "angrily," are not themselves actions in the sense of personal projects.
>
> The person who is acting angrily and the other who may be witness of the relevant actions and modes may not realize consciously that he or she

is acting that way. In principle, however, one and all *could* infer it. This is so because, as there is in action language no entity emotion but only emotion-actions and emotion-modes, there can be no ultimately privileged access to anger: there can only be observation, reasoning, and communication made more or less consciously and knowledgeably by people. (Schafer, 1976, pp. 282-283).

In some respects Schafer's position is similar to that of Skinner. The similarity, however, is limited. The type of analysis advocated by Skinner relies primarily on eliciting conditions, instrumental responses, and contingencies of reinforcement; the type of analysis advocated by Schafer, while also recognizing the importance of instrumental responses (actions), places primary emphasis on the *meaning* that a given response has for an individual.

The constructivist view of emotion being developed in the present volume bears certain similarities to the psychoanalytic position as advocated by Schafer. There are, however, important differences. For example, when a psychoanalyst speaks of the meaning of a response, he typically refers to the way that response fits into broader systems of behavior defined at the individual (psychological) level of analysis. By contrast, we have analyzed emotional meanings in relationship to sociocultural systems. Also, in their search for hidden motives and goals (usually related to sexuality), psychoanalysts often overlook more obvious determinants of behavior in the immediate situation. In this respect, the orientation of the present analysis is perhaps closer to that of Skinner and the social-learning theorists.

In Chapters 9 and 10 we will see that anger can be expressed in an indefinite variety of ways—physical attack, withdrawal, verbal abuse, symbolic gestures, the denial of some benefit, crying, raising one's voice, talking things over with or without hostility, telling a third party, and many other ways besides. In fact, it is difficult to say what a typical expression of anger is. That is one reason why we have defined anger—and other emotions—as syndromes, that is, as variable sets of responses, no single element of which is essential to the whole. Depending on the individual and the circumstances, instrumental responses may predominate in an episode; in different circumstances, expressive reactions may be more in evidence. In this respect instrumental responses and expressive reactions stand in relation to one another as parts (subsets) to a whole (the emotional syndrome). Neither kind of response, in and of itself, is more essential or a truer indication of emotion than is the other. The same could also be said, of course, about other components of an emotional syndrome, such as physiological changes and subjective experiences.

Involvement in Emotional Roles

As described earlier, emotional syndromes can also be conceptualized as transitory social roles. This provides another way of looking at the way emotional syndromes are organized. Roles may be enacted with varying degrees of involvement. At low levels of involvement enactment is mainly a formality, and instrumental responses predominate. A common expression of emotion at this level is a simple verbal statement, for example, "Don't do that again, it makes me angry." Such statements are not necessarily insincere just because they are largely instrumental and lack a great deal of feeling. They are generally appropriate to the situation and sufficient to achieve the desired end. In fact, the person who becomes too involved in an emotional role when the situation does not call for it may be considered insincere or affected.

As involvement increases, more elements of an emotional syndrome may be activated, such as physiological arousal and expressive reactions. Research has shown that the mere belief that one is physiologically aroused may enhance the experience of emotion, whether or not that belief is accurate (e.g., Nisbett & Valins, 1971). This is perhaps one reason why people often try to work themselves into a state of physiological arousal when emotional. It is as though without such arousal the emotional episode would not be experienced as convincing—either by oneself or by others.

At the highest levels of involvement behavior becomes stereotyped and unresponsive to both situational constrains and personal needs. The dictates of the role are paramount. One of the most dramatic illustrations of a high degree of involvement in an emotional role is the case of voodoo death (Cannon, 1942). The person who has been hexed enters into the role of a dying person—and dies. Needless to say, everyday emotional roles do not place such extreme demands on the individual.

Most emotional episodes proceed at rather low levels of involvement, where instrumental responses predominate, if the emotion is even expressed at all. Does this not place most episodes outside of our definition of emotion, which stipulates that the responses be interpreted as a passion rather than as an action? Not necessarily. There are at least two reasons why an episode at a low level of involvement might be interpreted as a passion, even though the individual is in full control of his behavior.

First, the more extreme occurrences of an emotion may serve as prototypes, helping to determine how milder occurrences will be interpreted.[11] For example, a violent attack on one occasion helps determine how a mild threat will be interpreted on another occasion. If the former is interpreted as a passion, then so too may be the latter. The second reason is actually a variation or elaboration on the first. The cultural prototype of most emotional reactions represents a high degree of involvement. Such involvement carries with it certain commitments and exemptions. If a person wishes those commitments and exemptions to apply to any particular response, then the response must be interpreted as part of an emotional role, no matter how minimal the involvement. A few examples will serve to illustrate this point. The young man who tells his sweetheart that he loves her may be quite insulted if she interprets the remark as premeditated or deliberate, regardless of how unpassionate he happens to feel at the time. He meant the remark to be interpreted as part of an emotional syndrome, which implies a degree of commitment that is often lacking in more deliberate ("calculated") responses. Or, to take another example, the parent who says to the child, "Don't do that again, it makes me angry," intends that the expression of anger be taken literally, even if the remark is not accompanied by a great deal of physiological arousal or other signs of involvement.

---

[11] A detailed discussion of the significance of the prototypic attributes for the categorization and interpretation of emotional reactions can be found in Chapter 14.

In short, the actual behavior exhibited (thoughts, remarks, etc.) represents only one factor contributing to the interpretation of a response as a passion. The other factor is the meaning of the emotional role. When a person interprets a perfunctory remark as the manifestation of an emotion, he is asking that the remark be understood and judged by standards that apply to emotional reactions and not by standards that apply to deliberate, rational behavior.

Anger and Aggression

One more topic needs to be discussed briefly before concluding this chapter, namely, the relationship between anger and aggression. Actually, we will be returning to this issue frequently in subsequent chapters, and hence only a few remarks are needed at this point by way of introduction.

Anger has often been defined as the subjective experience that accompanies certain forms of aggression, as a state of physiological arousal that enhances the probability of aggression, or as an intervening (drive) variable that mediates the effects of frustration, say, on aggression. By now it should be evident that none of these formulations is congruent with the present analysis. Anger, as here conceived, is the name of an emotional syndrome; aggression—a response intended to inflict pain or discomfort upon another—is one way in which anger is sometimes expressed.

Ryle (1949) tells the following fictional anecdote about a foreign visitor to Oxford University. After being shown a number of colleges, libraries, playing fields, museums, scientific departments, and administrative offices, the visitor asks, "But where is the university?" It then has to be explained to the visitor that the university is not some hidden counterpart to what he has seen. Rather it is the way in which all that he has seen is organized, and how the components function together in the conduct of research, the education of students, and so forth. The visitor has made what Ryle calls a "category mistake." That is, he has taken the university to be another member of the category of which it is the whole.

Similarly, the assumption that anger is a subjective experience, a state of physiological arousal, or whatever, is a category mistake. Anger represents the entire syndrome, the way these various elements are organized with respect to some end or goal. An analysis of anger, then, must focus primarily on the rules by which the syndrome is organized, and the functions that anger serves. Following our definition of anger as a *socially constituted* syndrome (i.e., a transitory social role), the relevant rules are the social norms related to anger, and the functions are to be found primarily on the social level of analysis.

Much of the remainder of this volume will be devoted to an analysis of the norms and functions of anger. In approaching this task, however, we also will have much to say about aggression. To a certain extent this is by necessity. When dealing with the possible biological bases of anger (Chapter 2), for example, we must necessarily focus on aggression, for that is the aspect of anger that has been most investigated on the animal level. Similarly, when examining anger cross-culturally (Chapter

3), we cannot focus on anger per se, but only on what is common to a variety of angerlike syndromes, namely, aggression.

Historical teachings (Chapter 4) and the legal treatment of crimes of passion (Chapter 5) also focus on the more violent expressions of anger. And finally, most of the experimental (psychological) research relevant to anger has actually involved aggression as the dependent variable (Chapter 6). Indeed, it is not until we analyze data with regard to the everyday expression of anger (Chapter 9) that we get a more balanced picture. As we shall see then, aggression—real or fantasied—is often absent from, or is of only secondary importance in, most angry episodes.

The preoccupation of psychologists with aggression as opposed to anger stems, of course, not only from methodological necessities and available sources of data. From a practical point of view, aggression is a much more pressing problem than is anger. But anger is also of considerable practical and theoretical interest in its own right. It is one of the most frequently experienced of all emotions, one intimately connected not only with our sense of well-being but also with our sense of fairness and justice. Does anger serve no purpose, have no function, except in relation to aggression? Is the concept of anger so inherently ambiguous, so permeated by value judgments, that it is immune to scientific analysis? As the following chapters will demonstrate, the answers to these questions is a definite no.

Concluding Observations

In this chapter we have presented in broad outline a constructivist view of emotion. The remainder of this volume will be devoted to filling in the details of that view, using anger as a paradigm case. At first anger might seem to be an inauspicious choice for such a purpose. More than most emotions, anger is often condemned as antisocial. Among young children, angry outbursts are usually punished by parents, teachers, and others in authority. And among adults, anger is typically regarded as an unpleasant or negative emotional experience. Yet anger is among the commonest of emotions. How can that be, unless anger is indeed an uncontrollable (instinctive) remnant of our phylogenetic past?

The remainder of this volume is an attempt to answer that question. If a constructivist view can accommodate the facts of anger, then its extension to most other emotions should be relatively straightforward. Let us begin our analysis by examining and reconceptualizing the biological bases of anger and aggression.

Chapter 2

Anger and Aggression in Biological Perspective

From a constructivist point of view, anger can be defined as a socially constituted syndrome, or transitory social role. One advantage of a definition in terms of social roles is that it allows a consideration of biological factors without resorting to a crude reductionism. As Newcomb (1950) has observed: "Protoplasm meets society as human organisms learn to perceive themselves and one another in terms of shared norms and become motivated to interact with one another by means of role behavior." (p. 331) Of course, it is one thing to say that protoplasm meets society in terms of shared norms and role behavior; it is quite another thing to say how that meeting takes place. That is the major prupose of the present chapter.

In general, I have little sympathy for the romantic notion that human beings are basically a pacific species and that, were it not for the corrupting influence of society, humans would live peacefully and harmoniously with one another. Although there are records of a few primitive societies in which aggression appears to be minimal or absent, that at best provides a hope for the future and not a testimony to the past. For the most part, the paleontological, anthropological, and historical record is disconcertingly gloomy as far as human aggression is concerned.

However, when considering the evolutionary-historical record and its implications for the study of anger, one important fact must be kept in mind. Human beings may indeed be an aggressive species "by nature." But without doubt, the greatest biological adaptation of humankind is the ability to transform and, to a limited extent, to transcend biological imperatives. In a real sense, biology has only provided humans with a first nature; society has provided a second. And neither is more fundamental than the other. Anger, to the extent that it is a socially constituted syndrome, belongs to our second nature.

In view of the above fact, a thorough discussion of anger from a biological perspective would have to take into account the evolution of human cognitive capacities, symbolization, and cooperative social living, as well as the evolution of aggression. However, such a broad-ranging review is beyond the scope of the present chapter. At the risk of perpetuating a one-sided conceptualization of anger, we will focus primarily on the aggressive elements in anger.

One final point by way of introduction: In Chapter 1 it was suggested that all behavior is hierarchically organized into systems, subsystems (syndromes), and elements, and that each level of organization can be analyzed from a sociocultural, psychological, and biological perspective. Thus, at the "highest" level of organization we may speak of sociocultural systems, psychological systems, and biological systems. Of course, no actual system of behavior is purely sociocultural, psychological, or biological. These are abstractions, projections, so to speak, on the axes of a three-dimensional life space.

We will begin this chapter by illustrating what is meant by a biological system of behavior. This will provide the background for discussing biological systems related to anger and aggression. We will then examine briefly the neural mecahnisms mediating anger and aggression, and the theoretical implications of this line of research. The final section of this chapter is devoted to an analysis of one class of biological elements—innate expressive reactions—which have figured prominently in traditional theories of emotion.

Biological Systems of Behavior

A concrete example will help to illustrate what is meant by a biological system of behavior. The kittiwake, a species of gull, has an unusual pattern of nesting behavior (see Cullen, 1957, and Tinbergen, 1960, for a complete description). Unlike most gulls, the kittiwake lives in the open sea outside of the breeding season, and when it does visit the land to breed, it nests on tiny cliff ledges which are sometimes only 4 inches wide. Cliff nesting in the kittiwake forms a coherent system of behavior that is related to a major biological adaptation—defense of the young against predation.

As a complex system of behavior, cliff nesting comprises a number of subsystems and elements. To take but a few examples, female kittiwakes sit down during copulation and newborn chicks tend to face the wall of the cliff. These behavioral elements help prevent falling off the ledge. Another behavioral element is the "choking" display used by male kittiwakes to attract a mate. This response is probably derived from movements originally involved in nest building. (The male kittiwake's territory is little more than his nest site.)

Elements such as the above represent new adaptive specializations on the part of the kittiwake. Other characteristics peculiar to the kittiwake can be viewed as the relaxation of antipredator defenses common in other gulls. For example, kittiwakes do not attack predators, alarm calls are rare, chicks are not camouflaged, and eggshells (which might attract predators) are not removed from the nest.

The defense of the kittiwake against predation illustrates the following four features of biological systems:

1. A biological system is defined in terms of its "goal" or adaptive significance. The ultimate goal of a biological system is, of course, the preservation of the species. But this goal can be achieved through a series of intermediate steps or subgoals. The delineation of a biological system can thus be made at different levels of generality. The antipredator system of the kittiwake has been defined at a

very general level. It could be broken down into subsystems serving more proximate goals, for example, nest building, pair formation, mating, or parental behavior.

2. A biological system consists of a variety of semiautonomous response elements, many of which are adaptive specializations in their own right. Such elements are genetically correlated. There is, however, no core feature (a specific neurological circuit, say) that ties the various elements together. Indeed, when the biological system involves a social network, different elements of the system may occur in different individuals (e.g., the choking display of the male kittiwake, the posture of the female during copulation, and the tendency of the chicks to face the wall of the cliff). In this respect, the notion of a biological system differs from the older notion of an instinct, for example as adumbrated by McDougall (1936).

3. Any particular response may be an element in more than one biological system. For example, the regurgitation of food serves to rid the stomach of undesirable contents. In the kittiwake, as well as in many other species of birds, regurgitation is also a means of feeding the young. And the llama of the Peruvian Andes has harnessed regurgitation for even more interesting purposes—it vomits in the face of an attacker. Needless to say, response elements differ in their relative accessibility; not any element can be incorporated into any system with equal ease. But as the above examples illustrate, even an organ such as the stomach is capable of rather diverse adaptive specializations.

4. In the absence of maintenance inputs, biological systems tend to undergo progressive relaxation. That is, the individual elements gradually become more loosely connected and independent of one another. The opposite of progressive relaxation is systematization, that is, the strengthening of preexisting relations and/or the addition of new elements and relationships into a system. Both processes are evident in the cliff nesting of the kittiwake, which involved the relaxation of antipredator defenses found in other gulls as well as the evolution of new adaptive specializations. In biological systems progressive relaxation may result from such genetic processes as mutation, independent assortment, recombination, and the like, while natural selection acts as the major systematizing influence. Natural selection is not, however, the only means of systematization. Even in lower organisms, individual experience in a particular environment may be an important factor in determining how response elements will become coordinated into an organized whole. Imprinting and learning are essential to the operation of most biological systems. And as we ascend the phylogenetic scale, biological systems become increasingly relaxed on a genetic level, and individual experience assumes ever greater importence as a systematizing factor.

The Relationship Between Biological Systems and Emotional Syndromes

There is a long tradition within psychology of identifying emotional syndromes with biologically based systems of behavior. However, there has been little agreement with regard to what constitutes a biological system and on the nature of the relationship of such systems to specific emotions. Therefore, before turning to our own proposals in this regard, it may be helpful to describe briefly the suggestions of another theorist. Plutchik (1980) has constructed a list of primary biological systems and their associated emotions. This list is presented in Table 2-1.

To qualify for inclusion in Plutchik's list, a biological system has to fulfill a basic adaptive function evident at all levels of the phylogenetic scale, from amoeba to human being. It follows that the corresponding emotions also exist at all levels and hence cannot be identified with particular body parts or specific response elements. The myriad of emotions recognized in human beings are, according to Plutchik, combinations or mixtures of the primary emotions. (For example, pride is presumably a mixture of anger and joy.) In this regard, Plutchik draws an analogy between emotional mixtures and color mixtures, that is, all the colors of the (emotional) spectrum can be obtained by combining a limited number of primaries.

There is no need here to review in any detail the theoretical rationale of empirical evidence for the type of position advocated by Plutchik. Suffice it to say that his views are not unrepresentative of a broad class of theories that relate emotional reactions more or less closely to a small number of biological systems (cf. Tomkins, 1962, 1963, 1980, 1981, 1982; Scott, 1969; Izard, 1977). The constructivist point of view being advocated here necessitates a somewhat different stance on the relationship between biological systems and emotional syndromes. This stance can be summarized in the following six propositions.

1. It is meaningful to speak of biological systems only on the species level. Of course, there are occasions when it may be useful to treat broad adaptive functions in the abstract, as does Plutchik. However, the same adaptive function can often be achieved by very different means. For example, protection of the young is an important adaptive function for all but the simplest of species. Yet knowledge of cliff nesting in the kittiwake, for example, is not very informative

Table 2-1. Plutchik's Structural Model of the Relationship Between Biological Systems and Emotional Reactions

Biological system	Behavioral manifestation	Emotional experience
Protection	Withdrawing, escaping	Fear, terror
Destruction	Attacking, biting	Anger, rage
Reproduction	Mating, possessing	Joy, ecstasy
Reintegration	Crying for help	Sadness, grief
Incorporation or affiliation	Pair bonding, grooming	Acceptance, trust
Rejection	Vomiting, defecating	Disgust, loathing
Exploration	Examining, mapping	Expectancy, anticipation
Orientation	Stopping, freezing	Surprise, astonishment

Note. In order to maintain consistency with the text, the headings in this table have been modified from those presented by Plutchik (1980, p. 154). The three columns, according to Plutchik, represent different "languages" for the description of emotion. The terms in the first column represent a functional language, that is, they describe the goals or functions of the emotions, biologically speaking. The second column describes the kinds of behavior that (depending upon the species) might be involved in fulfilling the corresponding functions. Finally, the third column contains words used to describe the subjective experience of emotion in humans.

about how that same function is achieved by such very different species as turtles and baboons. Even when we are dealing with more narrowly defined systems, such as mating behavior, generalization from one species to another can be made only on the basis of a detailed knowledge of the specific responses involved (Beach, 1976). And what is true of biological systems is even more true of emotional syndromes (subsystems), which are based on sociocultural and psychological, as well as on biological, systems of behavior. But more of that shortly.

2. An indefinite number of biological systems can be identified, depending upon the purpose of the investigator and the level of generality desired. For example, Plutchik relates anger and aggression to a single biological system (destruction), the prototype of which is the attempt to destroy a barrier to the satisfaction of some need. By contrast, Moyer (1976) has identified six different systems related to destructive or aggressive behavior. Moyer's scheme will be discussed in some detail later in this chapter. For the moment, suffice it to note that there is no set number of basic or primary biological systems. The number of systems identified depends in part on the point at which one chooses to enter the behavioral hierarchy, that is, on the level of organization that is of primary interest.

3. To complicate matters even further, biological systems are organized in a heterarchical as well as a hierarchical fashion. That is, the same behavioral element may form part of one biological system on one occasion and part of a different system on another occasion. Stated somewhat differently, biological systems tend to shade into one another "horizontally" as well as "vertically." Hence, even at a given level of organization, the distinction among biological systems is inherently arbitrary.

4. As we ascend the phylogenetic scale, biological systems become increasingly relaxed on a genetic level and individual experience assumes greater importance as a systematizing influence. This point has already been mentioned, but it deserves reemphasis, for it is central to a constructivist view of emotion. Specifically, elements from biological systems (and sociocultural and psychological systems, as well) are combined into specific emotional syndromes on the basis of learning and socialization. Take grief as an example. Some of the elements of grief (e.g., loss of appetite) may be largely of biological origin; other symptoms (e.g., certain mourning practices) may be primarily cultural in origin; and, of course, each individual experiences grief in a unique fashion, depending upon his or her own psychological makeup. The only point that needs emphasis here is that an emotional syndrome such as grief is the product of a complex interplay of factors, and it cannot be "reduced" in any simple fashion to a biological system.

5. It follows from the above considerations that there is no straightforward relationship between biological systems and specific emotional syndromes. Different emotions may be fashioned from the same biological system; and conversely, elements from different biological systems may be incorporated into a single emotion. Moreover, the various human emotions differ in how closely they are related to biological systems. Some very simple emotional reactions, such as startle to a loud noise, can be accounted for largely in biological terms. Other emotions, such as hope, courage, and envy, are more the product of socio-

cultural than biological evolution. One of the central themes of the present volume is that anger belongs with the latter group.

6. As a final point, it might be noted that the mere involvement of a biological system does not make a response emotional. Rozin (1976) has analyzed "intelligence" as a complex biological system consisting of a hierarchy of adaptive specializations, that is, specific solutions to specific problems in survival. The interpretation of a response as either "emotional" or "intelligent" depends on factors other than (or in addition to) the presence or absence of biologically based elements. Some of these other factors were described in Chapter 1, including the unusualness of the response, the attribution of responsibility, and degree of commitment implied.

Biological Systems Related to Anger and Aggression

Moyer (1976) has distinguished among six different biological systems related to aggression, namely, predatory, intermale, fear-induced, maternal, irritable, and sex-related aggression. Each kind of aggression is identifiable primarily in terms of the type of stimulus that elicits an attack, the topography of the response, and/or underlying physiological mechanisms (neuronal and endocrine). In addition, systems of aggression may differ in their reinforcing properties and in their relationship to other biological systems. For example, predatory aggression is linked to the neural substrate for hunger and is positively reinforcing, whereas fear-induced aggression is independent of hunger and is negatively reinforcing. The following is a brief description of each aggressive system.

Predatory aggression involves attack against prey. Although obviously related to hunger, the relationship is not invariable. Satiated animals will frequently hunt and attack prey without eating the victim; and hungry animals without adequate experience may starve in the presence of prey. In most species, predatory aggression is readily distinguishable from other forms of aggression in terms of response topography. The cat, for example, will stalk its prey and direct its attack (e.g., to the neck of the prey) in a manner quite distinct from the feline "rage" reaction, which is characterized by an arched back, piloerection, unsheathed claws, and so forth.

Intermale aggression occurs, as its name implies, between male conspecifics. With few exceptions, the male of most species is more aggressive than the female, and the target of the aggression is another male of the same species. The topography of intermale aggression is often highly stereotyped, consisting of threat displays and attacks against well-protected portions of the opponent's body. The male sex hormone (androgen) is critical for the development and maintenance of this form of aggression.

Fear-induced aggression can be differentiated from other forms by the fact that it is always preceded by attempts to escape. In some animals, it is also distinguishable in terms of the topography of the response, which involves autonomic reactions and defensive threat displays. However, not all defensive aggression is fear induced; for example, animals will often attack well before they are cornered or even attempt to flee. Novelty is an important factor in fear-induced aggression. Little is known about its endocrine and neurological bases, although it can be elicited by electrical stimulation of the brain.

Maternal aggression occurs in many, but not all, vertebrate species. The eliciting conditions involve some threat to the mother's young. The probability of attack depends on the stimulus characteristics of the young and the hormonal status of the mother. In primates, this type of aggression seems to be less dependent on hormones than in lower species, and more dependent on stimuli associated with the young (e.g., distress calls). Consequently, maternal aggression in primates may be displayed by females other than the mother and by males.

Irritable aggression may be elicited by a very broad class of stimuli, including pain, physiological dysfunction, deprivation, frustration, discomfort, and the like. In its pure form, irritable aggression involves attack without prior attempts to escape from the object being attacked. Males tend to show irritable aggression more than females; and in the latter, irritable aggression may fluctuate in association with the reproductive cycle.

Sex-related aggression is elicited by the same stimuli that elicit sexual behavior and is found primarily (but not exclusively) in the male. In some species, the initial stages of mating show a superficial resemblance to intermale or even predatory aggression. Of course, the consequences of aggressive courtship and true fighting are quite different. Nevertheless, sex-related aggression in animals sometimes occurs independently of reproductive behavior, as when males attack females in estrus.

Interrelationships Among Aggressive Systems

One might argue with the specifics of the above classification scheme. Irritable aggression, for example, appears to be a very broad and ill-defined class, and with increased research it may be possible to identify still other aggressive systems. Of even greater importance is the fact that each species shows its own unique pattern of aggressive behavior. Thus, not all species are predatory; in some the female is as aggressive as the male; and so forth.

But in spite of the above caveats, the general thrust of Moyer's analysis is surely correct: From a biological perspective, aggression is not a unitary phenomenon. Different kinds of aggression can be identified, each with its own adaptive significance, underlying physiological mechanisms, and so on. This statement does not mean, however, that the various kinds of aggression are completely independent of one another. As discussed earlier, the same response element may enter into more than one biological system, thus blurring any sharply defined boundaries. This is certainly true of aggressive systems. Moyer (1976) has described the situation as follows:

> There is no theoretical reason why behavior should not be under the influence of more than one set of physiological processes. It is, in fact, probably the most common state of affairs. The possible interactions among the different kinds of aggression and other motivational states are extremely complex... [for example,] the tendency to predatory behavior may be

inhibited by factors that activate the physiological processes associated with fear. However, the behavioral components of predation may be facilitated by those factors that activate the mechanisms for irritable aggression. At the same time, however, the predator is at some stage of food deprivatation and the physiological processes underlying that state are also contributing an input to the behavioral tendency that may be either facilitating or inhibiting, depending on the aomunt of deprivation. The animal is also in some state of sleep deprivation, which may also make some contribution to the behavioral outcome, and so on, almost ad infinitum. (pp. 207-208)

Anger and Agression

To which biological system, or combination of systems, might human anger be related? Moyer (1976) implies that human anger is most closely related to the class of irritable aggression. But that is not the only possibility. Men often become angry at other men in competitive and dominance situations (intermale aggression); mothers become angry at insults to their children (maternal aggression); men and women may become angry when threatened (fear-related aggression); and anger is not unknown during sexual encounters (sex-related aggression). With a little stretch of the imagination, anger may even be related to predatory aggression. Wolf (1965) has noted that the Romans considered the stomach to have aggressive connotations. For example, Horace referred to the *stomachum* (wrath) of Achilles—*Pelidae stomachum cedere nescile.* Wolf's own investigations indicate that the Romans may not have been entirely fanciful in this regard. Patients with stomach fistulas show an engorgement of the stomach lining with blood and increased gastric secretion when angry or hostile.

The above observations illustrate the futility of trying to relate a human emotional syndrome, such as anger, to any *specific* biological system of behavior. Indeed, we know very little about the evolution of human aggression in general, not to mention human anger in particular. Did humans evolve as a carniverous hunting species, as Ardrey (1976) and others have suggested, or are the roots of human aggression to be found in other biological systems? At the present time, one can only speculate.

Bigelow (1973) has argued that the rapid evolution of human beings (*Homo sapiens*) from early hominids was the result of two interrelated factors. The first factor was the development of *intragroup cooperation,* which facilitated protection and education of the young, defense from attack, and so forth. Such intragroup cooperation required an effective communication system (language), the control of biological urges, planning for the future, in short, intelligence. The second factor was *intergroup competition* for favored locations, game, and other resources. The existence of small groups allowed for diversity, that is, genetic changes were not submerged in a large population. Strange but similar individuals were probably attacked most readily, since they would provide the most competition. Hence, there has been only one evolving species of humans, with less adept groups (in terms of intragroup cooperation) being killed off.

The details of Bigelow's argument are not of concern to us here. All that is important to note is the close dialectical relationship that he postulates between the evolution of intelligence and aggression. Some theorists would like to deny the existence of such a relationship as though it represented some kind of original sin that, if true, would condemn the human species to perpetual strife and misery. But that implication is unwarranted. To the extent that aggression facilitated the evolution of intelligence, it also provided the means for its own transcendence. If aggression is prevalent in modern societies, it is not because of some biological imperative. It is, rather, due to conditions within society that encourage and maintain aggressive responses.

This brings us back to a point made earlier. In humans, biological systems have undergone progressive relaxation on a genetic level, while individual experience and social custom have assumed primary importance as systematizing factors. Thus, elements from different biological systems may combine with socially determined responses to form an almost indefinite variety of specific syndromes, of which anger is one example. Other examples of culture-specific aggressive syndromes will be discussed in Chapter 3. For the moment, suffice it to note that there is no contradiction in the contention that anger may indeed be related to one or more biological systems, and that anger is nevertheless a social construction.

Central Neural Mechanisms Mediating Anger and Aggression

Most of the aggressive systems discussed above can be activated by direct electrical or chemical stimulation of the brain. In the cat, for example, stimulation of the lateral hypothalamus may elicit a predatory attack against a rat; on the other hand, stimulation of the ventromedial hypothalamus may lead the cat, in a fit of feline "rage," to ignore the rat and attack the experimenter instead. The relevant research findings have been summarized in considerable detail by Moyer (1976). Our concern here is not with the details of such findings but with their implications for a theory of human anger and aggression. Therefore, the present discussion will be limited to a few illustrative studies involving primates, both infrahuman and human.

With regard to the organization of aggressive behavior in primates, perhaps the most informative series of studies is that by Delgado and his colleagues (Delgado, 1967, 1970; Delgado & Mir, 1969). Delgado has proposed what he calls a "theory of fragmental representation of behavior." According to this theory, some areas of the brain are responsible for the organization of behavioral fragments, such as autonomic responses, vocalization, facial expression, and tonic and phasic motor activity. Other neural structures help to organize these fragments into more complex behavioral episodes (e.g., a well-directed attack). Finally, the same response element or fragment may enter into more than one kind of behavioral category (e.g., sexual arousal and aggression), whereas other fragments, such as certain facial displays and vocalizations, may be specific to a single behavioral category.

Delgado's "theory" of behavioral fragmentation is basically an alternative conception of biological systems of behavior, a conception couched in neurological rather than genetic or evolutionary terms. Let us see how such a conception applies to the aggressive behavior of monkeys and men.

Delgado (1967) equipped *Macaca mulatta* monkeys with remote-controlled intracerebral electrodes. The brains of these monkeys could be stimulated by radio while the animals were isolated or roamed freely in their colonies. In agreement with Delgado's theory of behavioral fragmentation, stimulation of some brain sites elicited such elementary responses as opening the mouth, baring the teeth, and vocalizations. Stimulation of other areas of the brain elicited responses that, while still fragmentary, were more complex and sequentially organized. Examples included walking around the cage, circling, climbing, and the like. Such responses were indistinguishable from spontaneous acts and they were sensitive to changes in the environment; however, they remained divorced or isolated from the remainder of the animal's behavior. Finally, at a still higher level of organization, stimulation of the brain could trigger well-coordinated and purposeful attacks against other members of the colony.

Well-coordinated aggression of the latter type was dependent on the social status and past experiences of the animal. For example, when stimulation was applied to the "boss" or highest ranking monkey, he chased the subordinate animals around the cage, often striking and biting at them. But the aggression was not indiscriminate. Males with whom there had been previous clashes were the most frequent targets. "Friends" were less likely to be attacked.

The dependency of aggression on the social context is perhaps best illustrated by the behavior of one monkey, Lina, whose social status was manipulated by the substitution of dominant and submissive animals within a four-member colony. The same area of the brain (a point in the nucleus ventralis posterior lateralis of the thalamus) was stimulated on all occasions. When Lina was the lowest ranking member of the colony, brain stimulation triggered only a small number of attacks. In fact, rather than being the aggressor, Lina became the target of attack by the more dominant members of the colony whenever her brain was stimulated. When Lina's social rank was improved by the substitution of a subordinate monkey for one of the dominant animals, stimulation elicited a greater number of attacks by Lina, directed mainly at the newcomer. With further substitution of submissive for dominant animals, Lina's rank was raised to second in the four-member colony. Electrical stimulation of her brain now resulted in increased aggressiveness, and she ceased to be the target of attack by others.

In summary, aggressive systems—like other biological systems of behavior—are composed of semiautonomous or fragmentary responses. These response elements can be elicited by direct stimulation of neuronal groups within the central nervous system. Other neuronal groups, located in different areas of the brain, help to integrate the response elements into organized wholes. Stimulation of the latter structures does not elicit specific responses, but rather an "intent." Whether or not the intent is manifested depends on the animal's assessment of the situation and on previous experience.

It is a long evolutionary step from *Macaca mulatta* to *Homo sapiens*. Nevertheless, the principles of organization described by Delgado for the monkey seem to hold—with some important qualifications to be discussed below—for the human also.

Over the past several decades, numerous patients suffering from epileptic and other neurological disorders have had electrodes implanted in their brains for diagnostic or treatment purposes. The following is the verbatim report of an interview with one such patient as a 5-mA current was being passed through an electrode located in the amygdala.[1]

Interviewer: "How do you feel now?"

Subject (voice much higher in tone): "I feel like I want to get up from this chair! Please don't let me do it! (There is a change to strong voice inflection and a marked alteration in facial expression to express pleading.) Don't do this to me. I don't want to be mean!"

Interviewer: "Feel like you want to hit me?"

Subject: "Yeah, I just want to hit something. (Appears and sounds aroused and angry.) I want to get something and just tear it up. Take it so I won't! (Hands her scarf to interviewer; he hands her a stack of paper, and without further verbal exchange she tears it to shreds.) I don't like to feel like this!"

At this point, the level of stimulating current was reduced, and a short time later increased again.

Subject (voice loud and pleading): "Don't let me hit you!"

Interviewer: "How do you feel now?"

Subject: "I think I feel a little better like this. I get it out of my system. I don't have those other thoughts (her pre-existing mental symptoms) when I'm like this. . . . Take my blood pressure. Make them cut this thing off, it's killing me! Take my blood pressure, I say! (Strong voice inflection and facial appearance of anger.) Quit holding me! I'm getting up! You'd better get somebody else if you want to hold me! I'm going to hit you!" (Raises arm as if to strike.)

After the stimulating current was turned off, the interview was directed toward a detailed review of what had gone on.

Interviewer: "Did you see anyone? Your husband?"

Subject: "No, I didn't. I didn't even think about my husband."

Interviewer: "Did you feel any pain?"

Subject: "No, it's just a feeling in my body. No pain."

Interviewer: "Would you like to go through that again?"

Subject: "No. It didn't pain, but I don't like the feelings."

Interviewer: "Can you describe them?"

Subject: "I can't describe it, just can act it. I felt better in a way; I wasn't worried any more." (Her mental complaints.)

As the last statement by this patient illustrates, the subjective experiences resulting from electrical stimulation of the brain are often difficult to describe. In a hospital setting, the staff is generally supportive and sympathetic, giving little reason for anger. Thus, when a desire to attack does occur, it tends to have an unreal quality. The patient does not know how to interpret his or her own experience.

---

[1] This interview originally appeared in an article by King (1961, p. 485).

A variety of neurological and metabolic disorders may result in abnormal "stimulation" of the brain under natural conditions. The following case history, reported by Mark and Ervin (1970), is an example. As a young man, Thomas R. suffered brain anemia as a result of a ruptured ulcer and a resultant prolonged drop in blood pressure. Being a highly intelligent and creative individual, he was still able to educate himself to be an engineer. However, his behavior became increasingly unpredictable and at times psychotic. His major problem was uncontrollable anger. He harbored grudges and interpreted as insults even minor incidents. For example, if another car cut in front of him, he might take it as a personal affront, speed after the driver, and force him or her to the side of the road. If the driver was a man, Thomas would assault him; if it was a woman, he would insult her.

The most frequent target of Thomas's anger was his wife. An assault on his wife was typically preceded by an experience of severe abdominal or facial pain. Thomas might then take as an insult some innocuous remark, or accuse his wife of indiscretions, all the while becoming more enraged. The entire episode would culminate in a physical assault against his wife and sometimes his children. After such an outburst, Thomas would experience remorse and claim not to have any recollection of what he had done.

Thomas had been treated by a psychiatrist for 7 years, but to no avail. Antiseizure drugs and other medications also had little effect. The decision was therefore made to treat the illness with stereotaxic surgery. Electrodes were implanted in the amygdala of both hemispheres. When the medial area of the amygdala was stimulated, Thomas complained of pain and had a feeling of losing control; both reactions were prodromal to a typical onset of violence. Stimulation of the lateral amygdala produced a cessation of facial pain and a feeling of extreme relaxation. Bilateral lesions were made in the medial amygdala, following which the violent attacks ceased. However, Thomas continued to have an occasional epileptic seizure with periods of confusion and disorderly thinking.

Examples such as the above could be multiplied almost indefinitely, but one more brief case history will suffice for our purposes. Elliott (1978) has given the following description of a patient suffering from epilepsy.

> An intelligent woman of 38, with a warm and pleasant personality, developed temporal lobe attacks. In only two of these did she lose consciousness. Most of the attacks consisted of a momentary dreamy state during which external objects appeared unfamiliar. Over the same period she became subject to attacks of what she called insane rage. She was unaware of any external or internal reason for her anger. She might go down to the celler and start breaking things or she would scream at her children or her husband for no reason at all. These attacks disturbed her greatly as she had been under psychotherapy for eight years without benefit. (pp. 174-175)

An electroencephalogram showed epileptic spikes in all leads. Her symptoms, including the attacks of explosive rage, disappeared entirely when she was given medication (400 mg of phenytoin daily). Interestingly, however, another "symptom" appeared. All of her life, the patient had been without ordinary fear (e.g., when out alone in a bad neighborhood). With phenytoin she developed a normal sense of fear and apprehension.

Findings such as the above leave little doubt that biological systems related to aggression are represented in the human brain. It is not possible at the present time to differentiate human aggression into subtypes on the basis of underlying physiological mechanisms, as Moyer (1976) has done in the case of animal aggression. This is not due simply to a lack of relevant research on the human level. It is also due to the fact that human intellectual and symbolic capacities assure that whatever biological systems of aggression do exist are inevitably amalgamated, not only with one another, but with socially constituted responses as well. Thus, there is no isomorphic relationship between human aggressive syndromes and biological systems of behavior.

This point deserves particular emphasis. It is all too easy to assume that the results of neurophysiological investigations are irrelevant to *normal* human emotions; or to assume the contrary, namely, that an emotion such as anger exists "pre-programmed" within the nervous system, needing only an appropriate trigger in order to be released. Far more difficult is to conceive of how neurological, psychological, and sociocultural factors interact to produce emotional syndromes *sui generis*. For the latter, Delgado's "theory of fragmental organization of behavior" must be supplemented with a "theory of the organization of behavioral fragments." With this in mind, let us explore in somewhat more detail the nature and implications of the above findings.

Perhaps the first thing to note is that the mere elicitation of a response by electrical stimulation of the brain, or the elimination of a response through medication, tells us very little about how that response came to be organized the way it is. The pioneering studies of Penfield are particularly informative in this respect (Penfield, 1975; Penfield & Roberts, 1966). Unlike the studies described above, which involved the stimulation of subcortical areas, Penfield's investigations were limited primarily to the cerebral cortex. He found that stimulation of the secondary sensory areas could produce lifelike visual and auditory experiences. For example, one mother told of suddenly becoming aware, as the electrode touched her neocortex, of being in the kitchen listening to the voice of her little boy playing outside. A young man found himself in a concert hall listening to music; he could even hear the different instruments. Another woman heard a melody each time the same point was stimulated—for 30 times!

Memories are not limited to the type of visual and auditory images described by Penfield's patients. More abstract ideas, including internalized social norms and rules, are also encoded in neural tissue. Abstract ideas are not the stuff of immediate experience; their presence is "felt" primarily in the way they help to guide and regulate behavior. The following case, humorous and yet pathetic, illustrates how a lesion in the brain can destroy the practical memory for one of the most elementary rules of conduct in this society. A 62-year-old bank executive was suffering from intractable pain as a result of advanced cancer. Medication did not relieve the pain, and so a lesion was made in the white matter of the frontal lobe. Mark and Ervin (1970) describe the result as follows:

After he recovered from the operation, he went back to his normal routine as if nothing had happened. He said that he felt well, and he insisted that he and his wife go to an opera opening. He dressed himself immaculately in formal evening attire and walked with his wife from their house to the theater. His conversation was witty and urbane. About halfway there, he said, "Excuse me," and in full view of oncoming traffic and pedestrians, he urinated in the street! (pp. 142-143)

The images reported by Penfield's patients and the indiscretion of the bank executive are quite different from the emotional outbursts described earlier. Indeed, there do not appear to be any areas of the neocortex that are specifically associated with states like anger, fear, or joy. It would be wrong to conclude, however, that only limbic and subcortical structures are relevant to emotional reactions per se, and that the neocortex is the provenance of "higher" mental functions only. Quite the contrary: the amygdala, hippocampus, and other subcortical and limbic structures play as important a role in memory formation as they do in emotional reactivity; and it should go without saying that no emotion could occur in a truly human sense without the involvement of the neocortex. The nervous system is just that—a *system* in which no part functions in isolation of the others. And emotional reactions, like any other complex pattern of behavior, depend upon a hierarchical integration of cortical and subcortical activity. It makes little sense to speak of the emotions as though they were localized in one part of the brain or another.

This brief discussion of the neural mechanisms mediating anger and aggression has extended the previous discussion of biological systems to include their representation in the central nervous system. To parody a phrase by Delgado, we might speak of a "theory of the organization of behavioral fragments." Such a theory, as applied to human emotions, would contain at least the following three propositions (in addition to the six outlined earlier in connection with the evolution of biological systems):

1. The neural mechanisms mediating emotional reactions must be at least as variable as the behavior being mediated. Although emotional reactions may appear stereotyped relative to more deliberate, "purposeful" forms of behavior, they are nevertheless exquisitely variable. For example, not only are the situations that elicit anger quite varied, owing to the ability of humans to invest events with meaning, but so too are the responses. With the possible exeption of some expressive reactions, which will be discussed later in this chapter, anger can be manifested in an indefinite number of ways. Even if we limit consideration to direct physical aggression, an angry person may hit, kick, shoot, stab, bite, and so forth. But more indirect forms of aggression, such as a verbal retort or the withdrawal of some reward, are even more common during anger, as are a variety of nonaggressive responses. (The nature of the responses during anger will be discussed in detail in Chapter 9.)

2. The factors that bind responses into coherent syndromes are to be found within the environment as well as within the nervous system. This fact is amply illustrated by studies involving electrical stimulation of the brain. Except for elementary sensory and motor "fragments," the behavior elicited depends as much on

the environmental context as on the site of the electrode. In general, it may be said that emotional syndromes, including anger, represent evnironmental-behavioral units, and as such they are dependent upon, but not reducible to central neural mechanisms.

3. Experientially induced growth of cell fibers can alter the structural relationship among neurons, thus establishing new functional mechanisms within the central nervous system (cf. Luria, 1973; Pribram, 1971). In other words, the environmental factors that lend coherence to behavioral syndromes need not be current. The past experience of the individual—and of society, through the socialization of the individual—help to create behavioral syndromes *sui generis*. Of course, some nerual networks are less modifiable than others; that is, some elements of behavior may be "preprogrammed" in the central nervous system. But these behavioral fragments must be incorporated into larger units before they can play a role in adaptive behavior. And from a psychological viewpoint, it is the larger unit, that is, the behavioral syndrome rather then the behavioral element, that is the primary unit of analysis.

In spite of the implications of this last proposition, one class of behavioral elements—expressive reactions—has played a central role in theories of emotion. It is therefore important to consider this kind of response in somewhat more detail.

Expressive Reactions as Elements in Emotional Syndromes

Expressive reactions may be defined as stereotyped and rather discrete responses that are not intentionally directed toward any goal. Weeping, laughing, frowning, and other facial expressions are good examples. Some expressive reactions are learned and hence are idiosyncratic to an individual or to a culture. Others are genetically determined, either directly or indirectly. Our concern here is with the latter, which may be called *biological expressors*. By definition, biological expressors are elements of biological systems; they also may enter into specific emotional syndromes. An analysis of biological expressors may therefore help clarify the relationship between emotional syndromes and biological systems.

By way of background it will be helpful to review briefly two current theories of emotion that place a good deal of emphasis on biological expressors. Izard (1977) has defined an emotion as "a complex process with neurophysiological, neuromuscular, and phenomenological aspects" (p. 48). At the neurophysiological level, emotions consist of genetically determined patterns of electrochemical activity within the nervous system. At the neuromuscular level, facial expressions are the primary constituents of emotion, with bodily responses (postural-gestural, visceral-glandular, and vocal) playing a secondary role. Finally, at the phenomenological level, emotions help to amplify and sustain motivated behavior. More specifically, "when neurochemical activity, via innate programs, produces patterned facial and bodily activities, and feedback from these activities is transformed into conscious form, the result is a discrete fundamental emotion which is both a motivating and meaningful cue-producing experience" (p. 49).

Drawing on a number of sources, including his own cross-cultural research on the recognition of facial expressions, Izard (1977) argues that there are eight discrete fundamental emotions: enjoyment-joy, anger-rage, digust-revulsion, distress-anguish, surprise-startle, interest-excitement, shame-humiliation, and contempt-scorn. Our primary concern here is, of course, with anger. "In the human being," Izard states without equivocation, "the expression of anger and the experiential phenomenon of anger are innate, pancultural, universal phenomena" (p. 64). We shall return to this contention shortly.

Much of the best research on expressive reactions has come from the laboratory of Paul Ekman (for general reviews, see Ekman & Friesen, 1975; Ekman, Friesen, & Ellsworth, 1972). Although primarily concerned with nonverbal behavior in general, Ekman has also considered in some detail the relationship between expressive reactions and specific emotions. In a recent summary of research findings, Ekman and Oster (1979) conclude that there is unambiguous evidence of universality in the expressions for happiness, anger, disgust, sadness, distress, and combined fear/surprise. In literate cultures the latter two emotions (fear and surprise) are typically distinguishable from one another, but Ekman and Friesen (1971) found that among the South Fore of New Guinea, expressions of fear tended to be confused with expressions of surprise. Ekman and Oster also question Izard's data on the recognition of interest and shame, but basically they leave open the question whether future research may reveal universal facial expressions for these and other emotions.

Some theorists, such as Birdwhistell (1979), have denied that there is any evidence for universals in the facial expression of emotion. Ekman (1977) notes that one source of the disagreement on this issue is the frequent failure to specify exactly what is meant by emotion. Ekman's own conception of emotion resembles that of Izard. (The resemblance is not coincidental, for both draw heavily on the earlier theorizing of Silvan Tomkins, 1962, 1963.) Ekman explicitly rejects the notion that there is some *sine qua non* for emotion, whether visceral reactions, cognitive appraisal, or facial responses. Nevertheless, he, like Izard, postulates a limited number of neural "affect programs" which are genetically based and closely associated with the innervation of the facial musculature. An affect program is triggered by the appraisal of an appropriate stimulus; in turn, the affect program may set off memories, images, instrumental coping responses, and so on. Both the appraisal of emotional stimuli and the associated coping responses are primarily the product of cultural conditioning, but not the affect program itself.

> Biology has shaped the affect programme, determining which facial movements are likely to occur with one or another of the emotions, and perhaps also the timing of those movements. The particular combination of facial movements and the corresponding changes in visual appearance are not arbitrarily associated with each emotion but, for at least some emotions are the same for all people. (Ekman, 1977, pp. 65-66)

If the analyses of Ekman and Izard are correct, then anger cannot be viewed as a social construction except in a rather superficial sense. That is, culture might help determine the kinds of situations that elicit anger and the coping responses a person makes while angry. However, there would be a genetically determined core to the emotion, namely, the affect program and its associated expressive reactions. Except for borderline or incomplete instances, anger would indeed be "innate, pancultural, and universal."

At this point, it might be helpful to describe a representative study on the recognition of expressive reactions. We can then consider in more detail exactly what has and has not been demonstrated about the universality of emotional expressions.

In order to assure maximum cross-cultural generality, Ekman and Friesen (1971) tested the ability of people from a preliterate isolated culture (the South Fore of New Guinea) to identify the emotional expressions of Westerners. None of the subjects had ever seen a movie, worked for a Caucasian, or lived in a government town. The stimuli they were asked to judge consisted of 40 photographs of both posed and spontaneous emotional reactions. All the stimulus persons were Caucasians, both male and female, adult and child. The photographs were taken from previous research by Ekman and Friesen and others (e.g., Frois-Wittmann, (1930; Izard, 1968). Six different emotions were portrayed: happiness, anger, sadness, surprise, disgust, and fear.

The study consisted of a series of trials. On each trial the subject was presented with a set of three photographs and a brief story describing an emotion. The task was to select the photograph that matched the story. For example, on one trial the subject might be asked to pick the photograph of the person who is "angry and about to fight." On another trial, using another set of photographs, the story might refer to a person whose "child has died and feels very sad."

Because of the great number of possible combinations, not every emotion was contrasted with every other. Rather, a conservative procedure was employed in which each triad of photographs depicted emotions that, on the basis of prior research, were most likely to be confused with one another. Thus, anger was always contrasted with disgust, fear, and/or sadness, but never with happiness or surprise. Each triad of photographs was judged by variable number of subjects, ranging from 31 to 66.[2]

The results can be summarized briefly. With the exception of fear and surprise, which tended to be confused, subjects were readily able to match the photographs with the appropriate stories. For example, between 80 and 90% of the subjects selected the angry photograph when they were read the angry story.

The above results demonstrate quite convincingly that some facial expressions have a universal (pancultural) meaning. However, their significance for a theory of emotion is much less clear. Consider the case of anger. Subjects were asked to pick

---

[2] In addition to the data described here, Ekman and Friesen also showed photographs (in sets of two) to Fore children. The results were basically the same as those for adults. In still another aspect of this study, Ekman and Friesen asked a different set of Fore adults to indicate how they would look if they were the person being described in the emotion stories. Videotapes of some of these poses were shown to college students in the United States. The students had little difficulty identifying the expressions for anger, disgust, happiness, and sadness. However, fear was often confused with surprise, and vice versa. This was the same kind of mistake that the Fore made when judging Caucasian facial expressions.

the photograph in which the person is "angry and about to fight" (appropriately translated into the Fore language). None of the other stories or emotional labels had an aggressive connotation. Similarly, among the photographs only one aggressive display was depicted. In a strictly empirical sense, therefore, Ekman and Friesen have only demonstrated that certain expressive reactions connote aggressive intent, and that such expressions are recognizable across cultures. Such a demonstration tells us very little about anger as a specific emotional syndrome. This is because, in the study under consideration, the concept of anger was used in its most generic sense to refer to almost any aggressive tendency; no attempt was made to distinguish anger per se from a myriad of other aggressive syndromes (some examples of which will be described in Chapter 3).

The above "criticism" is not limited to the study by Ekman and Friesen. Quite the contrary, it is applicable to all studies that have demonstrated the recognition of emotion from facial expressions alone. In order to acheive accurate identification of expressive reactions, investigators have found it necessary to provide subjects with only a few generic labels or broad emotional categories from which to choose. When asked to make fine discriminations (e.g., between anger and jealousy) or when given the opportunity to generate their own descriptions, subjects typically fail to agree on the meaning of a facial expression.

The presence, then, of a given expressive reaction is not a *sufficient* condition for the attribution of emotion, since the same expression might be incorporated into a variety of different emotional and nonemotional syndromes. This is true even if the expression is spontaneous and sincere. The possibility remains, however, that perhaps expressive reactions are a *necessary* condition for the recognition and/ or experience of certain "fundamental" emotions, such as anger. This would seem to be the position of Izard (1977) and Tomkins (1962, 1963), among others. There is little evidence that bears directly on this issue (cf. Ekman & Oster, 1979), but some data from a study that will be reported in detail in Chapter 9 are tangentially relevant. In that study, only about 40% of the subjects reported that they felt any impulse toward physical aggression during a typical episode of anger. This would suggest that expressive reactions indicative of aggressive impulses may not be particularly common—no less necessary—during anger. Of course, a person might make an expressive reaction, perhaps in a very abbreviated or modified form, without recognizing or feeling any corresponding impulse. But then one would have to question the practical and theoretical significance of responses that are so fleeting that they often go unnoticed, both by the self and by others.[3]

From a constructivist viewpoint, biological expressors are just one kind of element that enters into emotional syndromes, and not the most important kind at

---

[3] For additional laboratory research that calls into question any necessary relationship between expressive reactions and the experience of emotion, see Tourangeau and Ellsworth (1979), together with a series of rebuttals and rejoinders by Izard (1981), Tomkins (1981), Hager and Ekman (1981), and Ellsworth and Tourangeau (1981). More than anything else this exchange illustrates the difficulty of testing the assumption that certain expressive reactions are a necessary, or even very important, part of so-called fundamental emotions, including anger.

that. As previously discussed, in human beings biological systems have undergone considerable relaxation. The various elements that constitute a system are therefore "free" to enter into a variety of more specific syndromes as a function of individual experience and social custom. The entire syndrome consists of cognitive appraisals, instrumental responses, socially as well as biologically determined expressive reactions, physiological changes, and the person's own reflective interpretation of the ongoing experience. To single out biological expressors as somehow more fundamental than the other components is a decision based on theoretical preconceptions; it is not a decision dictated by emprical evidence.

One final question remains: How do expressive reactions and other biological responses become incorporated into specific emotional syndromes? This is a difficult question, the answer to which can only be hinted at here. Anyone who has observed a very young child is aware of how expressive reactions may occur in keleidoscopic and rapidly changing arrays. The child may cry one moment and laugh the next, and sometimes is even startled at his or her own inconsistency. At this early stage of development the biological systems of which the expressive reactions are a part are still pretty well fractionated. With increasing experience (and perhaps maturation) the child acquires some control over these involuntary responses, and they gradually become organized into meaningful patterns closely attuned to the social situation. At this stage the child who has fallen may wait patiently for the approach of a sympathetic adult before bursting into tears. Eventually, after responses have been organized into a coherent pattern, their activation may become dissociated from consciousness, undergoing a secondary loss of voluntary control. It is only when this stage has been reached that we can properly speak of standard emotional syndromes. (We shall have more to say about emotional development in chapter 14.)

Concluding Observations

Behavior is subject to evolution, as are anatomical structures. It is thus possible to speak of biological systems of behavior, that is, species-wide patterns of response the elements of which subserve some common adaptive function. In humans, most biological systems have undergone considerable relaxation on the genetic level, and individual experience and social custom have become the primary systematizing factors. This means the elements of biological systems are relatively free to combine with other individually and socially constituted elements to form specific syndromes. Anger is one such syndrome.

The elements of a biological system are encoded within the nervous system and can be elicited as behavioral "fragments" by electrical stimulation of the brain. These fragments are hierarchically and heterarchically organized; there is, however, no core neural structure that binds them together as thread binds together the beads of a necklace. Rather, the fragments are more like the interlocking pieces of a puzzle. But unlike the pieces of an ordinary puzzle, behavioral fragments are dynamic structures the "shape" of which is constantly changing as a function of social (symbolic) as well as biological (genetic) factors.

Biologically based expressive reactions represent one class of response element or fragment. There is good evidence that some facial expressions are universally recognized as aggressive; that is, they are elements of one or more biological systems related to aggression. It is also evident that biological expressors have become incorporated into more specific aggressive syndromes, including anger. However, several caveats must be added in order to place these findings in proper perspective. For one thing, it is not known how common or important innate aggressive displays are for the everyday experience of anger. Certainly, they play a less visible and obvious role than do culturally determined (e.g., symbolic) gestures. For another thing, it is not known how frequently aggressive displays occur in nonangry situations.

Because of the theoretical significance that traditionally has been attached to biological expressors, it is perhaps worth emphasizing that what is true of one kind of a response element is not necessarily true of an entire behavioral syndrome. Thus, simply because some expressive reactions are innate and pancultural it does not follow that an emotion such as anger is also innate and pancultural.

As discussed in Chapter 1, emotional syndromes are interpreted as passions rather than as actions, that is, as something that happens to us as opposed to something we do. One possible source for the experience of passivity during emotion is the activation of elements of a biological system. Since such elements are, by definition, genetically determined, they have an automatic quality that seems to place them beyond a person's control. For example, it is difficult not to startle at a loud noise or to lash out at the source of pain. As a general principle, the more numerous or salient the biological elements in a given behavioral episode, the easier it is to interpret the entire response pattern as a passion rather than as an action. However, it would be wrong to conclude from this fact that the experience of emotion is invariably linked to biological systems, as a number of theorists have maintained (cf. McDougall, 1936; Plutchik, 1980).

The experience of emotion is an interpretation, a product of second-order monitoring. Thus, the activation of biological elements does not assure that a response will be experienced (interpreted) as emotional. Recall the statement of the woman, described on p. 43, who became aggressive as her brain was being stimulated through implanted electrodes: "I can't describe it [the nature of the experience], just can act it." The context (e.g., the hospital setting, the supportive behavior of the interviewer, and the knowledge that her brain was being stimulated artificially) provided no basis for this patient to interpret her experience as, say, anger. By contrast, given an adequate provocation or a tendency toward paranoid associations, artificial stimulation of the brain can indeed produce a full-blown angry episode. This is particularly true if the nature of the stimulation is unknown to the individual (e.g., because it is due to a tumor or epileptic discharge).

It is not just the activation of central neural mechanisms that facilitate the interpretation of a response as emotional. As Schachter (1971) and others have shown, the artificial induction of peripheral physiological arousal can have a similar effect; so too can the inducement of facial expressions (Laird, 1974). In general, it may be said that whenever one element of a behavioral syndrome is elicited, other elements of the syndrome will tend to be "recruited," and the entire episode will be interpreted in a manner appropriate to the context. (This is true, incidentally, whether or not the elements in question are parts of a biological system or whether they are socially constituted responses.) We shall have more to say about this issue, especially as it relates to peripheral physiological arousal, in Chapter 6. But it is time now to consider the contribution of sociocultural systems to aggressive syndromes.

Chapter 3

Cross-Cultural Variations in Aggressive Syndromes

Sociocultural systems of behavior can be defined in much the same way as biological systems, although the principles of organization are of course different. On the broadest level, one may speak of *the* social system, using the generic singular to refer to a given society in its entirety. The biological equivalent would be the species. On a somewhat less general, but still very broad, level of organization, one may speak of certain institutionalized ways of behaving that help maintain a given social order. Examples within our own society would include the judicial system, the banking system, and the legislative system. As social systems and subsystems become more and more narrowly defined, we eventually come to the level of the social role. This is the level of organization that is most relevant to an analysis of emotional syndromes.

In Chapter 1 emotions were defined as transitory social roles. There is no need to recapitulate that discussion here. The purpose of the present chapter is not to provide an analysis of emotional roles, but to illustrate their nature with concrete examples. In particular, we will consider four different aggressive syndromes: (1) wild-man behavior, a relatively nondangerous hysterical-like response observed among New Guinea highlanders; (2) *amok,* a deadly frenzy that occurs in a number of Southeast Asian societies, particularly in Malaysia, Indonesia, and the Philippines; (3) *to nu,* a response of the Kaingang Indians of Brazil that has some resemblance to both fear and anger; (4) and *ikari,* the closest equivalent to anger among the Japanese. After a brief description of each syndrome, its implications for the study of emotion in general, and anger in particular, will be discussed.

Wild-Man Behavior

Among the peoples who inhabit the highlands of New Guinea there is a syndrome that has variously been called "wild-man" behavior (Newman, 1964). "hysterical psychosis" (Langness, 1965), "possession" behavior (Koch, 1968; Salisbury, 1968), and "temporary madness" (Clarke, 1973). As these terms imply, the behavior does not represent a normal emotional response, although it does illustrate in exaggerated form many of the features of more standard emotions. Newman's term, wild-man behavior, is perhaps the most descriptive and theoretically neutral way of referring to the syndrome. The Gururumba, the group studied by Newman, are even more picturesque; they call the syndrome "being a wild pig."

There are no undomesticated pigs in the area of the highlands where the Gururumba live, and the analogy is to domesticated pigs that have escaped and run wild. The Gururumba do not understand why domesticated pigs sometimes run wild, but they believe that through proper procedure and ritual, the animal can be redomesticated. And so it is with a person who is afflicted with "being a wild pig": He has temporarily broken the bonds of human control and must be reintegrated into society.

Being a wild pig involves a variety of aggressive acts, including looting, shooting arrows at bystanders, and so forth. The aggression is not serious, however, and potential victims are seldom injured. Among the Gururumba such behavior may continue for several days, until the affected individual disappears into the forest where he destroys what he has taken (usually inconsequential objects left for him to steal). He may then return in a normal condition, neither remembering anything of his previous behavior nor being reminded of it by the villagers. Alternatively, he may return still in a wild state. In this case, he is captured; and in a ceremony similar to that performed for pigs that have gone wild, he is "redomesticated."

The Gururumba believe that being a wild pig is caused by the bite of a ghost of a recently deceased individual. These ghosts are malevolent, destructive entities; they reflect the qualities of men before the achievement of advanced culture, that is, before men lived in social groups, had domesticated animals, and so forth. The Gururumba view of human nature is not that of the "noble savage": Primeval man attacked, stole, and raped on whim. The Gururumba believe that they would behave likewise if it were not for social control. When bitten by a ghost, such control is lost and more pirmitive impulses are set free.

On a deeper and less well-articulated level, the Gururumba seem to recognize that it is not just a ghost which causes a person to behave like a wild pig; it is also the inability of the individual to cope with frustrations imposed by society. Only males between the ages of approximately 25 and 35 exhibit the syndrome. This period is especially stressful for the Gururumba male. He must forgo the considerable freedom of his youth and accept economic and social obligations related to marriage (prearranged and often unstable at first) and also participate in other group-coordinated enterprises. His success in these ventures determines not only his personal prestige and power, but also that of his clan. According to Newman (1964), being a wild pig is one way a person can call attention to difficulties in meeting such social obligations. Following an episode, members of the society apparently reevaluate the afflicted individual, and expectations are adjusted accordingly.

Langness (1965) has described a variety of wild-man behavior that he observed among the Bena Bena, a group that lives about 40 miles from the Gururumba. The Bena Bena call the syndrome *negi negi*. In most respects, *negi negi* is similar to being a wild pig, although there are also seemingly important differences. For example, the Bena Bena perform no special ritual to reintegrate the person into society after an attack. Nor are the expectations of the group for the afflicted individual necessarily lowered following an episode of *negi negi*. Langness reports the case of one man who was afflicted with *negi negi* on three different occasions, and yet who was made a tradiditional leader of his clan.

Salisbury (1968) observed eight cases of wild man behavior among the Siane, another highland group. In addition to young men, who are most prone to be affected, the sample included a young woman and the village headman, an older man of about 55. Although a few of these individuals evidenced signs of psychopathy, most were described by Salisbury as well-balanced, intelligent, nonexcitable individuals with leadership qualities. This led him to conclude that "for the Siane at least, and by extension for the other groups, possession behavior per se cannot be taken as an indication of psychological malfunction but as appropriate behavior for abnormal circumstances" (p. 87).

Salisbury thus opts for a largely sociological explanation of wild-man behavior. He notes that New Guinea highland societies are very closely knit. Communal living and cooperative enterprises require a great deal of conformity. An individual cannot play different roles on different occasions; rather, a person is expected to show continuity and consistency in all aspects of his or her behavior. This makes it difficult to make a decision that is not in keeping with past performance or group expectancies. Salisbury argues that wild-man behavior is a way of "announcing" to the group that a nonconforming decision has been made, without the individual having to assume responsibility for the decision. For example, if a person wishes to move to another location, be rid of a wife, renounce certain obligations, and so on—actions that might be blocked by the group in normal circumstances—being possessed by a ghost is a way of dramatically underscoring the decision. As support for his argument, Salisbury reports that affected individuals may chase a pig into the woods at night or walk past a grave, places also frequented by ghosts.

Salisbury also makes the important observation that instances of wild-man behavior typically occur within a short time after an untoward event, such as an unexpected death. Following such an event there seems to be a positive expectattion on the part of the group that *someone* will become afflicted; and according to Salisbury, "the usual pattern is for the person who performs the office of patient to be a somewhat distant friend of the deceased, or an individual who is not under most emotional strain as a principle in the ceremony" (p. 92). This might explain why so many of the persons who exhibit wild-man behavior also show leadership qualities under more normal conditions. It does not explain, however, why such individuals frequently have a nonconforming decision to "announce" while possessed.

The theme of wild-man behavior as the "performance of an office" is carried even further by Clarke (1973). He describes an outbreak of wild-man behavior among a group—the "Ap-ngai clan" —of Maring-speaking people in the Bismark Mountain region of New Guinea. On the basis of his own observations, as well as of a review of the previous literature on the topic, Clarke concludes that wild-man behavior is a form of theater. "Considered as theater, the interaction between the Ap-ngai wild man and his community becomes that between actor and audience, and the behavior is seen to provide both wild man and community with enough rewards to make the actor-audience system self-reinforcing" (p. 208). In addition to its entertainment value, Clarke speculates that wild-man behavior, like many other festivals or rituals, may serve to bridge discontinuities in the life of the actor or of the group.

Implications

There are three major implications that I would like to draw from the foregoing description of wild-man behavior. These have to do with (a) the experience of passivity during emotion, (b) the supposed primitiveness of emotional syndromes, and (c) the social function of emotional behavior.

The experience of passivity. In Chapter 1 we noted that emotions are interpreted as passions rather than as actions. Actions are things we do—rational, deliberate, and/or voluntary responses. Passions, on the other hand, are things that happen to us; we are "possessed" by our emotions.

The experience of passivity as it occurs in rather extreme instances of emotion is well illustrated by wild-man behavior. The wild man cannot control his behavior in the ordinary sense; typically, he cannot even recall an episode after it has passed. Even more important, he is not viewed by the society as completely responsible for his behavior. Yet it is quite clear that the experience of passivity on the part of the wild man is a kind of illusion. The wild man is enacting a social role, part of the meaning of which is that the behavior is beyond self-control.

The "primitiveness" of emotional reactions. That emotions are interpreted (and sometimes experienced) as passions rather than as actions has often led to the assumption that emotional reactions are biologically basic or primitive responses. As discussed in Chapter 2, for example, there is a common tendency within our own culture to view anger (as well as other forms of emotionally aggressive behavior) as remnants of man's phylogenetic past. According to this view, a person cannot control his anger when provoked any more than he can control his righting reflex when tripped. This view of emotions as biologically primitive and animal-like stems in part from the unfavorable contrast between emotional reactions and "higher" forms of behavior. Within the Western intellectual tradition, rationality and free will have been considered hallmarks of humanity; consequently, there has been a tendency to regard the seemingly irrational and impulsive as at best animal-like and brutish, and at worst pathological (for a historical review of the influence of such symbolism on theories of emotion, see Averill, 1974).

Of course, value judgments such as these are not limited to Western societies; no group could endure if in practical matters it emphasized the irrational and the impulsive. One might therefore expect emotional responses to be considered primitive in most, if not all, cultures. This situation is epitomized by the Gururumba name for wild-man behavior, "being a wild pig." The Gururumba believe that the behavior of the affected individual is similar to that of humans before they became socialized, when men presumably stole, raped, and killed at whim. It is clear, however, that being a wild pig is primitive only in an evaluative sense—no infrahuman animal could engage in such behavior, only a highly (perhaps overly) socialized person.

The social functions of emotional behavior. To say that a response involves the enactment of a trasnitory social role implies that it has some social function. If Newman's analysis of being a wild pig has any validity, we might almost view this syndrome as a form of community mental health. That is, when societal pressures become too great for an individual to handle, a kind of psychological bankruptcy can be declared. After a man has behaved like a wild pig, the group presumably reevaluates his needs and capacities, bringing expectancies more into line with reality. By providing an involuntary "out," the society can thus maintain pressure on individual members to conform voluntarily to social norms. Of course, if the out is to serve its function, it must be used sparingly and only in extreme cases. Therefore, although in one sense accepted, being a wild pig is not condoned.

These observations do not depend on the validity of Newman's particular analysis. The case of *negi negi* described by Langness, for example, does not seem to conform to Newman's hypothesis; and Salisbury has offered a still different interpretation for wild-man behavior among the Siane (e.g., announcing a nonconforming decision). For our purposes, however, it is not important what particular function wild-man behavior serves. Indeed, its functions probably vary somewhat from one group to another, depending on differences in social organization. And even within a single group, multiple functions may be served. For example, one might ask why (according to the local interpretation of the behavior) the bite of a ghost—rather than some other event—causes a person to become a wild man. To answer this question, an examination has to be made of the role played by ghosts in New Guinea societies. According to Langness (1965), ghosts are primarily of recently deceased kinsmen, and they may be either benevolent or malevolent, depending on the quality of the prior relationships. Thus, if a person quarrels with a kinsman before the latter dies, the ghost or the dead person may seek retaliation. This helps maintain amicable social relationships, especially toward the elderly, who sometimes threaten younger persons with ghostly retaliation if they do not act properly. The threat of being attacked by a ghost, as well as wild-man behavior itself, may thus be used to society's advantage.

In emphasizing the potential benefits of wild-man behavior, I do not wish to imply that all responses—simply because they have become in some sense institutionalized—are functionally significant. To illustrate this point, we will consider briefly a much more deadly syndrome than being a wild man.

Running Amok

The term *amok* refers to an aggressive frenzy observed in several different Southeast Asian societies, particularly in Malaysia. Aggressive frenzies are, of course, found in many different cultures (e.g., the *"berserk"* reaction attributed to old Norse warriors), but amok is probably the most studied of these syndromes. It has been described by van Wulfften Palthe (1936) as follows:

Suddenly, without warning, without those around him being in any way prepared for it, a native springs up, seizes the first weapon he can lay hands on, usually a sword or knife, and rushed like one possessed through his house and garden into the street. Like a mad dog, he attacks every living thing that gets in his way, and succeeds with marvelous skill in dealing deadly stabs and blows: his mental eye may, indeed, be clouded (the natives call the condition "*meat gelap*", clouded eyes), but his primary motor and sensory functions have in no way shared in the clouding, and it is not seldom that an amoker will in a moment or two leave five or six dead or desperately wounded persons on the ground in his wake! His mad lust for attack is not restricted to human beings, he will chop into carabaos (draft cattle) posts, and, in short, anything and everything that he meets. With wild cries of "Amok! Amok!" everyone in his neighborhood seeks safety in flight. When there is nothing left for him to kill, he turns his spirit of destructiveness against himself, so that if he is not previously "knocked out", the most terrible self-inflicted wounds may be the result; he is finally overpowered, when he has become exhausted, with his throat cut or with his belly laid open, and often, too, with horribly mutilated genital organs. The true amoker does not become satiated, he does not stop of his own accord. Those in the neighborhood *know* that fact all to well, and will, if they get the chance and are plucky enough to attempt it, do everything in their power to make an end of the amoker (if this is done by the police or military, who usually shoot him down, the newspapers will report it as "neerleggen", or "knock out"). For this reason, it is very seldom that an amoker is overpowered while still living and not too seriously injured to come to examination. (p. 529)

Superficially, running amok might appear to be a bizarre and idiosyncratic response; it is, however, closely attuned to the social setting. Van Wulfften Palthe reports cases of amok among Arabs, Chinese, and Europeans living in what was then called Netherland India; on the other hand, he knew of no case of a Malay running amok while living in a European country. Moreover, an episode of amok is generally preceded by a period of withdrawal or "meditation," during which the person may mutter religious texts and rhythmically sway back and forth. Other phases of the responses are also standardized, so the people know—to a certain extent, at least—what to expect of a person running amok.

The above description applies to what might be called "classical" amok. Actually, the syndrome has undergone considerable changes since it was first described by Western observers in the 15th and 16th centuries. (See Murphy, 1973, for a review.) In the earliest reports, amok was described as a deliberate and courageous form of self-sacrifice, motivated by revenge or humiliation. The response was socially approved, and if the individual happened to survive, he might be accorded considerable fame and honor for his heroics.

By the 19th century amok had evolved into the classical pattern described by van Wulfften Palthe in the passage quoted above. That is, it became a dissociated reaction on the part of otherwise normal individuals, with indiscriminate rather than directed attacks. Yet threads of continuity are evident. A loss of prestige or honor was still a major precipitating factor, and a person who was placed in a particularly shameful position was almost expected to run amok. The response was sufficiently common during the early part of the 19th century that all villages kept a long pole with a fork on the end for immobilizing an amok runner.

More recently, running amok has undergone further change. The incidence has become much less frequent, and the majority of persons who now run amok appear to be suffering from long-term psychopathology, such as general paresis or paranoid schizophrenia (Schmidt, Hill, & Guthrie, 1977). Nevertheless, instances of the classical syndrome of "true" amok are still observed, especially among persons of peasant or lower class origin who have had little education. In an analysis of amok among Laotions, Westermeyer (1972, 1973) observed no marked differences in the pre-morbid personality of 20 amok runners as compared with 12 other persons who had committed homicides for other reasons. He therefore conlcuded that psycho-pathology (e.g., psychosis) does not provide a parsimonious explanation for the more traditional forms of amok. Social factors, on the other hand, do seem to play an important role. Westermeyer argues that amok is particularly common in times of economic or social change, such as when a young man moves away from home, enters an occupation different from that of his father, suffers the loss of a job, or is deserted by a wife or a girlfriend.

In commenting on the findings by Westermeyer, Cheng (1972) has related amok to the broad social control exerted by the group over the individual in oriental societies. According to Cheng, running amok is an externalization of the conflict between ego and the "social" superego represented by the group. One difficulty with this hypothesis is that running amok is seldom observed among Chinese populations living in Southeast Asia. Schmidt et al. (1977) ascribe this fact to the strongly directive upbringing of Chinese children, which may better prepare them for the frustrations of adult life. In Malay-related cultures, by contrast, children are allowed a more free and undirected upbringing. As adults, however, the Malay place great stress on status and personal dignity, as well as on the concealment of frustration and resentment. Under these conditions, it is not surprising that a young man who has also lost the social support of his family or kin group (e.g., because of social and economic change) might "lose control" and become violently aggressive.

Implications

One of the basic assumptions underlying the analysis of emotion outlined in Chapter 1 is that emotional reactions are institutionalized responses that have meaning only within a particular social context. To speak of a response as institutionalized or as "having meaning within a particular social context" implies that emotions are functional, that is, that they serve some end within the society. In general, I believe this is true. And in later chapters I will argue that anger is a socially constituted response that has functional significance within our own society. There are, however, limits to such a functionalist approach, and those limits may be illustrated by reference to amok.

It is tempting to speculate on the possible functions that amok might serve, but such speculation will be resisted. Functional arguments are notoriously difficult to prove or disprove, and in the case of amok, there is insufficient evidence even to build a reasonable case. Indeed, for the sake of argument, I will assume that running amok serves no function, at least in its more modern manifestations. Why, then, has amok become institutionalized? And what implications does this have for the study of more standard emotional reactions? Before attempting to answer these questions, let me address briefly some more general objections to functional explanations in social psychology.

Many psychologists do not need to be reminded of the limits of functional analyses; they are already convinced that functional explanations are flawed in principle. Such skepticism stems from both the theoretical "right" and "left." By the right I mean the positivists, who believe that any explanation that is not ultimately reducible to statements about efficient causes must be superficial at best and meaningless at worst. Functional analyses, which make reference to goals and end states (final causes), are thus not to be taken seriously. But this objection is based more on prejudice than on fact. As Taylor (1970), Nagel (1979), and many others have pointed out, there is nothing inherently fallacious about functional explanations. Whether or not a particular type of explanation is adequate to a given phenomenon is as much an empirical as it is a logical question; certainly it is not an issue that can be decided beforehand by fiat.

The skepticism about functional explanations that stems from the left is more vague, and hence more difficult to deal with. It is an objection based not so much on logic as on the fear that functional explanations can be used to support a conservative ideology. For example, if a behavior that is deemed undesirable from the critic's point of view can be demonstrated to have functional significance, then attempts to change the behavior might be diffused. But this fear is largely irrelevant, if not entirely unwarranted. That a particular response has a function does not imply that the same function could not be better served in some other way, or even that the function could not (and should not) be eliminated by altering the underlying circumstances.

In short, functional arguments are not inherently flawed, although any particular functional argument may, of course, be wrong. With this in mind, let us return to the case of amok. As described earlier, amok is an institutionalized form of behavior, a social product, so to speak. Does this mean that it serves a social function? Not necessarily. A response can be socially constituted in either of two ways—as a product of use in its own right, or as a by-product of other processes that do have use. Perhaps an analogy will help to clarify this distinction. Garbage is a by-product. It is not something that is produced for its own sake because it has some functional value. Of course, once a by-product is produced, a use may be found for it. Thus, garbage may be used to fuel a power plant, thereby becoming an important resource in its own right. But whether garbage is ever employed usefully or simply remains a by-product of other processes, it is nevertheless a social product.

Some emotional syndromes appear to have functional significance in their own right, and hence can be viewed as social products in a primary sense. Other emotions seem to be by-products of other social processes, by-products that may or may not have secondary functional significance, depending on the situation. Among the syndromes discussed thus far, wild-man behavior probably belongs to the first category and running amok to the second.

In subsequent chapters I will argue that anger is a social product, not simply a by-product. In this respect, anger is more like wild-man behavior than it is like running amok. If we wished to draw a comparison between amok and a standard emotional reaction in our own culture, envy would provide a better analogy than anger. According to an analysis by Sabini and Silver (1978), envy is the by-product of a social comparison process. They argue that a person's status, as evaluated by himself, is inherently comparative: The greater the achievements of significant others, the less one's own accomplishments may seem. Sabini and Silver also assume that the maintenance of one's sense of worth is an important goal of most people. One way for a person to maintain or enhance his worth is to increase his own efforts to succeed; another way is to undercut or diminish the accomplishments of others. The latter course is a manifestation of what we call envy. If this analysis is correct, envy does not itself have a social function, although it is socially constituted. And like garbage, envy is almost universally viewed with distaste, a very common—if not entirely necessary—evil. In certain circumstances, of course, envy may be put to social use. For example, envy may be encouraged in order to pit one group against another. Depending on one's attitude toward the cause being espoused, this may be regarded as either demagogy or consciousness raising. Schoeck (1969), in an extended analysis of the consequences of envy, has argued that this emotion is often used to enforce conformity among members of a group.

To Nu

Wild-man behavior and running amok are unusual responses, even within their respective cultures. The third example of a culturally specific aggressive syndrome that we shall examine is more typical of everyday emotional syndromes. Among the Kaingang Indians of Brazil, a person may either flee a threatening object or attack and destroy it. The accompanying emotional state is called *to nu*. According to Henry (1936), *to nu* is "fear-anger, one emotion with two facets." The following story, recounted by Henry, illustrates this fear-anger syndrome:

> When Patkle died Kangdadn built a pyre for him and tried to burn him, but Patkle fell off the pyre when only his hands and feet were consumed, thus showing that he was supernaturally dangerous and a terrible threat to everyone. Because of this, the story runs, "they [his relatives] became angry and went away. Four days later I [the informant] went and put his bones in the ground. They feared him and therefore they went away. He is vai [supernaturally dangerous] to them and they may die. He showed them that they were going to die right there. That is why he fell in the direction of the place where they were going to die. Then they became angry. "He is supernaturally dangerous (vai) to us," they said. (p. 254)

In other words, when Patkle's body did not burn, his relatives took it as an omen of supernatural danger and became *to nu*, which Henry translates as "angry." Henry cautions, however, that this is not a literal transaltion. By itself the expression *nu* means "dangerous," while the element *to* means "direction toward." Thus, *to nu* literally means "dangerous toward." Note that the connotation of the English concept of anger is quite different than the connotation of *to nu*. If an American says, "I am angry with you," an appropriate response might be, "What did I do wrong?" "I am sorry," "I didn't mean it," "It was an accident," or the like. On the other hand, when a Kaingang says, "I am angry [*to nu*] with you," Henry describes the reaction as

> not contrition or repentance, or any kind of "negative self-feeling," but rage. This happens because even though he may know that you do not intend bodily harm, there is an aura of danger about anger [*to nu*] and danger creates fear, which in turn begets anger. (p. 256)

Differences between the concepts of anger and *to nu* reflect differences in social organization. As will become apparent in subsequent chapters, the expression of anger in our own culture is in part an accusation of wrongdoing. *To nu*, on the other hand, is more of a direct threat and does not necessarily imply any wrongdoing on the part of the target. In fact, according to Henry, the Kaingang seldom make direct accusations against one another. Because of this it is sometimes difficult to follow a Kaingang quarrel, for the antagonists may not mention what they are quarreling about or insinuate who is responsible.

Implications

Henry (1936) entitled his analysis of *to nu* "The Linguistic Expression of Emotion," and that is the issue that I wish to pursue. What is the relationship between language and emotion? Actually, we touched on this issue in Chapter 1, where it was argued that emotional terms are not simply labels that become attached to internal states (either physiological or subjective). Rather, the language we use to communicate about an emotion epitomizes the meaning of the emotional role. When a Kaingang Indian says that he is *to nu*, or an American that he is angry, the person is entering into a social relationship. Moreover, the social relationship (e.g., the mutual expectancies and intersubjective meanings) determines not only the behavioral manifestation of the emotion, but the subjective experience as well. It would seem to follow from these considerations that emotions are relative to particular cultural-linguistic groups—a contention that requires close examination.

In examining the relationship between language and emotion it will be helpful to begin with a phenomenon that is simpler, and less tied to a specific culture, than *to nu*. Specifically, we will use the phenomenon of pain to illustrate what is sometimes called an *expressivist* theory of meaning (in contrast to a referential theory, where the meaning of a term is taken to be the object or state of affairs to which the term refers). We may then expand the expressivist theory so that it encompasses more complex emotional meanings, such as *to nu*.

Consider the following observation by Wittgenstein (1953): "A child has hurt himself and he cries; and then adults talk to him and teach him exclamations and, later, sentences. They teach the child new pain-behavior" (#244). What Wittgenstein wants to illustrate by this example is the developmental continuity between a child's cry, an exclamation such as "Ouch!" and the sentence "I have a pain." Each has a meaning as an expression of pain.

Note that the relationship between a psychological state and its expression is quite different than the relationship between an object and its label. The latter relationship is arbitrary; different lables can be attached to the same object without affecting the latter in any important way. The same is usually not true of the relationship between a psychological state and its expression. A psychological state stands in relationship to its expression as a whole to its parts. (This is implicit in the definition of a psychological syndrome outlined in Chapter 1.) One implication that follows from these considerations is that a change in expression can change the nature of the entire syndrome—provided the expression is sufficiently fundamental, as verbal expressions often are.[1] Even a relatively "simple" and physiologically based phenomenon such as pain can be altered as a function of its expression. Or perhaps it would be more accurate to say that both the experience of pain and its expression are interdependent aspects of an ongoing stream of activity, the entire course of which is determined by the significance of the situation for the individual, including his or her intentions and desires (Beecher, 1959; Melzack & Casey, 1970; Spanos & Hewitt, 1980).

Pain provides a good introduction to an expressivist theory of meaning, but it can also be misleading in its simplicity. In particular, the term *expressivist* should not be interpreted too literally when applied to an analysis of meaning in general. From a broader perspective, it may be said that the meaning of a word derives from the use to which it is put and not just from the feeling it expresses.

An example from Wittgenstein (1953) may be used to explicate this point also. A builder and his assistant agree that whenever the former says the word "Slab!" the assistant will hand him a flat stone. In this way, the expression "Slab!" is given a certain use (meaning) in connection with the work they are doing. The example illustrates what Wittgenstein calls a "Language game." The notion of a language game focuses attention on the fact that words have meaning only as part of a larger activity in which a person is engaged. Of course, language games are not games in the ordinary sense of that term, nor are they as circumscribed as the example of the construction boss and his assistant might suggest. Rather, they are part of the "natural history" of the group (Wittgenstein, 1958, p. 98).

The definition of emotions as transitory social roles is clarified by reference to Wittgenstein's notion of a language game. In the example, the expression "Slab!" was given meaning in the context of a set pattern of interaction between the construction boss and his assistant. Should the assistant quit the project, another might be hired to take his place, and likewise for the boss. Being boss and assistant on a construction project are social roles, of which the expression "Slab!" is one mani-

---

[1] Of course, verbal expressions are not the *sine qua non* of emotional syndromes. Nor are verbal expressions the result of some introspective process by which a person reveals the inner workings of his mind. What makes verbal expressions unique is that they symbolize the syndrome—encapsulate its meaning, so to speak.

festation. These social roles are, in turn, only one aspect of a larger social network that helps determine the division of labor, the kinds of material used in construction, and so forth.

Now consider again Henry's description of *to nu*. The person who says that he is *to nu* can expect some kind of response on the part of the target of his emotion (an attempt to escape, perhaps, or an attack). And likewise, the person who knows that he is the target of *to nu* can expect further behavior on the part of the angry/fearful person. In a sense, the two participants have entered into transitory social roles vis-à-vis one another. The meaning of the roles transcends the particulars of the individuals involved and the immediate circumstances.

At this point an objection might be raised. Return for a moment to the example of the construction boss and his assistant. A critic might grant that the expression "Slab!" epitomizes the social roles of the participants in this particular language game. Yet the slab itself—as a peice of stone or building material—does not change as a function of how the construction boss and his assistant interact. Similarly, this critic might maintain, *to nu* has its own (innate) characteristics that do not change in any fundamental way as a function of how it is expressed (verbally or behaviorally) in social circumstances.

The foregoing objection would have some merit if human behavior were as rigid and unyielding as a piece of building material. But that is not the case. As the examples of wild-man behavior, amok, and *to nu* illustrate, human behavior is remarkably malleable and variable. But we do not even have to consider cross-cultural variations in behavior to make this point. Even a single syndrome, such as anger in our own culture, is exquisitely vairiable. As will become evident in subsequent chapters, a person may become angry for many different reasons, some constructive and others malevolent, and anger may be expressed in innumberable ways. The belief that there is some specific thing or event to which the term *anger* must refer (e.g., a feeling, neurological circuit, or whatever) is based on a implicit acceptance of a referential theory of meaning (i.e., on the view that words serve mainly as labels or names of objects). If one adopts, on the other hand, an expressivist theory, then the meaning of a term such as anger is determined not by what it refers to, but by the way it is used in social interaction. Going further, it may be said that the meaning of an emotional concept is determined by the same rules that help constitute the entire emotional syndrome as a transitory social role.

I am not suggesting that there must be a word for every kind of emotional experience. It is not uncommon for members of a cultural-linguistic group to have a concept for a certain category of experience without there being any word in the language to represent that category explicitly. This state of affairs has been described by Berlin, Breedlove, and Raven (1973) with respect to folk taxonomies (e.g., the classification of plants and animals). Such "covert categories" are usually expressed by circumlocutions, or they may be manifested in nonlinguistic modes of behavior only. It is not unreasonable to expect that most societies also have covert categories of emotional experience, especially within the aesthetic and religious domains. (Varieties of mystical experience might be a case in point.) And, of course, our conceptual world is not static. New categories of experience are constantly being developed and old ones transformed (see the historical changes in amok, described in the preceding section).

While recognizing the existence of covert and transitional categories of emotional experience, which may in some respects be "indescribable," I find it difficult to imagine an emotional experience that is not informed by prior conceptualizations of *any* kind. And although nonverbal modes of communication may be extremely important in conveying the precise meaning of an experience,[2] words are the most common and efficient way of representing concepts. Therefore, when we come across two different words, such as *to nu* and *anger*, that express emotional states, the most reasonable assumption is that we are dealing with two different kinds of experience, and not with one emotion to which two different labels have become attached.

This does not mean, of course, that an American cannot understand what a Kaingang Indian means by *to nu*, and conversely for *anger*. On a superficial level, at least, such understanding is relatively easy. To actually experience the emotion, however, the relevant concept would have to become an integral part of one's own way of thinking, and that would require a thorough understanding and implicit acceptance of the relevant aspects of the culture.

In Chapter 14 we will discuss in more detail the nature of emotional concepts and their relationships to social norms. But for now let us consider one final example of an aggressive syndrome from another culture.

Ikari

Ikari[3] is a commonplace emotional experience among the Japanese. The word *ikari* is typically translated into English as "anger." As will be seen below, there are some difficulties with this translation; but before discussing the meaning of *ikari*, it will be helpful to consider briefly some characteristics of the Japanese culture as it relates to aggressive behavior and to an individual's sense of self-identity and group identity.

Reischauer (1964) has observed that, as a result of a long history of social regimentation,

---

[2] Henry (1936) makes special note of the fact that the Kaingang often convey nuances in meaning through intonation, gesture, and facial expression. The richness and flexibility of many Kaingang concepts could not be inferred from the manifest content of their language alone.

[3] I wish to express appreciation to Barbara Sabol, Jeremy Giddings, and Yasuko Fukumi for assistance on gathering data, checking translations, and providing insights into Japanese culture relevant to *ikari*. A group of 28 Japanese students and teachers visiting the University of Massachusetts, Amherst, also kindly completed questionnaires describing typical incidents of *ikari* and comparing *ikari* with other closely related syndromes. Needless to say, any errors of interpretation that remain are my own.

the Japanese have become a people who live together in their cramped islands with relatively few outward signs of friction. Nowhere in the world is proper decorum more rigorously observed by all classes in all situations than in Japan, and nowhere else is physical violence less in evidence.

Reischauer quickly adds, however, that the Japanese

are as emotionally excitable as any people, and when they meet a situation to which their accustomed patterns of courteous conduct no longer apply, they are likely to react more violently than other people. (p. 94)[4]

The tendency of the individual to submerge his or her identity in that of the group, and to avoid conflict, has been commented on by a number of native Japanese scholars as a deeply ingrained trait. Thus, Doi (1973) has observed that

by his very nature man seeks the group, and cannot survive without it. If the rejection of the "small self" in favor of the "larger self" is extolled as a virtue, it becomes easier for him to act in concert with the group. In this way friction in human relations within the group is kept to a minimum, and the efficiency of group activity enhanced. It is this, chiefly, that accounts for the way the Japanese have been able since ancient times to pull together in times of national danger. . . . Another expression of the same trait may be seen in the general dislike of the Japanese for any conflict of opinions and their liking for at least an appearance of consensus when any decision has to be taken. (pp. 135-136)[5]

From the observations of Reischauer and Doi it might seem that emotional responses related to anger and aggression would be rather rare in Japanese society, except in situations where social conventions do not provide rules for courteous behavior. However, such an assumption would be a gross oversimplification.

Ueda (1960, 1962) has published several studies on *ikari* (anger), using the controlled diary method. In the first of these studies, 317 students (164 men and 153 women, mostly freshmen) at Nara Gakugei University recorded all instances of *ikari* that they experienced during a 1 week period. The recordings were made each evening before the students went to sleep. The average incidence of *ikari* was 5.3 episodes per week, with no significant differences between the sexes. The second study reported by Ueda (1962) involved an additional sample of 116 students (67 men and 49 women) who also kept a diary for a 1 week period. The average incidence of *ikari* was 3.3 episodes per week, with women reporting significantly more episodes of *ikari* at the higher levels of intensity.[6]

---

[4] Reprinted by permission of Alfred A. Knopf, Inc. Copyright © 1964 by Alfred A. Knopf, Inc.

[5] Reprinted by permission of Kodansha International Ltd. Copyright © 1973 by Kodansha International.

[6] This sex difference was perhaps due to situational factors; that is, the women in Ueda's sample may have found themselves in a more stressful situation as freshman at a university. Also, in Japan, as in the United States, overt emotional behavior is more acceptable among women; this might extend to the admission of *ikari* on a questionnaire. Still, the greater incidence—or admission— of *ikari* among women

The incidence of *ikari* reported by Ueda is roughly comparable to the incidence of anger among American college students when the data are collected in a similar manner (e.g., Gates, 1926; Meltzer, 1933). This would seem contrary to the Japanese ethic, noted above, to avoid conflict and to seek consensus by submerging individual to group interests.

It could be that the students who participated in Ueda's studies were experiencing *ikari*, but not expressing it, thus preserving decorum. Minami (1953/1971) has commented on the tendency of the Japansese to suppress hostile feelings, even under conditions of rather extreme provocation. But although Japanese society encourages circumspection, it also provides many (often subtle) outlets for emotional feelings. Yuji Aida (1970) offers the following anecdotal example.

> The husband comes home. He looks at the flowers at the alcove arranged by the wife. There is something disorderly in the way the flowers are put together. He then senses something upsetting his wife and tries to understand what has happened. Even if such arrangement was deliberately made by the wife with the view of letting her husband know her feelings, this, I think, still shows Japanese character. For instance, the wife is in no position to talk against her mother-in-law and yet wants to have her husband understand her trying experience [with the mother-in-law]. This dilemma can be overcome by this means [flower arrangement]. (Quoted by Lebra, 1976, p. 47)

In the previous section, when discussing the implications of the Kaingang syndrome of *to nu,* we emphasezed the formative influence of verbal expressions on the experience of emotion. Of course, words are not the only way of expressing emotion, and a sensitivity on the part of the observer is often necessary for decoding the the experiences of another. This subtlety in both the expression and interpretation of emotional experiences undoubtedly contributes to what Ishida (1974) has called the "gentle pathos" of the Japanese, in contrast to the more turbulent passions of the West.

But let us return for a moment to the studies by Ueda (1960, 1962). Approximately 75% of the episodes of *ikari* reported by the students involved another person as the target, and about another 10% involved institutional factors (regulations, etc.) or personal inadequacies. *Ikari* would thus seem to be a largely interpersonal emotion, much like anger (see Chapter 8). Also like anger, *ikari* is most often aroused in situations involving some threat to one's sense of self (e.g., an insult or slight) or the frustration of some desired activity (e.g., a radio being played too loudly for sleep). Does this mean that *ikari* and anger are really the same emotion, perhaps differing only in their mode of expression?

Before answering this question, we must consider a little more closely the procedures used by Ueda to collect his data. Each night at bedtime, the students were

---

is somewhat surprising. Japanese women, like their American counterparts, are often depicted as relatively passive and unassertive in comparison with men. This stereotype, which may be true in certain spheres, cannot be accepted uncritically, as will become more evident in Chapter 13, where we examine in detail possible sex differences in anger and aggression.

instructed to record all instances of *ikari* experienced during the day, and to provide a brief description of each incident. This procedure was patterned after similar studies done in the United States by Gates (1926), Meltzer (1933), and Anastasi, Cohen, and Spatz (1948), each of whom used some variation of the controlled diary method. The results of these studies will be described in Part II of this volume. For the moment, it suffices to note that the instructions given to subjects in both the Japanese and American studies were quite open ended, that is, subjects were allowed to interpret the concepts of *ikari* and anger much as they saw fit.

In English, the word *anger* may refer very loosely to a variety of different aggressive (and nonaggressive) responses that are occasioned by a wide range of frustrating or undesirable conditions. In this generic sense, a number of more specific emotional syndromes (e.g., annoyance, irritation, aggravation, outrage, fury, and wrath), *as well as* anger proper, may be grouped under the general rubric of anger. Indeed, even the growling of a dog over a bone, the temper tantrum of a child, and the rioting of a mob may be taken as signs of anger, broadly speaking.

The same is true of *ikari*. In Japanese, it is the generic term for a broad class of related emotional states (cf. Boucher, 1980). *Ikari* is also the name of a specific emotional syndrome within that class.

Such duality of meaning is not uncommon in folk taxonomies, where a single term is often used to refer both to a general class of phenomena and to a specific member of that class (Berlin, Breedlove, & Raven, 1973). In this respect the classification of emotional reactions is no different than the classification of plants, animals, diseases, or whatever.

In the studies by Ueda (1960, 1962), Gates (1926), and the others using the controlled diary method, it is reasonable to assume that the subjects interpreted the concepts of *ikari* and anger in more or less their generic sense, and when so interpreted, the Japanese and English concepts appear to be roughly equivalent. However, this correspondence may be due as much to the vagueness (inclusiveness) of the concepts as to any similarities in the specific emotional states being denoted.

Indeed, when we examine the specific emotions included within the general categories of *ikari* and anger, the correspondence between the Japanese and English concepts tends to disappear. This is true even of *ikari* and anger per se, that is, when these terms are used to refer to specific emotions within their respective classes. For example, in the English translation of Minami's (1953/1971) book, *Psychology of the Japanese People,* the word *anger* appears in nine different passages. In only three of these passages (pp. 50-51, 69, and 82) does the original Japanese read *ikari*. In the other passages the following words or phrases are all translated as "anger": *ikidori* (p. 12), *atari chirasu* (p. 21), *ikimaku* (p. 23), *iro o nasu* (p. 24), *fungai* (p. 96), and *haradachi* (p. 115). In each case the translation is appropriate, as determined by the context. Given a slightly different context, however, each of these terms—*ikari* included—has a connotation somewhat different than anger.

Does this mean that the Japanese make finer distinctions among angerlike responses than do English-speaking peoples, just as the Eskimos make finer distinctions among grades of snow than do plains Indians? Not at all. The English language is as rich as the Japanese in terms related to anger and aggression. There is, however, no one-to-one correspondence between the terms in the two languages (nor, to the extent that behavior is determined by the way it is conceptualized, between the emotional syndromes which the terms signify).

Implications

From the theoretical perspective presented in Chapter 1, emotional syndromes are social constructions, and hence they can be fully understood only within the context of a given culture. Cultural specificity is quite apparent in cases such as wild-man behavior and running amok. The situation becomes more uncertain when we are dealing with standard emotional reactions, such as *to nu, ikari,* and anger. Is anger universal? The answer to this question depends on what one means by anger and related concepts in other languages. When used generically, there is probably a concept in every other language that can be roughly translated as "anger." But when such concepts are interpreted in their generic sense, cross-cultural comparisons can be more misleading than enlightening.

In Chapter 2 we noted one instance in which the generic use of emotional concepts may have led to inappropriate conclusions in cross-cultural research. To recapitulate briefly, research has demonstrated that certain facial expressions (presumably, elements of biological systems related to aggression) are universally recognized as indicative of anger—but only if the concept of anger, or its equivalent in other languages, is interpreted so broadly as to include almost any aggressive tendency.

Of course, speculations about the universality of behavior are not limited to the biological. Consider for a moment the frustration-aggression hypothesis. In the version of this hypothesis presented by Berkowitz (1962), anger is defined very broadly as the tendency to become aggressive following frustration. No one doubts that frustration is universal, a necessary consequence of our physical and social environments. Also, no one doubts that people sometimes become aggressive when frustrated, whether as a result of biological predispositions or of learning. It does not follow, however, that anger—as a specific emotional syndrome—is a universal response to frustration. This type of analysis simply begs too many important questions. What constitutes frustration in various societies? Under what conditions does frustration lead to aggression? What constitutes an aggressive response? And how does the presumed link between frustration and aggression relate to the emotional experience of the individual and to the norms and structure of society? Questions such as these have never been answered satisfactorily, even within the context of our own society, let alone in a way that would make cross-cultural comparison meaningful.

The frustration-aggression hypothesis has considerable intuitive appeal, in part because it accords well with the generic use of the concept of anger. But our concern at the moment is not with the frustration-aggression hypothesis per se, which will be discussed in more detail in Chapter 6. Other definitions of anger could be offered that are equally broad and hence equally "universal." The main point that I wish to make is that the question of universality depends, in large part, on the way a phenomenon is defined. The more abstract the definition, the more likely that it will imply universal principles—and be divorced from the specifics of everyday experience. Concepts from the vernacular, such as anger and *ikari,* are often ambiguous in this regard. They can be used in both an abstract (generic) and a specific sense. In order to avoid theoretical confusion, it is important to maintain a clear distinction between these two senses.

In the remaining chapters of this book we will be discussing anger as it has become institutionalized within Western societies. That is, our concern is with anger as a specific syndrome; hence, we will not be interpreting the concept of anger in its most generic sense. This leaves open the issue of how far the same conclusions that apply to anger also apply to related syndromes, such as *ikari*, in other cultures.

Concluding Observations

In this chapter we have described four aggressive syndromes—wild-man behavior, running amok, *to nu*, and *ikari*. Many other syndromes could have been discussed, but these four are sufficient to illustrate the diversity of forms that aggressive behavior may take. Human aggression may have roots in one or more biological systems, but syndromes such as those we have been considering are as much a product of sociocultural as of biological evolution.

Each of these four syndromes has also been used to illustrate some specific point of relevance to the study of emotion in general and of anger in particular. Thus, in connection with wild-man behavior we considered how even rather dramatic responses, where the person literally experiences being overcome, can be interpreted as a transitory social role that has functional significance within a given social context. Running amok served to remind us of some of the limitations of a functionalist approach, even in connection with responses that are clearly social products (or, more accurately, by-products). *To nu*, a more standard emotional syndrome that combines some of the features of both fear and anger, provided a vehicle for discussing the relationship between language and emotion. And finally, the Japanese syndrome of *ikari* raised the issue of the universality of angerlike responses.

Let us turn now to a more detailed examination of the nature and significance of anger within our own culture.

Chapter 4

Historical Teachings on Anger

In the present chapter we begin to explore in detail the social norms that help constitute anger. And, appropriately enough, we begin at the beginning, that is, with an analysis of historical teachings on anger. Our purpose is not to trace the history of ideas regarding anger; it is rather to examine, through the eyes of leading historical figures, certain issues that continue to be of significance today.

Western civilization has many roots, but two of the most important are Graeco-Roman secular philosophy and Judeo-Christian religious traditions. These two roots became fused during the Middle Ages, thus providing the basis for modern thought. From classical Greece and Rome we will consider the teachings of Plato, Aristotle, and Seneca; and from the patristic, medieval, and early modern periods we will examine the views of Lactantius, Aquinas, and Descartes, respectively. The time between Plato and Descartes is approximately 2,000 years; only about 350 years have elapsed from Descartes to the present. Our discussion thus spans the greater part of Western intellectual history. More contemporary teachings on anger (e.g., as exemplified by the law) will be discussed in Chapter 5.

To study a phenomenon historically is like studying it cross-culturally. In many ways, the differences between ancient Greece and Rome and medieval Europe, on the one hand, and contemporary American society, on the other, are greater than the differences between, say, contemporary Japanese and American societies. One would therefore expect to find major differences as well as continuities between the *orgē* of the Greeks, the *ira* of the Romans, and the anger of Americans. For our purposes, however, the continuities are more important than the differences. And the continuities are striking, in part, because the historical figures that we will be discussing had a direct influence on one another and on contemporary thought. But the continuities may also be due to more subtle and indirect factors.

Reflecting on his experiences in pre- and postwar Germany, the Japanese scholar Eiichiro Ishida (1974) described Western civilization as "an odd compound of inexhaustible goodwill and kindness on the one hand and an implacable severity in human relationships on the other" (p. 29). In particular, Ishida finds a "fierce intolerance and implacable hatred of the foe . . . deeply rooted in the psychologies of the peoples of Western civilization" (p. 30). Historically, he sees this trait not only in the epics of the Greeks and Romans, but also in the phantom *wütendes Heer* of Germanic warriors as they thundered through the sky on stormy nights, and in ancient Hebrews, whose God, Jehovah, set an example of stern and often wrathful judgment. Ishida contrasts the tendency of Westerners toward the extremes of good-will and intolerance, kindness and severity, with the more "gentle pathos" of the Japanese. He proposes that these Western characteristics can ultimately be traced to the warlike nomadic wanderings of the early Indo-Eurpoean and Hebrew peoples. This inference is, Ishida recognizes, highly speculative. But whatever the source, it is difficult to disagree with Ishida's basic observation that human relations in the West have often been marked by both intense goodwill and implacable intolerance. As will be seen below, these conflicting tendencies are readily apparent in historical teachings on anger.

An Overview of the Issues

There are two ways to approach historical teachings: The first is chronologically and the second is through specific issues. For the most part, we shall proceed chronologically, beginning with Plato and ending with Descartes. There are obvious advantages to such an approach, but also some major disadvantages. In particular, since each author emphasized somewhat different issues, or addressed the same issues in very different ways, it is easy to lose direction and miss the relevance of a particular train of thought. At the outset, therefore, it might be helpful to provide a brief overview of the major issues of concern. These can be grouped under three main headings.

1. The social nature and significance of anger. For the most part, historical teach-ings on anger were done within the framework of ethics or moral philosophy; their authors were as much concerned with what *ought* to be as with what actually *is* (or was). In the area of human affairs, at least, there is a dialectical relationship between "is" and "ought." What is tends to be regarded as what ought to be; and what ought to be becomes what is. All of this is a roundabout way of saying that historical teachings—to the extent that they have become woven into the fabric of society—are the social norms or rules that help constitute anger.

The social norms that are most constitutive of anger pertain to the object (insti-gation/target/aim) of the emotion. On this issue, there is considerable agreement: Plato, Aristotle, Seneca, Lactantius, Aquinas, and Descartes all agree that proper instigation to anger is a deliberate (or at least avoidable) slight or wrongdoing; that the proper target for anger is another person; and that the proper aim is punishment for, or correction of, the wrong. But these are broad generalities; when it comes to specifics, there is ample room for disagreement. What constitutes a deliberate slight or wrongdoing? Who is most likely to feel wronged, and under what conditions? Are some persons (e.g., by virtue of their status) less appropriate targets than are others? What should be the goal of punishment: to exact revenge or to instruct the wrongdoer? How should punishment be carried out? What is the locus and effect of bodily changes during anger? And what is the relationship between anger in humans and angerlike responses in animals? Questions such as these elicited no greater agreement historically than they do among contemporary theorists. However, historical debates often lay bare the logic of an argument in a much clearer fashion than do contemporary debates, if for no other reason than that we are less likely to be misled by the jargon and "self-evident" assumptions of past eras.

Perhaps the greatest point of disagreement among the authors we will be considering is whether anger is *ever* warranted, even when a person has been truly wronged. Seneca argues forcefully that, since anger is a passion (irrational and uncontrollable), it more often leads to harm than to good; and, moreover, that whatever good might be done in anger could just as well or better be done in a rational and deliberate manner. At the opposite extreme is Lactantius, who argues that anger was given by God for the protection of humankind. The remaining authors adopt a more middle ground, recognizing the excesses to which anger often leads but arguing nevertheless that anger is necessary for the maintenance of a just social order.

2. Grounds for interpreting anger as a passion. Historical teachings are particularly well suited to an explication of the meaning and significance of the notion of passivity. *Passion* was the traditional term for what we now call emotion, and all of the authors that we will be considering take as a fundamental given that anger is a passion (i.e., something an individual "suffers"). But there the agreement ends. Is anger a passion because it is a function of a "lower" (nonrational) level of the psyche or soul (Plato, Aristotle, Aquinas)? Or, from a somewhat different perspective, is anger an action of the body that is perceived (passively experienced) by the soul, as suggested by Descartes? There are other possibilities as well. Perhaps anger is a passion because it is a form of misguided judgment, an irrational—as opposed to a nonrational—response (Seneca). But then how could a supremely rational (not to mention incorporeal) being, namely, God, experience anger (Lactantius)?

The questions may sound strange, but the issues are familiar. What is the role of physiological change and instinctive reactions during anger? Is anger cognitive or noncognitive? Could a computer (a completely logical device) be programmed to "experience" anger? But let me be more specific. In Chapter 1 we discussed a number of primary and secondary grounds for interpreting anger as a passion. The primary grounds include biological, psychological, and social imperatives, as well as systemic conflict and cognitive disorganization. Among the secondary grounds are such "surface" characteristics as irrationality and commitment. Historical teachings help clarify and illustrate these various grounds as they have been applied—and misapplied—to the case of anger. Such teachings are particularly relevant to presumed biological imperatives (which have been used as a rationalization for anger since the time of the ancient Greeks), to social imperatives (as reflected in the injunction that persons should become angry under certain socially prescribed conditions), and to systemic conflict.

3. Contradiction and conflict in the norms related to anger. On the basis of the primary grounds for interpreting anger as a pssion, three broad classes of emotion can be distinguished, namely, impulsive, conflictive, and transcendental (see Chapter 1). Anger is representative of the class of conflictive emotions. The rationale for such a classification of anger is far from new or original. In particular, the distinction between anger, on the one hand, and the impulsive emotions, on the other hand, has its roots in Plato's distinction between the spirited and appetitive elements of the psyche, and in the medieval distinction between the irascible and concupiscible emotions (Aquinas). However, the nature of the conflicting norms that help constitute anger can perhaps best be seen, at least on the social level of analysis, in the diametrically opposed views of Seneca and Lactantius. As already described, the former condemned anger almost without reservation. Lactantius, by contrast, considered anger to be a gift from God. This difference of opinion reflects a deep and continuing division within the Western intellectual tradition on the nature of humankind and on how best to maintain the social contract. Anger, as it has become institutionalized in Western societies, cannot be fully understood except in light of these historical trends and controversies.

With this brief overview of some of the major issues as background, let us turn to a chronological review of historical teachings on anger.

Plato

Plato (427-347 B.C.) was born of a well-to-do aristocratic family. On his mother's side he was descended from Solon, the great Athenian statesman. His father's side was just as illustrious, counting among its ancestors the god Poseidon. Plato grew up in a time of political turmoil and social corruption following the defeat of Athens in the Peloponnesian War, and his long life was devoted to a search for values that would provide a firm and permanent foundation for a just society. His answers have sometimes been characterized as totalitarian, ruthless, and inhumane (e.g., Esper, 1964; Russell, 1945). There is some truth to such characterizations, but also a great deal of hyperbole.

In order to understand Plato's views on anger, we must consider first his general conception of human nature. Diogenes Laertius (1925) writing some five centuries after the death of Plato, tells the following anecdote.

> Plato had defined man as an animal, biped and featherless, and was applauded. Diogenes [the Cynic] plucked a fowl and brought it into the lecture-room with the words, "Here is Plato's man." In consequence of which there was added to the definition, "having broad nails." (Vol. 2, VI, 40)

Of course, the nature of man as envisioned by Plato was much more complex than this apocryphal story would suggest. In explicating Plato's position, we may begin with the intuitively obvious distinction between rational and impulsive behavior. In the *Republic* (IV, 439e) Plato notes that impulses and desires—the passions in a broad sense—can be inhibited by responses that arise "from the calculations of reason," as when a thirsty man refrains from drinking poisonous water. This demonstrates, Plato argues, that the human soul or *psychē* must consist of at least two parts—a rational and an irrational. Plato then introduces a third possible element, the *thymos* or principle of high spirit, by which we feel anger.[1] And he asks: Does this principle belong to the rational or irrational part of the *psychē*?

At first, the answer would seem obvious. Anger is a passion, and hence it must belong in the irrational part. However, Plato goes to considerable length to demonstrate that the *thymos* (and hence anger) is distinct from what he considers to be baser appetites, such as hunger, thirst, sexual desire, fear, and greed. His argument is much the same as that used to distinguish between the rational and irrational aspects of the *psychē*; namely, if two functions conflict, they can be ascribed to different principles. It often occurs, Plato notes in the *Republic* (IV, 440b), that a person desires to do something that he knows is wrong. On such an occasion, a person may revile and become angry at himself, thus restraining his desires. In other words, when reason and appetite are at odds, the spirited element (*thymos*) may become allied with the former against the latter. Hence, according to Plato, anger must be separate from the other appetites.

Anger also becomes allied with reason to protect the individual from wrongs perpetrated by others. When a man believes himself to be wronged, Plato asks, "does not his spirit in that case seethe and grow fierce . . . and make itself the ally of what he judges just? And in noble souls it endures and wins victory and will not let go until either it achieves its purpose, or death ends all, or, as a dog is called back by a shepherd, it is called back by the reason within and calmed" (*Republic*, IV, 440d).[2]

From these considerations it might seem that anger is not a passion after all, but rather belongs to the rational part of the *psychē*. Plato offers two main reasons for rejecting such a notion. First, children and animals often exhibit high spirit and rage in the absence of the ability to reason; and, second, adults sometimes become

---

[1] Plato used the term *thymos* in a quasi-technical sense to refer both to the spirited element of the *psychē* and to anger per se. In early (i.e., pre-Homeric) Greek usage, *thymos* evidently had the connotation of an especially violent passion, and it also referred to breath or a vaporous substance. Later, the term became extended to less violent emotions and to the "soul" or life principle (Kurath, 1921; Onians, 1951). When discussing anger, Aristotle generally used the more common term, *orgē*, or one of its variants, although he also used *thymos* at times. The Latin writers we will be considering (Seneca, Lactantius, and Aquinas) used *ira* for what Plato and Aristotle meant by *thymos* and *orgē*. Descartes, writing in the French vernacular, used *colère*. The latter term is derived from the Greek *Kholos*, via the Latin *cholera*, which meant "bile" and also "bitter anger." The English term *anger* stems from the Latin *angor*, meaning a constriction of the throat, and hence anguish or trouble.

It is interesting to note that the most widely used words for a particular emotion seldom have exact cognates or a common etymological root in the major branches of the Indo-European languages, even in cases where there has been a considerable amount of cultural continuity and diffusion (see Buck, 1949; Chamberlain, 1895). Thus, we have *anger* in Egnlish, *colère* in French, *ira* in Latin, *orgē* in Greek, to which we might add *zorn* in German and *gnev* in Russian. The psychological significance (if any) of this linguistic diversification is not clear.

[2] All quotations are from *The Collected Dialogues of Plato*, edited by Hamilton and Cairns (1961). For comparative purposes, the original Greek word for anger and related concepts has sometimes been inserted in the text.

angry in an unreasoning way. Nevertheless, Plato emphasizes that anger is the natural ally of reason unless it is corrupted by improper education.

In the *Timaeus* Plato makes a distinction between the immortal and mortal parts of the *psychē*. This is basically the same as his distinction between the rational and irrational aspects, although the implications are somewhat different. The principle of the immortal *psychē* is self-motion—anything that received its motion through outside forces can cease to move and hence may die. Self-motion is also the motion of rational thought; therefore the immortal and rational *psychē* are the same. In contrast, the mortal *psychē* is "subject to terrible and irresistible affections [*pathē-mata*]—first of all, pleasure, the greatest incitement to evil; then pain, which deters from good; also rashness and fear, two foolish counselors, anger [*thymon*] hard to be appeased, and hope easily led astray" (*Timaeus*, 69d).

Having drawn the distinction between the immortal (rational) and mortal (irrational) parts of the *psychē*, Plato goes on to localize them within the body. The immortal *psychē* is placed in the head, since this is the part of the body that most closely approximates a sphere, the most perfect figure. The placement of the mortal *psychē* then follows quite naturally. In order not to disturb rational thought any more than necessary, the mortal *psychē* is located in the trunk of the body, with the neck as a narrow isthmus separating it from the rational part. The mortal *psychē* is further divided into superior and inferior parts, located above and below the midriff, respectively. The superior part is, of course, the *thymos*, by which we feel anger. It is located in the chest so that, being near the head, it may be obedient to the rule of reason and may "join with it in controlling and restraining the desires when they are no longer willing of their own accord to obey the command issuing from the citadel" (*Timaeus*, 70). The inferior or appetitive part of the mortal *psychē* is located in the abdomen below the diaphragm so as to be "as far as might be from the council chamber, making as little noise and disturbance as possible, and permitting the best part to advise quietly for the good of the whole and the individual" (71).

This bit of fanciful physiology is important for our considerations for the following reason. Although the immortal *psychē* is located in the head, its habitat is temporary. Rational, self-initiated thought, being a function of the immortal *psychē*, is basically independent of specific bodily processes. The situation is different with regard to the mortal *psychē*. Its functions—the passions—are intimately conected with the body. Stated somewhat differently, it is because the *psychē* is connected with the body that it is subject to passions, including anger. We shall come across this theme repeatedly in subsequent discussions.

Turning now from the physiological to the societal, Plato argues that the state also has three aspects, and that these correspond to the three aspects of the individual *psychē*—the heads of state (rational element), the soldiers or guardians (spirited element), and the merchants and artisans (appetitive element). The just state, like the just individual, is one in which these various elements operate in harmony, each fulfilling its proper role. The role of the guardians is to protect the state from enemies, both without and within. In the education of the guardians, special care must be taken to stimulate the spirited element in their nature. Training must be both mental and physical. Too much emphasis on physical training alone, as among devotees of gymnastics, may produce a disposition that is unduly savage and hard; on the other hand, too much emphasis on the mental may produce overcivilized softness. The properly trained guardian is courageous, but also gentle and orderly (*Republic*, III, 410d).

In short, just as the state needs a segment of its population to guard against attack from without and insurrection from within, so too does the individual person need a passionate element (*thymos*) of the *psychē* that is roused to anger when he or she is provoked. But Plato also recognized the dangers. Like the military that defies authority and usurps power for itself, anger may sometimes defy reason, and being out of control, may lead to rash and cruel deeds. Seneca, whose views on anger will be discussed shortly, tells the story of how Plato once became angry with a slave and, bent upon flogging him, ordered the slave to bare his shoulders. Gaining control of his anger, Plato stayed his uplifted hand and stood frozen like a statue in the act of striking. When a friend who happened by asked Plato what he was doing, he supposedly replied, "I am exacting punishment from an angry man" (Seneca, A.D. 40-50/1963, p. 285).

Aristotle

Plato's most brilliant pupil, Aristotle (384-323 B.C.), is important for our inquiry for three reasons. First, he formalized the distinction between actions and passions as fundamental modes of thought (indeed, of all being), and he thus had a profound influence on later theories of emotion. Second, many of his ideas regarding the assignment of responsibility for acts committed during emotion were incorporated into later Roman law, from whence they came to influence the legal norms of much of Western Europe (Shalgi, 1971). (The legal treatment of anger will be discussed in detail in Chapter 5.) And finally, Aristotle had a considerable direct influence on later moral teachings regarding anger.

Let us begin with Aristotle's distinction between actions and passions, which was only one part of a larger scheme of categorization. Very briefly, in considering the relationship of language to events, Aristotle argued that all simple expressions refer to phenomena that belong to at least one of 10 fundamental categories: substance, quantity, quality, relation, place, time, position, state or acquired characteristic, activity, and passivity. For example, the noun *person* refers to a substance; *intelligence* refers to a quality; *to hit* refers to an action; *to be hit* refers to a passion. As these last examples illustrate, the distinction between actions and passions is related linguistically to the active and passive voice. However, passions can also be expressed by nouns. Thus, *illness* refers to a passion, something that happens to an individual. Since a person can be both ill, say, and intelligent, passions are in some respects like qualities. The difference between these two categories is described by Aristotle[3] as follows:

---

[3] All quotations are from *The Basic Works of Aristotle*, R. McKeon (Ed.), 1941. Original source: *The Oxford Translation of Aristotle*, W. D. Ross (Ed.), Vols. 1 (1928), 3 (1931), 9 (1925). Oxford: Oxford University Press. Reprinted by permission of Oxford University Press.

> Those conditions... which arise from causes which may easily be rendered
> ineffective or speedily removed, are called, not qualities, but affections
> [*pathē*, passions] : for we are not said to be such and such in virtue of them.
> The man who blushes through shame is not said to be a constitutional
> blusher, nor is the man who becomes pale through fear said to be consti-
> tutionally pale. He is said rather to have been affected. Thus such condi-
> tions are called affections, not qualities. (*Categories*, 9b30)

From this passage, it is clear that the emotions belong to the category of passivity, along with a variety of other temporary conditions that affect an individual.
Although Aristotle took a more cognitive view of the emotions than did Plato
(Fortenbaugh, 1975), the classification of the emotions as passions also has physiological implications. For example, it led Aristotle to ask, with respect to the passions,
"Are they all affections of the complex of body and soul [*psychē*], or is there any
one among them peculiar to the soul itself?" And he gives the following answer:

> If we consider the majority of them [the passions], there seems to be no
> case in which the soul can act or be acted upon without involving the body;
> e.g., anger [*orgizesthai*], courage, appetite, and sensation generally. Think-
> ing seems the most probable exception, but if this proves to be a form of
> imagination or to be impossible without imagination, it too requires a
> body as a condition of its existence. (*On the Soul,* 403a5)

Eventually, Aristotle does distinguish one kind of thinking—active as opposed
to passive reason—that he believes to be independent of bodily processes. As for
the emotions, however, they are "enmattered formulable essences"; that is, they
necessarily consist of both matter and form. Because of this dual nature, "a physicist
would define an affection of soul differently from a dialectician; the latter would
define, e.g., anger [*orgē*] as the appetite for returning pain for pain, or something
like that, while the former would define it as a boiling of the blood or warm substance surrounding the heart" (*On the Soul,* 403a30).

Aristotle uses the material substratum to explain why anger, and the other passions, sometimes may lead a person to act unwisely or unjustly, even though he or
she "knows" better.

> Outbursts of anger [*thymoi*] and sexual appetites and some other such pas-
> sions, it is evident, actually alter our bodily condition, and in some men
> even produce fits of madness. It is plain, then, that incontinent people [i.e.,
> those lacking in slef-restraint] must be said to be in a similar condition to
> men asleep, mad, or drunk. (*Nicomachean Ethics,* 1147a15)

Let us consider now how a dialectician, as opposed to a physicist or physiologist,
might analyze anger. In his *Rhetoric*, Aristotle describes for the prospective orator
the conditions under which various emotions might be aroused in an audience. In
this connection he defines anger (*orgē*) "as an impulse, accompanied by pain, to a
conspicuous revenge for a conspicuous slight directed without justification towards
what concerns oneself or towards what concerns one's friends" (1378a30). There
are two aspects of this definition that deserve brief comment. The first has to do
with the response, and the second with the provocation.

With regard to the response, Aristotle emphasizes that the angry impulse is toward a conspicuous or manifest revenge. Anger that is suppressed, or expressed only indirectly, can have little effect. Indeed, Aristotle claims that we do not even become angry "if we think that the offender will not see that he is punished on our account and because of the way he has treated us" (*Rhetoric*, 1380b20).

With regard to the provocation, Aristotle means by the word *slight* any kind of contempt (dismissing something as unimportant), spite (thwarting the wishes of another, not for personal gain, but to prevent the other from achieving his or her goal), and insolence (doing or saying things to cause another shame simply for the pleasure of it). The slight must have been either voluntary or due to negligence (e.g., forgetfulness), and it must have been unjustified. These last provisos are especially important, for according to Aristotle, a person does not—or should not—become angry at an event that is unavoidable and/or justified.

In addition to the nature of the provocation, Aristotle considers in some detail three other conditions that are important to the arousal of anger: (1) the type of person who commits the provocation; (2) the temporary state of mind or mood that predisposes a person to become angry; and (3) the character of the person who is prone to anger.

With regard to the first condition, Aristotle argues that we are most likely to become angry at inferiors, for they should show us respect; at friends, for they ought to treat us well; at those who usually treat us with honor, for a slight from them is especially onerous; and at those who owe us good treatment or who do not return a kindness. We do *not* become angry at people whom we fear or respect. This last assertion may seem somewhat contradictory, since we usually respect our friends. On the other hand, it is the case that we are less likely to appraise as a slight the actions of an individual whom we respect. And as to fear, everyday experience would seem to suggest that we can be both afraid and angry at the same time. But anger, according to Aristotle's definition, is an impulse toward *conspicuous* revenge. Such revenge is not likely to be felt toward those whom we fear, since "nobody aims at what he thinks he cannot attain," and "the angry man [*orgizomenos*] is aiming at what he can attain" (1378b3). This last point is also relevant to Aristotle's assertion that anger is always directed against a particular individual and not "man" in general. The revenge must be conspicuous so that the offender can see that he is being punished for his slight. Man in general can neither see nor learn from the expression of anger, except in a metaphorical sense.

With regard to the second condition, Aristotle maintains that "people who are afflicted by sickness or poverty or love or thirst or any other unsatisfied desires are prone to anger [*orgiloi*] and easily roused; especially against those who slight their present distress. . . . Further, we are angered if we happen to be expecting a contrary result: for a quite unexpected evil is specially painful" (1379a15). In other words, anger is especially likely to occur when an individual is in a state of need, or has an expectation, which can be thwarted.

Finally, with regard to the third condition, Aristotle considers the character of the angry person to be very important, particularly with reference to the attribution of responsibility for acts committed out of anger. By *character* Aristotle

means that by "virtue of which we stand well or badly with reference to the passions, e.g., with reference to anger [orgisthēnai] we stand badly if we feel it violently
or too weakly, and well if we feel it moderately" (Nicomachean Ethics 1105b25).
In other words, the virtuous person seeks the mean between the extremes of too
much and too little. Aristotle makes clear, however, that he is not talking about an
algebraic mean between two set quantities. Rather, a response that is excessive for
one individual may not be for another (e.g., because of different obligations and
abilities), and similarly with regard to the provocation and the target. The goodness
or badness of a response must therefore always be evaluated relative to the person
and the situation.

> For instance, both fear and confidence and appetite and anger [orgisthēnai]
> and pity and in general pleasure and pain may be felt both too much and
> too little, and in both cases not well; but to feel them at the right times,
> with reference to the right objects, towards the right people, with the right
> motive, and in the right way, is what is both intermediate and best, and
> this is characteristic of virtue. (Nicomachean Ethics, 1106b20)

One final point needs to be made with regard to anger. A lack of restraint in
respect of anger is less blameworthy than is a lack of restraint in respect of other
emotions and appetites. This, according to Aristotle, is for four reasons (Nicomachean Ethics, 1149a25ff). First, anger is based on a judgment, for example, that
we have been insulted or slighted; and to be overcome by such a judgment, even
though wrongly, is less blameworthy than to be overcome by appetite. Second,
anger is more "natural" than is a desire for excessive and unnecessary pleasures.
Third, anger is an open response, and not crafty or dissimulating. And fourth, anger
is accompanied by pain (e.g., due to the provocation) and is not engaged in simply
for the pleasure of it.

In sum, Aristotle—like Plato—viewed anger as closely allied with reason, and as a
natural, open response to a painful situation. We shall now consider a much more
pessimistic assessment of anger.

Seneca

Original psychological speculation on most topics tended to decline following Aristotle; this was not the case, however, with regard to the emotions. With first the
collapse of the Alexandrian empire, and then the rise of the Roman imperium, the
Mediterranean world was in constant change and turmoil. Not surprisingly, therefore, attention turned increasingly to ethical issues, including the nature of pleasure,
pain, and the passions in general. Perhaps no group was more prolific on this topic
than the Stoics, followers of Zeno. Zeno came to Athens shortly after Aristotle's
death, and the school he founded takes its name from the place where he taught—a
porch (stoa) or open colonnade in Athens. Stoicism subsequently became the dominant philosophy among the Romans; and among the greatest—although not the
most consistent—of the Roman Stoics was Lucius Annaeus Seneca (4 B.C.- A.D. 65).
Seneca also wrote the first complete work, De Ira, specifically devoted to the topic

of anger. But before turning to this work, a few words should be said about the Stoic view of emotion in general.

The Stoics regarded the emotions as diseases of the mind, analogous to diseases of the body. They did recognize certain positive affects, such as cheerfulness, discretion, and fear of dishonor, as beneficial. But these positive affects were set against the more turbulent passions, which the Stoics considered to be perverted or false judgments concerning matters of good and evil. The wise man should thus strive to be rid of the passions, which he can do by forming correct opinions.

Like Plato and Aristotle before him, Seneca emphasized the notion of passivity, or the inability of a person to control his own behavior while angry. "If once we admit the emotion and by our own free will grant it any authority, reason becomes of no avail; after that it will do, not whatever you let it, but whatever it chooses" (pp. 125-126).[4] But while claiming that it is the nature of anger to be "unbridled" and "ungovernable," Seneca rejects Plato's sharp distinction between the rational and irrational elements of the soul. Reason and passion are not distinct, according to Seneca, but are "only the transformation of the mind toward the better or worse" (p. 127). It follows that only human beings are subject to anger, "for while it is the foe of reason, it is nevertheless born only where reason dwells" (p. 115).

Seneca sees absolutely no value in anger; indeed, it is "the most hideous and frenzied of all the emotions" (p. 107). No provocation justifies it, no situation permits it, and no benefit is gained by it. Once allowed, anger entirely consumes its possessor and renders dull his capacity for reasoning and sensible action. It is the author of the most heinous crimes, on both the individual and state level, and can only harm human relationships. Above all other emotions, anger is to be feared, for it is the least able to be shackled, and the most akin to madness.

Assertions such as these, Seneca recognized, would surely meet with objection. He therefore attempted to answer his critics in advance:

Does not anger spur the warrior to bravery in battle? Sometimes, Seneca admits. But so too does drunkenness, lunacy, or even fear. Moreover, since anger is contrary to reason and self-control, it more often hinders than helps the idividual when faced with danger. For warriors, "skill is their protection, anger their undoing" (p. 133).

Should not a man become angry in defense of others, for example if his father is murdered or his mother outraged before his eyes? No, replies Seneca. "To feel anger on behalf of loved ones is the mark of a weak mind, not of a loyal one. For a man to stand forth as the defender of parents, children, friends, and fellow-citizens, led merely by his sense of duty, acting voluntarily, using judgement, using foresight, moved neither by impulse nor by fury—this is noble and becoming" (p. 139).

---

[4] All page references are to the Loeb Classical Library edition of *De Ira* (Seneca, A.D. 40-50/1963).

Should not a good man be angry at evil? The good man should try to rehabilitate the evildoer, just as the physician tries to heal the sick. And if that is not possible, then the evildoer must be removed from society. "Mad dogs we knock on the head; the fierce and savage ox we slay; sickly sheep we put to the knife to keep them from infecting the flock; unnatural progeny we destroy; we drown even children who at birth are weakly and abnormal. Yet it is not anger, but reason that separates the harmful from the sound" (p. 145).

But we do not have to be angry in order to punish wrongdoing? When inflicting punishment, we should act in the spirit of the law. In legal proceedings: "Reason grants a hearing to both sides, then seeks to postpone action, even its own, in order that it may gain time to sift out the truth; but anger is precipitate. Reason wishes the decision that it gives to be just; anger wishes to have the decision which it has given seem the just decision. Reason considers nothing except the question at issue; anger is moved by trifling things that lie outside the case" (p. 153).

In short, anything that can be done in anger can be better done following rational deliberation. Anger should therefore be eliminated. But how? The answer to this question requires an analysis of the conditions which give rise to anger. According to Seneca, anger involves a three-stage process:

> The first prompting is involuntary, a preparation for passion, as it were, and a sort of menace; the next is combined with an act of volition, although not an unruly one, which assumes that it is right for me to avenge myself because I have been injured, or that it is right for the other person to be punished because he has committed a crime; the third prompting is now beyond control, in that it wishes to take vengeance, not if it is right to do so, but whether or no, and has utterly vanquished reason. (p. 175)

The best way to avoid the devastation of anger, as Seneca sees it, is to appraise events in such a manner that the initial promptings are never aroused. The two general conditions under which anger is typically aroused are (a) if we think we have received an *injury,* and (b) if we think we have received it *unjustly.*

With regard to the first condition, Seneca restricts the concept of injury to a harmful event that has been done intentionally or through negligence. He therefore regards it as the "act of a madman" to become angry at an inanimate object or at dumb animals, for they can harm us but they cannot injure us. The same is true of most accidental events caused by other persons.

With regard to the second condition, not all injuries incite a person to anger. Some, as in the case of punishment for wrongdoing, may be deserved, and should be accepted. Anger is aroused primarily if the injury is interpreted as undeserved, unwarranted, or unjustified.

Seneca offers many examples of how an event that might superficially be appraised as an injury or as unjustified can actually be interpreted otherwise. For example, many offenses may be turned into farce or jest, others can be ignored as unworthy of our attention, and still others can be justified on some grounds or at least for-given. Seneca concludes that

> the really great mind, the mind that has taken the true measure of itself, fails to revenge injury only because it fails to perceive it. . . . Revenge is the confession of a hurt; no mind is truly great that bends before injury. The man who has offended you is either stronger or weaker than you: if he is weaker, spare him; if he is stronger, spare yourself. (p. 267f)

Of course, there are cases where an injury is unjust, and it would be foolish to appraise it otherwise. In those cases the initial prompting to anger cannot be avoided, but they need not be yielded to. Instead, reason should determine what, if any, punishment is called for.

It is clear that Seneca's assessment of anger is in important respects diametrically opposed to the views of Plato and Aristotle, who regarded anger as a potentially constructive ally of reason. The difference of opinion stems, in part, from Seneca's restriction of the concept of anger to those states in which the individual completely loses control of his actions. Thus, Seneca states that if "anger suffers any limitation to be imposed upon it, it must be called by some other name—it has ceased to be anger; for I understand this to be unbridled and ungovernable" (p. 130f). But while thus restricting the concept of anger, Seneca also extends the notion of "unbridled and ungovernable" in rather subtle ways. For example, he tells the story of Cambyses, King of Persia, who was much addicted to wine. At a banquet one of his closest friends, Praexaspes, urged him to drink more sparingly, declaring the drunkenness is disgraceful in a king. Taking offense, Cambyses drank even more heavily. He then ordered that the son of Praexaspes be brought before him and in order to demonstrate to the father that the wine did not affect his performance, he unerr-ingly shot the son throught the heart with an arrow (p. 295).

In what sense was Cambyses' behavior unbridled and ungovernable, a passion rather than an action? In order to answer this question, we must first take note of a distinction Seneca drew between anger and cruelty. The latter, he says, presup-poses no prior injury, and it is done for pleasure rather than vengeance. However, there is a close relationship between anger and cruelty, according to Seneca. If too often repeated or indulged in, anger destroys mercy and the bonds which unite human beings. When this happens, what was originally done out of anger may sub-sequently be done for pleasure. Moreover, the person who acts cruelly may seek out or fancy some injrury in order to justify his brutality.

In spite of the above distinction between anger and cruelty, most of the instances of anger cited by Seneca could just as well be classified as cruelty. Certainly this is true of Cambyses' behavior. The only thing that would allow Seneca to classify the killing of Praexaspes' son as anger rather than cruelty is the fact that Cambyses had taken offense at a presumably well-intentioned remark. In other words, what dis-tinguishes anger from cruelty is not so much that the former is uncontrollable, but rather that it is based on a certain type of judgment—a judgment that one has been injured and must be avenged, but also a judgment that might be described as irrational and/or unjust. Seneca makes this point explicit in his definition of a passion as "only the transformation of the mind toward the . . . worse" (p. 127).

Lactantius

Stoicism was ultimately replaced by Christianity as the major philosophical school of the Roman empire. Lactantius was an important figure in this transition. Born sometime around A.D. 250-260, Lactantius received a classical pagan education and subsequently became a teacher of Latin rhetoric. He converted to Christianity about the year 300, and most of his major works were written after that date. As a religious philosopher he exerted considerable influence during the formative years of Christianity. One indication of his renown even during his own lifetime is that he became a spokesman for the Emperor Constantine and tutor to his son.

By way of background to Lactantius' analysis of anger, it may by noted that anger has often been the subject of praise within the Judeo-Christian religious tradition. In the Old Testament, Jehovah is depicted as a wrathful God, inflicting severe punishment on those who disobey His will. Psalm 58, for example, reads in part[5]:

> Break the teeth of these fierce
>   lions, O God.
> May they disappear like water
>   draining away;
>   may they be crushed like
>   weeds on a path.
> May they be like snails that
>   dissolve into slime;
>   may they be like a baby born
>   dead that never sees the
>   light.
> Before they know it, they are cut
>   down like weeds;
>   in his fierce anger God will
>   blow them away
>   while they are still living.
>
> The righteous will be glad when
>   they see sinners punished:
>   they will wade through the
>   blood of the wicked.

---

[5] *Good News Bible, the Bible in Today's English Version.* Copyright © American Bible Society, 1976. Reprinted with permission.

> People will say, "The righteous
>   are indeed rewarded;
>   there is indeed a God who
>   judges the world."

In the New Testament the emphasis on the wrath of God is tempered, and greater stress in placed on the virtues of meekness, forgiveness, and love. But not even Christ is depicted in the Bible as immune from anger.

How could such biblical teachings be reconciled with the types of argument against anger raised by Seneca and other philosophers influenced by Stoicism? Or, to put the question in more absolute terms, how could a supposedly immutable, all-wise, and all-powerful God be subject to anger, a passion?

In his work *De Ira Dei*, Lactantius (313-314/1965) attempted to resolve this dilemma by distinguishing between two kinds of anger—just and unjust. Referring to the type of definition offered by Aristotle and Seneca, Lactantius criticized the notion that anger (*ira*) is the desire to avenge injury or to return pain for pain. That, he maintained, refers to unjust anger, which could better be called either fury (*furorem*) or rage (*iracundiam*). Furious anger does not exist in God, who cannot be injured or suffer pain. Nor should it exist in man, where it can be the source of great evil. It can, however, be found in infrahuman animals. Just anger, by contrast, is not marked by vengeance. Rather, it is "a movement of a mind arising to the restraint of offenses" (p. 102). This kind of anger "ought not to be taken from man, nor can it be taken from God, because it is both useful and necessary for human affairs" (p. 102). In fact, without the threat of anger, civilized life would not be possible. Man would no longer consider his fellow man, but would seek his own selfish interests. Disorder and confusion would be prevalent and brute force would rule. Society would be reduced to chaos as men sought their own advantage, safe in the knowledge that they would reap no punishment.

Just anger is directed especially at those over whom we have authority. "When we see these offend, we are aroused to reprove them. For it is necessary that things which are bad should displease one who is good and just, and he to whom evil is displeasing is moved when he sees it done. Therefore, we rise to punishment, not because we have been injured, but in order that discipline be preserved, morals corrected, and license suppressed" (p. 101).

But what about the objection raised by Seneca that there is no need for anger, since punishment can be better administered, and offenses corrected, in a reasoned and dispassionate manner? A judge presiding over the law, Lactantius admits, should be dispassionate. However, the offenses brought before a judge have been committed elsewhere, and the guilt of the defendant must be proved, not assumed. Moreover, the judge must be moved not by his own opinions, but by the dictates of the law. The situation is different when an offense is committed directly before a person's own eyes. A good person is unable to watch calmly as another person commits an offense: "He who is not moved at all, either approves the faults, which is more shameful and unjust, or he avoids the bother of correcting them, bother which a calm spirit and quiet mind shuns and rejects unless anger has goaded and aroused it" (pp. 102-102).

Lactantius seems to recognize that this argument is not entirely convincing on strictly logical grounds. For those who are still skeptical he therefore suggests that they consult their own feelings. They will then recognize immediately that anger and chastisement are necessary for the exercise of authority; hence, whoever has authority (including God) must also be capable of anger (p. 114).

Lactantius also criticizes the notion, which he attributes to the Peripatetics, that the passions are best experienced in moderation. If the passions are vices, he argues, then they must be avoided entirely; but if they are good, then they should be fully experienced. Stated differently, it is not the intensity of a passion that determines whether it is good or bad, but the use to which it is put. Even a slight rejoicing over the misfortune of another may be evil, whereas great joy over a beneficial outcome may be virtuous. With regard to anger, we have seen that its proper use is the correction of wrongdoing. As such, it should be experienced to the extent called for by the offense.

The above argument is offered as a rebuttal to the Peripatetics, but it is not clear exactly whom Lactantius had in mind. (*Peripatetic* is a name given to the followers of Aristotle, because of the latter's habit of strolling with his students while teaching.) The views which Lactantius attacks are not an accurate representation of Aristotle's own position. As we have seen, Aristotle did not consider the emotions, in and of themselves, to be either virtues or vices. Moreover, he emphasized that "moderation" cannot be interpreted in an absolute sense, but is always relative to the situation and the individual. Thus, what is moderate in one context, or for one person, might be immoderate in another context or for another person. In this respect at least, it would seem that the difference between Lactantius and Aristotle is more one of tone than of substance.

This brings us to one final issue. Only a mutable object can suffer a passion, and God is by definition immutable. It would therefore seem that God is not capable of experiencing emotion, except perhaps in a metaphorical sense. However, according to Lactantius, we are not speaking metaphorically when we attribute anger to God; but neither do we mean that God is passively affected, or overcome, by anger. "Since God is possessed of the highest virtue, we ought to understand that He has His wrath in His power and is not ruled by it, but that He Himself governs the wrath as He wishes, which is not at all repugnant to a higher being" (p. 109). The situation is different in the case of man. In contrast to God, man is a feeble being who cannot always govern himself while angry. That anger is sometimes experienced passively is thus more a commentary on the nature of man than on the nature of anger.

As a Christian apologist for the wrath of God, Lactantius was forced to adopt a rather extreme position on the need for, and potential benefits of, anger. However, Lactantius certainly was no more extreme in his praise of anger than Seneca was in his condemnation. These two authors thus illustrate well the conflicting attitudes that have traditionally been associated with ethical teachings on anger. But in spite of all their differences, Seneca and Lactantius did agree on one important point:

Both regarded anger as a cognitive process which presupposes the ability to reason, even if the reasoning is faulty, as Seneca would maintain, or wise and just, as Lactantius would maintain.

Aquinas

The dominant philosophical orientation of the early Middle (or Dark) Ages was a Christian Neoplatonism with Stoic overtones. As far as speculation regarding anger is concerned, little new was added. St. Augustine (354-430) was the dominant intellectual figure during this period. Following the lead of Lactantius, he defined divine anger—and presumably human anger, too—as "a judgement by which punishment is inflicted upon sin" (*The City of God*, 15.25). Starting in the 12th century, the works of Aristotle were reintroduced into the Latin West, first through Arabic sources and then in the original Greek. This set the stage for St. Thomas Aquinas (1225-1274), whose synthesis of Aristotelian thought with Christian teachings represents one of the most significant intellectual achievements of the "high" Middle Ages.

Aquinas divided the basic emotions into two broad categories—the irascible and the concupiscible. The origins of this dividsion can be found in Plato's distinction between the spirited and the appetitive elements of the *psychē*. The concupiscible emotions—desire (*concupiscentia*), love, joy, hate, aversion, and sorrow—represent unobstructed tendencies toward or away from objects appraised as either good or evil. In the case of the irascible emotions, direct approach or avoidance is blocked. The dominant emotion that results is anger (*ira*), which gives the class its name. But other emotions may also ensue (viz., hope, despair, courage, or fear), depending on the circumstances.

This distinction between concupiscible and irascible emotions is related to the distinction introduced in Chapter 1 between impulsive and conflictive emotions. There, the impulsive emotions were defined as straightforward desires and aversions which are so automatic and compelling that they are not regarded as stemming from the self-as-agent. In other words, the impulsive and concupiscible emotions are basically the same. The conflictive emotions, however, are not the same as the irascible, and the difference is important for an understanding of anger. Therefore, a brief digression is in order.

In a sense, the concept of the irascible emotions represents a medieval version of the frustration-aggression hypothesis. If an impulse toward or away from some goal is blocked, a person may try to overcome the obstacle by aggression; or if that is not possible, he may give up in despair, retreat in fear, or hope for better success in the future. It is important to note, however, that a person need not experience conflict simply because he fights to overcome an obstacle. Conflict arises only if the person believes that in the situation aggression is wrong or dangerous. In other words, conflict involves incompatible response tendencies; it is not simply a straightforward response to frustration.

The difference between frustration and conflict may be expressed somewhat differently. Frustration may give rise to new impulses (e.g., toward aggression); conflict, however, involves a transformation of behavior due to incompatible impulses. Sometimes the response to conflict may resemble a simple impulsive reaction. But the resolution of a conflict always requires some compromise, or at least some justification as to why one response is acceded to while the other is not. In this respect what I have called conflictive emotions are more like socially constituted defense mechanisms than they are like the irascible emotions as traditionally conceived. But more of that shortly. Let us return now to Aquinas's analysis of anger.

Aquinas defines anger as "a desire to punish another by way of just revenge" (*Summa Theologiae,* 1a2ae. 47,1).[6] Of course, for revenge to be just, the original provocation must have been unjust. And, according to Aquinas:

> The greatest injustice is to injure someone by deliberate intent or effort, with conscious malice, as we read in the [Aristotle's] *Ethics.* That is why we are especially angry at those whom we believe have made a deliberate effort to injure us. If we think that the injury was done out of ignorance or emotion we are not angry with them, or at least not violently so. The injury is not as serious if it is motivated by ignoramce or emotion and in a sense calls for mercy and forgiveness. But those who do injury deliberately seem to be guilty of contempt, which is why they anger us so intensely. Aristotle says that *we feel no anger, or comparatively little, with those who themselves acted through anger; apparently, at least, they did not intend to slight us.* (1a2ae. 47, 2)

Since only persons can perform actions that are just or unjust, deliberate or undeliberate, it is only possible to become angry at specific individuals. Of course, we do sometimes aggress against inanimate objects which harm us. But such aggression is a kind of automatic reaction to painful sensory stimulation. It can be found in animals as well as man and does not presuppose the capacity to reason, as does true anger. Also, a group of people may injure us, in which case we tend to treat the entire group as a single individual if we experience anger.

The central feature of anger is the desire for revenge or punishment. But desire alone is not enough; revenge must also be possible. For example, if the person who provoked us is of very high station, then the reaction may be sadness rather than anger. It is important to note that Aquinas is not simply saying that anger will be suppressed when faced with powerful opposition, but that the actual provocation may be appraised in a fashion incompatible with anger.

It is evident from the above description that Aquinas draws heavily on Aristotle for his analysis of anger. Aquinas was, however, much more systematic than Aristotle, especially when it came to the virtues and vices of anger. Under what conditions is

---

[6] All quotations are from the *Summa Theologiae* by T. Aquinas. Copyright © 1964 by Blackfriars. Reprinted with the permission of McGraw-Hill Book Company. Quotations are cited by part, question, and article number.

anger virtuous and under what conditions is it vicious? In considering this issue, Aquinas distinguishes between what is sought (i.e., the object of anger) and how it is sought (e.g., the manner of being angry). The object of anger is to avenge an injury. The desire for vengeance is praiseworthy provided that it conforms to reason, and it is blameworthy if it does not conform. In particular, it is wrong "to seek to punish one who does not deserve it, or more than he deserves, or not according to the legitimate process of law, or not with the right intention, which is the correction of fault and the maintenance of justice" (2a2ae. 158,1).

As to the manner of being angry, "it should not be immoderatley fierce, either inwardly or outwardly. If this condition is not observed, anger will not be without sin, even when seeking just retribution" (2a2ae. 158, 1). In other words, the morality of anger must be considered not only in terms of its effects on the victim, but also in terms of its effects on the person who is angry. If the desire for revenge is so strong that it obscures reason, or disrupts other desirable behavior, then the anger is wrong even though it may have been warranted by the provocation. Stated somewhat differently—in nonmoralistic terms—there are socially appropriate ways of experiencing as well as of expressing anger.

Aquinas also considers it a vice *not* to become angry in appropriate circumstances. When anger conforms to reason, its object (revenge) may be considered the application of a temporary good (punishment) to an evil (the provocation). In this respect, anger can even be considered a form of judgment, the function of which is to correct faults and maintain justice. Not to make such judgments would be wrong. Moreover, a person cannot make a judgment regarding injustice, and will to correct the fault, without also experiencing certain feelings and undergoing physiological changes. This is because the lower "powers" of the soul (the sensory appetites) naturally follow the higher (reason and will). Such being the case, "sensory feelings of anger cannot be wholly absent except the will's motion of anger be withdrawn or weak. As a consequence the lack of high-tempered feeling will be wrong, as also the lack of the will to vindicate according to the judgment of right reason" (2a2ae. 158, 8).

And what about the passionate element in anger? In some instances, the bodily changes that normally accompany anger may become so tumultuous as to impede the use of reason. The person is then "overcome" by anger. Such a condition is to be avoided, for it can lead to excessive or inappropriate behavior. But since a person cannot be held fully responsible for actions performed when reason is impaired, neither can he be held entirely responsible for acts committed during anger.

The views of Aquinas on anger may be summarized in the following series of propositions. (1) Anger is initiated by the judgment that an offense has been committed which is both unjustified and deliberate. (2) If that judgment is correct, then anger is not only justified but also necessary, for unreasonable tolerance "nurses negligence, and invites the good as well as the evil to do wrong" (2a2ae. 158, 8). (3) But like any form of social control, anger may be abused: For example, the punishment may exceed the offense; anger may be used for personal gain and not to acheive justice; and it may be expressed out of hatred or for the sheer pleasure of revenge. (4) When anger is experienced and/or expressed inappropriately, it is itself subject to punishment. (5) However, if a person commits an offense out of anger, even though that anger was inappropriate, he will be judged less harshly than if he had acted deliberately.

Descartes

René Descartes (1596-1650) is the last historical figure whom we shall consider. His analysis of emotion is particularly interesting because he attempted to explain emotional reactions in completely mechanistic terms, that is, without regard to cognitive mediation.

Descartes rejected Aristotle's distinction between actions and passions as separate categories of being. Rather, he argued that any event can be both an action and a passion; it is an action from the perspective of the agent which causes it, and a passion from the perspective of the subject to which it happens. Thus, an action of the body, by affecting the soul, can be a passion of the soul.

Let us consider briefly how this process works. The body, according to Descartes, is a complex machine moved by particles of extreme minuteness, called animal spirits. (A very complicated steam engine would be a good modern analogy.) The soul, on the other hand, operates on fundamentally different—nonmechanistic—principles. The major function of the soul is thinking, broadly conceived, and thinking may be either an action or a passion. Actions of the soul are rational, deliberate thoughts, while passions are thoughts impressed upon the soul through its interaction with the body. This interaction takes place at the pineal gland (a small organ in the center of the brain), which serves as a kind of valve controlling the flow of animal spirits throughout the body.

Emotions are passions of the soul which are caused, maintained, and fortified by movement of the animal spirits. They differ from other passions of the soul—for example, external perceptions (scents, sounds, colors, etc.) and internal perceptions (hunger, thirst, pain, etc.)—in that emotions are subjectively referred to the soul itself and not to some specific stimulus. As an illustration of how emotions are produced, Descartes gives the following example. If the image of a frightening object strikes the retina, animal spirits are deflected by the pineal gland partly to the appropriate muscles, which produce flight, and partly to the heart and other bodily organs, which determine the quality of the animal spirits ascending to the brain. The resulting spirits are specially adapted for maintaining and strengthening the fear. This process is strictly mechanical and occurs in animals as well as man. In humans, however, the action of the spirits is communicated to the soul and hence, in respect to the latter, may be considered a passion.

Emotional responses may sometimes be initiated by actions of the soul, as when a person willfully conceives of an object that normally is associated with an emotion. In a similar manner, a person can learn to control his or her emotions by diverting attention away from an exciting object and/or by thinking of some object that elicits an emotion contrary to the one to be inhibited. However, a person has no *direct* control over the emotions. With the exception of the association of ideas just noted, the passions arise automatically following the perception of an appropriate object.

Not just any aspect of a perceived object will excite an emotion, but primarily those aspects that signify potential benefit or harm. According to Descartes, the emotions operate "in accordance with the institutions of nature" to maintain and enhance the well-being of the body. More specifically:

> The customary mode of action of all the passions is simply this, that they dispose the soul to desire those things which nature tells us are of use, and to persist in this desire, and also bring about that same agitation of spirits which customarily causes them to dispose the body to the movement which serves for the carrying into effect of these things. (Article LII[7])

It follows that in order to enumerate or classify the emotions, we need to examine the diverse ways in which objects may be significant to us. Being beneficial or harmful is, of course, the most fundamental way. But the benefit (or harm) may be past, present, or future; certain or uncertain; under our own control or the control of others; and so forth. On the basis of criteria such as these, Descartes distinguishes six primary emotions—wonder, love, hatred, desire, joy, and sadness. All other emotions he regards as combintaions of these six.

Before proceeding to a discussion of Descartes's analysis of anger, the similarity of his views to several current theories of emotion might be noted briefly. Although Descartes's physiological speculations appear today to be quite naive (indeed, they were outmoded even in his own day), the logic of his argument is similar in important respects to the James-Lange theory of emotion—and to some of its contemporary offshoots (e.g., Schachter, 1971). What these theories have in common is the supposition that feedback from physiological arousal adds the warm glow of emotion to the otherwise cold perception of an exciting event. Of all contemporary theorists, Descartes is perhaps closest to Silvan Tomkins (1970, 1980, 1981a). According to Tomkins, there are relatively few primary emotions, each based on an innate neural mechanism. Activation of an appropriate neural mechanism produces characteristic changes in the periphery, feedback from which helps to amplify and sustain adaptive responses to the eliciting stimulus.

Let us now turn to Descartes's analysis of anger (*colère*). Anger is a species of hatred; hence, the latter must be defined first.

> Hatred is an emotion caused by the [animal] spirits which incite the soul to desire to be separated from the objects which present themselves as hurtful. (Article LXXIX)

Two of the main species of hatred are indignation and anger. Indignation is felt when we perceive some evil done to another. Anger, by contrast, is a species of hatred that

> we have towards those who have done some evil to or have tried to injure not any chance person but more particularly ourselves. Thus it has the

---

[7] All references are to *The Passions of the Soul* (Descartes, 1649/1968).

same content as indignation, and all the more so in that it is founded on an action which affects us, and for which we desire to avenge ourselves, for this desire almost always accompanies it. (Article CXCIX)

Descartes further distinguishes two types of anger. The first type is rash and turbulent but easily appeased. It is the result of an "instant aversion" and afflicts "those who have much goodness and much love." Because of their love these persons take offense at injuries done to others as well as to themselves. There is no need to elaborate further on this type of anger, for it is very similar to the just anger described by Lactantius.

The second type of anger mentioned by Descartes is similar to what Lactantius called unjust anger. It afflicts those who are most proud, and/or who are base and infirm: the proud because they esteem themselves too highly; the base and infirm becasue they are dependent on others for the things they prize. Anger of this sort may not be apparent when first initiated, but its strength grows with time, "increased by the agitation of an ardent desire to avenge oneself excited in the blood" (Article CCII).

Descartes recognizes that anger "is useful in giving us strangth in repelling injury," but he cautions that "there is yet no passion an excess of which we should more carefully avoid." Like Seneca, he believes that the best defense against excessive anger is a "noble spirit," which causes

> us to esteem very little all the good things which may be taken away, and on the other hand to esteem highly the liberty and absolute dominion over self that we cease to have when we allow ourselves to be offended by someone. . . . The noble spirit thus has nothing but disdain, or at the most indignation, for those injuries which others are wont to resent angrily. (Article CIII)

In concluding this brief summary of the views of Descartes, two observations may be made. First, in spite of his ostensibly mechanistic approach to the emotions, when it came to practical teachings on anger Descartes could not avoid an emphasis on cognition (i.e., on actions as opposed to passions of the soul). Second, Descartes ostentatiously rejected prior analyses of emotion as clearly defective and of little value. Nevertheless, it is quite apparent that his own teachings on anger echo the general cultural themes found in previous writers. Indeed, these themes are so consistent and redundant that we will stop our historical survey with Descartes.

Summary and Implications

In addition to their intrinsic interest, historical teachings on anger can be used to help clarify a number of issues of contemporary concern. As previewed at the outset of the chapter, these issues include (a) the social nature and significance of anger, (b) the grounds for interpreting anger as a passion rather than as an action, and (c) the contradiction and conflict in social norms related to anger. Each of these issues will be discussed briefly.

The Social Nature and Significance of Anger

Let us begin by considering the instigation to anger. Plato, Aristotle, Seneca, Lactantius, Aquinas, and Descartes all agree that anger involves a moral judgment; that is, a determination that some harm has been committed and that the harm was either deliberate and unjustified or else was due to negligence. At first this might seem like a rather trivial observation, but if we take it seriously, its implications are rather far-reaching. For one thing, moral judgments presume the existence of social norms or standards of conduct. Theories that attempt to account for angry behavior in morally neutral terms (e.g., the frustration-aggression hypothesis) are thus bound to miss one of the most important aspects of the phenomenon they purport to explain.

Cognitively speaking, moral judgments are also highly complex. From this it follows that anger is a human emotion, for only human beings have the cognitive capacity to judge whether an instigation was unjustified, deliberate, negligent, and so forth. Animals and infants may become aggressive and high spirited in a manner reminiscent of anger; but when applied to animals and infants, the concept of anger is being used in a derivational or metaphorical sense. Plato and Descartes might disagree with this assertion, but Seneca probably expressed the matter best when he observed that "wild beasts and all animals, except man, are not subject to anger; for while it is the foe of reason, it is nevertheless born only where reason dwells" (*De Ira*, p. 115).

Finally, it may be concluded from these considerations that the typical target of anger will be another person, for only human actions can be judged in moral terms. This point was especially emphasized by Aristotle and Aquinas. Of course, we all sometimes become angry at inanimate objects, and at events that are either justified and/or beyond anyone's control. But in such circumstances we also typically feel somewhat foolish and embarrassed about our own anger. Hence, the exceptions tend to prove (test) the rule.

As regards the nature of the response, most historical teachings mention a desire for revenge and/or the correction of wrongdoing as essential features of anger. However, revenge and punishment may be exacted in an indefinite variety of ways, depending upon the individual and the circumstances. Indeed, given an adequate provocation, almost any response can be interpreted as a sign of anger, provided that it somehow communicates one's displeasure. This last proviso is important, for anger that is not expressed can have no positive function. That is why Aristotle defined anger not just as a desire for revenge, but as a desire for *conspicuous* revenge.

Among the authors that we have reviewed, only Seneca saw no good in anger. And his disagreement with the others on this issue was as much conceptual as empirical. That is, it had to do with the grounds for interpreting a response as anger, and hence as a passion rather than as an action.

Grounds for Interpreting Anger as a Passion

In Chapter 1 we discussed in some detail the distinction between actions and passions. The historical importance of this distinction should now be evident. We also described a number of primary and secondary grounds for interpreting emotional responses as passions rather than as actions. Irrationality has been perhaps the most important of the secondary grounds, historically speaking. Among the primary grounds, the role of biological and social imperatives and systemic conflict can also be clarified through historical teachings.[8]

Irrationality. The interpretation of anger as a passion because it involves irrational judgments was emphasized particularly by Seneca. Indeed, for Seneca, anger *is* a kind of false judgment. From Seneca's perspective, then, irrationality is not so much a ground for interpreting anger as a passion as it is part of what we mean by both anger and passion. But there is a problem with such an approach. For one thing, it does not conform entirely to everyday usage, as will be discussed below. For another thing, it does not even conform to Seneca's own usage. Recall the example of Cambyses, who shot his critic's son through the heart. If Cambyses' purpose was to demonstrate the steadiness of his hand while intimidating his critic, then his response was undoubtedly quite effective. The issue here is not so much one of rationality but of value. What Seneca considered to be wrong or immoral he also regarded as a "foe of reason," and hence as a passion rather than as an action.

Of course, Seneca was not alone in considering anger to be irrational, he was only the most radical in this regard. Plato, for example, also argued that anger is a function of the irrational part of the *psychē*; but Plato also recognized that anger is often closely "allied" with reason, that is, in those instances where anger is warranted and justified. It is not clear in what sense a response can be allied with reason and still be considered irrational. It might seem more appropriate to say that some episodes of anger are rational and others not. This appears to have been the view of Lactantius when he attributed just anger to God, a supremely rational being, and to the godlike element in man; in contrast, he attributed unjust anger (fury, rage) to dumb animals and to man's animal nature.

But even if we limit consideration to episodes of anger that would be regarded as irrational by ordinary criteria, we must still account for the source of the irrationality. A response may be irrational because of ignorance (not knowing what is best), faulty logic, unconscious motivation, or blind adherence to custom or habit; or, as will be discussed next, because of uncontrollable bodily changes.

Biological imperatives. One might not expect to find much reference to biological imperatives in historical teachings. Evolutionary theory (as opposed to some form of creationism) is distinctly modern; and our understanding of the physiological bases of behavior, poor as it is, makes the speculations of Plato and even Descartes seem exceedingly crude. But our concern here is with ideas, not with the accuracy

---

[8] Other secondary grounds (e.g., impulsivity, intensity, persistence, unusualness, and commitment) could also be discussed from the perspective of historical teachings, but there is not space. Among the remaining primary grounds discussed in Chapter 1, psychological imperatives have not received a great deal of attention from historical writers, and cognitive disorganization is less relevant to normal anger than to transcendental emotional states (e.g., mystical experiences, acute anxiety attacks).

of specific hypotheses. And the idea that anger and other emotions as well stem from biological imperatives is very ancient. The idea appears in a number of variations: Anger is a function of the mortal (irrational) *psychē*, is attributable to man's animal nature, or is an action of the body impressed on the soul.

Perhaps the first thing to note about this line of reasoning is that it is based more on symbolism than on fact.[9] The second thing to note is that it is—or can easily become—quite circular. For example, to the extent that anger is irrational, it *must* (so the argument goes) be separated from reason physiologically as well as conceptually; and since anger sometimes leads to acts that are "brutish," "bestial," and "inhumane," it *must* be a function of man's animal nature. In other words, the presumed irrational and animal-like qualities of anger are used to infer that anger is—in modern terms—a biologically based response. The latter assumption may then be used to explain why anger is experienced as a passion rather than as an action of the soul or *psychē*.

To illustrate the inadequacies of this line of reasoning, let us consider a little more closely the contention by Aquinas that anger, being a function of the sensitive part of the soul (which humans share with animals) necessarily involves a certain amount of physiological arousal. When such arousal becomes too extreme, according to Aquinas, it may obscure reason and hence become "uncontrollable." This is not a very satisfactory explanation for the experience of passivity during anger for two reasons. First, phsiological arousal per se (e.g., as induced by exercise) does not typically interfere with higher cognitive processes; and second, anger can be quite unreasonable and excessive without involving a great deal of physiological arousal—as in the cold, vengeful kind of anger described by Descartes.

The above considerations suggest that the irrational or passionate element of anger lies in the cognitive processes themselves (as Seneca maintained), and not in man's animal nature or physiological makeup. But we already have noted the inconsistencies in Seneca's position. To help us out of this dilemma, we must examine briefly two other primary grounds for interpreting anger as a passion, namely, sociocultural imperatives and systemic conflict.

Sociocultural imperatives. With the exception of Seneca, all of the persons we have considered emphasized not only the right but also the *obligation* to become angry

---

[9] I do not wish to imply that all biological speculation regarding the emotions is groundless. From a constructivist point of view, the relationship between biological systems and elements of emotional syndromes was discussed in Chapter 2. The point that I wish to make now is that the traditional link between the emotions, on the one hand, and biological and physiological factors, on the other, is quite ancient; and that the link is often based on what I have called psychophysiological symbolism (Averill, 1974). This refers to the tendency to associate psychological with physiological processes on the basis of shared symbolic connotations rather than on the basis of empirical evidence. Historically, psychophysiological symbolism has exerted a strong influence on theories of emotion, and it continues to do so today.

in appropriate circumstances. This theme was expressed in many ways. Thus, for Plato the spirited element of the *psychē* is as necessary for the well-being of the individual as properly trained guardians are for the state. Aristotle emphasized the importance of feeling anger at the right times, toward the right people, with the right motives, and so forth. Lactantius believed that only the wicked or the very lazy are not aroused to anger at the sight of injustice. Similarly, Aquinas argued that too little anger could be as sinful as too much. Descartes, while less moralistic in tone, also spoke of the "usefulness" of anger in repelling injury.

Such sociocultural imperatives, if internalized, result in behavior that is interpreted (and experienced) as beyond personal control. That is, the virtuous person cannot help but become angry when circumstances "demand" it. Rational deliberation is not necessary (indeed, is contraindicated), and hence the behavior may also be regarded as irrational, or at least as nonrational.

Sociocultural imperatives are also closely related to another secondary ground for interpreting a response as a passion, namely, commitment. As described in Chapter 1, commitment (as opposed to simple intensity or perseverance) implies adherence to some general principles or to a particular conception of one's self. To the extent that anger is done "in order that discipline be preserved, morals corrected, and license suppressed" (Lactantius), it implies commitment. Commitment is also reflected in Aristotle's assertion that anger involves a desire for *conspicuous* revenge. There are, of course, occasions when it is better not to reveal our anger. But in general, hidden anger—like a commitment that is not openly expressed—is somewhat less than genuine.

Systemic conflict. Seneca, of course, would disagree with the notion that anger involves sociocultural imperatives, just as he would disagree with the contention that anger reflects biological imperatives. Also, a good deal of ambivalence about anger can be found among even its most ardent apologists, such as Lactantius. This brings us to perhaps the most important ground for interpreting anger as a passion, namely, systemic conflict. As described in previous chapters, systems of behavior can be defined at biological, psychological, and social levels of analysis. *Inter*systemic conflict occurs when, let us say, some biological impulse is aroused in a situation where social norms call for an imcompatible response. *Intra*systemic conflict is also common, as when two incompatible biological impulses are aroused. Both kinds of conflict are important in anger. For the sake of simplicity, however, we will focus on intrasystemic conflict at the psychological and sociocultural levels of analysis.

Plato made intrapsychic (i.e., intrasystemic conflict on the psychological level) central to his analysis of anger. His tripartite division of the *psychē* bears comparison with Freud's tripartite division of the mind into ego (rational element), superego (spirited element), and id (appetitive element). With regard to anger, the spirited element rouses the individual to action when there is a conflict between the rational and appetitive elements of the *psychē*, or when some external wrongdoing is perceived. In such instances, anger is allied with reason but still distinct from it.

By the Middle Ages, Plato's division of the irrational *psychē* into spirited and appetitive elements had evolved into the distinction between the irascible and concupiscible emotions (cf. Aquinas). As will be recalled, the concupiscible emotions represent unobstructed impulses toward or away from objects appraised as either good or bad; by contrast, the irascible emotions arise when direct approach or avoidance is blocked.

Descartes, "parting company with all those who have written on this topic before," rejected the distinction between irascible and concupiscible emotions. The distinction seemed to imply, according to him, that the soul has two faculties, one of anger and the other of desire. But why just these two? The soul also has faculties of wondering, loving, hoping, fearing, and thus of receiving in itself every other passion, or else bringing about actions to which these passions urge it" (Article LXVIII).

Certainly Descartes was correct in this criticism. Returning for a moment to Plato's analysis, if we take the mere existence of conflict as a criterion for distinguishing between the spirited and appetitive elements of the *psychē*, then by the same criterion we could also distinguish among various appetitive parts of the *psychē*, such as fear and sexual desire. Descartes regarded the consupiscible emotions (unobstructed impulses) as primary, and the irascible emotions as secondary or derivative; hence, he denied that the distinction between the two kinds of emotion is in any way fundamental. But in his denial, he may have thrown the proverbial baby out with the bath water. What happens when two impulses conflict, or the tendency toward some goal is blocked? Here, I believe, Plato and Aquinas exhibited greater insight than did Descartes. Nevertheless, their insight was still quite limited.

As explained in the section on Aquinas, the class of irascible emotions is in some respects similar to what I have called conflictive emotions. But there is this important difference. The resolution of a conflict typically involves a symbolic transformation of one or more response tendencies. Hence, what I have called conflictive emotions are more like conversion reactions in a Freudian sense than they are like irascible emotions in a Thomistic sense.

Conceptualized in this way, conflictive emotions may take many different forms, depending upon the nature of the underlying conflict. Wild-man behavior, discussed in the previous chapter, is a good example of a rather extreme conflictive emotional state—a socially constituted hysterical reaction, so to speak. Anger, I would maintain, is a less dramatic conflictive emotion within our culture.

Contradictions and Conflict in the Social Norms Related to Anger

Of course, an emotion like anger is not the same as a typical conversion (hysterical) reaction. In the case of the latter, the source of the conflict and its resolution is primarily intrapsychic and idiosyncratic to the individual. In the case of anger, the intrapsychic conflict is a reflection of a broader conflict within the social system.

The nature of the social conflict related to anger is perhaps best revealed in the opposing views of Seneca and Lactantius. Seneca assumed that human beings are basically good, that reason is man's highest quality, and that punishment for wrong-doing should be administered only after a careful weighing of the evidence. Lactantius, on the other hand, believed that man is basically evil (as the result of original sin), that human reason is limited in scope, and that swift punishment is often necessary for the maintenance of a just social order. Of course, there are countervailing themes in each author, for neither completely rejected the assumptions of the other. Thus, Seneca had no compunction about recommending the execution of criminals or the drowning of malformed infants—provided such acts of homicide were done in accordance with reason and for the benefit of society. And for his part, Lactantius embraced the Christian teachings of forgiveness, mercy, and love, not to mention a belief in the ultimate sanctity of human life.

In short, the disagreement between Seneca and Lactantius reflects two sets of norms, both of which are deeply ingrained in Western intellectual and moral traditions. One set condemns deliberate acts of violence as inhumane, while the other set calls for the forceful retribution of injustice. How might these conflicting norms be reconciled? One way would be to interpret the encouraged but condemned response as, in some sense, beyond control.

We have noted how, with the exception of Seneca, all of the authors whom we have been considering regarded anger to be a social imperative in appropriate circumstances. At the same time, they recognized that anger may sometimes lead to untoward consequences. But even in the latter instances an important proviso was added, namely, a person cannot be held as responsible for an act committed out of anger as for a similar act committed deliberately (cf. Aristotle and Aquinas, especially). The ostensible reason for this mitigation of responsibility was, of course, that anger is a passion and hence something over which a person has no real control. But the situation is more complicated than this.

Much of the behavior of the Greek hero, the medieval Christian, or modern man has been regarded by many as beyond personal control (e.g., due to fate, predestination, or scientific determinism, depending upon the prevailing word view). In most cases, however, this belief has not been considered relevant to the attribution of responsibility. Thus, interpreting a response as a passion rather than as an action is more than saying that the response was determined by forces outside of the individual's own control—it is one way of mitigating responsibility for the act.

Stated in this way, the question arises: Which came first, the chicken (the interpretation of anger as a passion) or the egg (the mitigation of responsibility for an act committed out of anger)? This is not a question that we can attempt to answer here, if indeed it has an answer. However, one point should be noted. In the case of behavior, the distinction between causes and consequences, chickens and eggs, is often moot, particularly when viewed from a developmental and/or historical perspective. To take a rather trivial example, the consequences of a rat's having pressed a lever on one occasion (e.g., the receipt of food) may become (developmentally speaking) a "cause" of the animal's pressing the lever on a subsequent occasion. Analogously, from a social-historical point of view. the mitigation of responsibility may be a cause as well as a consequence of interpreting anger as a passion. This is an issue about which we shall have much more to say in Chapter 5, when we consider the legal treatment of crimes of passion.

Concluding Observations

From historical teachings, the following picture of anger emerges: Anger is a highly complex emotion, often irrational but not noncognitive (i.e., anger presumes the capacity for rational thought, whether or not it conforms to the standards of rationality as typically conceived). Anger is also an *interpersonal* emotion; indeed, the experience of anger might better be regarded as intersubjective rather than as a private feeling on the part of a single individual. The social nature of anger is evident in other ways as well. Thus, the instigation to anger involves the violation of socially acceptable standards of conduct, whether willful or through negligence; and the aim (motive) for anger is revenge or punishment, which should be proportional to the provocation and done openly and not by subterfuge.

We have also seen how historical teachings help clarify some of the grounds for interpreting anger as a passion rather than as an action. Biological imperatives (e.g., physiological change, man's animal nature) have traditionally been used to explain an individual's presumed lack of control over anger. But from a historical perspective, the traditional association of emotional with biological processes appears to be more symbolic than factual. Part of the legitimation (social justification) of many emotions is that they are divorced from uniquely human qualities, such as rationality and choice. This, incidentally, is true not only within our own culture. In Chapter 3 we saw how wild-man behavior was legitimized as a reversion to an animal-like state ("being wild pig"), even though it is obviously an institutionalized pattern of behavior. The legitimation of anger has apparently followed similar logic.

The fact that anger is often a duty imposed on the individual by the group (sociocultural imperatives) also did not go unnoticed in historical teachings. Indeed, this is a central theme, but one frequently masked by the conflicting norms that relate to anger.

To a great extent, historical teachings can be viewed as attempts to establish rules for the proper experience and expression of anger. These rules are seldom specified very precisely—which is not too surprising, since the rules of anger must be instantiated differently depending upon the individuals and circumstances involved. However, the general nature of these rules is clear, for example, they have to do with the adequacy of the provocation, the appropriateness of the target, and the aim or objective of the response, as well as the mode of expression and the attribution of responsibility. The rules are "designed" to maximize the positive functions of anger (e.g., the punishment and/or prevention of behavior that is considered, by prevailing social standards, to be unjustified or negligent), while minimizing undesirable consequences (e.g., unnessary violence and the pursuit of personal gain).

In Part II of this volume we will examine the extent to which the everyday experience of anger conforms to the cultural ideals suggested by historical teachings. But first, two additional topics will be discussed. In Chapter 5 we will bring historical teachings up to date, in a sense, by examining the rules of anger as they are reflected in contemporary legal practices; and in Chapter 6, we will consider some of the nonnormative conditions (e.g., unavoidable frustration, physiological arousal) that influence anger.

Chapter 5

Anger and the Law

In the United States over 20,000 people are the victims of willful (nonnegligent) homicide each year. About three-quarters of these homicides are eventually "solved" with the arrest of one or more persons. The legal treatment of these defendants provides a great amount of information on the social norms related to anger and aggression.

By way of introduction, let us review briefly the law of homicide. In most jurisdictions, four categories of criminal homicide are recognized: First- and second-degree murder and voluntary and involuntary manslaughter. *First-degree murder* is a homicide committed with "malice aforethought," a somewhat misleading legal phrase that denotes not only the premeditated taking of life, but also any killing done during the commission of another crime (e.g., during a robbery), or the killing of a police officer during the performance of his or her duties. *Second-degree murder* is a vaguely defined category that also implies malice aforethought, but that also takes into account mitigating circumstances. *Voluntary manslaughter* presumably does not involve premeditation; it is the typical "crime of passion." Finally, *involuntary manslaughter* includes homicides committed by accident or misfortune, but for which there is some degree of criminal liability.

As will be described in detail later in the chapter, more defendants are convicted of voluntary manslaughter—a crime of passion[1]—than of any other type of homicide. The legal conception of a crime of passion is contained in the following definition (*Words and Phrases*, 1953):

---

[1] The crime of passion is not the only kind of voluntary manslaughter, but it is by far the most common, and the only kind that will be considered in this chapter. It might also be wondered why crimes of *passion* are considered *voluntary* manslaughter. The concepts of passion and voluntariness are, in one sense, incompatible. But in another sense, they are not. The person who is angry *wants* to attack his antagonist. What is not under voluntary control is the desire itself, or the ability to resist the desire.

"Passion," as used in a charge defining manslaughter as voluntary homicide committed under the immediate influence of sudden passion arising from an adequate cause, means any of the emotions of the mind known as "anger," "rage," "sudden resentment," or "terror," rendering the mind incapable of cool reflection. (pp. 658-659)

Actually, terror is seldom used as a defense for voluntary manslaughter; if a person is so terrorized as to kill his antagonist, and the terror is justified, then the person might just as well plead self-defense, which could bring complete acquittal. Only if the terror was based on mistaken judgment would a defense of voluntary manslaughter be warranted. For the most part, then, the typical crime of passion involves an act committed out of anger, rage, or sudden resentment.

A person who is convicted of a crime of passion is seldom sentenced to more than a few years in prison, and is often set free on probation without any prison term at all. The sentence for first-degree murder, by contrast, may be life imprisonment or even death. Obviously, the attribution of anger in a court of law is no trivial matter, either for the defendant or for society. Why are crimes of passion treated so leniently? How does a jury determine whether a defendant was in a state of passion at the time of a killing? These are some of the issues that will be addressed in the present chapter.

The chapter is divided into four sections. First, we will review briefly the historical development and current relationships between social custom and the law of homicide. Second, we will examine the incidence and disposition of homicide cases in the United States (and, to a lesser extent, in England). Third, we will consider in some detail the criteria for attributing passions to a defendant in a court of law. And finally, in the fourth section, we will discuss the plea of temporary insanity, which can sometimes substitute for a plea of passion and which illustrates many of the same underlying social and psychological dynamics.

And what does all of this have to do with anger? In the previous chapter on historical teachings, two broad sets of norms were identified. One of these sets, which forms the basis for the written law, condemns deliberate acts of violence. The other set, often called the unwritten law, calls for forceful vengeance in the defense of home and honor. The conflict between these two sets of norms may be resolved by a third set, the norms or rules of anger, which stipulate the circumstances and manner in which vengeance can be exacted without violating the prohibition against deliberately harming another. In crimes of passion, the rules of anger are exceeded —otherwise, there would be no crime. If they are not exceeded too egregiously, however, a plea of passion may be allowed, and responsibility for the crime mitigated accordingly. An examination of crimes of passion can therefore tell us much about the norms and social functions of anger.

The Relationship Between Social Custom and the Law of Homicide

The present analysis assumes that there is a close relationship between legal practices and broader social customs, so that the former may be used as a kind of magnifying glass to study the latter. How valid is this assumption? At the risk of caricature, two opposing points of view may be distinguished on this issue. The first, or "consensus," view maintains that the law is a codification of shared beliefs and values; the second, or "conflict," view maintains that the law represents an imposition of the standards of one group (e.g., the dominant socioeconomic class) on other groups within society. In contemporary American society, the consensus view would seem to be more valid, at least as far as the law of homicide is concerned. For example, Rossi, Waite, Bose, and Berk (1974) conducted a survey of the perceived seriousness of 140 possible criminal offenses, including 19 different types of homicide (e.g., planned killing of a person for a fee, impulsive killing of an acquaintance, killing of a pedestrian while exceeding the speed limit). Participants in the survey were selected on the basis of a household sample of people living in Baltimore, Maryland. There were few differences in the perceived seriousness of the various offenses due to such factors as educational level, ethnic background, or race; therefore, the results of the survey can be considered fairly representative of the public's perception of the seriousness of possible offenses. Our concern here is with the rankings of the 19 types of homicide.

The five types of homicide judged most serious would all be classified as first-degree murder, because they involved malice aforethought (i.e., were planned) or, in one case, the killing of an officer in the performance of his duties (even though the killing was described as impulsive). The next most serious homicides (ranked 6 through 11) would be classified as either second-degree murder or voluntary manslaughter, depending on the nature of the provocation (e.g., killing someone after an argument over a business transaction, impulsive killing of a spouse). An interesting exception was the seventh-ranked homicide, which involved assassination of a public official. Legally, this would be classified as first-degree murder unless there were serious mitigating circumstances, such as insanity. In the public's eye, however, an assassination is evidently not much different than the killing of an ordinary citizen following a serious argument. Most of the remaining types of homicide studied by Rossi et al. (i.e., those which were ranked 12 through 19) would be classified as either voluntary or involuntary manslaughter, or even as justified. These included, for example, killing someone in a barroom free-for-all, causing the death of an employee by neglecting to repair machinery, and killing a suspected burglar in the home.

Other data also suggest that in the case of crimes against persons, contemporary legal practices in American tend to reflect broad social consensus (Schwartz, 1978; Thomas, Cage, & Foster, 1976).[2] Throughout much of Western history, that has not been the case. Therefore, in order to place present practices in perspective, let us review briefly the historical development of the law of homicide.

Greek and Roman law placed considerable emphasis on the mental element in crime, recognizing a distinction similar to that between murder and manslaughter.[3]

---

[2] This is not to imply that there is little room for controversy or conflict, especially with regard to the application of the law in particular cases, the nature of the sentences imposed (especially the death sentence), and the effectiveness of the penal system.
[3] MacDowell (1978) provides a helpful review of Greek law, especially in classical Athens. Because of its subsequent influence on Western legal traditions, there are

However, with the breakup and ultimate collapse of the Roman empire in the West, after repeated onslaughts by various Germanic tribes (e.g., the Lombards, Goths, Franks, Vandals, Jutes, Angles, and Saxons), legal practices during the Middle Ages came to be based largely on Germanic folk customs. One of the most important of these customs was the blood feud. As in preclassical Greece and in Rome before the Republic, it was up to family and kin to suppress indiscriminate violence through the threat of retaliation. Bloch (1961) has described the situation in the following way:

> The Middle Ages, from beginning to end, and particularly the feudal era, lived under the sign of private vengeance. The onus, of course, lay above all on the wronged individual; vengeance was imposed on him as the most sacred of duties—to be pursued even beyond the grave. . . . The solitary individual, however, could do but little. Moreover, it was most commonly a death that had to be avenged. In this case the family group went into action and the *faide* (feud) came into being, to use the old Germanic word which spread little by little through the whole of Europe. (pp. 125-126)

Official codes of law were promulgated from time to time during the first half of the Middle Ages (i.e., from the 6th to the 10th centuries), but the bulk of the law existed in oral tradition. Our knowledge of German folk law is therefore inexact. In the case of homicide, it appears to have involved standards of strict liability. Premeditated homicide and killing in a chance affray were both subject to capital punishment, although the method of execution may have been more humane in the latter than the former case (e.g., by the sword rather than being broken on the wheel).

There are a number of reasons why Germanic folk law involved such strict standards. In the first place, one purpose of the law as it became codified was to suppress the blood feud. This it did, in part, by taking over the function of the feud, thus making private vengeance unnecessary (and, indeed, itself punishable by law). When the primary purpose of the law is to deter crime and to achieve retribution, rather than to reform the criminal, standards of strict liability tend to be applied. In the second place, during the Middle Ages the law had to be simple. Few people even among the aristocracy could read or write; books were rare and had to be produced laboriously by hand; and society was fragmented and in constant flux. Under such conditions statutes would naturally be reduced to their simplest and most easily comprehended form.

This does not mean that the mental element in crime was completely ignored in medieval law. Even in the case of the blood feud vengeance was supposedly permissible only when the homicide was intentional. In the case of unintentional homicide the family of the victim was supposed to be satisfied with monetary or other such compensation. However, blood feuds were not known for their respect of nuances; for example, vengeance could be wreaked on an "innocent" relative of a killer, as well as on the killer himself.

---

many excellent histories of Roman law, for example, Buckland (1966), Kunkel (1966), and von Bar (1916/1968).

During the 12th century, two factors were at work that markedly influenced Western legal traditions. First, Roman law became the subject of active scholarship in the universities; and second, canon or church law was systematized into a coherent body of doctrine. The influence of both Roman and canon law was to place an emphasis on the mental element in crime and on the moral guilt of the individual in determining culpability.

These influences had a more immediate and direct effect on continental European law than on English common law, which tended to maintain its standards of strict liability until about the 15th century. However, a distinction must be made between the letter of the law and its application. When a law tends toward stricter liability than custom permits, the law may be ignored or only selectively enforced. A study by Given (1977) on homicide in 13th-century England illustrates this point well.

By the 13th century English kings had managed to establish a virtual monopoly on the right to judge crimes that involved capital punishment. The blood feud was thus largely supplanted. Every few years the king's justices visited a county and, among other duties, inquired into all homicides committed since the last visitation or "eyre." Given (1977) analyzed 20 eyre rolls from seven English counties and cities and from various times during the 13th century. This sample of eyre rolls provided information on 2,434 homicide victims and 3,492 accused killers. Based on Given's estimate of the population at that time, this amounts to an annual median homicide rate of about 15 killings for every 100,000 inhabitants. The corresponding rate for the United States today is about 10 nonnegligent homicides per 100,000 population (*FBI Uniform Crime Reports*, 1980), and for contemporary England it is less than one per 100,000 (Gibson, 1975).

As already noted, the only penalty for a convicted killer in the 13th century was death. (An exception was made for clerics, who were turned over to church courts for trial and punishment.) However, only about half of the accused killers mentioned in the eyre rolls were ever brought to trial; and of those who were tried, about three-quarters were acquitted. Moreover, a substantial minority (19%) of those convicted were subsequently pardoned. Of almost 3,500 persons accused of homicide, only about 7% were executed as the law stipulated.

The fact that about half of the accused killers were never apprehended or brought to trial deserves brief comment. In some cases (accounting for about 10% of the total number of homicides), the murderers were brigands who had killed during the course of a robbery. However, it was common for an accused person to flee regardless of the circumstances surrounding the homicide, and such flight was generally aided by sympathetic family and friends. As Given (1977) observes: "In a society where the formal institutionalized means of settling conflicts were not numerous, a man who had made himself odious to his neighbors may not have aroused much concern when he was slain by a group of those same neighbors" (p. 104). Certainly, little effort was made to bring many an accused killer to trial, or to convict if a trial was held.

Perhaps more persons would have been brought to trial and convicted if the law had distinguished different categories or kinds of homicide and had allowed a more flexible range of punishment. But that did not occur in England until the early part of the 16th century, when English common law was brought more into line with social custom. Felonious homicide (i.e., that not due to self-defense or accident) was then divided into two main categories—that with and that without malice afore-thought. The first was designated as murder and was punishable by death. The second, which came to be known as manslaughter, was punishable by a year's imprisonment and branding on the brawn of the thumb. Much of the subsequent history of the Anglo-American law of homicide has to do with the establishment of criteria for distinguishing between murder and manslaughter, and with the creation of subdivisions within each category. (For reviews of this history, see Kaye, 1967, and Sayre, 1932.)

The great 17th-century jurist Coke defined murder as "when a man . . . unlaw-fully killeth . . . any reasonable creature . . . with malice forethought, either expressed by the party or implied by law." Manslaughter was described by Coke as being done "upon a sudden falling out. . . . There is no difference between Murder and Man-slaughter, but that the one is upon malice forethought, & the other upon sudden occasion" (quoted by Kaye, 1967, p. 365). As Coke emphasized, the notion of "malice forethought" was to be interpreted not only in its ordinary psychological sense, but also as "implied by law." Regardless of the forethought involved, it was murder to kill someone without provocation, to kill an officer in the performance of his duties, or to kill while engaged in an unlawful activity (e.g., robbery). Thus, the phrase *malice forethought* did not refer simply to premeditation, although that was its primary meaning.

In contemporary English law the definition of murder offered by Coke is still accepted (Gibson, 1975). In many jurisdictions in the United States murder of a "second degree" is also recognized, which takes into account the fact that not even all murders are equally villainous.

With regard to manslaughter, the main difficulty facing lawmakers after Coke has been the development of a means for testing the genuineness of a person's anger or "sudden falling out," and to distinguish this kind of homicide from that due to accident or negligence (which, also being without malice aforethought, is not included in the definition of murder).

Until recently, English common law recognized only four kinds of provocation as "adequate" for mitigating a charge of murder to voluntary manslaughter, namely, catching one's wife in the act of adultery, being violently assaulted by another per-son, being caught in a sudden but mutual quarrel, and being arrested unlawfully. Insulting words or gestures, no matter how humiliating, traditionally have not been considered adequate provocation, nor has trespass against one's land or goods.

The above categories of provocation, sometimes referred to as the 19th-century four, were generally incorporated into American common law, albeit with consider-able variation from state to state. Prior to 1936 in Texas, for instance, being informed that someone had insulted a female relative was sufficient to mitigate a homicide from murder to voluntary manslaughter. However, the same statute stipu-lated that words alone or gestures directed against the individual himself were not a sufficient provocation. After 1936 a new statute was adopted which did not men-tion the "words alone" doctrine, and the following year a Texas court ruled that insulting words and gestures might therefore constitute adequate provocation.

Texas is not alone in loosening up the requirements with regard to adequate provocation. The English Homicide Act of 1957 allows the jury to decide the circumstances in which a "reasonable man"[4] might become impassioned, and members of the jury may take into account everything that was both said and done. In the United States, the Model Penal Code (1962/1974) embodies language that also grants the "reasonable man" considerable leeway in how he appraises events. Specifically, it states that criminal homicide constitutes manslaughter when

> a homicide which would otherwise be murder is committed under the influence of extreme mental or emotional disturbance for which there is reasonableness or excuse. The reasonableness of such explanation or excuse shall be determined from the viewpoint of a person in the actor's situation under the circumstances as he believes them to be. (Article 210.3)

The old statutes, by specifying in advance what constitutes adequate provocation, tended to limit the kind of evidence that could be presented to the jury. However, these restrictions were often circumvented in one way or another. The newer statutes simply recognize what has often been the case, namely, that an adequate provocation is what the members of the community—represented by the jury—consider it to be.

The Incidence of Homicide

Before turning to a more detailed analysis of crimes of passion, let us consider briefly the incidence of the various kinds of criminal homicide. Surprisingly, statistics on the final disposition of homicide cases are not readily available. In part, this is because the legal classification of a homicide can be very misleading, thus rendering summary statistics rather meaningless. We have already noted, for example, that first-degree murder may include a variety of homicides other than those committed with malice aforethought. The other categories of homicide also represent rather heterogeneous groupings, particularly in jurisdictions where plea bargaining is common. With this caveat in mind, we will review briefly several representative studies.

Wolfgang (1958) examined all cases of potentially criminal homicides recorded in the city of Philadelphia during the 5-year period from 1948 to 1952. There were 588 such cases, approximately 90% of which resulted in the arrest of one or more suspects. The disposition of these suspects is presented in Table 5-1. To summarize briefly, of the 607 suspects arrested, approximately 64% (387) were convicted and sentenced by a court of record. About 24% were acquitted, that is, no charges were brought, the charges were dropped, or the suspect was found not guilty in a court trial. (Acquittal does not mean that the person arrested was not the killer. In most cases, it means that the homicide was considered justified for one reason or another, or that the evidence was insufficient to prosecute.) In addition to convictions and

---

[4] The concept of a "reasonable man" has a specific meaning within the context of the law, as will be explained shortly.

acquittals, 13% of the cases were disposed of in some other fashion (e.g., the suspect died or committed suicide before trial, or was declared insane).

Perhaps the most important thing to note about the data in Table 5-1 is that more suspects were convicted of voluntary manslaughter than of any other offense. Specifically, 23% of all those originally arrested were finally convicted of voluntary manslaughter; and if we consider only the 387 suspects who were tried and convicted of some crime, 36% were convicted of voluntary manslaughter.

A more recent study of homicide in Philadelphia has been published by Zimring, Eigen, and O'Malley (1976). These investigators examined the disposition of the first 204 homicides reported to the police in 1970 (which encompassed a 5-month period from January 1 through May 25). Arrests were made in 82% of the incidents. Of the 245 persons arrested, 170 were adults who pleaded guilty or who were convicted in a court trial. Zimring et al. break these 170 convicted adults into two subgroups. The first subgroup, consisting of 38 persons, committed homicide during the course of another felony (e.g., robbery or rape). The majority of these (87%) were convicted of either first- or second-degree murder. The 132 persons in the other subgroup were charged only with homicide. Of these, 3% were convicted of first-degree murder, 39% of second-degree murder, 45% of voluntary manslaughter, and 13% of some lesser offense.

In other words, the picture has not changed much in Philadelphia since Wolfgang (1958) did his original study—voluntary manslaughter is still the most common form of homicide. Moreover, according to the data collected by Zimring et al. (1976), the median sentence for voluntary manslaughter was less than 2 years in prison.

Turning now to a different jurisdiction, we consider the findings of Lundsgaarde (1977), who reviewed 268 cases of potentially criminal homicides that were committed in the city of Houston during the year 1969. Approximately 90% of these

Table 5-1. Disposition of 607 Suspects Arrested for Homicides Committed in Philadelphia during the Years 1948 to 1952

Disposition	Number of suspects	Percentage of total
Acquitted (no charges brought, charges dismissed, found not guilty in trial)	143	24
Convicted of		
First-degree murder	77	13
Second-degree murder	113	19
Voluntary manslaughter	138	23
Involuntary manslaughter	59	10
(Subtotal 387/63.7%)		
Other disposition (insanity, suspect died before trial, etc.)	77	13

Note. Based on data collected by Wolfgang (1958).

cases resulted in arrest, with the apprehension of 239 suspects. The disposition of those arrested is presented in Table 5-2.

Of the 239 suspects apprehended, 44% were acquitted (i.e., no charges were brought, the charges were subsequently dismissed, or the suspect was found not guilty by a jury). This is a much higher rate of acquittal than that reported by Wolfgang (1958) and Zimring et al. (1976) for Philadelphia. In commenting on the high acquittal rate in Houston, Lundsgaarde observes that the Texas penal code still embodies some of the norms of the Old West. For example, unlike in many other states, a Texan who is attacked need not retreat in order to avoid killing his assailant. Norms such as this help account for many acquittals.

In addition to those acquitted, 43% of the Houston suspects were convicted of some crime, while 13% of the cases were disposed of in some other fashion. The Texas statutes that applied to homicide in 1969 had eliminated the traditional distinctions between various degrees of murder and between murder and manslaughter. They retained, however, the distinction between malice aforethought and without malice as part of the instructions to the jury. If the jury concluded that a guilty defendant acted without malice aforethought, the punishment could not exceed 5 years imprisonment. As can be seen from Table 5-2, many of those convicted received probation or relatively light sentences. Indeed, of all persons arrested for homicide, only 25% were eventually sentenced to more than 5 years in prison. When those who were acquitted are combined with those on probation, the majority of suspects served no time at all. A light sentence, probation, or acquittal was especially likely if the killing occurred during the course of an argument between peers (e.g., marriage partners, lovers, friends, or acquaintances).

Table 5-2. Disposition of 239 Suspects Arrested for Homicides Committed in Houston During 1969

Disposition	Number of suspects	Percentage of total
Acquitted (no charges brought, charges dismissed, found not guilty in trial)	106	44
Convicted and sentenced to		
More than 15 years in prison or death	26	11
6-15 years in prison	20	8
3-5 years in prison	24	10
2 years or less in prison	9	4
Probation	23	10
(Subtotal 102/43%)		
Other disposition (insanity, suspect died before trial, etc.)	31	13

Note. Based on data collected by Lundsgaarde (1977).

To summarize briefly, the distribution of convicted offenders according to degree of homicide may vary considerably from one jurisdiction to another, and from one time to another, depending upon the overall crime rate, the availability of lethal weapons, local customs for settling disputes, the tendency of prosecutors to plea bargain, and so forth. Nevertheless, a general pattern is apparent. For the United States as a whole, about 70-80% of all homicides result in an arrest. One reason for this high clearance rate is that the most common occasion for homicide is an argument between relatives, friends, lovers, or acquaintances. Nearly 50% of all homicides are of this nature, whereas less than 25% are committed during the course of another felony, such as robbery (*FBI Uniform Crime Reports*, 1980). In many of the cases, then, the identity of the killer is easily ascertained.

For the person charged with homicide, the most likely disposition will be either acquittal or a conviction of voluntary manslaughter. Although a wide variety of different crimes can be included under the rubric of voluntary manslaughter, the crime of passion is the paradigm case.

The Attribution of Anger in Courts of Law

As already described, the legal concept of passion refers primarily to the emotion of anger. It is therefore obvious that the attribution of anger in a court of law is of considerable importance, both for the defendant and for society at large. Moreover, if we assume that the law of homicide, as it has evolved over the centuries, reflects broader social norms and customs, then the legal treatment of crimes of passion also bears upon the everyday conception of anger. For instance, can anger be conceptualized in strictly psychological terms? Or does the concept of anger have an irreducible social component, that is, a conception that extends beyond the mere presence (or absence) of certain subjective and behavioral features? And what is the relationship between the attribution of anger and the assignment of responsibility? These and related issues will be addressed in the remainder of the chapter.

In order for a homicide to be considered a crime of passion, and hence classified as voluntary manslaughter rather than murder, four requirements must be met: (a) The provocation must have been adequate; (b) the response must have been in the heat of passion; (c) insufficient time must have elapsed for the passions to have cooled; and (d) the provocation, the passion, and the killing must have been causally connected. We will consider each of these criteria in turn.[5]

The Adequacy of Provocation

The most important criterion for the attribution of anger in a court of law is adequacy of provocation, which traditionally is determined by the so-called reasonable-

---

[5] The four criteria for attributing passion to a defendant correspond in many respects to the four kinds of feeling rules discussed in Chapter 1. Thus, rules of appraisal relate to the adequacy of provocation; rules of behavior to the heat of passion; rules of prognostication to cooling time; and rules of attribution to causal connections.

man test. That is, would the provocation that led to the killing arouse passion in a reasonable man? This test is considered "objective" because it refers to a hypothetical norm and not the psychological state of the individual. If the defendant does not happen to be a reasonable man (e.g., because of insanity), then his defense must be based on some other grounds. But more of that shortly.

What kinds of provocation might provoke a reasonable man to commit homicide? We have already mentioned the traditional 19th-century four (catching one's wife in the act of adultery, being violently assaulted, etc.), and how these are considered too restrictive by contemporary standards. Most penal codes now leave it up to the court and the jury to determine the adequacy of provocation, based upon their judgment of what a reasonable person might do in similar circumstances.

Of course, few people are ever provoked to homicide. Some persons may not even become angry at situations that are considered highly provocative by the "reasonable" man. Conversely, other persons may become unreasonably angry—even to the point of homicide—at relatively minor provocations. For analytical purposes, therefore, it is useful to distinguish between a socially adequate and a psychologically effective provocation. The former is dependent upon social norms and customs as interpreted (in court proceedings) by the jury; the latter is dependent upon the individual's own appraisal of the situation, and is a function of his or her particular psychological makeup.

The reasonable-man test used in courts of law is a way of determining the social adequacy of a provocation. Because of this, court proceedings might seem irrelevant to a psychological analysis. But such a conclusion would be misguided. For the well-socialized individual there is a close correspondence between socially adequate and psychologically effective provocations to anger. And when such a correspondence is lacking—for example, when a person responds "angrily" in the absence of an adequate provocation—the claim of anger may be disallowed or else punished as unjustified. Thus, the person who commits homicide in the absence of an adequate provocation might be charged with second-degree murder rather than voluntary manslaughter, no matter how "impassioned" he was at the time of the killing. The inference is that something else (other than normal anger) must have been involved. A similar inference is typically made in everyday affairs. For example, when a person becomes angry for little or no reason, a common reaction might be, "What is he trying to achieve?" or "He must be crazy."

The Heat of Passion

The attribution of anger in courts of law—as in everyday affairs—depends on the nature of the response as well as the adequacy of the provocation. In the picturesque language of the law, the homicide must have been committed "in the heat of passion" and not in "cold blood."[6] In applying this criterion, the jury is supposed to

---

[6] Recall Aristotle's definition of anger (for the physicist) "as a boiling of the blood or warm substance surrounding the heart."

take into account the actual state of the defendant at the time of the killing, and not the behavior of some hypothetical reasonable man.

But by what evidence does a jury decide whether or not an act was committed in the heat of passion? If the person was highly agitated at the time of the killing, that would be *prima facie* evidence. But a great deal of agitation or physiological arousal is neither sufficient nor necessary for the attribution of anger in a court of law. It is not sufficient because, as was noted above, a claim of anger may be disallowed if the response is *too* vehement, that is, disproportional to the provocation. Conversely, in the proper circumstances even an apparently measured response may be regarded as heated. For example, in the case of *People* v. *Lewis* (1953), the New York appellate court ruled that

> the words "in the heat of passion" do not necessarily require the manifes-
> tation of violent rage. It is principally a state of mind in which there is an
> absence of design to cause death and an absence of a deliberate implemen-
> tation of such a design. (p. 84)

The key elements in this definition are the "absence of design," which implies irrationality, and the "absence of a deliberate implementation," which implies impulsivity. Seneca would feel quite comfortable with such a cognitively oriented definition of the heat of passion. But as we saw in Chapter 4, a strictly cognitive orientation also has its limitations.

In the final analysis, the judgment that a person responded in the heat of passion is based on social norms regarding the appropriateness (or at least the excusability) of the response. An interesting example of this fact (albeit one which has nothing to do with contemporary legal practices) has been offered by Bohannan (1960). He describes the case of a Spanish nobleman who was hanged because he castrated his wife's lover instead of slaying him in the conventional manner. Some ways of responding are not appropriate, regardless of the provocation.

It might be thought that psychologists and psychiatrists would be especially com-petent to testify about the emotional state of a defendant at the time of the homi-cide. In general, the courts have not seen it that way. Psychological testimony, in particular, has been rather restricted (being limited, until recently, mostly to the presentation of diagnostic test data). Psychiatrists have been given greater leeway to testify, but only if the plea is insanity and not voluntary manslaughter. Legal atti-tudes in this regard appear to be changing, however. For example, the Pennsylvania supreme court has ruled in the case of *Commonwealth* v. *McCusker* (1972) that the traditional restrictions on psychiatric testimony are no longer valid. The case involved one James McCusker, who slew his wife. Within the month prior to the slaying McCusker became aware that his wife was having an affair with his step-brother; within minutes of the slaying, he learned that his wife was perhaps pregnant with his stepbrother's child; and immediately before she was killed, the wife threatened to leave McCusker and take with her their only child. McCusker was convicted of second-degree murder. The appellate court overturned this verdict because the trial court had not allowed the introduction of psychiatric evidence regarding the mental condition of McCusker at the time of the slaying. The court ruled that once adequate provocation and insufficient cooling time had been shown, psychiatric evidence is admissible on the question whether the defendant actually acted in the heat of passion.

In writing the majority opinion in this case, Justice Roberts took note "of the tremendous advancement made in the field of psychiatry during the last several decades." In a dissenting opinion, Justice Eagen expressed the fear that "from now on in Pennsylvania every pet theory advanced by a psychiatrist will have probative value in determining criminal responsibility." Justice Eagen would prefer to rely on the practical wisdom of the jury in determining whether or not a homicide was committed in the heat of passion. And, professional chauvinism aside, it must be admitted that his concerns are not entirely without foundation. There is little agreement among psychiatrists and psychologists regarding the nature of emotion in general or of anger in particular. Under such conditions, psychological testimony is bound to reflect personal and theoretical biases. But there is perhaps an even more fundamental issue here. If emotions are primarily social constructions, as has been argued in previous chapters, then they can only be judged by reference to social norms and standards. In this respect, a jury of the defendant's peers may be more "expert" than most psychologists and psychiatrists.

Insufficient Cooling Time

This brings us to the third requirement for a homicide to be classified as a crime of passion—insufficient cooling time. Like the adequacy of provocation, this criterion is judged by the reasonable-man test. Not surprisingly, the more extreme the provocation, the longer the delay that is considered reasonable. However, time alone is not the critical factor. Rather, what the person does during the period between the provocation and the slaying is crucial. If he engages in deliberate, well-planned acts (especially if they are not related to the provocation, such as making a business call), then these acts may be taken as a sign that the passion has cooled, no matter how short the time (Perkins, 1946). On the other hand, notions such as suppressed anger may be used to bridge the gap between provocation and act, even over extended periods of time (*Drye* v. *State*, 1944). Essentially, insufficient cooling time is a matter for the jury to decide, and their decision is based as much on a moral evaluation of what the reasonable man would or should do as on what the defendant actually did do.

Causal Connections

The final requirement for a crime of passion is that there be a causal connection between the provocation, the passion, and the crime. For example, there can be no mitigation if the intent to kill was formed before the provocation, or if the wrath is vented on some innocent bystander. This criterion appears simple enough; but the appearance is deceptive. For one thing, the notion of "cause" as it is used in this context is very ambiguous. In what sense can a passion, such as anger, cause an event, such as homicide? This is a question about which we shall have more to say in the next section. For another thing, most homicides involve relatives, friends, or acquaintances, and often are preceded by a long history of antagonism. When does such a predisposition become a prior intention (perhaps unconscious), thus rendering the passion inauthentic? There simply is no diagnostic test by which such a question can be answered.

Summary and Implications

The above four criteria for the attribution of anger in courts of law have evolved over many centuries of litigation. In a sense, they represent a theory of anger. Perhaps the first thing to note about this theory is the emphasis it places on the nature of the provocation. The more adequate the provocation, the more varied the response may be and still count as anger; also, the greater the provocation, the longer the anger may endure (even if unexpressed); and finally, when the provocation is regarded as adequate, the appropriate "causal" linkages are also likely to be inferred. Conversely, if the provocation is considered inadequate, then a response—not matter how heated and immediate—may not be regarded as a legitimate passion. This fact reflects the practical wisdom that what appears to be a passion on one level of analysis (e.g., the overt behavior and subjective experience of the individual) may actually be a deliberate and purposeful act on another level of analysis. As contradictory as it may seem, people are supposed to control and express their passions appropriately; and when they do not, they cannot use as an excuse the fact that they were overcome by emotion.

A second point to note about the legal theory of anger is that two of the four criteria used to identify a passion (adequacy of provocation and insufficient cooling time) do not refer to the psychological state of the individual defendant at the time of the killing; they refer, rather to what a supposedly reasonable person would do in similar circumstances. In other words, from a legal point of view, anger is more a matter of social norms and customs than of individual psychology. In fact, only one of the four criteria (in the heat of passion) specifically refers to the psychological state of the individual. And even there, social norms would seem to be a central factor in identifying the response as anger.

An emphasis on the normative as opposed to the psychological is due, in part, to the primary function of court proceedings—the attribution of responsibility. I would suggest, however, that in everyday affairs the situation is not too different. We often respond, and only when the nature or purpose of the response is called into question do we call it anger (or by whatever other label might be appropriate). Whether or not we *really* were angry at the moment of responding may be a moot point. The reason for attributing anger is not to identify a particular psychological or physiological state that might otherwise have gone unrecognized; rather, it is to place the response in question within an appropriate context—like framing a picture.

At this point, the foregoing remarks may seem rather cryptic. But before attempting further clarification, it will be helpful to consider another aspect of the law of homicide, namely, the insanity defense. Many of the same considerations apply to both the plea of passion and the plea of temporary insanity. In the latter case, however, the defense is not so encrusted by legal tradition nor by the prejudices of the "reasonable" man. In some respects, therefore, the insanity defense can provide clearer insight into the social and psychological dynamics involved in the attribution of responsibility for acts of homicide.

Temporary Insanity

Insanity may be chronic (as in schizophrenia), or it may be temporary (e.g., a transient breakdown occasioned by extreme stress). Essentially the same legal considerations apply in either case, although the consequences for the defendant are obviously quite different—confinement to a mental institution versus freedom. Insanity is a complete defense, exonerating the defendant of all criminal liability. If it is determined, therefore, that the defendant was insane only at the time of the killing, and that he has since recovered, his release may be immediate. On what grounds can a person plead temporary insanity? And in what sense can temporary insanity be said to cause a person to kill? In considering questions such as these, we will proceed in much the same way as we did in the case of crimes of passion. That is, we will first review the history of the insanity defense. Some data on the incidence of temporary insanity will then be presented. Finally, we will examine the grounds for attributing temporary insanity to a defendant.

Historical Background

Historically, the notion of temporary insanity has been closely allied with the concept of emotion. "Pathology" and "passion" stem from the same root (*pathos*); and the emotions have often been regarded as diseases of the mind. This is particularly true of anger. Thus, according to Seneca (A.D. 40-50/1963), "certain wise men have claimed that anger [*iram*] is temporary madness [*insaniam*]" (p. 107). This same theme is embedded in our ordinary language, where the term *mad* may refer to anger or to insanity. And in the often archaic language of the law, anger is defined as a "short madness [which] when provoked by a reasonable cause excuses from the punishment of murder" (*Words and Phrases,* 1953, p. 658).

In view of the above considerations, it is not surprising that the history of the insanity defense parallels closely the history of the plea of passion. Insanity, at least in its more subtle and temporary forms, has been recognized as a separate defense largely as a result of advances in psychiatry and medicine.

Until recently, the determination of insanity in Anglo-American common law was based on the M'Naghten Rules. Daniel M'Naghten was a paranoid woodturner from Glasgow who, in 1843, shot and killed the private secretary to the Prime Minister of England. At his trial, the medical testimony was unanimous that M'Naghten was insane, and he was acquitted by the jury on that account. The country was outraged. The House of Lords thereupon convened 15 judges of the Queen's bench for the purpose of clarifying the legal criteria for insanity. Five questions were put to the judges, and their answers constitute the M'Naghten Rules.[7] In part, the Rules state that a person is not criminally liable if, at the time of committing the act,

> the accused was laboring under such a defect of reason, from disease of the
> mind, as not to know the nature and quality of the act he was doing; or, if

---

[7] For the complete text of the M'Naghten Rules, as well as a thorough analysis, see Gendin (1973).

he did know it, that he did not know he was doing what was wrong. (Gendin, 1973, p. 100)

Few legal opinions in the history of English and American jurisprudence have elicited as much controversy as the M'Naghten Rules. Almost from the start they were attacked as being too intellectualistic. Insanity, it was argued, is not so much a defect of the intellect (an inability to know right from wrong) as it is a defect of the emotions (an inability to control one's behavior). As a consequence, an "irresistible impulse" clause was often added to the rules, so that a person could be found insane if he was unable to distinguish right from wrong, or if, knowing the difference, he was nevertheless unable to contain his behavior.

But even with the addition of the irresistible impulse clause, the M'Naghten Rules have generally been considered too strict. Few persons are *so* mad or mentally defective that they cannot tell right from wrong, or cannot control their behavior to some extent. After all, mental hospitals have rules that patients are expected to understand and follow, and the patients are rewarded and punished (often subtly) to the extent that they conform to hospital regulations.

Particularly in the 1950s and 1960s new statutes were introduced with the intention of liberalizing the insanity defense and bringing it more in line with current psychiatric thought. Thus, almost all federal courts of appeal and many states have adopted some variation of the statute recommended by the American Law Institute's Model Penal Code (1962/1974), which states the following:

> 1. A person is not responsible for criminal conduct if at the time of such conduct as a result of mental disease or defect he lacks substantial capacity either to appreciate the criminality of his conduct or to conform his conduct to the requirements of the law.
> 2. The terms "mental disease or defect" do not include an abnormality manifested only by repeated criminal or otherwise anti-social conduct.

The difference between the statute recommended in the Model Penal Code and the M'Naghten Rules may seem rather subtle, especially when the latter were supplemented by an irresistible impulse clause. The law thrives on subtleties; juries, however, do not. Under the M'Naghten Rules, juries customarily relied on common sense and local custom as well as legal doctrine to guide them in determining who is insane. They will undoubtedly continue to do so under the newer statutes as well.

Incidence

Insane killings sometimes appear senseless, bizarre, and/or unusually gruesome. A verdict of "not guilty, by reason of insanity" is therefore liable to be met by a sense of outrage, as if justice has somehow been cheated. Outrage is especially great if the person is released and then commits another crime. Everyone can think of instances where this has happened, since such cases receive widespread publicity. And because the notorious can easily be mistaken for the norm, the belief is common that insanity is widely used by clever defense lawyers and their clients to subvert the law.

We have already noted how the M'Naghten Rules were originally formulated because of the outrage occasioned by M'Naghten's acquittal. And although the M'Naghten Rules have generally been viewed as rather strict by medical standards, the public has not always seen it that way. Over a century ago, Mark Twain (1875) wrote a satirical essay on the topic. After recounting a number of infamous cases in which the killer was acquitted on the grounds of insanity, he concluded that

> insanity certainly is on the increase in the world, and crime is dying out. There are no longer any murders—none worth mentioning, at any rate. Formerly, if you killed a man, it was possible that you were insane—but now, if you, having friends and money, kill a man, it is *evidence* that you are a lunatic. . . . Of late years, it does not seem possible for a man to so conduct himself, before killing another man, as not to be manifestly insane. If he talks about the stars, he is insane. If he appears nervous and uneasy an hour before the killing, he is insane. If he weeps over a great grief, his friends shake their heads, and fear that he is "not right". If, an hour after the murder, he seems ill at ease, preoccupied, and excited, he is unquestionably insane.
>
> Really, what we want now, is not laws against crime, but a law against *insanity*. There is where the true evil lies. (pp. 225-226)

In view of the controversy that has traditionally surrounded the insanity defense, a surprisingly small number of killers are actually declared insane. For example, of the 621 accused killers studied by Wolfgang (1958), only 17 (2.7%) were declared insane by the courts. After reviewing other representative studies, Wolfgang concluded that in the United States only about 2-4% of all homicide offenders are insane. Data reported by Nolan (1974) suggest an even smaller percentage. According to Nolan, defendants are reluctant to choose an insanity defense because it is so time consuming and costly, and commitment to a mental hospital may be no improvement over prison. Juries are also reluctant to acquit someone on the basis of insanity, for fear that he gains his freedom prematurely and repeat the crime. And finally, defense attorneys are reluctant to suggest the defense, since it involves an admission of the allegations made by the prosecutor.

For purposes of comparison, it might be noted that in Great Britain the percentage of killers who are determined to be suffering from some mental abnormality is considerably higher than in the United States. Thus, during the years 1967-1971 a total of 1,782 suspects were convicted of some form of homicide in England and Wales. Of this total, nearly 32% were classified as mentally ill or deficient (Gibson, 1975). This high percentage is partly the result of the more lenient classification of abnormality by English courts.[8] The major difference between the two countries is

---

[8] In Great Britain "abnormal" homicides are divided into a number of subcategories: the traditional insanity defense; "Section 2 manslaughter," in which there is a diminished responsibility due to arrested or retarded mental development (whether inherent or acquired); and infanticide, when committed by a mother "disturbed by reason of her not having fully recovered from the effect of lactation consequent upon the birth of the child" (Gibson, 1975). About 50% of all abnormal homicides are classified as Section 2 manslaughter.

due, however, to the overall difference in homicide rates—that in the United States being nearly 10 times higher than that in England. In terms of incidence per 100,000 population, the number of homicides attributable to mental abnormality is not much different in the two countries.

In most cases where a person is declared insane, the individual is suffering from a long-term disorder, such as schizophrenia, and there is relatively little disagreement over the diagnosis. Cases of temporary insanity, where the defendant was apparently normal up to the time of the slaying, and then recovered his sanity shortly thereafter, are particularly rare.

In view of the above considerations, why is the insanity defense perceived as frequent? And why does it elicit so much controversy? In part, the answer to this question has already been suggested; namely, some insane killings are particularly gruesome and senseless, and hence they receive wide notoriety. But that is not the entire story. In fact, as we shall see below, pleas of *temporary* insanity often involve cases for which there is widespread sympathy for the defendant and his actions. The main reason the insanity defense is so controversial is that it touches on issues of fundamental philosophical, scientific, and social concern: What is a mental disease? How can a disease cause a person to behave in ways that are illegal or immoral? If a mental disease can cause a person to behave in ways that are illegal, are there not other factors that might have similar effects? Indeed, is not all behavior ultimately determined by factors beyond a person's control? And if so, can anyone ever be held responsible for his or her behavior?

A consideration of these broader issues is obviously beyond the scope of the present chapter. However, a closer examination of the plea of temporary insanity will help clarify some of the points made earlier in connection with the crimes of passion.

Adjudication

As already noted, there are many similarities between the legal concepts of anger and temporary insanity; e.g., both refer to a "short madness" that (in the case of anger) mitigates responsibility or (in the case of insanity) completely absolves the individual of responsibility. But there are also important differences between these two legal categories. In theory, for example, a crime of passion is to be judged by the standards of the reasonable-man test, which does not take into account the idiosyncrasies of the individual defendant. In contrast, the plea of temporary insanity focuses explicitly on the mental state of the defendant and asks whether the homicide was the product not of adequate provocation, but of mental disease. In actual practice, however, the legal distinction between passion and temporary insanity is often vague and indistinct. Thus, the hypothetical reasonable man by whose standards the crime of passion is judged often becomes endowed with the characteristics of the specific defendant at trial, thus making this standard almost indistinguishable from the more subjective (individualized) standard used in the insanity defense (Goldstein, 1967). And conversely, since the legal concept of mental illness is intentionally vague, the court often looks to the nature of the provocation in order to determine whether the defendant should be considered insane at the time of the killing.

A frequently cited example of how a plea of temporary insanity may be used to excuse homicide is the case of *State* v. *Remus* (1928). The defendant, Remus, killed his wife during the course of divorce proceedings. No question of immediate provocation was involved, and hence it could not be claimed that this was a crime of passion. By setting up a defense of insanity, however, Remus was able to introduce evidence of his wife's infidelity and of a plan by her and another man to deprive him of his property. Expert witnesses for the prosecution unanimously declared Remus to be sane, but the jury found him not guilty by reason of insanity. In commenting on this case, Guttmacher and Weihofen (1952) have observed that

> cases such as this must be accepted as a normal concomitant of the jury system. Indeed, they can be said to be the justification of the jury system. No one would claim that a jury is more competent than the judge to pass upon the literal correctness or truth of the testimony presented; the only justification for getting a jury's reaction is that we want a community consensus. Taking the verdict of the jury allows the rule of law to be tempered by the public sense of justice in hard cases. This has in fact nothing to do with the defense of insanity as such. It is merely the case of a jury unwilling to apply the law as written, and using any excuse that happens to be at hand. (pp. 399-400)

Szasz (1968) has stated the matter even more dramatically. Referring to the novel *Anatomy of a Murder*, in which a husband is acquitted of the murder of his wife's lover on the grounds of temporary insanity, Szasz writes the following:

> While this sort of crime has, in my opinion, nothing to do with insanity, the jury's refusal to convict the defendant makes sense. Such a trial is a kind of modern morality play. Its message is to uphold the sanctity of marriage. The husband who kills his wife's lover is like the soldier who protects the fatherland from the enemy. If society wishes to promote this kind of morality, it will sanction this type of murder. The game is reasonable, although not necessarily one in which we might wish to participate (p. 139)

The simile of a soldier protecting his fatherland highlights the institutionalized nature of this kind of homicide. In the case of the soldier, however, there is no question of his breaking the law when he kills the enemy. In the case of the husband who kills his wife or her lover, the situation is quite different. He does need an excuse, one which will leave intact the general proscription against the deliberate and malicious killing of another (murder). Temporary insanity provides such an excuse. Szasz's allusion to a morality play is also insightful. It should not be taken to mean, however, that the person who pleads temporary insanity is only acting, nor that the jury which acquits on such grounds is engaging in a farce. The play—if one wishes to call it that—is also reality.

As we already have described, an insanity defense (whether under the M'Naghten or other competing rules) requires that the defendant be suffering from a disease or defect of the mind at the time of the killing. But what constitutes a disease of the mind, especially when no organic pathology can be demonstrated and the condition is only temporary? Consider for a moment the case of *State* v. *Guido* (1963). The defendant, Adele Guido, had been badly mistreated for a number of years by a violent and unfaithful husband. Although she seldom had been harmed physically, she feared for her life (according to her testimony). Following an argument in which her husband supposedly threatened to kill their child if she did not do as he wished, she decided to commit suicide, using her husband's pistol. At the last moment she changed her mind; but as she was putting the weapon away, she saw her husband asleep in a chair and fired the weapon at him until it was empty. She was convicted of second-degree murder and appealed.

The appellate court remanded the case for retrial. In part, the conviction was overturned because the testimony of defense psychiatrists was unfairly impugned by the prosecution, thus prejudicing the jury. After examining the defendant, the psychiatrists had declared her sane at the time of the killing. Later, however, they changed the diagnosis to temporary insanity even though no new data had been obtained. The prosecution contended that this was an instance of the psychiatrists changing their diagnosis to fit the needs of the defendant. The defense argued that the change had been made because the psychiatrists, in their original report, had misunderstood the concept of legal insanity, which they took to mean some form of psychosis. The psychiatrists had originally determined that Mrs. Guido was suffering from "a severe disorganizing degree of anxiety" at the time of the killing, but that she was not insane. After consultation with the defense attorneys, however, they concluded that the defendant "was unable to differentiate right from wrong and the nature and consequences of her act, by virtue of the ascendency of the unconscious drives which rendered her, in a legal sense, insane" (*State* v. *Guido*, 1963, p. 51).

Such a change in opinion, being based on a clearer conception of legal insanity, was legitimate in the opinion of the appellate court. The judges went on to add:

> The hard question under any concept of legal insanity is, What constitutes a "disease"? The frame of reference is criminal responsibility, and the issue is whether a given wrongdoer should be stamped a criminal because of his act. The postulate is that some wrongdoers are sick while others are bad, and that it is against good morals to stigmatize the sick. Who then are the sick whose illness shows they are free of moral blame? We cannot turn to the psychiatrist for a list of illnesses which have that quality because, for all his insight into the dynamices of behavior, he has not solved the riddle of blame. The question remains an ethical one, the answer to which lies beyond scientific truth. (p. 52)

The logic of this opinion is obscure but instructive. The argument begins with the premise that it would be "against good morals to stigmatize the sick" by holding them responsible for a wrongdoing caused by illness. It concludes, however, with the contention that the identification of those illnesses or conditions that relieve an individual of responsibility is an ethical question and hence "beyond scientific truth." This line of reasoning comes dangerously close to being circular. However, if one views temporary insanity (at least in some of its forms) as a socially constituted response dialectically related to the attribution of responsibility, then the opinion of the judges makes good sense.

From the above considerations, it is evident that temporary insanity does not cause a homicide in the same sense that a microbe, say, might cause a fever. But the law is not concerned with discovering causes in a scientific sense, except as the latter bear upon the assignment of responsibility. To say that a homicide was caused by temporary insanity is a way of saying that the defendant was not responsible for the act.

In contrast to crimes of passion, where rather clear criteria have evolved for the attribution of emotion (the adequacy of provocation, heat of passion, etc.), the criteria for identifying temporary insanity are vague and imprecise. This vagueness and imprecision often allows—even requires—that testifying psychiatrists and psychologists define temporary insanity by reference to social norms rather than medical guidelines. Yet the medical connotation of mental illness disguises what is occurring as scientific rather than social (cf. Hardisty, 1973; Morse, 1978). Recognition of this fact is one reason why some lawmakers, and even a few psychologists and psychiatrists (e.g., Szasz), question the appropriateness of the insanity defense in many of its applications.

It is important to recognize that some obfuscation is necessary if temporary insanity is to serve as a defense for homicide, relieving the individual of responsibility.[9] Nevertheless, there is a certain danger in this process. Given the appropriate social encouragement and rationale, a person may come to experience his own behavior as beyond control, and to act in a manner befitting the cultural stereotype of a temporarily insane person. It is not difficult to envision the institutionalization of some forms of temporary insanity in much the same manner as wild-man behavior has become institutionalized among the highlanders of New Guinea (see Chapter 3). In fact, I would suggest that something of this sort has occurred in the case of anger.

With some hyperbole, it may be said that anger is a socially constituted form of temporary insanity. Taken literally, this statement applies, at best, only to extreme instances of anger, such as those which result in crimes of passion. Nevertheless, many of the same considerations that apply to crimes of passion and to temporary insanity also apply to the everyday experience of anger.

Concluding Observations

In his study of homicides in Houston, the results of which were reviewed earlier in this chapter, Lundsgaarde (1977) notes that the pattern of killings indicates the involvement of two kinds of sanctions: "(1) the organized negative sanctions of criminal law and the public sentiment prohibiting the taking of human life; (2) the diffuse positive sanctions that approve of individual aggression and violence, includ-

---

[9] I do not wish to insinuate that temporary insanity is always used merely as an excuse for homicide. Under conditions of extreme stress, or as a result of a neurological disorder (e.g., brain tumor or lesion), a person may commit homicide while temporarily insane in a literal sense (psychologically speaking).

ing killing, given specific situations and acceptable motivational circumstances" (p. 17). These two kinds of sanctions correspond to the two conflicting sets of norms discussed in Chapter 4. Historical teachings on anger, it may be recalled, condemn deliberate acts of violence on the one hand, and yet call for retribution against perceived wrongs on the other hand.

To a large extent, the history of the law of homicide reflects an emphasis on the first of these two sets of norms (prohibiting aggression). This was particularly true during the Middle Ages, when the law was one of strict liability—in theory if not in practice. However, the contemporary law of homicide, particularly as it concerns crimes of passion and temporary insanity, can only be understood in light of the second set of norms (encouraging retribution). From the perspective of the latter, anger and the law can be viewed as complementary means of social control.

In this connection, it might be noted that the widespread use of police and other law enforcement agencies is of relatively recent origin, at least as far as the great masses of people are concerned. For most of Western history, it has been up to the individual to assure that justice is done in the conduct of daily affairs. Even today, only about half the criminal offenses which are committed are actually reported to the police by the victims. And it goes without saying that criminal offenses are numerically small in comparison to the vast number of irritations and provocations encountered in everyday interpersonal relations. Some informal means of social control, of which anger would seem to be an example, is still necessary and useful.

The above hypothesis regarding the complementary relationship between anger and the law is similar to one put forward by William McDougall (1936):

> Though with the progress of civilization the public administration of justice has encroached more and more on the sphere of operation of the anger of individuals as a power restraining offenses of all kinds, yet, in the matter of offenses against the person, individual anger remains as a latent threat whose influence is by no means negligible in the regulation of manners, as we see most clearly in those countries in which the practice of duelling is not yet obsolete. And in the nursery and the school righteous anger will always have a great and proper part to play in the training of the individual for his life in society. (pp. 251-252)

Of course, anger may violate as well as complement the law, as when it leads to homicide. But if the provocation is considered adequate, even the person who kills in anger may be treated with leniency.

By attributing his response to anger (or temporary insanity), an accused killer is in effect asking the jury to judge him not by the standards that prohibit the deliberate taking of life, but by the standards (sometimes called the "unwritten law") that encourage protection of home and honor. There is a problem, however. The proscription against homicide does not allow many exceptions. The killing itself must therefore be redefined: No longer is it the act of a normal human being; rather, it is the result of an irrational, animal-like impulse (anger) or the symptom of a disease (temporary insanity).

In sum, on the basis of both historical teachings and contemporary legal practices, anger may be conceptualized as the product of three sets of norms. Two of these sets do not refer specifically to anger; rather, they have to do with the general cultural proscription against deliberately harming another and the often contradictory demand for retribution against perceived wrongs. The conflict between these two sets of norms is resolved by a third set, which does refer specifically to anger. This set comprises the norms or rules of anger, about which we will have much more to say in subsequent chapters. These rules specify the conditions under and the manner in which anger may be experienced and expressed. If the rules of anger are met, the response may be interpreted as a passion rather than as an action. In this way, the demand for retribution can be fulfilled without violating the proscription against *deliberate* acts of violence. On the other hand, if the rules of anger are not met, then a claim of passion may be disallowed and the person held responsible for the consequences of his behavior.

It should go without saying that the above synopsis is overdrawn and incomplete. Historical teachings and legal practices tend to highlight the more dramatic and violent forms of anger. A more balanced picture will emerge as we review, in the next chapter, experimental research on nonnormative sources of anger and aggression, and in Part II of this volume, where we present detailed data on the everyday experience of anger.

Chapter 6

Nonnormative Sources of Anger and Aggression

In considering the legal treatment of crimes of passion we focused primarily on the criteria for attributing anger to a defendant and on the often complementary relationship between anger and the law. We should not lose sight of the fact, however, that crimes of passion are still crimes, and hence they cannot be completely explained in terms of social norms or rules. The same is true of the many "misdemeanors" of everyday life. On occasion, we all become angry when we shouldn't. Perhaps the car won't start, and we swear and kick the tire. Or perhaps the children are playing loudly, and we angrily snap at them. How can we account for such episodes? An appeal to social norms is of only limited help, for the behavior in question exceeds accepted standards. We must therefore look to nonnormative factors for an explanation. Similar considerations apply even when anger is legitimate. All behavior is overdetermined. The person who does not feel well, for example, may be more sensitive to provocation than the person who is in good health. Drugs such as alcohol may also lower the threshold for anger, as may a wide variety of environmental factors (e.g., noise, heat, and crowded conditions).

In the present chapter we will examine some of the environmental and psychological variables that help "cause" a person to become angry, but which do not count as socially acceptable reasons for anger. No attempt will be made to discuss or even mention all of the many and varied factors that can contribute to an angry outburst. Rather, we will focus on four main classes of variables that have served as important integrating constructs in prior theories of anger and aggression. These include (a) frustration, (b) physiological arousal, (c) aggressive stimuli, and (d) extrinsic motivation.

One further word by way of introduction. Most of the research that will be reviewed below involves the effects of variables such as frustration and arousal on *aggression*. In most of the studies described, subjects also have been *angered*, although anger per se typically has not been the major focus of interest. This creates a potential ambiguity. When a variable is found to increase aggression among subjects, can we say that the variable has influenced anger or only one of its modes of expression, aggression? We will discuss this issue in some detail at the end of the chapter, after we have reviewed the relevant research. For the moment, it is only necessary to point out this potential source of confusion. At times during the following discussion, a distinction will be made (or implied) between anger and aggression; more frequently, however, the concepts of anger and aggression will be used almost interchangeably, or the compound phrase "anger and aggression" will be used to indicate that either or both phenomena are under consideration. The context should make the meaning clear.

The Frustration-Aggression Hypothesis

Frustration has long been regarded as a major instigation to anger and aggression. For example, we saw in Chapter 4 how the medieval distinction between concupiscible and irascible emotions was based on the idea that the frustration of some desire (*concupiscus*) could lead to anger (*ira*) or to some other related response. Earlier in this century, Freud (1920) and McDougall (1923), among others, argued that anger and aggression are instinctive responses to frustrated impulses. In 1939 a group of social scientists—psychologists, sociologists, and anthropologists—published a small book in which they attempted to formulate in a rigorous and systematic fashion the relationship between frustration and aggression (Dollard, Doob, Miller, Mowrer, & Sears, 1939).

The basic postulate of Dollard et al. was that "the occurrence of aggressive behavior presupposes the existence of frustration and, contrariwise, that the existence of frustration always leads to some form of aggression" (p. 1). Frustration was defined as "an interference with the occurrence of an instigated goal-response at its proper time in the behavior sequence" (p. 7), and aggression was defined as any sequence of behavior the goal of which "is the injury of the person to whom it is directed" (p. 9). Following frustration, aggressive tendencies might be "temporarily compressed, delayed, disguised, displaced, or otherwise deflected from their immediate and logical goal," but "not destroyed" (p. 2). Much of Dollard et al. 's book was an amplification of this last assertion, that is, an attempt to specify the manner and conditions in which aggressive tendencies would be compressed, delayed, disguised, or displaced following frustration.

No psychologist today subscribes to the frustration-aggression hypothesis in its original form. Ample research has demonstrated that frustration is neither a necessary nor a sufficient condition for aggression. Nevertheless, many theorists still assume that frustration is a major, if not the major, source of aggression. The validity of this assumption will be examined below. But first we must consider how anger fits into the frustration-aggression hypothesis. In the original monograph by Dollard et al., *anger* is referenced in the index only once, and that reference is to a footnote that does not even mention anger specifically. In other words, as originally conceived by Dollard et al., anger is not a relevant consideration; frustration is what counts.

In a major reformulation of the frustration-aggression hypothesis, Berkowitz (1962) reintroduced the concept of anger, but in a way that stripped it of most of its meaning. According to Berkowitz, frustration leads to anger, which "serves as a drive heightening the likelihood of aggressive behavior" (p. 32). In other words, aggression is not the immediate consequence of frustration, anger is. "According to this conception, then, frustration creates a predisposition to make hostile responses by arousing anger" (p. 33).

There is no question that frustration often leads to anger, and that aggression is a common manifestation of anger. In fact, as will be reported in Chapter 8, frustration is one of the factors most frequently cited as being involved in the instigation to anger. However, this fact should not be overinterpreted. Anger ensues primarily when the frustration is occasioned by the actions of another person, actions which are appraised by the angry individual as unjustified or at least avoidable. Experimantal research has also demonstrated that it is primarily arbitrary (unwarranted) frustrations that arouse subjects to anger and/or aggression (e.g., Burnstein & Worchel, 1962; Cohen, 1955; Pastore, 1952; Zillmann & Cantor, 1976).

Based on the review of historical and legal teachings presented in Chapters 4 and 5, it is evident that unjustified and avoidable frustrations fall within the domain of socially sanctioned instigations to anger, especially if they interfere with highly prized goals. Our concern in the present chapter is, however, with nonnormative sources of anger and aggression. From the latter perspective, the question that must be asked is this: To what extent does frustration per se, that is, frustration that does not also involve the violation of socially approved standards of conduct, lead to anger and/or aggression?

A great deal of research has been conducted in an attempt to answer this question. Much of this research has used some variation of an experimental paradigm introduced by Buss (1961). It is often called the "teacher-learner" paradigm, although "evaluator-performer" might be a more descriptive phrase. Very briefly, a subject is placed in the role of an evaluator who delivers electric shocks or some other form of punishment to another person as a function of the latter's performance on some task. The number, intensity, and/or duration of the shocks ostensibly delivered to the performer are used to measure the subject's aggressive tendencies. In actuality, the performer is usually a confederate of the experimenter; his responses are preprogrammed and no shocks are received. But the subject does not know this.

A wide variety of experimental manipulations can be superimposed on the basic evaluator-performer paradigm. For example, the subject-evaluator may be frustrated while working on some prior task; his or her state of physiological arousal may be increased by means of films or physical exercise; the confederate-performer may act in a rude and insulting manner; and so forth. Different cover stories can also be used to mask the purpose of the experimental manipulations and to make the entire procedure seem plausible.

Using a variation of the evaluator-performer paradigm, Geen (1968) demonstrated that frustration per se (failure to solve a problem within a given time period) enhanced the punitiveness of a subject's subsequent evaluation of another's performance, even though the latter had nothing to do with the frustration (the problem was insoluble). It is noteworthy, however, that in this same experiment the most aggression occurred in a condition that involved no frustration (the problem was soluble), but that did involve an insult (subjects were accused of low intelligence and poor motivation by the person they were later to "evaluate").

Other studies (e.g., Buss, 1966; Taylor & Pisano, 1971, S. Worchel, 1974) have failed to observe an enhancement of aggression due to frustration per se. The results of several studies (Genty, 1970; Rule & Hewett, 1971) even suggest that frustration may sometimes inhibit subsequent aggression. Such inconsistent findings have led Baron (1977) to conclude that frustration "is not a very common or important [antecedent of anger or aggression] and is probably far less crucial in this respect than has widely—and persistently—been assumed" (p. 92). But Baron also adds a caveat. Most of the experimental research on this issue has involved relatively mild frustration. Baron makes the reasonable hypothesis that as the intensity of frustration increases, so too will the likelihood of anger and/or aggression.

An intense frustration may lead to anger and/or aggression for either or both of two reasons. First, by definition, an intense frustration involves the thwarting of some highly desired goal, one which the individual may be willing to "fight" to achieve. Second, when a goal is highly valued, its thwarting is more likely to be viewed as unreasonable or unjustified.

In summary, frustration is one factor that can contribute to the arousal of anger and/or aggression. Under ordinary conditions, it is not a particularly potent factor. This is because most everyday frustrations are mild and either legitimate or unavoidable (e.g., due to accident). However, even mild frustrations may sometimes combine with other more "adequate" provocations, thus increasing the likelihood of anger in response to the latter. This fact is worth emphasizing because frustrations are ubiquitous, and their effects may be cumulative. Moreover, should daily frustrations lose their cloak of legitimacy, what was formerly a minor contributing factor may be transformed into an adequate provocation in its own right. Since social living involves constant compromise, the potential for anger and aggression is always present. This was the theme adumbrated by Freud in *Civilization and Its Discontents*. It is a valid theme, but its theoretical significance should not be overdrawn or misconstrued, as was done in the case of the frustration-aggression hypothesis.

Physiological Arousal

As previously described, in Berkowitz's formulation of the frustration-aggression hypothesis frustration supposedly leads to a heightened state of physiological arousal ("drive") which, in the presence of appropriate environmental stimuli,[1] may lead to aggression. Berkowitz called this state of arousal "anger," and considered it to have aggression-eliciting properties; however, in later writings (e.g., 1972) he has made explicit the assumption that arousal from *any* source may enhance responsivity to aggressive cues. In the present section, we will review evidence relevant to this assumption. However, we do not wish to limit consideration to Berkowitz's formu-

---

[1] This proviso is very important, as will be discussed in the next section.

lation. We will therefore begin by describing several other theories that also emphasize physiollogical arousal as a major determinant of emotional behavior.

One of the most influential theories of emotion in recent decades has been that
proposed by Stanely Schachter (1964, 1971). According to Schachter, an emotion
is the joint product of two factors: physiological arousal and cognitive appraisals
(inferences) regarding the source of that arousal. More specifically, Schachter postulates that interoceptive feedback from physiological arousal provides nondiscrimina-
tive affective tone to experience, while the appraisal of situational cues determines
which, if any, emotion will be experienced. Thus, precisely the same state of physiological arousal might be experienced as anger, joy, sadness, or any of a variety of
other emotions, depending upon how the situation is appraised.

Zillmann (1978) has criticized Schachter's theory as being too cognitive. He
notes that a similar, but less cognitive, formulation has had a long history within
the behaviorist tradition. Hull (1952), for example, postulated a generalized drive
state that "energizes" whatever response happens to be prepotent at a given time.
Operationally, physiological arousal has often been taken as an indication of generalized drive. For the behaviorist, however, the response tendency is influenced
directly by the state of arousal, and not through the mediation of an inferential
step, as proposed by Schachter. Berkowitz's formulation of the frustration-aggression hypothesis, described earlier, falls within this behaviorist tradition.

In short, one of the most common assumptions in contemporary theories of
emotion is that physiological arousal from diverse sources may combine to enhance
whatever emotional experiences and responses might occur in a given situation. A
great deal of evidence supports this assumption (for reviews, see Dienstbier, 1979;
Schachter, 1971; Zillmann, 1979). Nevertheless, its theoretical significance should
not be overdrawn.

Consider an experiment by Zillmann (1971). Subjects were first provoked and
then shown one of three kinds of films designed to induce varying degrees of physiological arousal. The films depicted either travel scenes, a prizefight, or erotic (pre-
coital) behavior. Pretesting indicated that the travelogue was least arousing and the
erotic film the most arousing. After viewing the films, subjects had the opportunity
to retaliate against the person who had provoked them. (This experiment, like most
others discussed in this chapter, used a variation of the evaluator-performer paradigm described in the previous section). The results indicated that aggression
increased as a function of the arousing properties of the films; that is, subjects who
saw the travelogue aggressed least, and those who saw the erotica aggressed most.
The prizefight film had an intermediate effect.

Zillmann's study illustrates how physiological arousal, induced by an extraneous
source, can influence aggressive behavior. However, in order to keep these findings
in persepctive, three qualifications must be kept in mind.

1. In Zillmann's study, none of the films influenced the aggressive behavior of
   subjects who had not been provoked. In other words, it was only when subjects
   were set to aggress, because they were angry, that altering the levels of physiological arousal had any effect. This is a common finding. Konečni (1975) found,
   for example, that repeated exposure to aversive auditory stimulation designed to

increase the level of arousal had little effect on aggressive behavior unless the subjects had also been insulted and reported themselves to be angry. Konečni concludes that aggression is not enhanced by arousing conditions that are not also conducive to anger.

At first, it might seem that the above qualification is too obvious to even deserve comment. What is obvious, however, is often overlooked. We have seen a similar situation in the case of the frustration-aggression hypothesis. That is, frustration does not typically influence aggressive behavior unless the frustration is contingently related to some provocation, or else is provocative in its own right. Yet investigators have tended to ignore the nature of the provocation, focusing instead on frustration per se as the major source of anger and aggression. Similarly, there has been a tendency to place too much emphasis on physiological arousal as a cause of anger and aggression, while downplaying (or ignoring) the nature of the provocation.

2. States of heightened physiological arousal do not simply occur; they occur for some reason, and that reason typically has a greater influence on subsequent behavior than does the arousal itself. In the above study by Zillmann (1971), for example, physiological arousal was induced by films, one depicting a prize-fight and the other erotica. An experiment by Geen and Stonner (1974) also used a fight film to induce physiological arousal. Subjects were told that the fighting was motivated either by a desire for revenge, by professionalism, or by altruism. Subjects who had been told that the fight was motivated by revenge aggressed the most, provided they also had been provoked by the target of their aggression. In other words, the way subjects interpreted the arousing film was more important than the degree of arousal induced.

Similar findings have been observed in the case of erotica, the other kind of arousing stimulus used by Zillmann (1971). That is, studies have shown that erotic stimuli unrelated to the provocation may inhibit as well as enhance subsequent aggression (Baron, 1974; Baron & Bell, 1977; Donnerstein, 1980, Frodi, 1977). The explanation for these seemingly contradictory effects of erotica appears to lie in the nature of the stimuli used in different studies and in the subjects' attitudes toward those stimuli. Very briefly, mild erotica may distract a person's attention from the provocation, or encourage response tendencies incompatible with aggression. The modest amount of physiological arousal that is produced by mild erotica is not sufficient to counteract these aggression-reducing effects. More explicit erotica, on the other hand, not only increases physiological arousal, but is also somewhat distasteful to many subjects. Both the arousal and the aversiveness of the stimulus may serve to enhance aggression among subjects who have been provoked to anger (White, 1979). Finally, erotica that has aggressive as well as sexual connotations may have an especially marked effect; under some conditions—for example, where the victim is depicted as deriving some enjoyment from the assault—such erotica may lead nonangered as well as angered subjects to respond aggressively toward a female target (Donnerstein & Berkowitz, 1981).

Our concern here is not with the possible effects of viewing violence and pornography on aggression, although these are important topics in their own right. Our interest in the above studies is more prosaic. Stimuli that induce physiological arousal may have important effects on subsequent aggression, effects that are independent of—and typically stronger than—the effects of physiological arousal per se.

3. To complicate matters even further, it is not simply the nature of the arousing stimulus that is important, but also the perceived connection between the stimulus and the person's state of arousal. "Transfer of excitation" (to use Zillmann's phrase) occurs most readily when a person is unaware of the true source of his or her arousal and misattributes it instead to the provocation (in the case of anger). This is the kind of situation originally investigated by Schacter and his colleagues. In their classic experiment, Schachter and Singer (1962) injected subjects with epinephrine and either (a) misinformed them, (b) gave them no information about the arousing side effects of the drug, or (c) gave them correct information about the reactions (e.g., increased heart rate) they might experience. The former groups of subjects, who did not know the true source of their arousal, presumably interpreted their physiological symptoms as being due to situational factors, and became angry or mirthful, depending on the behavior of a stooge. Subjects who were informed of the true effects of the drug, and hence had an explanation for their arousal, were not so influenced by situational cues.

Other investigators have devised a variety of ingenious techniques to produce physiological arousal in such a way that subjects would be unaware of its true source. For example, Zillmann, Johnson, and Day (1974) took advantage of the fact that recovery from physical exercise proceeds more slowly on a physiological than on a psychological level. That is, a person may think that he has recovered from exercise while physiological activity remains above the resting levels. Zillmann et al. reasoned that such residual physiological arousal would be available for "transfer" to another situation. As a test of this hypothesis, subjects were either provoked or treated in a neutral fashion. After a 6-minute delay, they were given an opportunity to aggress against the person with whom they had interacted. The experimental manipulation was introduced during the delay period. Specifically, half of the subjects engaged in strenuous physical exercise at the beginning of the period; the other half at the end. In the former case, it was presumed that by the end of the delay period, the subjects would have recovered psychologically but not physiologically from the exercise, and hence would have a certain amount of unexplained arousal which might be misattributed to the original provocation. By contrast, subjects who exercised toward the end of the delay period would realize the source of their arousal, and hence would experience no transfer effect. The results were as predicted. Subjects who were provoked and exercised at the beginning of the period retaliated more than the subjects who were provoked and exercised at the end of the period. Exercise had no effect on the behavior of unprovoked subjects.

In most of the studies cited thus far, the arousing stimulus was introduced after the provocation but before the subjects had an opportunity to retaliate; or else the provocation and responses proceeded contemporaneously. In either case, extraneous physiological arousal might have exerted an influence by "energizing" the prepotent response to the provocation. Can arousal from an unrelated source also influence the appraisal of a provocative event (e.g., the input as well as the output side of the emotional sequence)? In an attempt to answer this question, Zillmann and Bryant (1974) manipulated subjects' level of physiological arousal before they experienced any provocation. Subjects engaged either in physical exercise, as in the study by Zillmann et al. (1974) described above, or in a nonstrenuous task (disk threading). Half of the subjects in each group were then provoked, but no retaliation was allowed until sufficient time had elapsed for physiological recovery to occur. When given the opportunity to retaliate, subjects who had been provoked while in an aroused state were more aggressive than those who were provoked in a nonaroused state. Zillmann and Bryant interpreted this result to mean that residues of excitation during provocation enhance the experience of anger; and when angry, a person commits himself to an aggressive course of action that may be executed at a later time. In a further test of this hypothesis, Bryant and Zillmann (1979) demonstrated that the commitment or predisposition to respond aggressively can be quite enduring. In this experiment, several weeks elapsed between the provocation and the opportunity to retaliate. In spite of this long delay, subjects who were more aroused (as a result of viewing a film) at the time of the provocation were more aggressive when unexpectedly given the opportunity to retaliate several weeks later.

Let us now summarize the results of the research reviewed in this section. In the absence of a provocation to anger, increased physiological arousal typically has little influence on aggressive behavior. If a person is provoked, however, then his or her reactions may be amplified by the transfer to physiological arousal from extraneous sources. Transfer of arousal occurs primarily when the person is unaware of the source of the extraneous arousal and misattributes it to the provocation. But even when the connection between the exciting stimulus and the resulting state of arousal is disguised, the nature of the stimulus may still influence the course of the angry episode. For example, if the exciting stimulus is itself irritating, if it causes the person to ruminate over perceived wrongs, or if it legitimizes retaliation, then anger and aggression may be enhanced. On the other hand, if the stimulus is pleasant, distracts from the provocation, or induces incompatible response tendencies, then anger and aggression may be reduced.

From the above considerations, it is not surprising that the transfer of arousal has proven to be a subtle phenomenon. Even under the best of conditions, its effects may be slight and easily disrupted. One illustration of this fact is the difficulty researchers have had in replicating Schachter and Singer's (1962) original study (Marshall & Zimbardo, 1979; Maslach, 1979). Of course, failure to replicate a specific study—even one so central—does not call into question the reality of the transfer-of-arousal phenomenon, the existence of which has been amply demonstrated. However, it does call into question the generality or importance of the phenomenon for a general theory of emotion.

Aggressive Stimuli

In the preceding section note was made of the importance of extraneous stimuli in determining whether or not an aggressive response would occur to provocation. In the present section we will pursue this issue further. Our concern, however, is not with just any type of extraneous stimulus. Rather, we will focus on the effects of stimuli that seem to "pull" for aggression because of their meaning or connotation (e.g., as opposed to any side effects they might have on physiological arousal). Such stimili can be divided into two broad categories: (a) target characteristics, and (b) situational cues. We will discuss each category separately, although many of the same considerations apply to each.

Target Characteristics

Aspects of a person's physiognomy, behavior, dress, and so forth may heighten the probability of an angry or aggressive response. One particularly tragic illustration of this fact can be seen in the pattern of child abuse. Parents who abuse their children often describe themselves as acting out of anger (Gil, 1973). However, the norms of anger (e.g., retribution against the willful wrongdoing of another) do not apply to the behavior of infants and very young children. Nonnormative factors must therefore be invoked to explain child abuse. Among the factors that place a child at risk are such personal characteristics as its sex (males are more likely to be abused than females), unattractiveness, prematurity, developmental delay or abnormality, and even the sound of its cry (for reviews, see Frodi & Lamb, 1980; Gil, 1973; Parke & Collmer, 1975).

   Some possible reasons why such such cues might elicit aggressive responses will be discussed shortly. But first let us consider several additional examples of how target characteristics facilitate angry and aggressive responses. Any good defense lawyer knows that the appearance of a defendant can influence a jury's verdict of guilt of innocence, although strictly speaking it should not. It would certainly be surprising if the everyday experience of anger, which also involves an attribution of blame for some presumed wrongdoing, were not even more influenced by irrelevant target characteristics. Of course, to the extnet that a particular characteristic places an individual in a socially recognized category (e.g., with regard to status, or as a member of a group subject to discrimination), then the facilitation of anger and/or aggression may be partly normative. In many instances, however, the influence of target characteristics is much more subtle, and the effects cannot be attributed social norms (or prejudices).

   Studies by Berkowitz and Geen (1966; Geen and Berkowitz, 1966) can be used to illustrate this last point. Subjects were provoked and then shown a film clip of a bloody prizefight in which the loser was portrayed by the well-known actor Kirk Douglas. After seeing the fight, subjects were given the opportunity to retaliate against the person who had provoked them. Retaliation was greater if the provocateur's name was ostensibly the same as the movie name of the character who lost the prizefight (Kelly) or of the actor who protrayed the character (Kirk). Retaliation was less if the provocateur was given the name of the winner of the fight or an irrelevant name.

A variety of explanations can be offered to account for the influence of target characteristics on aggressive behavior. In the above studies, for example, the character portrayed by Kirk Douglas was generally viewed as deserving to lose the fight. The names associated with the loser might therefore have served as a disinhibiting factor, for example, by implying that retaliation was justified. On the basis of other studies, some of which will be described below, Berkowitz (1974) prefers an explanation in terms of associative learning (classical conditioning). That is, if a name (or other extraneous stimulus) has previously been associated with aggression, then it may acquire the properties of a conditioned stimulus. Frodi and Lamb (1980) adopt a position similar to that of Berkowitz in an attempt to account for the effects of target characteristics in child abuse.[2]

In other contexts, psychodynamically oriented explanations of the effects of target characteristics might be appropriate. For example, a person who frequently becomes angry at his boss for no apparent reason may be responding to some unresolved conflict involving his father, whom his boss resembles. The hallmark of a psychodynamic explanation, as opposed to an explanation in terms of associative learning, is the role attributed to symbolic transformation; the manifest target is not simply associated with, but comes to *stand for*, the latent or "real" target.

For the sake of completeness, it might also be noted that certain physiognomic or other characteristics of the target may serve as biological releasers for aggressive responses. Such releasers have been well documented in lower animals, although their possible influence (or even existence) has not been demonstrated on the human level—a fact that may relfect the biases of most investigators as much as the actual state of affairs. ("Releaser" is perhaps an inappropriate term to use with respect to humans, for it suggests too much automaticity. At most, priming and not releasing mechanisms might be involved.)

But our concern here is not with possible mechanisms. Since target characteristics do not form a natural category (i.e., are not all of a kind), no single explanation can account for their influence on anger and aggression.

Situational Cues

Let us turn now to the second category of stimuli mentioned earlier, namely, situational or contextual cues. These, too, do not form a natural category, and hence we will not speculate about possible mediating mechanisms. It suffices for our purposes to illustrate the effects of such stimuli and to assess their importance for

---

[2] Actually, there is little *direct* evidence for an interpretation of aggressive stimuli in terms of classical conditioning. In a test of this model, Swart and Berkowitz (1976) attempted to condition aggressive responses to a previously neutral stimulus. The results were, however, equivocal. For a thorough review and criticism of this line of theory and research, see Zillmann (1979, pp. 221 ff.).

the everyday experience of anger and aggression. In order to keep the discussion short, we will use as a paradigm the so-called weapons effect. It is difficult to think of a stimulus that might be more effective than a weapon in pulling for an aggressive response. Hence, any conclusions (especially limitations) that apply to the weapons effect should also apply *mutatis mutandis* to the effect of other aggressive stimuli.

In an experiment by Berkowitz and LePage (1967), it was found that angered subjects delivered more and longer shocks to a provocateur when a gun—rather than a neutral object (e.g.,a badminton racquet)—was present in the room. The experimental design was such that subjects had no reason to believe that either the gun or the neutral objects had any relationship to events occurring in the study. Several other sudies have obtained results similar to those of Berkowitz and LePage (Fraczek & Macaulay, 1971; Frodi, 1975). On the other hand, Page and Scheidt (1971) and Turner, Layton, & Simons (1975) failed to find a consistent weapons effect; and still other studies (e.g., Buss, Booker, & Buss, 1972; Turner & Simons, 1974) have actually obtained the opposite effect, that is, subjects were less aggressive in the presence of weapons.

In considering the apparent elusiveness of the weapons effect, Berkowitz (1974) mentions three main factors that might account for the inconsistent findings. First, people differ in the way that they interpret stimuli. If a person considers a gun to be dangerous or odious, then the presence of a weapon may hinder rather than facilitate aggression. Second, even when an extraneous stimulus such as a weapon facilitates aggressive tendencies, the effect may be masked by other cues in the situation that are inhibitory. Indeed, the mere arousal of an aggressive tendency may trigger a counterreaction if the person believes that aggression is an inappropriate response in the situation. Finally, and perhaps most important, any tendencies prompted by an extraneous cue, such as a weapon, are usually weak. The presence of a weapon should therefore have an effect only if the person is already set to attack for some other reason.

The above three points could, of course, be made about the effects of any extraneous situational cue (or target characteristic). Undoubtedly, extraneous stimuli sometimes have an unwarranted influence on anger and aggression. Experimental research is not needed to demonstrate such an effect. Experimental research does suggest, however, that the effect of situational cues—even a cue as potent as a weapon—is rather limited.

Berkowitz (1974) has argued that the influence of extraneous cues helps explain many instances of *impulsive* (angry) as opposed to *instrumental* aggression, including the types of crimes of passion discussed in Chapter 4. Berkowitz's argument is that people sometimes are carried away by certain features of their environment, and that this accounts for the partly involuntary nature of an angry response. However, if research on the weapons effect can be taken as respresentative, then it is doubtful that extraneous cues go very far in explaining crimes of passion or the everyday experience of anger. As in the case of the frusutration-aggression hypothesis and the transfer-of-arousal paradigm, too much is being asked of too little, theoretically speaking.

Extrinsic Motivation

Traditionally, there has been a close conceptual relationship between emotions and motives. It has, however, been a relationship marked by ambivalence, with sometimes the one (emotions) and sometimes the other (motives) being assigned the primary role. For example, emotions have often been conceptualized as "drives" which serve to motivate behavior (see Berkowitz's formulation of the frustration-aggression hypothesis discussed earlier). Conversely, the emotions themselves have frequently been viewed as motivated, rather than as motivating, as when an angry episode is attributed to (perhaps unconscious) desires or wishes.

In the present section we will consider some possible motives for anger. Our major concern is with the influence of motives that are extrinsic to anger, for these represent a nonnormative source of anger and aggression. A motive is extrinsic to anger if it involves an objective that is unrelated to the provocation. An example would be the husband who gets angry at his wife over a trivial incident in order to get out of taking her to a party. By contrast, a motive is intrinsic to anger if it involves an objective that is socially accepted and recognized as a legitimate goal of anger. Some examples of intrinsic motives have been discussed in Chapters 4 and 5, for example, revenge for wrongdoing and the correction of faults.

In Part II of this volume, particularly Chapters 8 and 10, we will present additional data on the motives for anger. To adumbrate briefly, a typical episode of anger involves such motives as asserting authority or independence, getting the instigator to desist from the provocation (often for the instigator's own good), and/or strengthing a relationship with the instigator. Motives such as these can be considered intrinsic, since they conform to social norms and rules concerning the proper objectives of anger. However, the data reported in Chapters 8 and 10 also indicate that extrinsic motives are involved in many episodes of anger. For example, it is not uncommon for people to report that one goal of an angry episode is to get the instigator to do something for them (something unrelated to the instigation), or conversely, to get out of doing something for the instigator.[3]

It might be objected that people cannot report accurately the motives for their anger. Indeed, the whole idea that anger can be motivated (whether intrinsically or extrinsically) might appear to involve a logical contradiction. In ordinary discourse, we can speak about the motives for a person's actions. It is typically odd, however, to speak about the motives for a passion. For example, it makes little sense to ask about the motive for John's hunger. Does it make any more sense to ask about the motive for John's anger? The answer to this question bears not only

---

[3] The infliction of pain or suffering on the victim has sometimes been postulated as a primary motive for anger; and in fact, indication that the target has been hurt can have a reinforcing effect on the aggressive behavior of angered subjects (see Baron, 1977, pp. 260 ff., for a review of relevant research). Nevertheless, the infliction of pain is typically a means to achieve some other end, such as revenge. The person who *only* wishes to inflict harm is acting out of cruelty or sadism, not anger.

on the issues being discussed in this chapter, but also on analyses to be presented in subsequent chapters. Therefore, a brief digression is in order.

Models of Motivation

The notion that emotional reactions can be motivated has been voiced by many theorists of diverse persuasion. Among philosophically oriented theorists, for example, Sartre (1948) has maintained that emotions are actions (judgments) that help to transform reality in a "magical" way. A similar theme has recently been expressed by Solomon (1976), who argues that

> every emotion is also an ideology, a set of demands, "how the world ought to be." It is not only an interpretation of our world but a projection into its future, filled with desires which sometimes become intentions and commitments. (p. 280)

Among the "classical" analysts, Adler (1954) was perhaps the most insistent that a person's emotions could be viewed as part of a larger plan or set of goals; and as described in Chapter 1, Schafer (1976)—a contemporary psychoanalyst within the Freudian tradition—has argued that the emotions be viewed as "disclaimed actions," that is, as goal-directed responses for which the individual disclaims responsibility. Finally, to take an example from within a more academic tradition, Arnold and Gasson (1968) have suggested that emotions are "instruments in pursuit of our purposes" (p. 212).

On the other hand, Lyons (1980) has argued that contentions such as the above are logically muddled, and that it is untenable to suggest that emotions are purposive. Moreover, he cites an equally impressive array of authors to support his views.

There is obviously not space here to enter into this dispute in any depth. Part of the problem lies in the different ways that various authors have used the concepts of motive, purpose, intentionality, and the like. About the most that we can accomplish here is to indicate how the concept of motive is being used in the present analysis.

Motives are theoretical constructs introduced to explain behavior. There is thus no "correct" concept of motivation. Rather, motives can be conceptualized in different ways, depending upon the overall nature of the theory being considered. We will mention here two possible formulations that are compatible with the constructivist view of emotion outlined in Chapter 1.

According to one formulation, motives might be conceived of a short- or long-term dispositions to respond in a particular way in the presence of an appropriate incentive (Atkinson, 1964). The basis for the disposition presumably lies in psychologocal structures, for example, "defense mechanisms," "plans," or cognitive "schemata"; and, ultimately, in the structural properties of the nervous system (either innate or acquired). For the person who is disposed to respond in an angry fashion, the motivation is intrinsic if the incentive is related to the provocation in a socially acceptable manner and extrinsic if the incentive is extraneous to the provocation.

Another way to view motivation is in terms of a behavioral hierarchy. By behavior I mean an instrumental response defined with reference to some goal object. The behavior or a rat in a Skinner box can be used to illustrate the nature of a behavioral hierarchy. At one level the rat's behavior might be described as lever pressing. At a higher level of organization the same response might be described as food-getting or shock-avoidance. Continuing even higher in the hierarchy, food-getting might be subsidiary to a more encompassing pattern of behavior, such as hoarding.

How does motivation fit into this scheme? We could, as previously described, posit various dispositions and incentives that might account for the rat's behavior. For many purposes, however, a somewhat simpler approach is feasible, one that does not entangle us in controversies about potentially unobservable states of the organism, and yet one which remains relatively true to our everyday concept of motivation. Consider again the rat in a Skinner box. In ordinary language, it might be said that the rat is pressing the lever in order to obtain food, and that it is obtaining food for the purpose of hoarding. These motivational ascriptions ("in order to," "for the purpose of") do not rely for their meaning on the identification of some internal conditions of the organism. Rather, they refer to the way behavior is connected or organized with respect to goal objects of increasing generality.

On the human level, Chein (1972) has been the most explicit in applying a hierarchical model of behavior to the problem of motivation. According to Chein, a superordinate act can be considered the motive for an act lower in a behavioral hierarchy if the latter is necessary for the completion of the former. A related, though somewhat more cognitively oriented, approach to motivation may be found in Kelly's (1955) theory of personal constructs. A construct is a way of interpreting events. In Kelly's system a higher-order construct determines subordinate constructs in much the same way that a superordinate response (a motive, in Chein's sense) determines subsidiary responses.

According to the above analysis, all behavior is both motiviating (when treated as a superordinate act) and motivated (when treated as a subsidiary response). For example, an episode of anger may be considered a motive for a variety of subsidiary responses (e.g., yelling, striking). But looking upward rather than downward in the behavioral hierarchy, one may speak of the motive (superordinate act) of which the episode of anger is a subsidiary response. If that superordinate act does not include anger as a socially acceptable subsidiary, then the motive can be said to be extrinsic to anger, and conversely for intrinsic motives.

The nature of extrinsic motives can be further clarified if we keep in mind that an episode of anger is not a unitary phenomenon. In particular, as was discussed in Chapter 1, a distinction can be made between a response (e.g., an act of aggression) and the interpretation or reflective experience of that response (e.g., as anger). A response and its interpretaion can be subsidiary to different motives. Thus, a person who has become aggressive for one reason may interpret (and even experience) his behavior as anger for quite a different reason (e.g., in order to shift blame from himself to the target). In such a case, we sould say that the anger episode was, at least in part, extrinsically motivated.

During the normal course of socialization, a child (or adult) learns both how to respond and how to interpret the response in an appropriate fashion. In this way, individual motives are made consonant with social norms. When they are not consonant, the attribution of anger may be disallowed, and the response attributed to ulterior (extrinsic) motives. But socialization is never complete, and even if it were, the norms of anger only set broad limits on behavior. There is thus considerable latitude for extrinsic motives to influence the course of an angry episode.

We will have more to say about the issue of motivation in subsequent chapters. But let us return now to our discussion of nonnormative sources of anger and aggression and their implications.

Implications

We have considered four nonnormative sources of anger and aggression, namely, nonarbitrary frustrations, extraneous physiological arousal, aggressive stimuli unrelated to the instigation, and extrinsic motivation. Other sources of equal importance could have been discussed. For example, there are stable individual differences in the tendency to view the world in an aggressive and/or hostile fashion (Edmunds & Kendrick, 1980) and to engage in aggressive behavior (Olweus, 1979). It is no more legitimate for an aggressive person to become angry than it is for a mild-mannered person to become angry; hence, such individual differences—to the extent that they influence a person's reaction to provocation—represent a nonnormative source of anger and aggression.

Drugs, particularly alcohol, are another major factor contributing to angry and aggressive outbursts. But there is no need to continue adding to the list. Rather, let us consider the practical and theoretical significance of nonnormaitve factors, regardless of their source.

Perhaps the first thing to note is that some of the factors that have figured most prominently in past theories of anger and aggression actually seem to have relatively little influence in their own right. Frustration is perhaps the best example of this. Although the frustration-aggression hypothesis has dominated the field for many years, in well-controlled laboratory studies it has been difficult to demonstrate *any* effect of frustration on aggression unless the subject has also been provoked to anger, for example, by making the frustration arbitrary (unwarranted) or by adding insult.[4] Of course, it might be argued that laboratory manipulations are necessarily

---

[4] A provocation to anger is not the only way of providing subjects with a "justification" for aggression—cf. Milgram's (1974) experiments on obedience to authority. The aggression-enhancing effects of frustration, physiological arousal, and the like could thus be studied in contexts other than anger. As a matter of fact, however, most experimental research on the influence of such variables has included an angry condition as part of the experimental design, even though (or perhaps because) anger per se has seldom been a primary focus of interest.

too mild to produce marked effects. In one sense that is certainly true. A person cannot be frustrated in the laboratory in a way that can match some of the extreme frustrations that sometimes occur in everyday life. But the opposite argument can be—and has been—made. Specifically, field studies suggest that laboratory research has tended to overestimate the effects of mild frustrations on aggressive behavior (Fawl, 1963).

Of course, it is not entirely appropriate to consider any single factor in isolation. In Berkowitz's formulation of the frustration-aggression hypothesis, for example, aggression is linked not only to frustration, but also to physiological arousal (from whatever source) and to the presence of aggressive stimuli. Certainly, these three variables together are more conducive to anger and aggression than any one alone. If we add to the equation extrinsic motives, an aggressive outburst is greatly increased, *given even a minor provocation.*

This last proviso is extremely important, for without a provocation (real or fancied) it is difficult to interpret—or experience—a response as anger, as opposed to some other form of aggression. And in this connection it is noteworthy that one of the most consistent findings of the research reviewed in this chapter is that subjects typically do not engage in aggressive behavior unless they also believe they have reason to be angry, or else are given some other justification for aggression.

Up until this point I frequently have used "anger" and "aggression" almost interchangeably. That is because most of the research we have been revieweing either has not made a clear distinction between these two phenomena, or has used the concept of anger in an extremely broad (generic) sense. When it has been necessary to distinguish between anger and aggression, I have relied upon the context to make my meaning clear. That strategy is becoming increasingly awkward. In the remainder of this discussion, therefore, a clear line will be drawn between anger as a specific emotional syndrome and aggression as one of its common manifestations (recognizing, of course, that not all aggression is a manifestation of anger).

The influence of nonnormative factors on the experience and expression of *anger* may be summarized in the following three propositions:

1. *Any factor that lowers the threshold for perceived wrong or injury will also lower the threshold for anger.* For example, if a person is already frustrated, in an aroused state, or annoyed by unpleasant conditions, then he may interpret even a casual remark as an affront, or view any further obstruction as an unwarranted infringement on his rights. This proposition is rather trivially obvious. The next two are not.

2. *Any factor that increases the likelihood of an aggressive response will also increase the likelihood of anger.* Whereas Proposition 1 focuses on the appraisal components of an angry syndrome, Proposition 2 focuses on the response components. The two propositions thus complement one another. Underlying both is the assumption that whenever one component of a syndrome is activated, other components will also be recruited. This is obviously true in the case of appraisals, but it is also true of responses as well (although not necessarily to the same degree). In any case, extraneous stimuli that model or encourage aggression may facilitate anger, as may any aggressive response that results from frustration, arousal, extrinsic motivation, drugs, or whatever.

3. *Any factor that requires a person to justify his behavior may turn "simple" aggression into an angry episode.* Proposition 3 deals not with the initial appraisal of an instigation or the (coordinated) response, as do Propositions 1 and 2, but with a person's interpretation of his or her own behavior. A person who reacts in an untoward fashion to an unavoidable frustration, or who aggresses against another for ulterior motives, may be called upon to justify his behavior, if not by others, then by his own sense of values. Anger provides a justification in two ways. First, it places the blame for the incident on the presumed instigator; and second, since anger is a passion, it implies that the person is not entirely responsible for his behavior anyway. Of course, once a response is interpreted as anger, that interpretation may further influence the course of events. A behavioral syndrome and its interpretation stand in a dialectical relationship, each influencing the other. In the case of anger and aggression, a truly vicious cycle can sometimes be formed wherein an initial response creates a need for justification (anger), which in turn encourages further aggression and even greater anger.

Concluding Observations

Aggression and violence exact a terrible toll, not only from the victims, but from society as a whole. Many of the more egregious forms of violence—from child abuse to mass homicide—are often attributed to anger, especially by persons sympathetic to the perpetrator (though not necessarily to his actions).[5] Clearly, we cannot account for such violence—nor even the much more numerous instances of pettiness and hurtful actions that plague our daily lives—by reference to the norms of anger. Nonnormative factors play an important, and sometimes predominant, role in the instigation to anger.

Taken singly or in isolation, the various nonnormative factors that we have been considering (frustration, arousal, etc.) seem to have only subtle and often inconsistent effects. However, such factors are ubiquitous, and their effects may be cumulative and multiplicative. Their subtlety can thus belie their importance. Still, it is easy to overemphaize the influence of nonnormative factors on anger and aggression, as has been the case in much recent research and theory. Pepitone (1976) has observed, without exaggeration, that "in the research conducted by psychologists over the past 35 years there is scarcely any reference to *normative values and beliefs* associated with roles and cultural groups as to the origin, direction, inhibition, and form of aggression" (p. 645, italics added).

---

[5] The response of social critics to riots often provides a good illustration of this point. Those who wish to blame societal conditions for a riot generally describe the rioters as angry. Those who wish to hold the rioters responsible typically blame hooliganism, greed, or criminal elements for the riot. As we saw in the case of crimes of passion (Chapter 5), the attribution of anger is as much a matter of social as of psychological analysis.

The lack of emphasis on normative factors stems in part from an understandable desire to explain aggression in general, as opposed to specific forms of aggression, such as that which sometimes occurs out of anger. But the desire may be misguided, as illustrated by the following analogy.

If anger is compared to a disease, then the nonnormative sources of anger may be likened to extraneous variables (pollutants, stress, constitutional predispositions, etc.) that increase susceptibility to, and the severity of, an illness. It would be extremely difficult to demonstrate the influence of any single extraneous variable on the health of human subjects following short-term and relatively mild exposure in a laboratory setting. Nevertheless, epidemiological studies leave no doubt about the cumulative and interactive effects of extraneous variables on the incidence of disease.

But no matter how many extraneous variables (pollutants, stress, etc.) are implicated, and no matter how important their effects, they cannot account for the occurrence of a specific disease—pneumonia, let us say. Pneumonia is an organized set of reactions to a particular pathogen. Similarly, no matter how many extraneous (nonnormative) factors are taken into account, they cannot explain the occurrence of anger, which is an organized set of responses to certain kinds of provocation.

Pursuing the analogy one step further, consider what it would be like to construct a theory applicable to all respiratory diseases, not just pneumonia. *Ex hypothesi*, such a theory would have to focus primarily on variables that are extraneous to any particular disease, that are of common occurrence, and that usually have little efficacy in their own right. Similar considerations apply to theories of aggression. Just as there are many types of respiratory diseases, so too there are many types of aggression; angry aggression is only one variety. To construct a theory of aggression while ignoring specific forms would be like constructing a theory of disease while ignoring specific diseases. The result would necessarily be highly abstract and divorced from the realities of everyday life.

Part II
Empirical Studies of the Everyday Experience of Anger

Chapter 7

Overview and Methods

This brief chapter introduces Part II of our analysis. The purpose of the chapter is twofold: first, to review some of the methodological shortcomings of current research on anger and aggression; and second, to provide an overview of five studies, the results of which will be presented in subsequent chapters.

Some Observations on Past and Current Research

The previous chapters have often used rather extreme examples of anger and related states (e.g., wild-man behavior, the instances of cruelty cited by Seneca, and crimes of passion) in order to make some theoretical point. Considerable insight into the nature of anger and aggression can be had from such examples, but they can also be misleading in important respects. Ultimately, the functional significance of anger—if it has any—must be found on the level of everyday affairs. A crime of passion may be dramatic; but its effect, fortunately, is far removed from most of us. However, most people do become mildly angry almost on a daily basis, and may experience another's anger nearly as often. The effects of such episodes are not dramatic; indeed, the typical episode of anger may not even be remembered a short while after it has occurred. Nevertheless, the cumulative effects of innumerable small episodes may be more significant than the consequences of an isolated but dramatic outburst.

Recently, social psychologists have devoted considerable attention to the way the proverbial man in the street may be led astray by focusing attention on singular events (see Ross, 1977, for a review of this issue). For example, if a tourist has a holiday ruined by unusually stormy weather, he may form a negative opinion of the place he has visited, quite ignoring the numerous positive experiences of most visitors. Of course, it is easy to denigrate the man in the street for being somewhat naive in his theorizing; for example, for placing too much weight on the dramatic or unusual, for ignoring base-rate data, for overlooking the informational value of non-occurrences, or for imposing preconceived ideas on observations. But are social scientists any more immune to these shortcomings than the man in the street? One would hope so; however, at least as far as theories of anger and aggression are concerned, the answer is doubtful.

Psychology is a science, but it is not a science like chemistry or physics, and psychologists often feel defensive about the difference. In psychological theorizing, therefore, great weight is often placed on phenomena that are unusual and counterintuitive, and/or that seem to offer simple solutions to socially relevant problems. It might be objected that this assertion is true only of armchair psychologists, that *experimental* psychology has built-in safeguards to prevent the influence of such biases.

But an experiment is itself an unusual state of affairs. Consider for a moment the evaluator-performer paradigm, on which many of the findings reported in the previous chapter were based. The subject (typically a college freshman or sophomore fulfilling a course requirement) is brought into a laboratory, deliberately provoked by a relative stranger and then given the opportunity to retaliate by administering shock to the provocateur, ostensibly as punishment for the latter's poor performance on some learning task. At various points in the procedure, the subject may be asked to exercise, be shown erotic films, or be subjected to some other manipulations designed to influence the degree of frustration, physiological arousal, or whatever.

I do not mean to make light of such research. Most laboratory studies are well designed, and they yield information that would be difficult to obtain in any other way. Yet there is a problem here that should not be glossed over. Lubek (1979) examined all of the articles on aggression and related topics that appeared between 1968 and 1977 in two leading American social-psychological journals—the *Journal of Personality and Social Psychology* and the *Journal of Experimental Social Psychology*. During this 10-year period 102 articles on aggression were published. About 65% of these used the evaluator-performer paradigm or related techniques.[1] Lubek also noted a marked tendency among the authors of the articles to cite their own work or that of a small expert group, and also not to cite research more than a decade old.

The tendency for research on anger and aggression to rely so heavily on a particular methodology is disquieting. As discussed in Chapter 6, laboratory research has tended to focus on nonnormative factors or mechanisms. Some of these mechanisms —such as frustration—have formed the basis for comprehensive theories of anger and/or aggression. We have also noted, however, that the proposed mechanisms may actually account for very little of the variance in everyday aggressive behavior. This

---

[1] These data are derived from Lubek's Table 4 (p. 290). The value of 65% includes all studies that used the delivery of electric shock as the dependent variable. Most of these studies would have involved some variation of the evaluator-performer paradigm, although other paradigms have been devised that also used electric shock as a dependent variable (e.g., Taylor, 1967). On the other hand, 65% undoubtedly underestimates the conformity in current social-psychological research on aggression, which is predominantly experimental. Most laboratory studies share certain features in common, whether or not they utilize shock as a dependent variable. And our concern at the moment is as much with the limitations of laboratory research as it is with any specific paradigm within that tradition.

point is sufficiently important that it will be reinforced by one further example. In an experimental situation, Barker, Dembo, and Lewin (1941) observed that children were easily frustrated in the laboratory, and that when frustrated they responded in a wide variety of ways, including aggression. In a field setting, on the other hand, Fawl (1963), a student of Barker, not only found fewer instances of frustration than would be expected on the basis of laboratory studies, but when frustration did occur, the consequences were generally different than those observed in the laboratory. Aggression, in particular, was an infrequent response to frustration.

In view of the above considerations, it would seem desirable to supplement laboratory research with field studies of the everyday experience of anger. However, field studies (involving direct observation) are usually not practical, for a variety of reasons. First, many episodes of anger do not occur in public, and hence cannot be observed. Second, when anger does occur in a public setting, it may not be expressed openly. Third, the incidents that precipitate many episodes of anger involve events in the past history of a relationship, a history that is seldom known to an external observer. And finally, ethical considerations limit the extent to which people can be observed without their knowledge or consent. For these reasons, some form of self-report or questionnaire technique would seem to be the most appropriate method for obtaining data on the everyday experience of anger. And in the chapters that follow, the results of a series of such studies will be reported.

Somewhat surprisingly, there have been few previous surveys of the everyday experience of anger based on questionnaires or interviews. As part of his series on Child Study, Hall (1899) asked "nearly 900 teachers, parents and others" to provide descriptions of anger and related states (e.g., "wrath, ire, temper, madness, indignation, sulks, sours, putchiness, crossness, choler, grudge, fume, fury, passion, to be or fall out with"). Hall received a total of 2,184 descriptions. One teacher alone collected descriptions from 244 persons, of which 121 were original observations on children, 92 were reminiscences, and 28 were based on secondhand information. From this wealth of data, Hall culled numerous brief vignettes illustrating various aspects of anger, particularly in children. But although the vignettes are interesting and often suggestive, the study itself is practically worthless as far as providing representative data is concerned.

In a much more systematic study, Richardson (1918) asked 12 persons (10 of whom were graduate students in psychology at Clark University) to observe and keep daily records of "all instances of anger . . . no matter how minute." Richardson was primarily interested in "mental behavior" (thoughts, feelings, etc.), and each person kept a record for at least 3 months. Gates (1926) had 51 women students, members of introductory courses in psychology at Barnard College, record all their experiences of "anger and extreme irritation" during a 1-week period. The focus in this study was primarily on overt behavior and eliciting conditions. Meltzer (1933) and Anastasi, Cohen, and Spatz (1948) used a technique similar to that of Gates. Meltzer obtained reports from 93 Oregon State College students (both men and women), while Anastasi et al. collected data from 38 Barnard College women. Anastasi et al. focused primarily on eliciting conditions, as opposed to responses.

McKellar (1949, 1950) asked a group of several hundred members of adult education classes in the London area to complete a questionnaire describing two recent episodes of anger or annoyance, and he supplemented these data with his own self-observations as well as with in-depth interviews of a small number of additional subjects. McKellar was interested primarily in the conditions that elicit anger and the "voluntary behavior" (e.g., aggression) that accompanies anger.

Where relevant, the results of the above studies will be described in some detail in subsequent chapters. For our present purposes, it is sufficient to note the brevity of the list.[2] While hundreds of laboratory studies have been conducted on anger and aggression, the number of detailed surveys of the everyday experience of anger can be counted on the fingers of one hand.

One reason for the paucity of surveys of the everyday experience of anger is a concern with the validity of self-report data. To a certain extent the concern is quite justified. It would seem, however, that a healthy skepticism and caution about self-reports have resulted in an unhealthy form of self-censorship, in which psychologists have cut themselves off from a potentially useful source of information.

Some limitations to the use of self-report data will be discussed later in this chapter. But first it will be helpful to have a brief overview of the series of studies, the results of which will be presented in the chapters that follow.

Studies of the Everyday Experience of Anger

Based on the substantive issues involved, the series can be divided as follows: Study I—Anger as experienced by the angry person (Chapters 8 and 9); Study II—Experiencing another person's anger (Chapter 10); Study III—Differences between anger and annoyance (Chapter 11); Study IV—Temporal dimensions of anger (Chapter 12); and Study V—Differences between men and women in the everyday experience of anger (Chapter 13). All of these studies are based on detailed questionnaires, and each is logically related to the others. It is therefore convenient to provide an overview of the various studies—their purposes, methods, and analyses—all in one place. Additional details will be presented as appropriate in subsequent chapters.

Study I. Anger as Experienced by the Angry Person

The first and the most fundamental study of the series had as its primary purpose the gathering of descriptive data on the everyday experience of anger *from the perspective of the angry person*. A total of 160 subjects participated in the study; 80 of these were community residents ranging in age from 21 to 60 years; and 80 were undergraduate students recruited from introductory psychology courses at the University of Massachusetts, Amherst. The details of the sampling procedures, the

---

[2] There is no assurance that this list is complete, but it does include most, if not all, of the readily available studies. Other research could be cited in which anger was included as one of several emotions surveyed (e.g., Allen & Haccoun, 1976), but even these studies would not add greatly to the list.

nature of the population sampled, and so forth will be described more fully in Chapter 8.

Each participant in the study completed a detailed written questionnaire on the everyday experience of anger, a copy of which is contained in Appendix A. (Hereafter this questionnaire will be referred to as Questionnaire A in order to distinguish it from the questionnaire used in Study II. A copy of the latter is contained in Appendix B.) Very briefly, Questionnaire A consists of 88 items, focusing on the most intense episode of anger experienced by the subject during the preceding week (or, if the person did not become angry during the week, on the most recent experience before that). All but a few participants reported becoming angry at least once during the week; and in any case, no episode was included in the final analyses if it occurred more than 1 month earlier. This helped assure not only accuracy of recall, but also a representative sample of angry incidents. That is, most persons do not experience an extreme or unusual episode of anger during any given week or even month.

As an examination of Appendix A indicates, the questionnaire is quite comprehensive. The topics covered include, among other things: the target of the anger; the nature of the instigation; background conditions; the intensity and nature of the response, both desired and actually expressed; the objectives of the response, that is, what the subject thought he or she might accomplish by becoming angry; the perceived reactions of the instigator; and the continuing affective reactions of the subject following the initial response.

In terms of format, the questionnaire contains a mixture of forced-choice and open-ended items. The forced-choice items specify in an explicit fashion many of the more common characteristics of a typical angry episode, along with logically possible alternatives. The open-ended questions scattered throughout the questionnaire provide the opportunity for further elaboration and explanation. This format allows the questionnaire to be comprehensive but not onerous. Indeed, in response to a direct question at the end of the questionnaire, only 6 out of 180 subjects indicated that it was boring; a few also indicated that they had some difficulty in being so specific about their anger, especially if the incident was mild. For the most part, however, the response to the questionnaire was overwhelmingly positive. This is worth noting, for too often it is presumed that persons are reluctant or unwilling to report their emotional experiences. Such skepticism is not altogether warranted, at least not in the present instance.

Study II. Experiencing Another Person's Anger

The primary purpose of Study II was to obtain normative data on the reactions *of the target* to another person's anger. For this purpose, a second questionnaire was constructed, a copy of which is contained in Appendix B. In constructing Questionnaire B, items from Questionnaire A were "turned around" whenever possible. For example, instead of asking a subject whether *you* (the angry person) aggressed against the offender, the subject was asked in Questionnaire B whether the angry person aggressed against *you* (the target). Of course, some items that are relevant to the experience of one's own anger are not relevant to experiencing another person's anger, and vice versa. Thus, Questionnaires A and B do not correspond in all respects. Moreover, even when it was possible to construct corresponding items for both questionnaires, the response format sometimes had to be changed. Items on Questionnaire A typically were followed by 3-point rating scales (0 = not at all, 1 = somewhat, 2 = very much). On Questionnaire B a fourth category (? = don't know) was added to the rating scales for those items which required the subject (the target) to make an inference about the behavior or state of mind of the angry person.

Only students participated in Study II; that is, Questionnaire B was not sent to community residents. Subjects (80 in all) were recruited at the same time and in the same manner, as the students who participated in Study I.

The reactions of the target to another person's anger are important for both theoretical and methodological reasons. Theoretically, the present analysis assumes that an emotion such as anger is maintained within the social system because it has positive as well as negative consequences. In evaluating this assumption, the reactions of the person who is the target of anger are of prime importance. How often and under what conditions does anger elicit contrition, say, as opposed to defiance? A major objective of Study II was to obtain data relevant to issues such as this.

From a more methodological standpoint, the results of Study II can be used to check on certain biases that might have confounded the data from Study I. For example, a participant in Study I might say that he became angry at an *unjustified* act on the part of another, thus presenting himself in a socially desirable light. However, if social desirability is a major factor in determining responses to the questionnaires, then the opposite pattern of results should be obtained in Study II. That is, social desirability would encourage the target to say that an instigation was *justified*, thus impugning the other person's anger as illegitimate.

Study III. Differences Between Anger and Annoyance

One of the best ways to analyze a phenomenon is by contrasting it with a closely related phenomenon. That was the purpose of Study III, which contrasts anger with annoyance. It might be thought that the primary difference between these states is simply a matter of degree. But that is not the case. To be very annoyed is not just a degree less than being a little bit angry. While anger often presupposes annoyance, it presupposes other things as well. For example, there is a moral connotation to anger, an attribution of blame that is not necessarily associated with annoyance. There are other important differences between anger and annoyance as well (see Chapter 11).

Study III not only helps set anger in relief by contrasting it with a closely related state, it also provides additional information on the everyday occurrence of anger. In Studies I and II subjects were asked to recall an incident of anger that occurred during the previous week. In Study III the subjects (48 students) kept a diary record of all their experiences of anger and annoyance for a 1-week period. This is basically the controlled diary method employed by Anastasi et al. (1948), Gates (1926), and Meltzer (1933). At the end of the week, the subjects were asked to select the most intense episode of anger and the most intense episode of annoyance. They then filled out questionnaires describing each of these two experiences in detail. Except for minor changes in the introductory sections, this was the same as Questionnaire A, with "annoyance" being substituted for "anger," depending upon the type of episode being rated.

Study IV. Temporal Dimensions of Anger

Emotional syndromes are dynamic, not static, states of affairs. Once initiated, an emotion develops, changes (sometimes subsiding, only to well up again), and eventually terminates. Although this fact is widely recognized, issues related to the duration and time course of anger and other emotions have received little explicit attention in the psychological literature. And when considered, such issues have often been made subsidiary to theoretical assumptions regarding the nature of emotion. For example, a theorist who emphasizes bodily changes or expressive reactions may link the time course of emotion to the duration of specific bodily processes.

Study IV explores matters related to the duration of anger, beginning not with preconceived theoretical assumptions, but with the way subjects describe a typical angry episode. The procedure was similar to that of Study I, except that the incidents of anger were limited to episodes occurring within an ongoing interpersonal relationship (e.g., between friends or acquaintances). Special emphasis was placed on factors that might influence the time course of anger, and the relevant items in Questionnaire A were reformulated to provide greater detail on these issues. The subjects in this study consisted of 235 undergraduate students.

The results of Study IV are presented in Chapter 12. Conceptual issues related to the temporal dimensions of emotion are also considered at that point. In particular, a conception of emotional episodes as short-term dispositions is adumbrated.

Study V. Differences Between Men and Women in the Everyday Experience of Anger

It has become almost a cliché in both the popular and psychological literature to assert that women are less able than men to experience and/or express anger. Two lines of argument are often used to support this assertion. From a biological perspective, note may be made of the fact that the males of most primate species are more aggressive than the females; and that cross-culturally men also appear to be more aggressive than women. If anger is closely related to aggression, it would seem to follow that men should be more prone to anger than are women. From a more sociological perspective, many feminist writers disavow any inherent differences in the capacity for men and women to become angry, but claim instead that women are not *allowed* (in a male-dominated society) to express their anger openly and directly. What is the evidence?

In Studies I, II, and III described above, the subject samples were divided equally between men and women. In Study IV no attempt was made to achieve an equal distribution between the sexes; and, as is often the case in the recruitment of subjects, more women than men volunteered (160 vs. 75). These four studies provide a considerable amount of data relevant to possible sex differences in the everyday experience of anger. An analysis of these data, together with a review of the relevant clinical and experimental research, constitute Study V, the results of which are presented in Chapter 13. As will be seen then, sex differences in the experience and expression of anger are not nearly as great as might be expected on the basis of either the biological or the feminist argument. This fact has important implications for understanding the origins and functions of anger (as opposed to aggression) and for clarifying the relationship between anger and ideology.

Approaches to the Analysis and Presentation
of the Results

For the most part, presentation of the data will be in the form of descriptive statistics (means, percentages, and the like). To illustrate relationships among variables, a variety of parametric and nonparametric statistical techniques also have been employed, including multivariate and univariate analysis of variance, regression analysis, factor analysis, and chi-square. In not all cases were the assumptions of a statistical test met in a strict sense. For example, the 3-point scales used for most variables often resulted in skewed distributions. However, for samples of the size used, even parametric tests can be applied with little distortion to dichotomous data that are moderately skewed (D'Agostino, 1971; Glass, Peckham, & Sanders, 1972; Lunney, 1970). Similarly, the chi-square test has been shown to be reasonably accurate even when marginal probability distributions are as disproportionate as .9 versus .1 (Bradley, Bradley, McGrath, & Cutcomb, 1979).

The robustness of these tests does not extend to all levels of significance. Beyond the traditional .05 and .01 levels, statistical tests become more sensitive to violations of underlying assumptions. For this reason only the .05 and .01 levels of significance are reported in the presentation of the results. Also for this reason, as well as to preserve some semblance of a readable style, the complete details of specific statistical tests (e.g., F ratios) are not generally reported unless the results seem somehow controversial, or unless the statistic itself adds substantively to the conclusion.

The major problem is not with the choice of appropriate statistics; the problem is rather the sheer number of analyses that can be applied to the data collected. The questionnaires are complex and allow subjects to be divided into many different categories of potential theoretical and practical interest. For example, one might ask how responses vary as a function of the target of, or motives for, anger. When a great number of different analyses are performed, some "significant" findings can be expected simply on the basis of chance, regardless of the analyses used. An attempt has been made to control for this problem by procedural as well as statistical means. As already described, the different studies that compose the series were designed to complement one another; and it is the overall pattern of results that is ultimately important, not the result of any particular test. Thus, individual analyses performed on segments of the data should be interpreted in the spirit of descriptive and exploratory statistics, rather than as confirmatory.

The results of Study I (anger as experienced by the angry person) and of Study II (experiencing another person's anger) will be presented in the most detail, occupying the next three chapters. Specifically, Chapter 8 focuses on the three major aspects of the object of anger (the target, instigation, and objective or motive); Chapter 9 examines the modes of expression and consequences of anger. Chapter 10 explores these same issues, but from the target's point of view. Each of these chapters is largely descriptive, presenting not only the results of Studies I and II; but, where relevant, a review of previously published research as well. The reader who is not particularly interested in details might want to skim these chapters.

In presenting the results of Study III (anger vs. annoyance), Study IV (the temporal dimensions of anger), and Study V (differences between men and women), less emphasis is placed on the tabulation of data, except as these clarify and extend the results of Studies I and II, and greater emphasis is placed on the implications of the findings. Chapters 11-13 are thus broader in scope and more conceptually oriented than are Chapters 8-10.

Limitations of Self-Report Data

At the outset of the present chapter, some of the limitations of much contemporary research on anger and aggression were discussed. We are now in a position to discuss some of the limitations of the type of self-report data that form the basis for Studies I-V. One limitation, though serious, will be mentioned only briefly, for it is not peculiar to self-reports. That is the problem of sampling. With the exception of the community residents surveyed in Study I, the subjects who participated in these studies were university students. Obviously, students are not representative of the population at large. This limitation is, however, typical of most psychological research, including almost all laboratory studies of anger and aggression. Moreover, the sample of community residents who did participate in Study I allows some check on any peculiarities in the data due to the use of students as subjects.

A more serious limitation that must be considered has to do with the accuracy of self-reports of emotional states. Subjects cannot always assess accurately the determinants of their behavior; and even when they can assess those determinants, they may not report them accurately on a questionnaire. Let us consider the latter issue first, that is, the failure of subjects to report their "true" feelings due, say, to a desire to present a favorable social image. Many of the items on the questionnaires ask subjects to make value judgments, for example, whether the precipitating incident involved a justified or unjustified act on the part of the instigator. Other items concern the goals or motives that the person had in becoming angry, for example, to break off or to strengthen a relationship. Most previous research on anger (whether surveys or laboratory experiments) has tended to eschew issues of this type for the sake of objectivity. Self-reports of value judgments and motives are particularly subject to distortion due to social desirability. Nevertheless, it is precisely when we ask about such issues that we touch upon the norms and functions of anger.

In the present series of studies, an attempt was made to overcome distortions due to social desirability and other response biases by assuring anonymity, by making the questionnaire items quite specific, and by asking the subject to explain after each set of items the reasons for his or her responses. But even more important is that the five studies were designed to check and balance one another. Thus, the comparisons between community residents and students, between the angry person's own experience of anger and the target's experience of another's anger, between anger and annoyance, between short-term and long-term anger, and between the experiences of men and women all provide useful checks on various kinds of biases that might distort the results.

But even if response biases can be held to a minimum and/or their effects assessed, a major problem still remains. It is possible that subjects cannot assess the determinants of their behavior, and hence are unable to provide accurate self-reports regardless of any biases that might further distort the results. For example, Mandler (1975) has pointed out that self-reports can be based only upon what appears in consciousness, and that the contents of consciousness are always modified by cognitive processes of which a person is unaware. It follows, according to Mandler, that "people's reports about their experiences, their behavior, and their actions are very frequently, and may always be, fictions or theories about those events" (p. 52). In a similar vein, Nisbett and Wilson (1977) have argued that "when reporting on the effects of stimuli, people may not interrogate a memory of the cognitive processes that operate on the stimuli; instead, they may base their reports on implicit, a priori theories about the causal connection between stimulus and response" (p. 233). In support of this contention, Nisbett and Wilson have reviewed a considerable amount of evidence suggesting that people are typically unaware of, and hence unable to describe, the variables in a situation that are influencing their behavior; and in the absence of such awareness, self-reports may simply reflect preconceived notions about what stimuli should, or usually do, influence the behavior in question.

Nisbett and Wilson's analysis has been sharply criticized on both conceptual and technical grounds (see Rich, 1979; Smith & Miller, 1978; White, 1980). There is no need to repeat such criticism here. Suffice it to say that the frequent derogation of self-reports is based, to a certain extent, on misunderstanding. No one denies that people are often unable to describe the cognitive processes that mediate behavior. However, people are typically able to describe the reasons for their behavior, that is, the rules that help guide their responses. An example used by Smith and Miller will serve to illustrate this point. If asked how they solved a problem by long division, most elementary school pupils would be able to state the appropriate rules. Such a report would be perfectly accurate, even though the pupil did not, in the words of Nisbett and Wilson, "interrogate a memory of the cognitive processes that operate on the stimuli." (Indeed, in this context, it is difficult to imagine what such an interrogation might entail.) Similarly, people may be able to describe the reasons for their behavior while angry without having any special access to underlying cognitive processes. The fact that the reasons offered in such an instance may reflect social norms and rules is no ground to derogate the self-reports—particularly if the purpose of the research is to elucidate those social norms and rules, as it is in the present case.

This brings us to another problem, not with the use of self-reports per se, but with the proclivity of social scientists to be fascinated by what is unusual and counterintuitive. No one wants to discover what the man in the street already knows. And yet that is precisely what the outcome is liable to be when we study the reasons people give for their everyday social behavior. If the self-reports are accurate reflections of social norms, then the results should be intuitively obvious to anyone who shares those norms, whether that person is a social scientist or the man in the street. However, such analyses are not thereby rendered trivial. For one thing, simply because everybody "knows" something does not mean that they can articulate that knowledge in a clear and systematic fashion. The latter is one of the tasks of social science. For another thing, as was noted in the introduction to this chapter, both scientists and laymen are often led astray in their theorizing by an emphasis on unusual and singular events. Analyses of everyday occurrences, even if the results turn out to be intuitively obvious, provide necessary moorings for more speculative belief systems—whether popular fictions or scientific theories.

Concluding Observations

There is no single method that is most appropriate for investigating a complex phenomenon such as anger. In previous chapters we have considered the possible contribution of biological systems to anger, cross-cultural variations in angerlike syndromes, historical (ethical) teachings on anger, the legal treatment of crimes of passion, and experimental research on the psychological mechanisms mediating anger and aggression. All of these sources provide valuable information. Ultimately, however, questions regarding the nature and significance of anger must be addressed on the level of everyday experience. It is in day-to-day interactions that anger exerts its major influence, for good or ill. But how often do people typically become angry? At whom? For what reasons? And what are the consequences? Surprisingly, elementary and simple questions such as these cannot be answered at the present time. One reason for this state of affairs is a traditional skepticism among social scientists about findings obtained from questionnaires (self-report data); another reason is a predilection for the unusual and counterintuitive. Of course, any methodology has its limitations. This is certainly true of surveys using questionnaires; but it is also true of laboratory experiments, field observations, and the like. Moreover, well-designed questionnaires can provide information that would be difficult or impossible to obtain in any other fashion.

With the above considerations in mind, a series of surveys was undertaken. The present chapter has provided a brief overview of the rationale for, and the methods used in, these studies. The next six chapters are devoted to a presentation of the results and a discussion of their implications.

Chapter 8

Anger as Experienced by the Angry Person: Targets, Instigations, and Motives

In the first part of this chapter we describe the subjects who participated in Study I and the general characteristics (e.g., intensity, duration, typicality) of the incidents they reported. The remainder of the chapter is devoted to the three aspects of the object of anger described in Chapter 1: the target—the person or thing at whom the anger is directed; the instigation—the events that precipitated the anger; and the objective—the motive or aim of the angry response.

Participants

Two samples of subjects completed Questionnaire A. The first sample was recruited from the city of Greenfield, Massachusetts, and surrounding communities. Greenfield itself has a population of 18,000 and is located 20 miles north of the University of Massachuesetts, Amherst. Incorported in 1753, it is a county seat and center for agriculture and light industry (taps and dies, cutlery, hand tools, and the like). More than most communities, it is a microcosm of New England.

The second sample consisted of students enrolled in introductory psychology courses at the University of Massachusetts, Amherst. This is a large (approximately 23,000 students) state-supported university located in the Connecticut Valley region of central Massachusetts. The introductory psychology courses help fulfill general education requirements, and hence draw students (mostly freshmen and sophomores) from many different departments of the university. Students are encouraged to participate in psychological research as part of their learning experience, and most do volunteer.

Community Residents

The community residents were recruited in the following manner: First, names were randomly selected from the Greenfield area telephone directory, and letters were sent explaining the project. In order to assure an equal distribution of men and women, half of the letters were addressed to "Mr." and half to "Mrs." After allowing time for receipt of the letters, each potential subject was contacted by phone. If he or she agreed to participate, a questionnaire was sent together with a $4.00 check for remuneration. Subjects were requested to return the questionnaires within 1 week, although this schedule was not rigidly adhered to. The questionnaire itself was completed anonymously, and a postcard with the subject's name was returned separately. If the postcard was not received within 3 weeks, a follow-up letter was sent with an additional questionnaire, in case the original had been lost or destroyed.

A goal was set to obtain 80 subjects who were (a) native-born Americans; (b) between the ages of 21 and 60; (c) married (although widowed and divorced subjects were also included). One hundred and fifty-six persons (78 men and 78 women) who met these criteria were contacted by letter and telephone. Of these, 84 persons (54%) returned usable questionnaires. This is a remarkably high rate of return for a questionnaire of such complexity (cf. Linsky, 1975). The 84 subjects included 40 men and 44 women. Four of the women were eliminated at random, equalizing the sexes at 40 subjects each.

Of the remaining 72 eligible subjects who were contacted, 44 refused to participate, while another 23 agreed to participate but either returned the questionnaire unanswered or did not return it at all. An additional 5 subjects indicated that they had not become angry recently, and they described either an incident of annoyance or a very intense and/or dramatic incident of anger from the past (up to 6 years previously). Since the goal of the survey was to obtain data on typical episodes of anger, it was decided to exclude these subjects and to set a 1-month time limit on the recency of the incident reported. That is, an incident of anger had to have occurred within the previous month in order to be included within the survey. (Nearly three-quarters, 74%, of the participants described an incident that occurred during the week prior to completing the survey, the median time being 5 days prior).

The ages of the 80 community residents included in the final sample ranged from 21 to 60 years, with a mean of 40. Throughout this age range, the distribution of subjects was approximately rectangular. Most of the subjects (94%) were currently married; one man and two women were divorced, and one man and one woman were widowed. Most (75%) of the men and women also had children living at home.

As far as educational background in concerned, 11% of the community residents never completed high school, 46% were high school graduates, 20% had some training beyond high school, 11% were college graduates, and 11% had some training beyond college.

Nearly half the men (47%) could be classified as blue-collar workers (mechanics, carpenters, policemen and firemen, and factory workers). White-collar workers (salesmen, clerical workers, etc.) made up 30% of the male sample, and 18% could be classified as professional. (The remaining 5% could not be classified.)

The majority (70%) of the women in the sample also held jobs outside the home (i.e., only 30% described their occupation as housewife). Of the 28 working women, 7 were employed in teaching, 6 in nursing and health-related professions, and the remainder in a variety of different positions.

Student Participants

The student sample was recruited through announcements in the introductory psychology courses. Interested students picked up the questionnaire at meetings arranged for that purpose, or from the project secretary's office. When picking up a questionnaire, each student left his or her name and phone number; when the questionnaire was returned, the student's name was crossed off the list. All participants were encouraged to return the questionnaire within 1 week. If after 3 weeks a name was still not crossed off, the student was telephoned and urged to complete the questionnaire. Recruitment continued until 80 students (40 men and 40 women) had returned usable questionnaires.

To be eligible to participate a student had to be 21 years old or less (mean age = 18.5) and single. As in the case of the community residents, the anger incident described had to have occurred within the past month in order to be counted. Five questionnaries were discarded for failing to meet this criterion and another had to be discarded beacuse it was incompletely filled out. Approximately 7% of the students who took questionnaires never returned them.

The above procedure was hardly "random" in the ordinary sense of the term Nevertheless, it did result in a fairly representative sample of students, and certainly a sample that is comparable to that used in most psychological research in a university setting.

The vast majority (90%) of the students were living in dormitories (usually two students per room) at the time of the survey. Only four students were living at home, and another four had some other living arrangement (e.g., an apartment or cooperative housing).

From the above descriptions it is clear that the students differed from the community residents in several important respects (including age, marital status, and living arrangements, not to mention"occupation"). There also were some more subtle differences between the two groups. In terms of religious background, for example, 44% of the students described themselves as Catholic, 31% as Protestant, and 21% as Jewish. The corresponding figures for the community residents were 39%, 55%, and 3%. In general, the student sample was drawn from more recent immigrant groups to the area (e.g., Irish and Eastern European) than was the sample of community residents. This is also illustrated by the fact that only 3 (4%) of the students described their ethnic background as "New England Yankee," whereas 23 (29%) of the community residents did so.

Our concern here is with the general cultural norms that help constitute the emotion of anger, and not with the way those norms apply to particular subgroups or settings. In the discussion that follows, therefore, the community residents and students will be treated as a single sample of subjects (n = 160). On those items where the community residents and students did differ, appropriate note will be made. For the moment, suffice it to say that none of the differences between the two groups call into question the basic conclusions that will be presented during the course of the discussion.[1]

The Angry Incidents

The first section of the questionnaire (see Appendix A) asked subjects to indicate the number of times they had become angry and annoyed during the previous week. Subjects also were asked to describe the incident in which they were most annoyed (but not angry), the incident in which they were most angry, and the difference between the two. The remainder of the questionnaire then focused on the most angry incident. In presenting the results, we will begin with data on the relative frequency of anger and annoyance and on the intensity, duration, and typicality of the angry incident.

The Frequency of Anger and Annoyance

The frequencies of anger and annoyance as reported by the participants are presented in Table 8-1. The majority of persons (105, or 66% of the total sample) reported becoming angry "1 to 2 times during the week," with the frequency falling off drastically on either side of that modal value. As might be expected, annoyance was more frequent than anger, with nearly half (71) of the subjects becoming annoyed at least once a day.

The values presented in Table 8-1 must be interpreted with considerable caution. Many minor incidents of anger and annoyance are quickly forgotten. Moreover, the wording of the questionnaire may have suggested to participants how frequently they "should" have become angry. That is, participants were asked not only to recall the frequency of their anger, but also to describe the most intense experience that occurred during the past week (or the most recent experience before that). This wording implies that most people do become angry at least once a week; and if participants were influenced by this implication, it might help account for the fact that so many reported becoming angry "1 or 2 times during the week."

---

[1] Some of the data for the community residents have been presented separately elsewhere (Averill, 1979). Among the community residents there were no appreciable differences due to age or socioeconomic status, although there were not a sufficient number of subjects to detect nuances in the data as a function of these variables. As mentioned, there were a number of significant differences between the anger of community residents and students, which will be noted at appropriated points in the text. These differences can be accounted for largely in terms of the living conditions of the students and are of little theoretical interest. Somewhat surprisingly, there were fewer differences between men and women than between students and community residents. The implications of this fact will be discussed in Chapter 13.

Table 8-1. Frequency of Annoyance and Anger as Reported by Participants

Frequency	Annoyance[a]	Anger
Not at all during the week	1	26
1-2 times during the week	28	105
3-5 times during the week	59	18
About 1 time each day	17	4
About 2 times each day	22	2
About 3 times each day	15	1
About 4-5 times each day	14	3
About 6-10 times each day	3	0
More than 10 times each day	0	1

Note. n = 160.
[a] One subject did not indicate a frequency for annoyance, hence this column adds to 159.

In this connection, it might be useful to describe some of the results of Study III that will be reported in detail in Chapter 11. In that study (which was designed to explore the differences between anger and annoyance), 48 students were asked to keep *daily* records of each experience of anger and annoyance. An average of 7.3 incidents of anger, and 23.5 incidents of annoyance were recorded each week.

If anything, then, the data presented in Table 8-1 represent an underestimate of the actual incidence of anger. Some people, because of either a benign disposition or favorable circumstances, may go for weeks without experiencing anger.[2] However, most persons experience one or more moderately intense episodes of anger per week; and if daily records are kept, so that relatively minor and easily forgotten incidents of anger are recorded, then the average frequency may be more like one episode per day.[3]

Some Characteristics of the Most Intense Incident

Let us turn now to a consideration of the most intense incident of anger experienced by the subjects during the week prior to completing the questionnaire, or if no incident occurred during that period, then of the most recent incident prior to

---

[2] For example, 10 subjects (5 community residents and 5 students) did not report an incident of anger that occurred within a month prior to completing the questionnaire. As previously mentioned, these subjects were excluded from the final sample. The incidents they described were for the most part quite extreme, suggesting that these subjects were interpreting the concept of anger in an overly restrictive fashion.
[3] In this connection, the results of several earlier studies of anger might also be noted. Subjects studied by Richardson (1918) and Gates (1926) reported between 2 and 3 incidents of anger and/or annoyance per week; Meltzer's (1933) subjects reported about 5 incidents per week; and Anastasi, Cohen, and Spatz (1948) found 16 incidents per week. Obviously, the self-reported frequency of anger varies greatly, depending upon the way the data are collected. But whatever the method, it is also obvious that anger is a very frequent experience.

that. These incidents form the major focus of the present study, and hence it is important to consider at the outset how representative they are of anger in general. We will begin by considering the rated intensity of the angry episodes.

Intensity. On a 10-point scale ranging from "very mild" (1) to "very intense—as angry as most people ever become" (10), the mean rating of the incidents was 7.1. Moreover, the large majority (79%) of the responses fell above the midpoint of the scale. On the whole, subjects did not report incidents that they considered trivial or inconsequential.

The intensity of an angry episode correlated with its duration ($r = .39$), but with few other variables (e.g., response tendencies). This is not particularly surprising, since the way a person responds when angry depends upon a host of factors—the social setting, the target, the nature of the provocation, what the person wishes to accomplish, and so forth. By itself, therefore, the intensity of the experience—unless extreme—cannot be expected to account for a great deal of the variance in behavior.

Duration. The duration of the anger incidents was bimodally distributed, with 26 subjects (16%) saying their anger lasted for from 5-10 minutes and 33 subjects (21%) saying their anger lasted more than 1 day. The median duration was about 1 hour. The factors that influence the duration of anger will be discussed in Chapter 12 in connection with Study IV.

Loss of control. In previous chapters, emphasis has been placed on the fact that emotional concepts connote individual passivity, that is, a loss of personal control. In the questionnaire an attempt was made to tap this aspect of the experience of anger by asking subjects to rate how able they were to control the outward expression of their anger (what they said and did) and also their inward experience (what they thought and felt). Essentially the same rating scales, but with somewhat different wording, were asked at two different points in the questionnaire—once near the beginning and again after the subjects had described in detail their responses (both overt and felt). For purposes of analysis, these two sets of ratings were combined. Two scores were thus obtained, both representing the mean ratings on two 10-point scales. One score represents the perceived loss of behavioral control, while the other represents the perceived loss of internal control (thoughts and feelings). An "index of inhibition" was also calculated by taking the difference between these two scores. A positive value on this index indicates the extent to which overt behavior was more controlled (inhibited) than internal experience.

The mean ratings on each of these variables were 4.2 for the loss of behavioral control, 5.9 for the loss of internal control, and 1.8 for the inhibition of behavior. Not surprisingly, there was a significant correlation between intensity of anger and the loss of both behavioral ($r = .38$) and internal ($r = .53$) control. There was no relationship between intensity and degree of inhibition. There was, however, a significant correlation ($r = .33$) between the duration of the incident and inhibition—the more inhibited the expression, the longer the anger lasted (or vice versa). Some possible implications of this relationship will be discussed in Chapter 9, which deals with the responses and consequences of anger.

Representativeness

One reason for asking subjects to describe the most intense incident of anger that occurred during the preceding week was to ensure that the episode would be fairly typical—that is, not an extreme or unusual event. To check on this, subjects were asked to rate how typical the precipitating incident was "to what makes people in general angry," and how typical their responses were to "how other people generally respond when angry." With regard to the precipitating incident, 52 (33%) thought it "very" typical, 85 (53%) thought it "somewhat" typical, and only 23 (14%) believed it to be "not at all" typical. With regard to their responses, the corresponding figures were 28 (18%), 115 (72%), and 17 (11%). A large majority of the subjects obviously believed that the incidents described were fairly representative of anger in general. An inspection of the open-ended descriptions provided by subjects leaves no reason to doubt this conclusion.

Summary

Most persons become angry at least once a week, and nearly everyone at least once a month. (If relatively mild or easily forgotten incidents are counted, the incidence may jump to once a day.) Many of these everyday experiences are by no means trivial or unimportant. In the present study the "most intense" incident within the prior week received a mean rating of about 7.0 on a 10-point scale, where 10 meant "as angry as most people ever become." With regard to the experience of passivity, subjects generally reported being less in control of their thoughts and feelings than of their behavior. The duration of the incidents, which was correlated with both intensity and the degree of behavioral inhibition, tended to be biomodal; that is, there were more incidents of relatively short (less than 10 minutes) and relatively long (one day or more) duration than there were of intermediate time periods.[4]

The Target of Anger

The remainder of this chapter will be devoted to an analysis of the objects of anger. The typical object has three aspects—the target, the instigation, and the objective or motive. We will consider the target first.

---

[4] On these preliminary analyses there were several statistically significant differences (all p's $< .05$) between the community residents and students. Specifically, the students rated their experiences as more intense than did the community residents (7.6 vs. 6.7). The students also were more likely to report that they still became angry when thinking about the incident (56 students vs. 35 community residents) and that they experienced a greater loss of control over their thoughts and feelings (6.3 vs. 5.6, on a 10-point scale). Finally, the students had a higher index of inhibition (2.1 vs. 1.5). This was due primarily to the lack of control over their thoughts and feelings; there was virtually no difference between the groups in the degree of control they experienced over their overt behavior.

Human Versus Nonhuman Targets

Of the 160 community residents and students who completed Questionnarie A, 140 (88%) indicated that the target of their anger involved another person. In the majority (126) of these instances, the other person was the primary target whereas in the remainder (14) the human target was secondarily involved. In the latter instances, a nonhuman target was the recognized source of the anger, but the response became focused on some person associated with the incident.

There were 20 episodes that did not involve another person as part of the target. But in 11 of these, the respondents had become angry at a human institution or at themselves. This means that only 9 episodes (6% of the total) did not involve a human being or institution as an integral part of the target. And even in these 9 instances, indirect reference was often made to another person, and/or the non-human target was itself treated as though it were a person. For example, a student became angry at a car she was using when it malfunctioned, "after my sister had told me it drove fine." The student made it clear that she was not angry *at* her sister, but it was also evident that the assurances of her sister contributed to her anger. Another student became angry at the fact that he had no money for food, but added that he would not have been in the predicament had he "not *carelessly* gambled my money away" (emphasis in original). He was not angry at himself, strictly speaking, but he did impute some blame to himself as part of his anger.

The interpersonal nature of anger is even more starkly illustrated by several examples of anthropomorphism (i.e., the tendency to treat an inanimate object as though it were human). One woman became angry at being seriously ill and actually envisioned a little man (personifying her illness) at whom she could direct her anger. And a plumber who became angry at a trap he had installed (after it developed a hairline leak) described his response as follows: "I made the hole in the trap bigger, as if to say—'That's what you should look like if you're going to leak.' " When describing his motives, he added: "Silly, but if I'm doing my job, why can't the trap do its job?"

In short, there can be little doubt that anger is primarily an interpersonal emotion. Of course, at times we all do become angry at inanimate objects, and at impersonal circumstances; but that is not normative, and following such episodes, we may feel a little silly or embarrassed.[5]

One reason why anger is directed primarily at other persons is that people are typically the major source of pain and frustration in our lives. But there is perhaps an even more important reason. As will become more evident below, the typical episode of anger involves an attribution of responsibility, an accusation, so to speak, that the target has done something wrong. It follows that the target of anger must be a person or object (e.g., a human institution) to whom responsibility can be assigned.

---

[5] When daily records are kept, so that more mild episodes of anger are recorded, then the proportion of incidents involving a human target decreases. Nevertheless, the proportion remains high—70% or more (see Study III, Chapter 11).

The Type of Person Who Becomes the Target of Anger

If we limit consideration to the 140 incidents that involved another person, we may ask: What was the relationship between the angry individual and the target? This question can be answered both in terms of affectional relationships (e.g., whether the target was liked or disliked) and in terms of status relationships (e.g., whether the target had greater or less authority than the angry person).

Affectional relationships. In popular conception, anger and hate are closely related notions. This is also true in psychological theory. Thus, McDougall (1936) defined hate as "the general name of all sentiments in the structure of which the affective dispositions of anger and of fear are incorporated" (p. 436). Similarly, Izard (1977) suggests that hate is an "affective cognitive orientation" in which the affective component consists of some combination of anger, disgust, or contempt (pp. 95-96). However, when we examine the target of anger, as indicated by the responses of participants in the present survey, a somewhat different picture emerges. In 46 instances (33% of the episodes that involved another person), the target of anger was a "loved one." In another 30 instances (21%), the target was "someone you know well and like." Thus, in over 50% of the episodes, there was a positive affectional relationship between the angry person and the target. With regard to the remaining instances, 36 (26%) involved an acquaintance (e.g., a colleague or neighbor), and 17 (12%) involved a stranger. In only 11 episodes (8%) was the target "someone you know well and dislike."[6]

There are a number of reasons why a person is more likely to become angry at loved ones and friends, as opposed to strangers and/or disliked others; For example, close and continual contact with loved ones (friends, etc.) increases the chances that a provocation will occur; transgressions committed by loved ones are more likely to be cumulative and distressing; there is a stronger motivation to get loved ones to change their ways; and knowledge of what to expect from loved ones leads to greater confidence—less inhibition—in the expression (and experience) of anger.

The above reasons are not independent, and each is undoubtedly important in certain circumstances. But whatever the reason, it is of theoretical interest that, of the 140 subjects who became angry at another person, over 50% became angry at a loved one or friend, whereas less than 10% became angry at someone whom they disliked. Evidently, anger is more often associated with love than with hate. That is perhaps what La Rochefoucauld (1665/1959) had in mind when he observed that "if love be judged by most of its visible effects it looks more like hatred than friendship" (Maxim #72).

Of course, if the provocations that lead to anger are repeated often enough, that is, if anger is not effective in inducing change, then love may turn to hate (cf. McKellar, 1950). But that is not the ordinary course of events. Usually anger does

---

[6] Students were more likely than the community residents to become angry at someone who was well known and liked (22 vs. 8 episodes, $p < .01$). Community residents, by contrast, were more likely than students to become angry at loved ones (27 vs. 19 episodes) and at acquaintances (22 vs. 14 episodes).

lead to a satisfactory resolution. And in such instances, feelings of friendliness toward the offender may actually increase. Thus, Richardson (1918) observed that after a successful expression of anger there is often a desire to bestow favors on the offender, and he quotes Spinoza to the effect that "an act of offense may indirectly give origin to love."

This quotation by Spinoza, as well as the earlier one by La Rochefoucauld, suggest that close affectionate relationships are marked by a good deal of ambivalence. Goldstein (1975, p. 64 ff.) has also emphasized this point in accounting for the high incidence of violence (e.g., spouse abuse, crimes of passion) among family members and close friends. The establishment of a close relationship necessarily involves some loss of autonomy and freedom, and requires tolerance for the negative as well as the positive attributes of the other person. Anger is one way of coping with the conflict generated by the accommodations necessary to establish and maintain a close relationship. Given an "adequate" provocation, anger can—and usually does— have a beneficial outcome, as we shall see in Chapter 9. However, when ordinary anger fails, or the stress of accommodation becomes too great, violence may ensue.

Status relationships. According to Aristotle, we are most likely to become angry at inferiors, and least likely to become angry at those whom we fear or respect. A similar theme was also expressed by other historical figures, especially Lactantius and Aquinas (see Chapter 4). The contention receives some partial support from the present survey. Anger at "someone who had authority over you" was relatively infrequent (34 cases, or 24% of the episodes in which the target was another person). However, anger at "someone over whom you had authority" was even less frequent (23 cases, or 16% of the episodes). In the majority of the cases (81, or 58%) the target of anger was "an equal or peer."

Before interpreting these figures, it should be noted that the students in the sample had little opportunity to become angry at a subordinate; moreover, student culture legitimizes a certain amount of anger and aggression against instructors and other authority figures. It is therefore not surprising that only 1 student reported becoming angry at a subordinate, whereas 20 indicated that the target of their anger was a person who had authority over them. Among community residents the corresponding figures were 22 (for low-authority figures) and 14 (for high-authority figures). In this respect the data of the community residents are probably more representative. Other laboratory and field studies have also found that anger is more likely to be aroused by the actions of persons of low status than by similar actions on the part of high-status individuals (e.g., Doob & Gross, 1968, Harris, 1974).

On a psychological level, this effect is probably mediated in two ways: First, a provocation by a superior is more likely to be appraised as justified or legitimate than a similar provocation by a peer or subordinate; and second, even if a provocation by a superior is appraised as unjustified, it may lead to indifference or depression, rather than anger, if some form of direct or indirect action is not seen as a viable response.

Summary

Anger is primarily an interpersonal emotion. Even when anger is directed at an inanimate object, the target is liable to be personified. The most common target of anger is a loved one, friend, or acquaintance. Anger at strangers and at those whom we dislike is not usual (in part, perhaps, because we tend to give strangers the benefit of the doubt and to avoid those whom we dislike). The target is also liable to be an equal or peer, or else someone over whom we have authority. High status and authority, by contrast, seem to confer on a potential target a degree of immunity from anger.

The Instigation to Anger

We may love another "for himself," but we cannot be angry at another simply for himself. The object of anger involves not only a target but also an instigation. Indeed, in some cases, as when a person becomes angry at some perceived injustice, the instigation may even be divorced from any specific target; or, what amounts to much the same thing, the instigation may serve as its own (abstract) target. Because of the importance of the instigation in determining the object of anger, and hence for distinguishing anger from other emotional states, we will begin with a review of previous attempts to classify the instigations to anger.

The Nature of the Instigation

In Richardson's (1918) study, 12 persons (10 graduate students at Clark University and 2 others) were asked to observe and keep daily records of their anger for period of at least 3 months. A total of 600 incidents were recorded. Richardson divided the instigations into two broad categories—*irritation* (frustration, pain, etc.) and *negative self-feelings* (humiliation, hurt feelings, etc.). He found that the latter type of instigation was more directly and immediately related to anger, although he presents no exact figures.

Several other attempts to classify the instigations to anger are presented in Table 8-2. In each of these studies, subjects were asked to keep a daily record ot their anger or to provide a brief open-ended description of recent incidents. The instigations were then divided into mutually exclusive categories. Gates (1926) and Meltzer (1933) treated all instances of anger as the result of some kind of frustration or thwarting of routine activities (e.g., the interruption of sleep or habitual responses) and the thwarting of self-assertive impulses. Following a scheme developed by Woodworth (1921), self-assertion was further divided into three subcategories: (a) "defensive reactions to persons," provoked by threats to self-esteem, attempts at domination by others, and the like; (b) "aggressive reactions to persons," provoked by disobedience, refusals of a request, or other attempts by the target to resist the influence of the angry person, and (c) "defensive reactions to things," provoked by inanimate objects (e.g., equipment malfunction) which interfere with "mastery" or ego-involving behavior.

As can be seen from Table 8-2, most of the instigations reported by Gates and Meltzer involved frustration of self-assertive activities. This is particularly true of the Meltzer study. (The difference between the two studies in this regard may be

Table 8-2. Instigations to Anger as Classified in Previous Studies

Study	Sample	Number of incidents reported	Nature of the instigation	Percentage of incidents
Gates (1926)	51 college students; female	All incidents during 1 week; total = 145	Frustration of routine activities	37
			Frustration of self-assertive activities 1). defensive reactions to persons (36%) 2). assertive reactions to persons (7%) 3). defensive reactions to things (21%)	64
Meltzer (1933)	93 college students; male and female	All incidents during 1 week; total = 393	Frustration of routine activities	14
			Frustration of self-assertive activities 1). defensive reactions to persons (38%) 2). assertive reactions to persons (13%) 3). defensive reactions to things (35%)	86
Anastasi, Cohen, and Spatz (1948)	38 college students; female	All incidents during 1 week; total = 598	Thwarted plans	52
			Inferiority and loss of prestige	21
			Schoolwork	13
			Family relationships	10
			Abstract problems	5
McKellar (1949)	200 adult education students; male and female	1 or 2 recent incidents; total = 379	Need situations	47
			Personality situations	53

Note. From Averill (1979).

due to the fact that Meltzer defined frustration of routine activities somewhat differently—and more narrowly—than did Gates.) According to Gates, a defensive reaction to persons is particularly characteristic of the most intense episodes of anger.

Anastasi, Cohen, and Spatz (1948) did not impose a logically consistent classification on their data; rather, they attempted "to adhere as closely as possible to the subject's own reports." The result was a fivefold classification: thwarted plans; inferiority or loss of prestige (e.g., sarcastic comments); schoolwork (e.g., lengthy assignments); family relations (e.g., sibling rivalry); and abstract problems (e.g., seeing a classmate cheat or witnessing intolerance toward others). These five categories accounted for 52%, 21%, 13%, 10%, and 5%, respectively, of the anger reported by subjects.

As a final example, McKellar (1950) distinguished between *need situations* and *personality situations* in the instigation to anger. Need situations, which accounted for approximately 44% of the incidents analyzed by McKellar, included any interference with the pursuit of a goal, such as missing a bus. Personality situations, which accounted for 54% of the instigations, included the imposition of physical or mental pain or the encroachment upon personal values, status, possessions, and the like. Examples of such situations were criticisms of ideas, work, clothing, or friends. (Of the cases reported by McKellar, 2% could not be classified in either of these two categories.)

From this brief review of previous research it is evident that the classification of "typical" instigations to anger is no simple matter. Most classifications seem to be either too broad (e.g., the dichotomies of Richardson and McKellar) or too specific to a given population (e.g., the "schoolwork" category of Anastasi et al.) or to be based on a priori schemes of questionable validity (e.g., the threefold division of self-assertive needs used by Gates and Meltzer). One source of difficulty has been the tendency to focus on the specific kinds of incidents that arouse anger (e.g., the interruption of some activity, criticism, an extended work assignment) rather than on the manner in which such incidents are evaluated by the individuals involved. For example, did the angry person consider the interruption (criticism, etc.) to be justified? Could the precipitating event have been avoided with a little care and foresight? And so forth.

Let us turn now to the results of the present survey. Subjects were asked to evaluate the incident that made them angry, first in terms of its fortuitousness and/or justification, and then in terms of its specific characteristics. With regard to the former, four mutually exclusive categories were presented in the questionnaire, and subjects were asked to select the category which best described the incident that made them angry. The results are presented in Table 8-3. The vast majority of subjects indicated that the incident was either voluntary and unjustified (51%) or a potentially avoidable accident or event (31%). Relatively few persons became angry at events which they considered voluntary but justified (11%) or unavoidable (7%).

That half the subjects appraised the instigation as "voluntary and unjustified" implies that moral fault or blame is commonly involved in the instigation to anger.

Table 8-3. Instigation to Anger Described in Terms of Justification

Justification	Percentage of incidents ($n = 160$)
1. Voluntary and unjustified: the instigator knew what he/she was doing, but he/she had no right to do it.	51
2. Potentially avoidable accident or event: the result of negligence, carelessness, or lack of foresight	31
3. Voluntary and justified: the instigator knew what he/she was doing and had a right to do it.	11
4. Unavoidable accident or event: it could not have been foreseen or was beyond anyone's control.	7

This finding is, of course, quite consistent with the historical teachings on anger reviewed earlier. It also is consistent with incidental observations made by Richardson (1918), who noted that irritation is more likely to develop into anger if there is a breach of fairness or justice. Richardson further observed that "in some extreme cases the subject may assume a make-believe attitude and trump up reasons to suit his own ends regardless of the facts" (p. 17). McKellar (1950) also has reported that anger is likely to be severe, and may even develop into long-term attitudes of resentment and hatred, if the instigation involves a morally unjustified act.

Moral fault or blame is not, however, the only factor involved in the instigation to anger. Nearly one-third of the subjects indicated that they became angry at a "potentially avoidable accident or event." This suggests that anger is commonly used to correct behavior, even when moral wrong is not implied. Drawing an analogy with the law (see Chapter 5), it might be said that angry appraisals are like judgments rendered in civil as well as criminal cases.

The above considerations illustrate one reason why it is so difficult to specify with any precision and finality the nature of the instigation to anger. Almost any potential harm may provoke anger if it is appraised as unjustified and/or avoidable. Conversely, any circumstance which makes an event appear justifiable and/or unvoidable will help mitigate the instigation. And it should go without saying that what is considered justifiable (or unavoidable) is dependent in large measure on social norms and customs, and hence may vary from one group to another, from one context to another, and from one time to another.

This does not mean that the specific nature of the precipitating event is devoid of practical or theoretical interest. If anger serves as an informal means of social control, then certain kinds of instigations should be more important than others, regardless of their justification. Violations of social and/or personal norms, for example, should be more important than the thwarting of routine activities. To gather data on this issue, six specific factors were described in Questionnaire A, and subjects were asked to rate *each* on a 3-point scale depending upon whether it was (0) "not at all," (1) "somewhat," or (2) "very much" involved in the incident that made them angry. The six factors are listed in Table 8-4, rank ordered by degree of involvement.

Frustration, or the interruption of some ongoing or planned activity, was the single factor most frequently mentioned. This is not particularly surprising. As discussed in Chapter 6, frustration has often been postulated as a major instigation to anger. But frustration by itself is seldom a sufficient condition for anger. Thus, of the 129 subjects (81% of the total) who mentioned frustration, nearly all—124— indicated that one or more of the following factors also were somewhat or very much involved in their anger: violation of important personal expectations or wishes (90 subjects), violation of socially accepted ways of behaving (81 subjects), a loss of personal pride (81 subjects), possible or actual property damage (23 subjects), and possible or actual physical injury (19 subjects).

The above results might be interpreted in a number of different ways. For example, the violation of personal and social norms, the loss of pride, potential injury, and so on could be interpreted as causes of frustrations, varieties of frustration, or factors in addition to frustration.These different interpretations are possible because frustration is a very elastic concept—one that can be stretched to fit almost any circumstance. For scientific purposes, it might be helpful if we could get rid of the concept of frustration entirely. That however, it not likely to occur. The safest conclusion would therefore seem to be that frustration is an important but seldom sufficient condition for anger.[7]

After frustration, three kinds of instigation were mentioned with almost equal frequency (by about 65% of the subjects). These were (1) a loss of self-esteem, (2) a violation of personal wishes or expectations, and (3) a violation of socially accepted ways of behaving.[8]

In considering the first of these factors it is important to take into acount a person's customary level of self-esteem as well as the particular instigating circumstance. A number of investigators have observed that persons of low self-esteem are especially prone to anger and aggression (e.g., Rosenbaum & DeCharms, 1960; Veldman & Worchel, 1961; Toch, 1969; Worchel, 1960). Presumably such persons are especially vulnerable to further threats to their already fragile sense of personal

---

[7] Experimental research related to frustration was discussed in Chapter 6. There, too, it was concluded that frustration per se seldom leads to anger or aggression, unless the frustration is particularly severe and/or arbitrary.

[8] This rank ordering of instigations is, of course, dependent on the list of options presented in Questionnaire A, as well as on the actual occurrence of events. In Study IV (Chapter 12), possible instigations were described somewhat differently than they were in the present study; and in that case, the most frequently mentioned instigation (by 87% of the subjects) was "an action which was not in keeping with the kind of relationship you have or would like to have with [the instigator], or with what you expect from [the instigator]."

Table 8-4. Instigation to Anger Described in Terms of Intrinsic Characteristics

Factors involved in the instigation to anger	Mean rating[a]	Percentage of subjects marking "somewhat" or "very much"[b]
1. Frustration or the interruption of some ongoing or planned activity	1.38	82
2. An event, action, or attitude which resulted in a loss of personal pride, self-esteem, or sense of personal worth	1.02	64
3. Violation of expectations and wishes which are important to you but which may not be widely shared by others	.99	68
4. Violation of socially accepted ways of behaving or widely shared rules of conduct	.90	63
5. Possible or actual property damage	.29	19
6. Possible or actual physical injury and/or pain	.23	14

[a] 0 = not at all; 1 = somewhat; 2 = very much.
[b] n = 160.

worth. However, the relationship between a person's customary level of self-esteem and the instigation to anger is undoubtedly complex. For example, persons with very low self-esteem may perceive a threat as justified (e.g., as congruent with their own self-image), or they may not believe that they are capable of an effective response. In either case, such a person would more likely respond with anxiety and/or depression than with anger. At the other extreme, persons with high self-esteem are less likely than others to perceive as threatening minor slights or rebuffs. There may thus be a curvilinear relationship between level of self-esteem and susceptibility to anger. Though for opposite reasons, persons of very low and very high self-esteem may not respond with anger unless an insult is particularly severe and unambiguous.

Let us turn now to the violation of personal expectations and wishes, which was also mentioned by about 68% of the participants. The examples in the questionnaire that were used to illustrate this type if instigation emphasized such incidents as someone disregarding "one of your pet likes or dislikes," a child or spouse not acting "in line with your expectations," or dislike for "a neighbor's life-style." In line with these examples, the kinds of incidents which subjects most frequently des-

cribed in connection with the item were the breaking of family rules or understand-
ings (especially by children); being let down by friends or co-workers; disagreeing
with the opinions and attitudes of another; and the like. The thrust of these responses
is thus toward the violation of personal norms or standards and not simply toward
the interruption or frustration of some activity.

When personal expectations are widely shared by others, we may speak of social
norms. The violation of social norms (i.e., of socially accepted ways of behaving)
was mentioned by 63% of the subjects as a factor in their anger. This is a rather high
percentage, especially in view of the fact that Anastasi et al. found that only 5% of
the incidents of anger they surveyed involved "abstract problems," a category that
corresponds roughly to the violation of social norms (see Table 8-2). The reason
for the wide discrepancy between the results of Anastasi et al. and the present findings is perhaps twofold. In the first place, people often do not become very angry
at "abstract problems" unless such problems affect them personally, for example,
by interfering with some planned activity or by threatening their self-esteem.
Therefore, when Anastasi et al. divided the instigations into mutually exclusive
categories on the basis of the "most important" factor involved, relatively few
would have fallen into the cateogry of abstract problems. In the second place, the
subjects in the present survey—and not the experimenter, as in Anastasi's study—
chose what factors were involved in the instigation, and they were not constrained to
choose a single most important factor. It is apparent from the open-ended responses
that many subjects viewed nearly any frustration, chastisement, or threat to the self
as a violation of social norms, provided that it also was regarded as unjustified and/
or unavoidable.

For the sake of completeness, note should also be made of the relatively low
incidence of possible or actual physical injury and property damage as precipitating
factors (see items 5 and 6, Table 8-4). Obviously this does not mean that such factors are unimportant when they occur. However, they occur relatively infrequently
in everyday affairs, whereas psychological and/or interpersonal threats are quite
common.

Summary

The instigations to anger are many and varied, and they defy any simple classification scheme. Frustration, loss of self-esteem, or a threat to an interpersonal relationship (see Chapter 12) seem to be the major "umbrella categories" that people
use to describe the events that make them angry. But these categories are too broad
and vague to be very informative. The major factors involved in the instigation
to anger appear to be normative. Normative standards may be involved in at least
two ways. First, any frustration, loss of self-esteem, and so on may violate general
social norms if the incident is considered unjustified or avoidable (e.g., due to negligence or lack of foresight). In the present study, approximately 80% of the subjects
regarded the instigation to be either unjustified or avoidable. Second, the instigation
may consist of a violation of some specific social and/or personal expectancy. A
breach of etiquette or the breaking of an agreement would be examples. Each of

these categories (i.e., the violation of social and/or personal expectancies) was marked by about 65% of the subjects.

Motives for Anger

Motives help constitute the third aspect of the object of anger, namely, the objective. This aspect is more complicated, both conceptually and empirically, than either the target or the instigation. The objective is what the instigation calls for, and the target "affords," by way of response. But that is looking at it from the side of the eliciting conditions. From the subject's side, the objective corresponds roughly to the motive, aim, or goal of the response.

In the present section, we will consider the motives that subjects had (or believed they had) for becoming angry. The general relationship between motivation and emotion has been discussed in Chapter 6. To recapitulate briefly, behavior is here viewed as forming a heirarchy of superordinate and subsidiary responses. Following Chein (1972), a superordinate act can be considered the motive for an act lower in the hierarchy if the latter serves to complete the former.

In order to clarify on an intuitive level the ways in which anger can be motivated, it was explained to subjects in the questionnaire that

> sometimes when we become angry, we may simply want to get back at the person or thing that angered us. Often, however, additional motives are involved in our anger. For example, we may become angry at a child for running into the street in order to protect him/her from injury; or we may become angry in order to get someone to help us out with some work. Although such motives are quite common, *we typically are not fully aware of them at the time of our anger.* It may only be in looking back and thinking carefully about the incident that we come to realize all that was involved in our anger.

Subjects were then asked to read through a list of 11 motives, each of which was accompanied by several examples. After reading the enitre list, subjects rated each motive on a 3-point scale, indicating how much it was involved in their anger (0 = not at all; 1 = somewhat; and 2 = very much). The list of motives, ranked according to the mean ratings, is presented in Talbe 8-5.

As can be seen, the most frequently endorsed motive (by 63% of the subjects) was "to assert your authority or independence, or to improve your image." This makes sense in view of the fact that the frustration of some ongoing or planned activity, a loss of pride or self-esteem, and/or the violation of personal expectations were the most frequently mentioned instigations to anger. On a very broad level, then, it would seem that anger is often subsidiary to the more inclusive goal of achieving personal control over a situation and reestablishing the sense of personal worth that is often associated with such control. This is one of the most fundamental motives of human behavior, and it incorporates many subsidiary responses, not just anger.

Table 8-5. Motives Subjects Offered for Becoming Angry.

Motive	Mean rating[a]	Percentage of subjects marking "somewhat" or "very much"[b]
1. To assert your authority or independence, or to improve your image	.86	63
2. To get back at, or gain revenge on, the instigator for the present incident	.79	57
3. To bring about a change in the behavior of the instigator primarily for your own good	.78	54
4. To bring about a change in the behavior of the instigator primarily for his/her own good[c]	.70	49
5. To strengthen a relationship with the instigator[c]	.66	46
6. To get even for past wrongs by the instigator	.54	39
7. To let off steam over miscellaneous frustrations of the day which had nothing to do with the present incident	.50	37
8. To express your general dislike for the instigator	.38	28
9. To get the instigator to do something for you	.28	22
10. To break off a relationship with the instigator	.24	18
11. To get out of doing something for the instigator	.18	13

[a] 0 = not at all; 1 = somewhat; 2 = very much.
[b] $n = 160$.
[c] There were statistically significant differences between the mean ratings of community residents and students on these motives. Specifically, the community residents expressed a stronger desire to bring about a change for the instigator's good ($mr = .84$ vs. .56) and to strengthen a relationship with the instigator (.84 vs. .48). For additional details, see Footnote 9, p. 178.

The next most frequently mentioned motive (by 57% of the subjects) was "to get back at, or gain revenge on, the instigator for the present incident." It is somewhat surprising that this motive was not endorsed by even more subjects, for it can almost be taken as a definition of anger. (Compare, for example, Aristotle's definition of anger as an impulse "to conspicuous revenge for a conspicuous slight"—see Chapter 3.) Perhaps some subjects did not endorse this item because it seemed too universally applicable, and hence did not relate the episode to any broader concerns the subjects may have had.

The third and fourth most frequently endorsed motives had to do with changing the behavior of the instigator, either for the angry person's own good (54%) or for the instigator's own good (49%). These two motives are, of course, not incompatible. Since most of the angry incidents were directed at loved ones, friends, or acquaintances (e.g., associates, neighbors), many of the things that the angry person might consider good for himself or herself could also be considered good for the instigator, and vice versa. This is illustrated by the fact that the next most frequently endorsed motive (45%) was "to strengthen a relationship with the instigator." Also, if anger serves as an informal means of social control, one of its ultimate goals should be a change in the behavior of the instigator for mutual good. In the next chapter, we shall examine how well this goal is achieved.

Not all anger focuses on the immediate incident. For example, 39% of the subjects indicated that they wanted "to get even for past wrongs," and 37% wanted "to 'let off steam' over miscellaneous frustrations." Nor was all anger constructively motivated. A sizable minority of subjects wanted "to express dislike for the instigator" (38%). "To get the instigator to do something for you" (e.g., through intimidation) was endorsed by 22% of the subjects, while 18% wanted to break off a relationship with the instigator. Finally, 15% of the subjects indicated that they wanted to get out of doing something for the instigator.[9]

Before analyzing the above results further, a possible objection should be considered. Self-reports of psychological—and especially motivational—processes have long been suspect. Some of the difficulties inherent in the use of self-reports have already been discussed in Chapter 7. At this point, only a few additional comments will be made. Specifically, how do we know that the reasons offered by people for becoming angry represent true motives and are not simply post hoc rationalizations for their behavior?

---

[9] A multivariate analysis of variance was performed on the list of motives, using the sample of subjects (community residents vs. students) as the independent variable. The overall F ratio was only marginally significant ($p < .10$). Two of the univariate analyses did, however, yield statistically significant results. Specifically, the community residents were more likely to say that they wished to strengthen a relationship with the instigator ($p < .01$) and that they became angry for the instigator's own good ($p < .05$). These results are consistent with those noted earlier, namely, that the community residents were more likely to become angry at a loved one, and that their anger was likely to be less intense. It does not follow, however, that the community residents were less expressive of their anger than were the students. As will be seen in Chapter 9, just the opposite was the case.

In answering this question, it should first be noted that the concept of motivation as used here does not refer to some internal cognitive process or hidden "drive."
Rather, it refers to the way in which behavior is interconnected, with lower order
responses being subsidiary to higher order responses.[10] Of course, like any complex
set of circumstances, the interconnectedness of behavior is not always apparent or
easy to recognize. Therefore, people often impose meaning on their behavior after
the fact in order to make their responses appear more rational or socially desirable
than was actually the case. Take, for example, a motive like getting the instigator
to change for his or her own good. Some subjects who endorsed this item took a
rather broad view of what was for the instigator's good. It is as though they reasoned
somewhat as follows: "From my point of view, the instigator was acting in an
unjust or obnoxious way. Moreover, my point of view is basically correct (i.e., it
reflects the way people should behave). Therefore, if the instigator changes because
of my anger, then it will have been for his or her own good."

A neutral observer might not agree with the premises of such an argument (e.g.,
that the subject's point of view is basically correct), but the logic is not unsound.
Perhaps the most that can be said is that the conclusion of the argument assumes a
greater interconnectedness of behavior than actually exists.

The above considerations do not mean, of course, that the responses of subjects
can be naively taken at face value. In Chapter 10, therefore, we will explore the
motives for anger from the perspective of the target. As will be seen, the major
conclusions of the present analysis do not require revision as a function of whether
the incident is described from the point of view of the angry person or the target.

Returning now to the list of motives presented in Table 8-5, we see that most
subjects indicated that more than one motive was involved in their anger. To help
identify common patterns of motivation, ratings of the 11 motives were intercorre-
lated, and a factor analysis (principal components) was performed. Three factors
had eigenvalues greater than unity, and these were rotated orthogonally, using the
varimax method. The results are presented in Table 8-6.

The first factor presented in Table 8-6 seems to represent a kind of *malevolent*
anger. It is best characterized by such motives as "to express dislike," "to break off
a relationship," and "to gain revenge for the present incident." "To get even for
past wrongs," and "to bring about a change in the behavior of the instigator for
your own good" also had moderately high loadings on this factor. These motives
are not, however, unique to malevolent anger.

The second factor represents a more *constructive* use of anger. "To strengthen a
relationship" is the motive that best characterizes this dimension. "To assert
authority, or imporve your image," "to bring about a change in the behavior of the
instigator for his or her own good," and "to get the instigator to do something for
you" also had moderate loadings on this factor. Constructive anger thus appears to
be a complex blend of self-centered and altruistic motives.

---

[10] In the present context, *response* refers to a goal-directed act. That is, responses
are defined in terms of their effects upon the environment as well as in terms of
topography (the specific movements made). See Chapter 6 for a more complete
discussion of this and related points.

Table 8-6. Rotated Orthogonal Factor Loadings for the Complete List of 11 Motives

Motive	Rank order of endorsement	Factor A (malevolent anger)	Factor B (constructive anger)	Factor C (fractious anger)
To express dislike for the instigator	8	.77		
To break off a relationship	10	.49		-.31
To gain revenge for the present incident	2	.44		-.40
To get even for past wrongs	6	.44	.31	
To bring about a change for your own good	3	.35	.43	
To strengthen a relationship	5		.63	
To assert authority or independence	1		.43	
To bring about a change for the instigator's good	4		.32	
To get the instigator to do something for you	9		.37	
To let off steam over miscellaneous frustrations	7			.32
To get out of doing something for the instigator	11			

The third factor represents a kind of *fractious* anger. It is not motivated by revenge, nor does the angry person wish to break off a relationship. Rather, fractious anger involves "letting off steam" occasioned by miscellaneous frustrations that are unrelated to the precipitating incident.

Although the three kinds of anger described above—malevolent, constructive, and fractious—make sense logically as well as statistically, it should also be noted that together they account for only 47% of the variance in the factor solution presented in Table 8-6. Evidently there was a considerable amount of variability in the patterning of motivation. One source of such variablility might be the target of anger. A second factor analysis was therefore performed, using only those episodes where the target involved another person (n = 140). Malevolent and fractious anger again emerged as separate dimensions. Constructive anger, however, divided into two independent factors. One of these factors was defined by the following three motives (with loadings in parentheses):

To get even for past wrongs (.52)
To get the instigator to change for your (the angry person's) own good (.49)
To gain revenge for the present incident (.34)

This is a kind of revengeful anger, reflecting long-standing discontents as well as reaction to the immediate incident. It is "constructive" only in the sense that there is no suggestion of dislike for the instigator (as in the case of malevolent anger). The other factor into which constructive anger decomposed retained more of the qualities of the original. It was defined by the following three motives:

To assert authority or independence (.58)
To strengthen a relationship (.53)
To get the instigator to do something for you (.31)

Of course, even among human targets the nature of the motivation might vary depending upon whether the individual was a loved one, a stranger, and so on. In order to explore this possibility, analyses of variance were performed in which the relationship with the target was the independent variable and the motives for anger were the dependent varables. Motives which showed significant differences as a function of the target are shown in Table 8-7.

As can be seen, the three motives most characteristic of malevolent anger ("to express dislike," "to break off a relationship," and "to gain revenge for the present incident") tended to be focused primarily on persons who were well known but disliked. The motive "to get even for past wrongs," which loaded on both the malevolent and constructive factors, was also endorsed most frequently when the target was disliked. Not surprisingly, the desire to "strengthen a relationship" was most common when the target was a loved one or someone who was well known and liked. This is the primary motive defining constructive anger.

It will be noted that the motive that best defined fractious anger ("to let off steam") is not listed in Table 8-7. It received approximately equal ratings regardless of the target. This supports the notion that fractious anger has more to do with the frustrations and concerns of the angry person than with the precipitating incident. Other motives also did not vary significantly as a function of the target. This is true, for example, of the most frequently endorsed of all the motives, namely, "to assert your authority or independence, or to improve your image." A person can assert authority, and so forth, in order to break off a relationship as well as to strengthen it. Obviously, one must be cautious about interpreting any given motive as intrinsically malevolent or constructive. Much depends on the circumstances.

Table 8-7. Differences among the Mean Ratings[a] of Motives as a Function of the Target of the Anger

Motive	Loved one (n = 46)	Know well and like (n = 30)	Know well and dislike (n = 11)	Acquaintance (n = 36)	Stranger (n = 17)	F ratio
Express dislike	.09$_a$	.17$_a$	1.36$_c$	.39$_{ab}$	.71$_b$	14.76***
Break off a relationship	.24$_a$	.10$_a$	1.18$_b$	.19$_a$	.18$_a$	9.54***
Gain revenge for present incident	.93$_{ab}$	.80$_a$	1.55$_b$	.72$_a$	.71$_a$	2.89*
Get even for past wrongs	.48$_a$	.67$_{ab}$	1.36$_b$	.50$_a$	.41$_a$	3.84**
Strengthen a relationship	1.09$_b$	.83$_{ab}$	.27$_a$	.56$_a$	.24$_a$	6.27**

Note. For any given motive, values with the same subscript do not differ significantly from one another, using the Tukey α procedure.
[a] 0 = not at all; 1 = somewhat; 2 = very much.
*$p < .05$.
**$p < .01$.
***$p < .001$.

Summary

The typical angry episode forms part of a behavioral hierarchy, that is, is motivated by the broader concerns of the individual. On the basis of the motives involved, three kinds of anger may be distinguished—malevolent, constructive, and fractious. Malevolent anger perhaps best fits the popular conception of this emotion. Its objective is to express dislike and to break off a relationship. Malevolent anger is, however, less frequent than constructive anger, both in terms of the motives involved and in terms of the typical target (e.g., someone who is disliked). Constructive anger, by contrast, is characterized by a desire to strengthen a relationship with the instigator, who is typically a friend or loved one. This kind of anger is, however, rather poorly defined, and tends to decompose into subvarieties. Also, it should not be concluded that the motives for constructive anger are necessarily altruistic. Anger tends to be self-centered even when constructive. But in a close interpersonal relationship, the angry person is liable to believe that what is good for himself is also good for the target, and vice versa. Finally, with regard to fractious anger, this is a diffuse response, a kind of letting off of steam, and perhaps should not even be called anger except in a metaphorical sense.

Concluding Observations

Anger is a very common emotion. Among the participants in the present study, approximately 85% indicated that they had become angry *at least* once during the prior week; and that is undoubtedly an underestimate, since many minor incidents of anger are quickly forgotten or are later reinterpreted as some other state (e.g., irritation, annoyance). The most frequent target of anger is a loved one, friend, or acquaintance. Opportunity is undoubtedly an important factor here—we tend to avoid contact with those whom we dislike, and strangers seldom threaten us. But opportunity does not negate the fact that anger is more frequently associated with those we like (e.g., a parent, spouse, child, friend) than with those we dislike. One consequence of this fact is that anger is, more often than not, constructively motivated—the objective is not primarily to harm or inflict pain on the target, but rather to change the conditions that led to the instigation. This may involve getting the target to recognize one's own rights and autonomy, or in some other way to change his or her behavior for the betterment of the relationship.

Regardless of the target or the motive (objective), the instigation to anger—in the overwhelming majority of cases—involves some perceived wrong. This might be an action on the part of the instigator that is potentially hurtful (either to the angry person, to the instigator himself, and/or to a third party) and that is regarded as unjustified by the angry person; or the instigation might be an act that, while not intentional, could have been avoided with sufficient care and forethought.

The findings that anger is typically initiated by an appraised wrong, is directed toward a friend or loved one, and is constructively motivated are consistent with the notion that anger serves a positive social function by helping to regulate interpersonal relations. But there are still other aspects of anger that must be considered before such a conclusion can be accepted—for example, the manner in which anger is typically expressed and the consequences of anger.

Chapter 9

Anger as Experienced by the Angry Person: Responses and Consequences

Anger can be expressed in a great variety of ways. The present chapter explores the meaning and significance of some of those ways. We will begin by reviewing prior research on the everyday expression of anger, and then continue with our presentation of the results of Study I.

In order to lend some substance and organization to the discussion, it will be helpful to have a foil to serve as a contrast. That foil is the common assumption that the fundamental response tendency during anger is to strike out or to engage in some form of physical aggression. This assumption stems, in turn, from an even prior assumption, namely, that anger is a biologically primitive response. According to Izard (1977), who represents this point of view, the biological significance of anger "lay in its ability to mobilize one's energy and make one capable of defending oneself with great vigor and energy" (p. 333). Izard recognizes, of course, that anger does not usually result in physical aggression; but this, he believes, is the result of social adjustment. In order to meet social and ethical standards, we learn "to respond to anger with words and with enough tact to keep from angering the other person and cutting off communication" (p. 334).

In previous chapters I have presented a number of theoretical and empirical arguments against the kind of position adumbrated by Izard, and I have argued instead that anger is basically a social construction. It is very difficult, if not impossible, to prove or disprove either point of view in a rigorous or definitive way. Nevertheless, the tendencies people feel, the responses they typically make, and the perceived outcomes of those responses are certainly relevant considerations.

A Review of Prior Research

Since responses during anger are so variable, it is necessary to review previous research, not only to place the results of the present study in context, but also to identify any consistent trends in the data. Let us begin with Richardson's (1918) study or 12 persons, each of whom kept a record of his or her anger over a period of at least 3 months. A total of 600 angry incidents were recorded, in which 1,468 different responses were made (i.e., there was an average of 2.4 responses per incident).

Richardson was primarily interested in "mental behavior" rather than the overt expression of anger. Therefore, most of the responses he studied were the thoughts and feelings of subjects. He divided these into three main kinds: *Attributive reactions* (any hostile thought or impulse); *contrary reactions* (a friendly or overpolite attitude, or search for mitigating circumstances); and *indifferent reactions* (apathetically ignoring the offense, or taking an "I don't care" attitude). The relative frequencies of these three types of response are shown in Table 9-1.

According to Richardson: "The initial reaction to anger is always of the attributive type." This would seem to confirm the close linkage between anger and aggression. However, the ubiquity of the attributive response as reported by Richardson is due, in part, to the broadness of the category. Richardson counted as attributive any hostile impulse, no matter how inhibited, disguised, or indirect its expression. Richardson actually observed no real attack "in which blows were struck except with those persons who have the correction of children" (pp. 33-34). He also observed "few real quarrels" on the verbal level. The most common attributive reaction was an imaginary attack, either verbal or physical, but primarily the former. The relative preponderance of verbal as opposed to physical aggression, even on the imaginary level, is an important issue about which we will have more to say later in the chapter. Other common attributive reactions reported by Richardson were witticisms, irony, irascible play or mock attacks, an imaginary exaltation of the self (but without necessarily humiliating the offender), a resolution to do something about the situation in the future, and so forth.

In spite of the ubiquity of the attributive (hostile) reaction, a contrary (friendly) response was also observed in more than 40% of the episodes. A contrary reaction was especially common in situations where the instigator was an intimate friend or someone with whom the angry person had to get along. According to Richardson, the contrary reaction is secondary to the attributive reaction. "After the anger has gone so far, the subject suddenly assumes a friendly attitude as if there were no emotion. . . . [But] whenever the attributive reaction is satisfactory, the contrary reaction is not resorted to" (pp. 47, 48).

Table 9-1. Types and Relative Frequencies of Anger Responses ("Mental Behavior") Based on Observations by Richardson (1918).

Type of response	Number of responses (total = 1,468)	Percentage of total responses	Percentage of episodes[a] (n = 600)
Attributive (hostile)	1,042	71	100
Contrary (friendly)	264	18	44
Indifferent	162	11	27

[a] The percentage of episodes in which a particular kind of response occurred is an estimate based on Richardson's assertion that an attributive reaction was an invariable accompaniment of anger and on the assumption that only one contrary or indifferent reaction occurred per episode.

Finally, when there was nothing else that could be done, the angry person often adopted an attitude of "What's the use?" or "I don't care." Such indifferent reactions occurred in about a quarter of the episodes. Richardson also noted that if an indifferent reaction occurs during the initial stages of anger, the emotion does not fully develop.

To summarize, Richardson's findings illustrate the close link between anger and aggressive impulses. It is important to note, however, that the aggression he observed was primarily verbal or symbolic (even when unexpressed). Overt physical aggression seldom occurred, and then mostly in connection with the correction (punishment) of children. In approximately 44% of the incidents, anger also led to a contrary or friendly reaction, particularly if the offender was a friend or acquaintance and/or if an attributive reaction appeared to be counterproductive. If nothing at all could be done about the situation, anger was sometimes (in about 25% of the incidents) replaced by indifference or apathy.

The above results are, of course, limited by the small sample of subjects (12) studied by Richardson, by the broadness of his categories, and by his emphasis on "mental behavior" as opposed to the actual expression of anger. A more fine-grained, but in many respects conceptually less satisfying, picture of anger is provided by Gates (1926). As described in Chapter 7, Gates asked 51 undergraudate students at Barnard College (all women) to keep a diary of each time they became angry during a 1-week period. In addition to information about eliciting conditions, the students were asked to list the responses they made. A total of 300 responses were recorded, an average of 2.1 for each of the 145 episodes of anger experienced by the subjects. Gates organized the responses as in Table 9-2.

In Gates's own words, the data in Table 9-2 present "an amusing picture of the responses of the young college girl to offending persons or objects and also an enlightening commentary on the inefficiency of human instinctive reactions" (p. 332). It is difficult to argue with this assessment. Nevertheless, Gates's observation contains two important—and questionable—assumptions. It assumes, first, that anger is characterized by "instinctive reactions" (direct aggression against the offender, presumably); and second, that the responses displayed by the subjects were, for the most part, ineffective substitutes for, or degraded versions of, those instinctive reactions. Actually, Gates does not present any direct evidence on the efficacy of the behavior displayed; for example, on whether making an angry exclamation or refusing to speak had its desired effect.

There are several other features about the data reported in Table 9-2 that deserve brief comment. First, it will be noted that some form of verbal behavior (excited talking and/or an angry retort) occurred in 40% of the episodes, whereas physical aggression was rare (2%). This agrees with the general trend of the data reported by Richardson. In contrast to Richardson, however, Gates observed few contrary reactions and no indifferent reactions. This probably reflects, in large part, differences in recording biases in the two studies; instructions about what kinds of responses to record also accounts for the frequent report of expressive and physiological reactions on the part of Gates's subjects. We shall have more to say about these kinds of responses later.

Table 9-2. Characteristic Responses During Anger Based on Data Reported by Gates (1926)

Type of response	Number of responses (total = 300)	Percentage of total responses	Percentage of episodes (n = 145)
Gross bodily responses directed at offending object:			
Excited talking or angry exclamation	32	10.7	22.1
Angry, sarcastic, sulky retort	26	8.7	17.9
Restless behavior (e.g., pacing, tossing in bed, shifting in chair)	20	6.7	13.8
Refusal to speak or to look at the offender	18	6.0	12.4
Violence to inanimate objects	10	3.3	6.9
Sudden exit from room	7	2.3	4.8
Grimace or glaring and staring at offender	5	1.7	3.4
Violence to offender (slap, shake)	3	1.0	2.1
Pleasant reply	3	1.0	2.1
Refusal of food	2	.7	1.4
Part total	126	42.0	86.9
Expressive movements:			
Unpleasant facial expression (frown)	30	10.0	20.1
Biting of fingers or lips	13	4.3	9.0
Clenching teeth or hands	12	4.0	8.3
Body tense	10	3.3	6.9
Stamping foot	8	2.7	5.5
Tears in eyes	8	2.7	5.5
Eyes flashed, stared, popped	3	1.0	2.1
Part total	84	28.0	57.9
Activities of sympathetic system and adrenal glands (mainly)			
Gasp, heavy or rapid breathing	28	9.3	19.3
"Hot" feeling	19	6.3	13.1
Flushing	13	4.3	9.0
Fast heartbeat	12	4.0	8.3
Swallowing, choked feeling	4	1.3	2.8
Nausea or "sinking" in stomach	4	1.3	2.8
Trembling, weak feeling	4	1.3	2.8
Cold hands, dry lips	2	.7	1.4
Loss of desire to eat	2	.7	1.4
Headache, dizziness	2	.7	1.4
Part total	90	30.0	62.1

In addition to the responses actually made, subjects in Gates's study also reported a wide variety of impulses felt. The most important of these were "to make a verbal retort" (in 37% of the episodes), "to do physical injury to the offender" (in 28% of the epidsodes), "to injure inanimate objects" (in 14% of the episodes), and "to run away, leave the room" (in 8% of the episodes).

Let us turn now to a more recent study, using a very different methodology. Davitz (1969) has constructed a "dictionary" of 50 emotional concepts. Each "definition" consists of a series of descriptive phrases that were endorsed by a group of subjects as being representative of a particular emotion. More specifically, subjects were asked to recall instances in which they had experienced various emotions. In the case of anger, for example, they described a specific incident and then read through a list of 556 items, checking each item that characterized the experience. The list contained items referring to overt behavior, physiological symptoms, perception of the situation, cognitive responses, and thoughts about oneself and others. Fifty subjects participated in the study (25 men and 25 women). All were college graduates, the majority either full- or part-time graduate students at Columbia University, although some were members of the secretarial and administrative staff. Thirty-four items were checked by over one-third of the subjects as characteristic of anger. These items are presented in Table 9-3, together with the percentage of endorsement.

Among the general response tendencies, the most frequently endorsed item (by 64% of the subjects) was to be "easily irritated, ready to snap." The next most frequently endorsed response tendency (by about 50% of the subjects) involved physical aggression (e.g., hitting, smashing, striking out). Only 42% of the subjects indicated that they wanted "to say something nasty." From these data it would appear that Davitz's subjects placed greater emphasis on physical aggression than did the subjects surveyed by Richardson and Gates. Some reasons for this apparent discrepancy will be discussed in a later section, when we consider in more detail the relative frequency of verbal and physical aggression during anger.

As in the earlier study by Gates (see Table 9-2), the largest category of responses endorsed by Davitz's subjects refer to expressive and/or physiological reactions. But aside from general bodily tension and some kind of frown or scowl, there is not a great deal of overlap between the reactions listed in Table 9-3 (Davitz) and those listed in Table 9-2 (Gates). In general, Davitz's subjects placed greater emphasis on cardiovascular symptoms (e.g., a rise in blood pressure) while Gates's subjects reported more respiratory and gastrointestinal changes. This illustrates a point that will be discussed more thoroughly in a later section; namely, most persons feel tense or aroused when angry, but whether they experience (and/or report) that arousal in terms of cardiovascular, respiratory, gastrointestinal, or muscular involvement is dependent upon a host of individual and situational factors and hence says little about the nature of anger per se.

Finally, it will be noted that several kinds of responses appear in Table 9-3 (under the heading "thoughts and feelings") that have not been discussed before. These refer primarily to cognitive processes such as thinking about and focusing attention on the events that caused the anger and on what can be done to rectify the situation. As will become evident below, a need for understanding appears to be an important aspect of the everyday experience of anger. There is, in fact, a sense in which anger can be viewed as a form of problem-solving (as opposed to a form of aggression). But more of that shortly.

Table 9-3. Characteristic Responses during Anger as Reported by Davitz (1969)

Type of response	Percentage of endorsement
General response tendencies	
I'm easily irritated, ready to snap.	64
There is an impulse to hurt, to hit, or to kick someone else.	50
An impulse to strike out, to pound, or smash, or kick, or bite; to do something that will hurt.	50
I want to strike out, explode, but I hold back, control myself.	46
I want to say something nasty, something that will hurt someone.	42
Expressive and/or physiological reactions	
My blood pressure goes up; blood seems to rush through my body.	72
My face and mouth are tight, tense, hard.	60
My whole body is tense.	60
There is an excitement, a sense of being keyed up, overstimulated, supercharged.	58
My pulse quickens.	56
My body seems to speed up.	54
There is a quickening of heartbeat.	52
My teeth are clenched.	52
My fists are clenched.	52
I feel that I will burst or explode; as if there is too much inside to be held in.	48
There is muscular rigidity.	40
My heart pounds.	40
There is a churning inside.	40
There is a tight knotted feeling in my stomach.	38
It's as if everything inside, my stomach, my throat, my head is expanding to the utmost, almost bursting.	34
Thoughts and feelings	
I seem to be caught up and overwhelmed by the feeling.	64
There is a sense of being gripped by the situation.	54
There is a narrowing of my senses, my attention becomes riveted on one thing.	52
I keep thinking about what happened over and over again.	44
The feeling begins with a sharp, sudden onset.	42
It's involved with other feelings.	40
I keep thinking of getting even, of revenge.	40
I can only think of what caused the feeling.	38
A confused, mixed-up feeling.	38
I'm completely wrapped up in the moment, the present, the here and now, with no thought of past or future.	36
I keep searching for an explanation, for some understanding; I keep thinking, "why?"	34
There is an intensified focus to my sensations.	34
My senses are perfectly focused.	34

As a last example of the kinds of responses typically displayed during anger, the study by McKellar (1949) may be cited. McKellar asked 120 members of adult education classes in the London area to describe two recent experiences of anger and/or annoyance, one that occurred within the last day or two and a second that occurred "recently." A total of 228 descriptions were obtained. The major form of response in each episode is presented in Table 9-4.

McKellar summarized his data at a rather high level of abstraction, and he explicitly focused on voluntary (mainly aggressive) responses. The few references to expressive reactions (e.g., weeping) represent only incidental observations. The picture of anger presented is therefore not as rich or detailed as that offered by Richardson, Gates, and Davitz. Nevertheless, it does contain some points of interest. Perhaps most important, it suggests that anger often goes unexpressed (in about 60% of the episodes); and that when it is expressed, a verbal retort is the most common kind of response. McKellar makes special note of the fact that although a human adult was stated to be the cause of anger in about 98% of the cases, a physical attack against an adult occurred in less than 1% of the cases. The most common objects of physical aggression were children and animals, presumably in the form of spanking or other forms of correction.

Summary

The foregoing review of previous research illustrates the diverse ways in which a person may respond while angry, and the equally diverse ways those responses may be classified. Indeed, it seems almost meaningless to ask, What is the typical response during anger? Such a question assumes that there is a typical response. If nothing else, the data reviewed thus far should make one skeptical about the validity of such an assumption; and as will be seen, the data to be reviewed below do little to alter that skepticism.

With this cautionary note as background, let us continue with a presentation of the results of the survey of community residents and students begun in the last chapter. In the survey, four very gross categories of responses were distinguished: (a) instrumental responses, in terms of both impulses felt and responses made; (b) expressive reactions and/or physiological responses; (c) cognitive reinterpretations of the eliciting conditions after the initial response; and (d) continuing affective reactions. Each kind of response will be discussed in turn; however, the major emphasis will be placed on the first category.

Instrumental Responses During Anger

For our purposes, an instrumental response may be defined as any act the goal of which is to alter the situation either by rectifying the instigation or by damping the emotional arousal. In their ideational aspect, instrumental responses correspond roughly to the "mental behavior" studied by Richardson; in terms of overt behavior,

Table 9-4. Responses During Anger Based on Data Reported by McKellar (1949)

Type of response	Number of episodes ($n = 228$)	Percentage of episodes
Anger left unexpressed		
With no substitute response	81	35.5
With a substitute response (e.g., going for a walk)	50	21.9
With amusement	4	1.8
Anger expressed later to a sympathetic listener		
But against the original object	9	3.9
Anger expressed at the time of the incident		
Verbal aggression	71	31.1
Physical attack	12	5.3
against an adult (2 incidents)		
against a child (5 incidents)		
against an animal (3 incidents)		
against an inanimate object (2 incidents)		
Weeping	1	.4

this category is more or less equivalent to what Gates called "gross bodily responses" and what McKellar termed "voluntary responses."

Eleven possible instrumental responses were described in Questionnaire A. Subjects were asked to read through the entire list and then to rate each item on two 3-point scales. One scale referred to how much the subjects felt like making the response (0 = not at all, 1 = somewhat, 2 = very much), and the second scale referred to what the subject actually did. The percentage of subjects who indicated that a particular response was at least somewhat invovled in their anger is presented in Table 9-5.

In the introduction to this chapter it was noted that in order to lend organization to the discussion of responses, some foil was needed. Such a foil is provided by the common assumption that the fundamental response tendency during anger is some form of physical aggression and, even more fundamentally, that anger is a biologically primitive response. The data presented in Table 9-5, together with results of prior research, allow us to examine these assumptions from a variety of different perspectives. We will begin by considering the inhibition of anger, that is, the differences between impulses felt and responses made. The data reported by Richardson (1918) and McKellar (1949) suggest that anger is inhibited the majority of the time. From a functional point of view, a response that is inhibited can be of little significance. The widespread inhibition of anger, if it occurs, would thus suggest that this emotion may indeed be a remnant of our biological past, no longer useful in everyday affiars.

Table 9-5. Instrumental Responses During Anger

	Percentage of subjects marking "somewhat" or "very much"	
Type of response	Impulses felt	Responses made
Direct aggression		
Verbal or symbolic aggression[a]	82	49
Denial or removal of some benefit	59	41
Physical aggression or punishment	40	10
Indirect aggression		
Telling a third party in order to get back at the instigator (malediction)	42	34
Harming something important to the instigator	25	9
Displaced aggression		
Against a nonhuman object or thing[a]	32	28
Against some person	24	25
Nonaggressive responses		
Engaging in calming activities[a]	60	60
Talking the incident over with a neutral party, with no intent to harm the offender[a]	59	59
Talking the incident over with the offender without exhibiting hostility	52	39
Engaging in activities opposite to the instigation of anger	14	19

[a]Multivariate analyses of variance of the mean ratings revealed significant differences between community residents and students in terms of both impulses felt ($p < .01$) and responses made ($p < .05$). Univariate analyses indicate that these differences were due primarily to the following variables: significantly more community residents than students said that they responded with verbal aggression (58% vs. 40%); on the other hand, significantly more students than community residents indicated that they felt like displacing their anger on some object (42% vs. 21%), that they felt like (74% vs. 46%) or actually did (71% vs. 49%) engage in calming activities, and that they felt like talking the incident over with a neutral party (70% vs. 48%). In short, the community residents were somewhat more open and direct in their expression of anger than were the students.

The Inhibition of Anger

An examination of Table 9-5 indicates that among the present sample of subjects, all types of interaction with the instigator tended to be inhibited during anger. In the case of direct and indirect aggression, impulses were felt significantly more often than expressed (all p's $< .01$). This was also true of the tendency to talk the incident over with the instigator without exhibiting hostility. On the other hand, displaced aggression and calming activities were expressed almost as frequently as the impulses were felt. The only response that was expressed more often than desired was "engaging in activities opposite to the expression of anger" ("contrary reactions," to use Richardson's term). The difference was not, however, statistically significant.

A brief digression on the correlates of inhibition. In chapter 8 an "index of inhibition" was described which consists of the difference between how "in control" subjects felt they were of their overt behavior as opposed to their thoughts and feelings. Subjects who received high scores on this index tended to display relatively less physical ($r = -.28$) and verbal ($r = -.34$) aggression but relatively more malediction ($r = .26$) than did low-scoring subjects. In other words, this inhibition index relates more to the suppression of direct than of indirect forms of aggression. Inhibited subjects also reported that their anger lasted longer ($r = .33$) and that they still became angry when thinking about the incident. More specifically, subjects who still became angry had a mean inhibition score of 2.3, whereas subjects who no longer became angry when thinking of the incident had a score of 1.3, a highly reliable difference ($p < .01$).

It is not clear from the above data whether people who inhibit the direct expression of their anger tend to remain angry longer and continue to be aroused by the original incident, or whether people who remain angry longer tend to inhibit their responses (e.g., so as not to drag out an argument or appear vindictive). In certain instances, it is clearly better to fume a little longer, rather than to act or to say things that may later be regretted. On the other hand, additional data will be presented in Chapter 12 (Study IV) which suggest that the absence of communication often prolongs anger.

Returning to the present study, we note that although some inhibition of behavior may have been common, the target was typically made aware of the angry person's feelings. If we consider only those episodes which involved another person ($n = 140$), the instigator knew (according to the subject) that he or she was the target of anger in 102 incidents (73%).[1] Such awareness was especially likely if the target was a loved one and the motive of the angry person was "to strengthen a relationship," "to get the instigator to do something," and/or "to get the instigator to change for his or her own good." Anger was least likely to be communicated if the target was a stranger and the motive was "to express dislike."

In short, the data presented thus far are neither favorable nor unfavorable to the assumption that anger is a biologically primitive response that is typically suppressed for social reasons. It is true that anger often results in an inhibition of all kinds of interaction with the instigator (nonaggressive as well as aggressive), but it is also true that inhibition is seldom complete, especially when the target is a loved one and the motives are basically constructive. Moreover, it is perhaps worth emphasizing that the functional significance of anger need not depend on its full expression. The threat of retaliation is often more effective than actual retaliation.

The Relative Frequency of Aggressive and Nonaggressive Responses

Let us turn now to a more detailed examination of some of the ways in which anger is typically expressed. We will consider first the extent to which anger is associated with aggressive, as opposed to nonaggressive, response tendencies. Anger has often

---

[1] This percentage was significantly higher for the community residents than for students—85% vs. 61% ($p < .01$, based on a chi-square analysis of the numbers involved).

been defined either as a form of aggression or as a motive for aggression. This identification of anger with aggression has important theoretical consequences, for if accurate, it means that explanations of aggression can be applied *mutatis mutandis* to anger, and vice versa. On the other hand, if anger involves nonaggressive as well as aggressive components, then different kinds of explanation must be invoked to explain anger as opposed to aggression per se.

In the present study 93% of the subjects indicated that they felt like engaging in some form of direct or indirect aggression against the instigator (i.e., verbal aggression, denial of benefit, physical aggression, harming something important to the instigator, and/or malediction); 83% of the subjects indicated that they actually made one or more of these responses. These figures tend to support the observation of Richardson (1918) that real or fantasized aggression is a nearly universal accompaniment of anger.

It is also clear from the present study, however, that nonaggressive responses are very common during anger—about as common, in fact, as are aggressive responses. For example, approximately 75% of the subjects reported that they not only wanted to, but that they actually did, talk the incident over, without hostile intent, either with the instigator or with a neutral party. In this connection, it may be recalled that subjects in the study by Davitz (1969) frequently reported that they were confused and kept searching for an explanation when angry (see Table 9-3). "Talking the incident over" is one way of resolving such confusion and of correcting the situation.

Some forms of direct and indirect aggression, as well as talking things over without hostility, can be viewed as attempts at problem-solving. Other kinds of responses during anger serve primarily to alleviate the emotional arousal itself. Such palliative responses can also be either aggressive or nonaggressive. For example, displaced aggression is largely palliative, as are calming activities. About 40% of the subjects reported that they felt like displacing and/or actually did displace aggression on some uninvolved person or object. On the other hand, 60% of the subjects reported that they engaged in nonaggressive calming activities.

In sum, aggressive and nonaggressive response tendencies are about equally common during anger. But rather than dividing the behavior of the angry person into aggressive and nonaggressive varieties, a more meaningful division might be in terms of problem-oriented versus palliative responses (see Lazarus & Launier, 1978, for a further discussion of this distinction as it relates to stress and emotion in general). From the latter perspective, anger might be viewed primarily as a form of problem-solving rather than as a form of aggression per se.

The Meaning of Aggression for the Angry Individual

This last observation raises the question: What do we mean by "aggression"? An important element in almost any definition of aggression is the motive of the individual doing the "aggressing." Consider, for example, a surgeon performing an operation. The surgeon may inflict considerable pain on the patient, but his or her behavior is not normally considered aggressive. In part, this is because the patient aggrees to undergo the pain. But even if the patient did not agree to the operation (e.g., because of mental incapacity), we would still be hesitant to call the surgeon's behavior an act of aggression if the operation were performed for the patient's own good. In other words, the motives of a person are of vital importance when classifying a response as aggressive.

In Chapter 8 we presented data on 11 possible motives for anger. Correlations were calculated between these motives and the responses subjects said that they made (or felt like making) while angry. For the most part, the correlations were quite low; in absolute value few exceeded .30, and most were less than .10. This means that ostensibly similar responses can be—and often are—associated with quite different motives. But in spite of their generally low values, the distribution of statistically significant ($r > .16$) correlations did form a meaningful pattern. Malevolent anger (as indicated, say, by the motive "to express dislike") was most associated with indirect aggression, for example, malediction and harming something important to the instigator, as well as displaced aggression against some person. By contrast, constructive anger ("to strengthen a relationship") was more associated with direct modes of response, such as verbal or symbolic aggression, denial of benefit, and talking the incident over with the instigator. There was no consistent relationship between physical aggression, either desired or expressed, and constructive anger. Finally, in the case of fractious anger ("to let off steam") subjects reported a desire to engage in calming activities, but tended to respond instead with physical aggression.

Because of its practical and theoretical importance, let us examine in more detail the circumstances in which subjects reported engaging in direct physical aggression. Among community residents, the actual expression of physical aggression occurred primarily in connection with the correction (punishment) of children. Specifically, 10 of the community residents indicated that they responded with physical aggression. In five of these instances, the target was a young child. Thus, 50% of the episodes that involved physical aggression had a child as the target. And, in another incident involving physical aggression, the target was the angry person's adolescent daughter.

Richardson (1918) and McKellar (1949) also noted that physical aggression, when it occurs, is most often directed at children. This does not mean that child beating or some other form of malignant aggression is common during anger. The aggression involved in these episodes was quite mild (a spank, shove, or slap), and in ordinary circumstances probably would not even be labeled "aggressive." The intent was to instruct and/or deter the child, not to harm.

Among the student sample, children were involved in only two episodes of anger, neither of which resulted in physical aggression. Of the six instances of physical aggression reported by the students, the target was a loved one (adult) in three instances, an inanimate object in two instances, and someone who was well known and liked in one instance.

There were no reported instances, either by community residents or students, where physical aggression was directed at a stranger or at someone who was well known but disliked. This undoubtedly reflects the combined influence of social ethics and fear of retaliation, for in terms of impulses felt (as opposed to responses made) there were no significant differences as a function of the target. That is, subjects reported that they felt like aggressing physically against strangers and disliked others as frequently as against loved ones, inanimate objects, and the like. In the case of strangers and disliked others, however, the impulses were never acted upon.

In short, physical aggression does not represent a uniform category. To slap a child as a form of punishment is obviously very different than to strike an enemy in hate. Even in fantasy (i.e., impulses felt), where physical aggression is as likely to be directed against someone who is disliked as against a loved one, the meaning of the impulse may differ greatly from one episode to another, and from one individual to another.

Verbal Versus Physical Aggression

Although aggressive responses may mean different things depending upon the context, it is nevertheless instructive to compare the relative frequency of verbal and physical forms of aggression. As discussed earlier, a biological perspective generally assumes that physical aggression or the threat of physical aggression is somehow fundamental to anger, and that verbal behavior represents a socially and ethically induced overlay (cf. Izard, 1977). From a contructivist point of view, by contrast, uniquely human and social forms of behavior are the fundamental aspects of anger; biologically based aggressive responses are, if anything, secondary.

We shall examine this issue by comparing the relative frequency of direct verbal and physical aggression. If other forms of "socialized" aggressive (e.g., denial of benefit) and nonaggressive responses (e.g., talking the incident over without hostility) were included in the analysis, the basic conclusions would only be strengthened.

Let us begin with the direct *expression* of physical and verbal aggression; we will then consider *impulses felt* but not necessarily expressed. Richardson (1918) observed few instances of physical aggression in 600 episodes of anger, and then mostly in connection with the correction of children. With regard to verbal aggression, on the other hand, Richardson suggests that "anger rarely, if ever, occurs without its vocal expression in some manner, if not by direct vocalization either by inner speech or voco-motor imagery" (p. 36). In a more quantitative analysis, Gates (1926) reported that some form of verbal behavior (excited talking and/or an angry retort) occurred in 40% of 145 episodes, whereas physical aggression occurred in only 2% of the episodes (see Table 9-2). Of the 228 episodes studied by McKellar (1949), 31% involved verbal aggression and 5% involved physical aggression (the most common target being children—see Table 9-4). Finally, in the present survey (see Table 9-5), some form of direct verbal and/or symbolic aggression occurred in 49% of the episodes, whereas direct physical aggression occurred in only 10%.

There is thus fairly good agreement that direct verbal aggression may occur in from 30 to 50% of angry episodes, whereas physical aggression typically occurs in less than 10%. Moreover, when physical aggression does occur, it is generally quite mild, for example, being directed at children in the form of punishment.

It might be argued that overt behavior is not indicative of anger per se, since physical aggression, especially, is liable to be inhibited. Therefore, let us look at the impulses felt. As already noted, Richardson (1918) believed that "inner speech or voco-motor imagery"is a universal characteristic of anger. Unfortunately, he gives no exact figures for the frequency of imagined physical—as opposed to verbal—aggression. In Gates's (1926) study subjects reported that they felt like making a "verbal retort" in 37% of the episodes, and doing "physical injury to the offender" in 28% of the episodes. Presumably Gates was defining the impulse to verbal aggression much more narrowly than was Richardson.

In the "Dictionary of Emotional Concepts" compiled by Davitz (1969), items that referred to striking out, hitting, pounding, smashing, kicking, and so on were endorsed by 50% of the subjects (see Table 9-3). A smaller number of subjects (43%) endorsed the item "I want to say something nasty, something that will hurt." This emphasis on physical aggression contrasts with the findings of Richardson and Gates. The reasons for the discrepancy are not entirely clear, but there are perhaps two main factors. First, the items used by Davitz are actually somewhat ambiguous—a person can "strike out" and "hurt" verbally as well as by hitting, kicking, pounding, smashing, and the like. In this connection it may be recalled that the most frequently endorsed response tendency in Davitz's study (by 62% of the subjects) was to be easily irritated and "ready to snap," which would seem to imply a largely verbal reaction. Second, the subjects studied by Richardson and Gates kept notes of their reactions as they occurred; Davitz's subjects were asked to recall an episode of anger, with no stipulations set on the recency of the occurrence. In recalling a specific incident of anger to describe, Davitz's subjects may have focused on particularly intense episodes, ones that stood out in their minds as especially noteworthy; and such episodes are more likely than usual to involve physical aggression.

Turning now to the results of the present study, 82% of the subjects indicated that they felt like aggressing verbally against the instigator, whereas only half that number (40%) felt an impulse toward physical aggression.

If we consider only the *highest* figures reported in all of the studies mentioned above, it seems safe to conclude that the impulse to verbal aggression occurs in about 80-100% of angry episodes (Richardson, the present survey), while the impulse to physical aggression occurs about 40-50% of the time (Davitz, the present survey). The gap between these two forms of aggression undoubtedly closes as the intensity of anger increases, but it is dfficult to argue from these data that physical aggression is somehow more "fundamental" than verbal aggression during anger. Indeed, instead of physical aggression being primary and verbal aggression secondary, the situation may actually be the reverse. Physical aggression is most likely to occur among individuals who lack verbal skills and/or in situations where the verbal expression of anger is no longer effective (Toch, 1969; Camp, 1977).

Summary

Because the instrumental responses during anger are so variable, it is difficult to draw a meaningful picture of the typical angry episode that does not also draw upon the instigating conditions and motives involved. Nevertheless, from the research reviewed thus far, the following conclusions seem warranted.

1. Angry behavior is frequently inhibited, but seldom entirely. When appropriate, anger is typically communicated to the instigator (73% of the time in the present study).
2. Some form of aggressive impulse (verbal, denial of benefit, physical aggression, etc.) is almost universal during anger; and the majority of the time (80% in the present study), one or more of these impulses are acted upon.
3. Nonaggressive responses are also very common during anger. For example, 75% of the subjects in the present study indicated that they wanted to, and actually did, talk the incident over with the instigator and/or with a neutral third party.
4. There is little relationship between the motives for anger and the type of response made. There is a slight tendency for indirect forms of aggression to be malevolently motivated. In general, however, any given response (such as direct physical aggression) can have very different meanings depending upon the target and the motives involved.
5. Impulses toward verbal aggression are experienced about twice as often as impulses toward physical aggression (roughly 80% to 40% in the present study). Denial of benefit, another highly socialized form of aggression, is also more common than physical aggression, in terms of both impulses felt and responses made.

In the psychological literature, anger has often been conceptualized as a form of, or motive for, aggression. Physical aggression, in particular, has been considered a fundamental attribute of anger. The data presented thus far call this assumption into question. They do not, however, resolve the issue regarding which kind of response, if any, is most fundamental to anger. Indeed, this may not even be a meaningful issue as posed, in spite of its apparent theoretical significance. A response may be considered fundamental for many different reasons, for example, because it is genetically based, because it is ontogenetically prior, or because it is higher (or lower) in a response hierarchy. As will be discussed in Chapter 14, there is also a logical sense in which aggression may be prototypic of anger without necessarily being fundamental in any of these other senses. However this issue is finally resolved, one thing is clear: Inferences about aggression, particularly physical aggression, cannot be applied without major qualification to anger, and vice versa. In many respects, anger might better be conceptualized as a form of problem-solving than as a form of aggression. Of course, anger is not problem-solving in just an intellectual sense; it also involves a commitment to action should the instigating circumstances not change.

Expressive Reactions and Physiological Symptoms

Instrumental responses during anger might be expected to reflect the influence of socialization. The theorist who wishes to maintain that anger is a biologically based response still has recourse to expressive reactions and/or physiological symptoms.

These, supposedly, are not as subject to socialization pressures, and hence they may provide a better index of the origins and nature of anger.

Because of methodological limitations, no attempt was made in the present study to assess in detail expressive reactions and physiological symptoms. Rather, subjects were simply provided with a list of seven reactions as examples. These ranged from the very inclusive (e.g., general tension) to the very specific (e.g., nervous laughter). Subjects were asked to rate these reactions, and also to specify any other responses that they might have experienced. The results are presented in Table 9-6.

The data presented in Table 9-6 should be considered in conjuction with similar data reported by Gates (see Table 9-2) and Davitz (see Table 9-3). Perhaps the most obvious fact to note is that most subjects experienced a moderate degree of tension or arousal during anger. It is evident, however, that such arousal may be manifested in a great variety of different ways. Some subjects report cardiovascular changes, while others describe respiratory, muscular, or even gastrointestinal disturbances.

It would be easy to dismiss such results simply because they are based on self-reports. However, controlled laboratory studies also provide little support for the notion that the experience of anger is based upon a unique pattern of internal physiological changes and/or expressive reactions. For one thing, most persons are not able to make fine discriminations among physiological responses (McFarland, 1975; Katkin, Blascovich, & Goldband, 1981; Whitehead, Drescher, Heiman, & Blackwell, 1977); and although a number of investigators have postulated that feed-back from facial expressions plays a major role in the experience of emotion,

Table 9-6. Expressive and/or Physiological Reactions While Angry

Reaction	Mean rating[a]	Percentage of subjects marking "somewhat" or "very much"
General tension	1.47	93
Restlessness[b]	1.01	74
Frowning[b]	.93	66
Flushing or rise in temperature	.79	63
Shaky, cracking voice[b]	.34	29
Crying	.32	23
Nervous laughter[b]	.15	13
Other[c]		

[a] 0 = not at all; 1 = somewhat; 2 = very much.
[b] Multivariate analyses of variance on the mean ratings indicated significant differences between student and community residents on these variables. This was due primarily to greater self-reported restlessness on the part of students (mean rating: 1.21 vs. .81; $p < .01$). Students also reported more frowning and nervous laughter (p's $< .05$), whereas the community residents were more likely to say they responded with a shaky, cracking voice ($p < .05$); but in the case of these variables the size of the differences was minor.
[c] Among "other" reactions listed were muscle tension (twice), clenching of fist (twice), swearing, shortness of breath, rise in blood pressure, blanching, nausea, gritting of teeth, hyperactivity, quietness, silence, touching of hair (a nervous habit), exaggerated enunciation, artificial seriousness, and a miscellany of more general affective states, such as frustration, depression, and irritability.

including anger, the hypothesis has proven to be very difficult even to test (Ellsworth & Tourangeau, 1981). For another thing, there is not even much evidence that anger is accompanied by specific physiological and expressive reactions. As discussed in Chapter 2, certain facial expressions do appear to be universally recognized as signs of aggressive intent. There is little reason to believe, however, that such expressive reactions are specific to anger, or even that they are especially common during anger. Similar considerations apply to internal physiological changes, including the norepinephrinelike response pattern that at one time was reported to be a reliable accompaniment of anger (Funkenstein, 1956; Schachter, 1957), but which recent evidence would seem to disconfirm (Frankenhaeuser, 1979).

In short, the great variability in the way people describe their physiological and expressive reactions while angry may reflect the actual state of affairs. Aside from general arousal, the changes that occur—and that are experienced, however, vaguely— probably vary a great deal as a function of individual differences in reactivity and, what is even more important, as a function of the instrumental responses an individual is making or would like to make.

Reappraisals of the Instigating Conditions

After becoming angry, a person may have second thoughts about the instigation and the appropriateness of his or her own responses. For example, Richardson (1918) observed that subjects made an "indifferent reaction" in 27% of the episodes he studied. An indifferent reaction, according to Richardson, occurs as a last resort and involves the adoption of an "I don't care" attitude. Other reappraisals are also common, as is illustrated in Table 9-7.

The most frequent reappraisal, especially among the student sample, involved a more benign interpretation of the motives or guilt of the instigator. Other common reappraisals were to diminish the importance of the instigator, and/or to reevaluate one's own role in the incident. The strategies listed in the "other" category were generally variations on these three themes, or else they involved a reassessment of the angry person's ability to cope with the situation. For example, several subjects decided, "I can't do anything about it anyway, so what's the use," whereas several others made, in effect, the opposite assessment, "I can handle this, so why become angry." Anger, it seems cannot flourish in soil that is either too poor to too rich in coping possibilities.

Folk wisdom has long held that humor is an excellent antidote against anger: "If you can't ignore a provocation, laugh at it." Recent psychological research also suggests that humor can mitigate anger (Baron, 1977, p. 263). It is therefore noteworthy that only 4 of the 160 subjects in the present survey indicated that they reinterpreted the incident humorously, even though this option was explicitly mentioned in the questionnaire. In ordinary circumstances, evidently, people are seldom able to find humor in the events that anger them.

Cognitive strategies such as those listed in Table 9-7 have long been advocated as a means for preventing and regulating anger (cf. the teachings of Seneca duscussed

Table 9-7. Reappraisals of the Angry Episode

Reappraisal	Percentage of subjects
Reinterpreted the motives or guilt of the instigator[a]	23
Decided the incident was less important than originally thought	18
Reinterpreted your own motives, guilt, or role in the incident	18
Minimized the importance of the instigator	13
Reinterpreted the event humorously	3
Some other reinterpretation[a]	19
Made *no* reinterpretation	38

[a]The students indicated that they were more likely to reinterpret the motives of the instigator than did the community residents (35% vs. 11%, $p < .01$), whereas the community residents were more likely than the students to say they made some other kind of reinterpretation (28% vs. 11%, $p < .01$).

in Chapter 4), and they are central to some modern therapeutic approaches to anger disorders (e.g., Meichanbaum & Novaco, 1978; Novaco, 1979). It is therefore of interest to compare the experiences of subjects who made some reappraisal ($n = 99$) with the experiences of subjects who made no reappraisal ($n = 61$). There was a large number of statistically significant differences between these two groups. The following is a summary.

Subjects who made some reappraisal also rated themselves as less intensely angry, as angry for a shorter duration, and as less likely to become angry again when thinking about the incident.

With regard to the target, reappraisals were more likely when the offender was a loved one or someone who was higher in authority. By contrast, if the offender was a stranger, a reappraisal was less likely.

With regard to the instigation, a reappraisal was less likely if the precipitating incident was perceived as voluntary and unjustified, and if it involved the violation of socially accepted ways of behaving. The violation of a social norm, it may be noted, respresents a more clear-cut provocation to anger than does, say, simple frustration, and hence reappraisals are less realistic in such circumstances.

Subjects who made some reappraisal were more often constructively motivated (e.g., they wished to strengthen a relationship with the instigator), or they simply wished to let off steam. These subjects also felt like engaging in, and actually did engage in, more activities opposite to the expression of anger. This does not mean that they were inhibited in the direct expression of their anger. On the contrary, a reappraisal of the instigating conditions tended to be associated with physical and verbal aggression toward the instigator; also, subjects who made some reappraisal were less likely to engage in indirect aggression, such as harming something important to the instigator.

One must be cautious about inferring cause-and-effect relationships from data such as the above. Nevertheless, the findings are consistent with results presented earlier (as well as other data that will be presented in Chapter 12), which suggest that the open and direct expression of anger often helps to clarify a situation, so that what was originally appraised as a "wrong" may subsequently be reinterpreted in a more benign way. This is particularly true if the anger is constructively motivated.

Of course, whether or not a reappraisal occurs depends on the responses of the target as well as on those of the angry person. In the present study, subjects were less likely to make a reappraisal if the instigator denied responsibility for the precipitating incident. This result is perhaps worth emphasizing, since a denial of responsibility on the part of the target, if legitimate, implies that the angry person was in the wrong. The angry person, evidently, is not likely to see it that way.

Two issues remain to be addressed before leaving this topic. First, are some reappraisals more effective than others in terminating an episode of anger? And second, how is anger resolved by those people who make no reappraisals? With regard to the first issue, no differential effects due to type of reappraisal were observed in the present study. Depending upon the person and the situation, one type of reappraisal was apparently as effective as any other in helping to bring the angry episode to a conclusion.

With regard to the second issue, it must not be assumed that a reappraisal of the instigation is necessary for the resolution of anger, or that it is even desirable in every instance. Some provocations are clearly unjustified and should not be reappraised; and in other instances a lack of interaction with the instigator may make any reappraisal difficult. Yet even such episodes of anger are typically brought to a satisfactory conclusion. Real or fantasied retaliation against the instigator may redress the perceived sense of injustice, restore self-esteem, or induce some change in the behavior of the instigator such that anger is no longer appropriate. And even if there is no change in the behavior of the instigator, thinking about the provocation, discussing the issue with a third party, and so on may be sufficient to clarify matters and restore a sense of equity. As Richardson (1918) noted: "Whenever the subject comes to a definite conclusion whether it refers to the emotional situation or a contemplated mode of behavior toward the offender, there is a reported sudden drop in the intensity of the emotion, even though the attitude is but a tentative and temporary one" (p. 58). Also, the affective relationship with the instigator is an important factor in bringing anger to a close. It is difficult to remain angry long at a friend or loved one without positive events intervening to mitigate the negative feelings. There is a danger, however. If the anger elicits no permanent change on the part of either the instigator or the angry person, then future incidents of the same type may lead to increasingly intense outbursts, and what was once friendship may turn to enmity. In Chapter 12 we will have more to say about these and other issues related to the termination of anger.

The Consequences of Anger

In the final analysis, the functional significance of a response is determined by its consequences, although not all consequences need have functional significance. In this section we will consider three types of consequences: continuing affective reactions on the part of the angry person; reactions of the target to the person's anger; and, most important of all, the overall beneficial or harmful effects of the episode as perceived by the angry person.

Continuing Affective Reactions

The typical episode of anger does not end abruptly, but merges into, or becomes mingled with, some other affective state. Such aftereffects are predominantly negative. For example, Meltzer (1933) found that 63% of the 189 angry episodes that he studied resulted in "dissociative" trends (continued irritability, disgust, nervousness, self-pity, and other negative reactions), whereas only 15% resulted in "integrative" trends (feelings of satisfaction, triumph, relief, calm, and the like). Meltzer's investigation of this issue was not, however, very systematic, as indicated by the fact that no afterreaction could be determined in 22% of the episodes.

Subjects in the present survey were asked to rate on a 3-point scale how they felt about their own anger after their initial response. Seven general categories of affective reactions were listed, each defined by a triad of closely related terms (e.g., anxious/jittery/nervous; relieved/calm/satisfied). Space also was provided for subjects to list any other reaction they might have experienced. The results are presented in Table 9-8.

Before discussing these results, a caveat must be mentioned. The instructions in the questionnaires asked subjects to rate how they felt about their own anger. How-

Table 9-8. Continuing Affective Reactions Following the Initial Response

Reaction	Mean rating[a]	Percentage of subjects marking "somewhat or "very much"
Irritable, hostile, aggravated	1.04	69
Depressed, unhappy, gloomy	.85	59
Anxious, jittery, nervous	.58	46
Ashamed, embarrassed, guilty	.44	33
Relieved, calm, satisfied[b]	.33	28
Good, pleased, glad	.26	21
Triumphant, confident, dominant	.19	16
Other[c]		

[a] 0 = not at all; 1 = somewhat; 2 = very much.
[b] Multivariate analysis of variance indicated that community residents felt more relieved following their anger than did students (mean ratings: .41 vs. .24; $p < .05$).
[c] Under the "other" category, the two most frequently mentioned reactions (by three subjects each) were "frustrated" and "justified." Also mentioned were "angry," "regretful," "upset," "confused," "dissatisfied," "concerned," "impatient," and "resigned."

ever, most subjects simply described their ongoing feelings following the initial response. These continuing affective reactions undoubtedly reflect a variety of factors, including the original appraisal of the instigation and any subsequent reappraisals, the reaction of the instigator (which will be discussed below), and the subjects' evaluations of their own behavior.

But whatever the source, it is clear that the subjective aftereffects of anger are largely dysphoric. Most subjects reported feeling irritable, depressed, anxious, and/or ashamed. Fewer than 30% of the subjects reported feeling relieved following the incident; and although the most frequently stated motive for anger was to assert authority/independence or to improve one's self-image, only about 15% of the subjects reported feeling triumphant afterward.

Of course, persons may have mixed feelings about their anger, feeling, for example, both irritable and yet relieved. In order to assess the overall balance of positive and negative feelings, the mean rating of each subject on the four negative affective scales (irritable, depressed, anxious, and ashamed) was subtracted from the mean rating of the three positive categories (relieved, good, and triumphant). The final score on this variable could thus range from -2 (completely negative) to +2 (completely positive). The mean rating for all subjects was -.47, with a standard deviation of .75. Only 53 subjects (33%) fell at or above the midpoint, that is, had an overall neutral or positive reaction.

It may be true, as Richardson (1918) observed, that "there are but few instances of anger that have no flash of pleasantness anywhere, in some degree before the motion is finally completed" (p. 76).Certainly people often find pleasure in thoughts of revenge. It is equally clear, however, that such pleasurable moments are not sufficient to offset the generally negative feelings that follow in the wake of the typical angry episode.

Reactions of the Target

One hundred and two subjects indicated that the instigators knew that they (the instigators) were the target of anger. The major reactions exhibited by the instigator in these instances are shown in Table 9-9. (Each reaction was rated on a 3-point scale.) Most often, the angry person perceived the instigator as responding with either defiance and/or indifference (about 45% of the time each). An apology was forthcoming in about 41% of the episodes, as was a denial of responsibility and/or hurt feelings. Anger (return hostility), surprise, and/or rejection were also commonly perceived reactions.

From the angry person's point of view, of course, an apology from the instigator would be a most desirable consequence. An overt apology, however, is not necessary for a beneficial outcome. An instigator who responds with a show of defiance, for example, may still be hesitant to repeat the provocation in the future. Also, what the angry person perceives as defiance may be experienced quite differently by the target. This is a matter about which we shall have much more to say in the next chapter.

Table 9-9. Reactions of the Target (n = 102) to the Subject's Anger

Target's reaction	Mean rating[a]	Percentage of subjects marking "somewhat" or "very much"
Defiance	.62	46
Indifference or lack of concern	.62	44
Denial of responsibility	.57	41
Apology or other sign of contrition	.56	41
Hurt feelings	.55	42
Anger or hostility	.51	38
Surprise	.38	30
Rejection	.35	28
Jokes, frivolity, or silliness	.17	14
Other[b]		

[a] 0 = not at all; 1 = somewhat; 2 = very much.
[b] Thirteen "other" reactions were mentioned. Five were negative or unresponsive to the situation (e.g., pretended ignorance, silence), three were positive (e.g., concern, understanding), and six were potentially either negative or positive (e.g., bewilderment, waiting to see what would happen next).

Overall Beneficial or Harmful Effects

In order to obtain a summary index of the beneficial or harmful effects of anger, subjects were asked the following question:

> Everything considered (the nature of the instigation, your response to it, the consequences of your anger, etc.), do you believe that this episode of anger was adaptive (beneficial) _____ or maladaptive (harmful) _____?

The ratio of "adaptive" to "maladaptive" responses was about 2.5:1. Specifically, 100 subjects found the incident benefical, 41 found it harmful, and 19 incicated that it was neither or both.

Of the 100 subjects who considered the incident beneficial, about 70% indicated that it helped to improve the situation. This was accomplished in either of three ways: (a) getting the instigator to change his attitudes and/or behavior toward the angry person (32 subjects); (b) increasing mutual understanding (16 subjects); (c) increasing awareness on the part of the angry person of his or her own strengths and weaknessess (23 subjects).[2]

---

[2] There was a greater tendency on the part of community residents to suggest that their anger had a direct influence on the target, while students—more than community residents—emphasized increased self-understanding. Since the remaining studies in this series all used students as subjects, this might be a convenient place to summarize some of the major differences between the responses of the students and the broader population. Very briefly, the anger of the community residents was less intense and more quickly resolved than that of the students, and was more likely to be directed at loved ones and acquaintances than at persons who were well known and liked. The anger of the community residents was also more openly

A number of subjects also indicated that their anger served to release tension. Approximately 15% of those who considered the episode beneficial gave this as the reason. The remaining explanations—15%—for the beneficial outcomes were too vague to classify.

Of the 41 subjects who considered the incident to be maladaptive or harmful, about 25% (10) indicated that it resulted in a deterioration of the situation. Others indicated simply that it was an unpleasant experience (30%), that it accomplished nothing (25%), or that their anger was not expressed (10%), and/or gave some miscellaneous reason for the harmful effects (10%).

The above figures must, of course, be viewed as very rough. The reasons subjects gave for the beneficial and harmful effects of their anger were often vague and difficult to classify. The fact of central importance is that the majority of subjects (by ratio of about 2.5:1) believed that their anger was more benefical than harmful. And if only those episodes of anger that resulted in some improvement in the situation (as opposed, say, to a simple release of tension) are compared with those episodes that resulted in an actual deterioration of the situation (as opposed to simply being an unpleasant experience accomplishing nothing), then the ratio of beneficial to harmful outcomes increases to approximately 7:1.

Summary

In terms of continuing affective reactions, the consequences of anger are largely negative. That is, people tend to feel irritable, depressed, and/or anxious after an angry episode. Also, the angry person tends to view the reactions of the target in a negative light (e.g., as defiance or indifference). There is reason to believe, however, that these immediate consequences of anger are not the most important ones, at least not from a functional point of view. (Calluses may be one consequence of shoveling snow, but not a functional consequence.) Taking a broader perspective, we see that the outcome of a typical angry episode is more often considered beneficial than harmful. This may be due, for example, to some change in the behavior or attitude of the target, to an increase in mutual understanding, or to an increased self-awareness on the part of the angry person of his or her own strengths and weaknesses. In Chapter 10 we will examine such consequences of anger in greater detail, but from the point of view of the target rather than that of the angry person.

---

and directly expressed, was more constructively motivated, and resulted in a greater sense of relief. In mentioning these differences, I should emphasize that the similarities between the two groups were much greater than the differences. But more important from the present theoretical perspective is that whatever bias might be introduced by reliance on students as subjects is a conservative one. That is, the social norms and functional significance of anger would be even more evident in an unselected as opposed to a student population. This is due, no doubt, to the peculiar living conditions in which most students find themselves, namely, as relatively transient residents in dormitories, away from family, and subjected to an academic routine.

Concluding Observations

Anger may be expressed in an almost indefinite number of ways. This is probably the reason why classical discussions of anger, such as those reviewed in Chapter 4, have focused on instigating conditions (e.g., the appraisal of wrongdoing) and on the motives of the angry individual (e.g., the desire for revenge, or the correction of misconduct). When it comes to the *behavior* of the angry individual, the greatest theoretical attention has focused on physical aggression. One reason for this focus of attention is that violent outbursts are particularly dramatic and often harmful. When interpreting a phenomenon, we often place undue weight on singular events that are highly dramatic, while downplaying or ignoring commonplace occurrences that may actually be more important in the long run (Nisbett, Borgida, Crandell, & Reed, 1976). That is perhaps one reason why a phenomenon such as anger tends to be conceptualized in terms of its most dramatic manifestations—physical aggression.

On the basis of the present and previous surveys, it is evident that actual physical aggression is rare during anger; even the impulse to physical aggression is not particularly common. A verbal retort or the denial of some benefit (or both) is the most common expression of anger. Of greater theoretical interest, however, is the fact that nonaggressive responses (such as talking the incident over with the instigator or with a neutral party) are about as common during anger as are aggressive responses. When these less dramatic manifestations are taken into account, anger could just as well be conceptualized as a form of problem-solving as a form of aggression.

But the difficulty with viewing angry behavior almost exclusively in terms of aggression (and especially physical aggression) is not only one of representativeness; it is also one of definition. Aggression may mean many different things, depending on the motives of the individual. As we saw in Chapter 8, the motives for anger can be divided into three broad categories—malevolent, constructive, and fractious. The direct expression of anger tends to be constructively motivated; and when aggression does occur, it can often be considered "aggressive" in only an extended sense. Malevolent anger, which conforms more to the traditional conception of this emotion, typically finds expression in indirect ways. These relationships make good logical as well as empirical sense. If anger is to be constructive (problem oriented), it must be communicated to the instigator, often in an emphatic ("aggressive") way. On the other hand, if the intent is malevolent, then indirect aggression may not only be safer, but also more hurtful.

Following a typical episode of anger, a person is liable to feel irritable, depressed, and in a generally negative mood. But in spite of this, the overall outcome of the typical angry episode is evaluated as positive. Like a medicine that leaves a bad taste in the mouth, anger may help restore balance to a relationship or achieve other ends unobtainable by more benign means.

Chapter 10

Experiencing Another's Anger

To the extent that anger is an *interpersonal* emotion, the experiences of the angry person can provide only part of the story; the experiences of the target are also important, particularly for an understanding of the possible functional significance of anger. It is, after all, primarily through the target that anger must exert its influence. The purpose of Study II, reported in the present chapter, was therefore to explore the reactions of the target to another's anger.

Procedural Considerations

In order to study the experiences of the target, a questionnaire (B) was constructed that paralleled in many respects the questionnaire (A) used in Study I. A copy of this second questionnaire is contained in Appendix B. The rationale behind its construction was explained briefly in Chapter 7.

Participants

Only students participated in Study II. Subjects were recruited at the same time and in the same manner as the student subjects who participated in Study I. As may be recalled, these subjects were limited to unmarried, native-born Americans who were 21 years old or less. Students who volunteered were given either Questionnaire A or Questionnaire B on a random basis. Among those who received Questionnaire B, 10 returned unusable questionnaires—7 because the incident described occurred more than a month previously and 3 because the questionnaire was improperly filled out. Approximately 7% of the students who received questionnaires did not return them at all.

Questionnaires continued to be collected until 80 students (40 men and 40 women) had completed Questionnaire A (for Study I) and a corresponding number had completed Questionnaire B (for Study II). There were no significant differences in demographic variables between the students who completed one questionnaire and those who completed the other.

Data Analyses

This chapter is devoted to a presentation of the results of Questionnaire B and, where relevant, to a comparison between Questionnaires A and B. All of the subjects who completed Questionnaire B were, of course, aware of the other person's anger. For purposes of comparison, therefore, a similar restriction was placed on the episodes described in Questionnaire A. Specifically, comparisons between the two questionnaires were done using only those episodes (n = 102) from Study I in which the subjects indicated that the targets were aware of their anger. Also, because of the differences between the community residents and students who participated in Study I, subanalyses were done using only student subjects.

All of the results reported below that involve a comparison between questionnaires utilize the combined data of the community residents and students from Study I. However, no differences are reported as statistically significant unless they were also at least marginally significant ($p < .10$) in the subanalyses involving only the students who participated in the studies.

The Angry Incidents

As in Study I, subjects completing Questionnaire B were asked to focus on the most intense incident during the previous week or on the most recent incident prior to that. Approximately 60% of the subjects (49) reported being the target of anger at least once during the week, and the median time that had elapsed between the incident described and the completion of the questionnaire was 5.8 days. The mean intensity of the "most intense" incident was 6.6 on a 10-point scale. This was somewhat lower than the corresponding rating (7.1) of one's own anger (Questionnaire A), but not significantly so.

In spite of their somewhat lower ratings in terms of absolute intensity, 61% of the targets felt that the other person's anger was more intense than the incident called for; by contrast, only 35% of the subjects describing their own anger felt that their responses were unduly severe. This difference is highly significant ($p < .01$). The target was also more likely to perceive the angry person's behavior as "uncontrolled" and "impulsive." That is, subjects who rated another's anger reported a greater loss of behavioral control on the part of the angry person than did subjects who rated their own anger (5.6 vs. 4.2 on a 10-point scale, $p < .01$).

In short, although people may perceive another's anger as less intense than it "really" is (from the angry person's point of view), they still believe the anger to be more intense and uncontrolled than is warranted.

The Relationship Between the Target and the Angry Person

As we saw in Chapter 8, people say they are more likely to become angry at loved ones and friends than at strangers or those who are disliked. An equally strong trend in the same direction appears when anger is viewed from the perspective of the target. Specifically, in 80% of the episodes the targets indicated that the angry person was either well known and liked (39 episodes) or a loved one (25 episodes); in the remaining 20% of the episodes the angry person was an acquaintance (9 episodes), someone who was well known and disliked (4 episodes), or a stranger (3 episodes).

The Nature of the Instigation

Among the subjects completing Questionnaire B, 95% said that the other person's anger resulted from something that they (the targets) had done. Thus, with only a few exceptions, the targets saw their own behavior as part of the instigation. But what was it about their behavior that elicited anger? We have seen how anger typically involves an imputation of blame, that is, the angry person perceives the target as having done something "wrong." In this respect, perhaps more than any other, we might expect the perceptions of the target to differ from those of the angry person; and that is the case, as can be seen in Table 10-1.

Targets, as opposed to angry persons, were much less likely to perceive the precipitating incident as *voluntary and unjustified*; by contrast, they were more likely to perceive the instigation as *voluntary and justified* or as an *unavoidable accident*. Still, it is important to note that half the targets did accept blame for the incident, that is, indicated that the instigation was unjustified or (if an accident) avoidable.

That a large number of targets (35%) said that the instigation was voluntary and justified deserves brief comment. At first, this would seem to contradict the con-

Table 10-1. Justification for Anger as Perceived by the Angry Person and by the Target

Justification	As perceived by		Significance of the difference
	Angry persons	Targets	
1. Voluntary and unjustified: The instigator knew what he/she was doing, but he/she had no right to do it.	59%	21%	<.01
2. Potentially avoidable accident or event: the result of negligence, carelessness, or lack of foresight.	28	28	ns
3. Voluntary and justified: The instigator knew what he/she was doing and had a right to do it.	12	35	<.01
4. Unavoidable accident or event: It could not have been foreseen or was beyond anyone's control.	2	15	<.01

Note. The results are presented in terms of the percentage of angry persons (n = 102) and targets (n = 80) who believed that the instigation fell into each mutually exclusive category. The descriptions by the angry persons (Questionnaire A) and the targets (Questionnaire B) refer to different incidents.

clusion reached in earlier chapters, namely, that the most "adequate" provocation to anger is an *unjustified* act. But the discrepancy is more apparent than real, at least as far as the underlying norms of anger are concerned. Most of the targets who said that the instigation was justified also recognized the apparent contradiction, and in their open-ended responses they offered further clarification. Some mentioned mitigating circumstances that would help justify the instigation; others described predisposing factors (e.g., fatigue, illness) that might explain why the angry person took affront. But the most common explanation—by about half of those who said that the instigation was justified—was an emphasis on their right to do what they did in spite of what the angry person thought. In short, nearly all subjects responded in some way to the imputation of blame implicit in the other person's anger, if only to deny the legitimacy of the claim.

Table 10-2 presents comparisons between the mean ratings of angry persons and targets on six specific factors (frustration, loss of pride, etc.) that are often involved in the instigation to anger. There was general agreement between the two groups on the relative importance of these variables. Both angry persons and targets indicated that frustration, loss of pride, and/or the violation of a personal expectancy or wish were the three factors most commonly involved. On only one factor did the two

Table 10-2. Mean Ratings of Six Factors Involved in the Instigation to Anger as Perceived by the Angry Person ($n = 102$) and by the Target ($n = 80$)

Factors involved in the instigation to anger	Mean ratings[a]		Significance of the difference
	Angry persons	Targets	
1. Frustration or the interruption of some ongoing or planned activity	1.25	1.15	ns
2. An event, action, or attitude which resulted in a loss of personal pride, self-esteem, or sense of self-worth	1.09	1.05	ns
3. Violation of expectations and wishes which are important to you but which may not be widely shared by others	1.08	1.20	ns
4. Violation of socially accepted ways of behaving or widely shared rules of conduct	1.02	.75	$< .05$
5. Possible or actual property damage	.25	.15	ns
6. Possible or actual physical injury and/or pain	.25	.14	ns

Note. The ratings by the angry persons (Questionnaire A) and the targets (Questionnaire B) are of different incidents.

[a] 0 = not at all; 1 = somewhat; 2 = very much.

groups differ significantly—the violation of social norms. Targets tended to view this as less important than did angry persons.

Perhaps the major generalization that can be drawn from the data presented in Tables 10-1 and 10-2 is that people tend to view another person's anger as less legitimate and more idiosyncratically determined than they view their own anger. It is also evident from the open-ended descriptions that the instigation to anger is not necessarily fixed at the outset; rather, it is constantly in the process of negotiation and clarification as the angry episode progresses. We shall have more to say about this issue later.

The Motives for Anger

Table 10-3 presents the motives of the angry person as perceived by the target. These data must, of course, be interpreted with caution; it is hard enough to recognize one's own motives, no less the motives of another individual. However, as was discussed in Chapter 8, the self-reports of one's own motives reflect, in part, the "implicit theory" that people have about anger. The data presented in Table 10-3 should be viewed in much the same way. That is, these reports indicate the aims that the target thought the angry persons would or should have, given the nature of the instigation, the responses exhibited, the relationship involved, and so on.

As a general statement, it may be said that the targets tended to view the other person's anger as selfishly and situationally determined. This is reflected in the three most frequently ascribed motives: to bring about a change for his or her (the angry person's) own good, to get back at you (the target) for the present incident, and to let off steam. Selfishness, however, does not necessarily imply malevolence. Only about 12% of the targets believed that the angry person wanted to break off a relationship and/or express dislike. On the other hand, 55% of the targets attributed to the angry person one or both of the constructive motives—to strengthen a relationship and to bring about a change primarily for your (the target's) own good.

It is difficult to compare these results directly with the motives angry persons attributed to themselves in Study I. If the "don't know" category is not counted, then targets are more likely than angry persons to attribute a typical angry episode to letting off steam. Also, targets are less likely than angry persons to believe that malevolent motives—for example, "to express dislike"—are involved.

However, if the percentage of targets who said that they did not know the motives of the angry person are added to those who said that a motive was "somewhat" or "very much" involved, then the above differences become exaggerated with respect to fractious anger and diminished with respect to malevolent anger. For example, only 33% of the subjects in Study I who said that the target knew of their anger indicated that letting off steam was one of their motives. Nearly twice as many targets either made this attribution (51%) or else stated that they did not know (10%). On the other hand, with regard to malevolent anger, 19% of the relevant subjects in Study I said that they wanted "to express dislike." Only 6% of the targets in Study II made a similar attribution. But the numbers involved are small, and the differences between the two studies largely disappear if the 9% of the targets who said that they did not know are also counted.

Table 10-3. Motives Attributed to the Angry Person by the Target ($n = 80$)

Motive	Mean rating[a]	Percentage of subjects marking	
		"Somewhat" or "very much"	"Don't know"
1. To bring about a change in your behavior primarily for his or her own good	.99	64	1
2. To get back at you, or gain revenge for the present incident	.90	61	4
3. To let off steam over miscellaneous frustrations	.85[b]	51	10
4. To assert authority or independence, or to improve his/her self-image	.79	53	11
5. To strengthen a relationship with you	.63	40	11
6. To bring about a change in your behavior primarily for your own good	.60	35	9
7. To get you to do something for him/her	.55	38	6
8. To get even with you for past wrongs	.53	31	4
9. To break off a relationship with you	.08[b]	5	6
10. To express general dislike for you	.07[b]	6	9
11. To get out of doing something for you	.07[b]	5	5

[a] 0 = not at all; 1 = somewhat; 2 = very much. Subjects who answered "don't know" were not included in the calculation of the mean ratings.

[b] On these motives there were insignificant ($p < .01$) differences between the attribution to another (by the target) and to oneself (by the angry person). The mean ratings were: to let off steam, .85 vs. .42; to break off a relationship, .08 vs. .25; to express dislike, .07 vs. .23; and to get out of doing something, .07 vs. .24. In other words, persons tend to view another's anger as more fractious but also as less malevolent than their own.

Summary

As far as the object of a typical angry episode is concerned (i.e., targets, instigations, and motives or objectives), both targets and angry persons appear to be in fair agreement. In the present study, the target stood in a positive affective relationship with the angry person (e.g., as a friend or loved one) in approximately 80% of the episodes. In 50% of the episodes the target admitted that the instigation was either an unjustified act or an avoidable accident; and in most of the remaining cases the imputation of blame was clearly recognized, even if denied. Finally, targets were no more likely—and perhaps even less likely—than angry persons to regard the motives for anger as malevolent. Targets recognized constructive motives in over 50% of the episodes, and in this respect also did not differ significantly from the angry persons who participated in Study I. The major difference between the two studies in terms of motives is that targets were much more likely to say that the angry person was letting off steam over miscellaneous frustrations.

Responses of the Angry Person as Perceived by the Target

In Chapter 9 it was concluded that anger cannot be identified too closely with aggression, particularly in a biological sense. This conclusion was based on two major findings. First, nonaggressive responses, such as talking the incident over with the instigator without hostility, were about as common as aggressive responses. Second, when aggression did occur, it was usually in a highly socialized form, for example, a verbal retort or the denial of some benefit customarily enjoyed by the instigator. Physical aggression was rare; even the impulse to physical aggression was not particularly common.

The above findings were, however, based on reports by angry persons of their own behavior. Targets have a less benign view of the behavior of angry persons, as evidenced by the data presented in Tables 10-4 and 10-5.

Table 10-4 presents mean ratings of all responses attributed to the angry person by the target. About 86% of the targets said that the angry person became verbally aggressive. The denial of some benefit or customarily enjoyed behavior (e.g., withdrawal of affection) was also a commonly perceived response—by over 60% of the targets.

For many of the responses listed in Table 10-4 the targets were often unsure whether or not the angry person actually engaged in the behavior described. These particular responses will therefore not be discussed further, for the data add no new insights to what already has been said on the topic. Rather, we shall focus attention on the four responses that involved a direct interaction between the angry person and the target, and hence for which there was no uncertainty on the part of the target that such a response was actually made. These responses include verbal aggression, denial of benefit, physical aggression, and talking the incident over with the offender. Table 10-5 compares the mean ratings of angry persons and targets on each of these four variables.

Table 10-4. Responses of the Angry Person as Perceived by the Target

Type of response	Mean rating ($n = 80$)	Percentage of subjects marking	
		"Somewhat" or "very much"	"Don't know"
Direct aggression			
Verbal or symbolic aggression	1.55	86	0
Denial or removal of some benefit	.84	61	0
Physical aggression or punishment	.30	20	0
Indirect aggression			
Telling a third party in order to get back at the instigator (malediction)	.34	23	10
Harming something important to the instigator	.10	8	3
Displaced aggression			
Against a nonhuman object or thing	.33	21	16
Against some person	.27	16	21
Nonaggressive responses			
Engaging in calming activities	.73	40	20
Talking the incident over with a neutral party, with no intent to harm the offender	.37	23	23
Talking the incident over with the offender without exhibiting hostility	.56	43	0
Engaging in activities opposite to the instigation of anger	.28	16	5

Table 10-5. Mean Ratings of Angry Responses as Perceived by the Angry Person ($n = 102$) and by the Target ($n = 80$)

Response	Mean rating[a]		Significance of the difference
	Angry persons	Targets	
Verbal or symbolic aggression	.97	1.55	$< .01$
Denial or removal of some benefit	.70	.84	ns
Physical aggression or punishment	.11	.30	$< .05$
Talking the incident over with the offender without exhibiting hostility	.78	.56	$< .10$

[a] 0 = not at all; 1 = somewhat; 2 = very much.

As can be seen from the data presented in Table 10-5, targets tended to view the angry persons as more aggressive, both verbally and physically, than the latter viewed themselves. Conversely, the angry persons were more likely to say that they talked the incident over with the offender, although the difference between the groups was in this case only marginally significant.

It must be kept in mind that different incidents were being described by the angry persons and targets; but that cannot account for the widely different perceptions on the part of the two groups of subjects. There were no indications, for example, in the open-ended responses, that the two sets of incidents actually differed in the amount of aggression involved. Rather, it seems that we are dealing with true differences in perception.

Brown and Tedeschi (1976) have demonstrated that the perception of a response as aggressive is dependent on the orientation of the observer and the nature of the instigating conditions. For example, an attack in response to an "adequate" provocation is perceived as less aggressive than an unprovoked attack. From the data presented in the previous section (see Table 10-1) it is clear that targets are more likely than angry persons to regard the instigation as either justified or unavoidable; that is, as an event that should not provoke anger. On this basis alone, one might expect that targets would perceive the behavior of angry persons as more aggressive. However, when the responses attributed to the angry persons were analyzed as a function of the perceived provocation, no significant differences emerged. That is, targets who believed the provocation to be justified or unavoidable rated the angry person as no more aggressive than did targets who believed the provocation to be unjustified or avoidable. Hence, factors other than, or in addition to, the perceived provocation must have influenced the target's ratings of the other person's anger.

We can only speculate on what those other factors might be, but the answer is perhaps quite simple. As we have seen, anger involves an accusation of wrongdoing, and it at least carries with it the threat of retaliation. On either ground, the mere statement "I am angry" could easily be interpreted as aggressive by the target, whereas the angry person could just as rightly view such a statement as more informative than aggressive.

In summary, there may be some truth to the assertion that the expression of anger is inherently aggressive, at least from the target's point of view. This truth, however, is based on only one of the many meanings of aggression; it does not necessarily support the view that anger and aggression are closely linked, for example, in a biological sense.

Recognizing Another's Anger

In earlier chapters, the instigation or provocation has been emphasized as a major criterion for the attribution of anger. This is particularly evident, for example, in courts of law, where the adequacy of provocation is the primary basis for classifying a homicide as a crime of passion as opposed to premediated murder. Of course, in court cases a violent act has already occurred, and hence response characteristics might be expected to be less informative than the instigation. In everyday affairs, by contrast, matters are often the reverse; that is, the instigation may be recognized as provocative before any overt response has been made. In such circumstances, what is the relative importance of situational as opposed to behavioral cues in the attribution of anger? And among behavioral cues, which are more important, instrumental responses (verbal or physical aggression) or expressive reactions?

In order to explore issues such as these, Questionnaire B contained a number of items designed to ascertain how the target first recognized the other person's anger. The target, it should be noted, is in a particularly advantageous position to weigh the relative importance of situational and behavioral cues in the attribution of anger, for aside from the angry person, few people are in a better position to be aware of all facets of the angry episode.

In Questionnaire B, subjects were provided with a list of several different types of cues on which the recognition of anger might be based. Table 10-6 indicates the extent to which each type of cue contributed to the target's initial impression of the other person's anger.

Nearly all targets mentioned some kind of expressive reaction, with the tone of voice being cited most frequently (by 89% of the targets). The content of what the angry person said (including verbal aggression) was also mentioned by 86% of the targets. With regard to nonverbal instrumental responses, the way the angry person acted was divided into two opposing categories—withdrawal and attack (physical aggression). The former, which was mentioned by about half the targets, was nearly twice as frequent as the latter. Finally, knowledge of the precipitating incident aided in the recognition of the other person's anger in 63% of the incidents.

The above results suggest that both instrumental responses (what a person says and does) and expressive reactions (the manner in which it is said and done) are

Table 10-6. Cues by Which the Target First Recognized or Inferred the Other Person's Anger ($n = 80$)

Type of cue	Mean rating[a]	Percentage of subjects marking "somewhat" or "very much"
Expressive reactions on the part of the angry person		
Tone of voice	1.54	89
Facial expressions	1.23	75
Body postures or gestures	.89	60
Content of what the angry person said	1.48	86
Way the angry person acted		
Became withdrawn or noncommunicative	.75	48
Became physically aggressive	.45	28
Precipitating incident	.89	63

[a] 0 = not at all; 1 = somewhat; 2 = very much.

important for the recognition of another person's anger. We cannot infer from these data which of these two aspects or kinds of behavior is typically more informative. Nevertheless, the evident importance of expressive reactions deserves brief comment.

A Further Note on Expressive Reactions

As discussed in Chapter 2, expressive reactions have traditionally played an important role in theories of emotion. Most speculation has centered on specific facial expressions and their possible evolutionary significance. It is therefore of interest to note that, in the present study, the most frequently mentioned expressive reaction was the tone of voice. The present remarks will therefore be limited to a few observations on vocal cues, although similar observations could be made with regard to other expressive reactions (and physiological changes) as well.

Scherer (1979) has made a comprehensive review of research on the nonlinguistic aspects of vocal expression during emotion. He concludes that

> we can be reasonably certain only about the vocal indicators of the two emotions studied most frequently: anger and grief/sadness. Anger seems to be characterized by high pitch level and wide pitch range, loud voice, and fast tempo, whereas the opposite ends of these vocal dimensions characterize grief/sadness: low pitch and narrow pitch range, downward pitch contour, soft voice, and slow tempo.

He goes on to note, however, that

> these vocal dimensions are also closely identified with the opposite poles of the activation dimension, inviting the conjecture that only the activation differences between simultations of highly agitated anger (as compared to the suppressed kind) and quiet grief/sadness (as compared to desperate mourning) have been measured by these parameters (p. 514)

In the studies reviewed by Scherer, vocal cues did not allow a distinction among various emotions except as the latter varied along a dimension of arousal, for example, from "quiet grief" to "agitated anger." In this respect, it might be recalled from Chapter 9 that the major—indeed, about the only—physiological symptom or "expressive reaction" that was consistently reported by a majority of angry persons was an increase in general tension or arousal. It is thus reasonable to assume that, in the present study, the vocal cues of most importance for the recognition of anger were the high pitch, wide range, loud voice, and fast tempo characteristic of aroused speech.

But even this last assumption requires qualification. Most of the studies of specific emotions reviewed by Scherer (13 out of 16) involved actors simulating the speech of persons who are supposedly angry, sad, and so on. Such a procedure can introduce artificial uniformity into the data. When vocalization is studied as a function of induced stress or arousal (either in the laboratory or natural settings), the results are quite variable. For example, whereas the pitch of the voice may rise for the majority of the subjects under stress, it may fall for a significant minority. Scherer concludes that "individual differences in vocal reactions are of such magnitude and importance that the study of the causes for such differences should be one of the major issues for further research" (p. 507).

The problem of individual differences is readily apparent in the open-ended responses of subjects who participated in the present study. The specific expressive reactions spontaneously mentioned by the subjects were often highly idiosyncratic to the angry person. For example, one target remarked: "I can tell whether she is happy or mad by if she talks a lot or not"; and another commented that "the first signs of her anger are always squinty eyes and she turns away." It will be recalled that in most of the episodes the targets knew the angry persons quite well. Such knowledge is evidently quite important in recognizing another's anger. Hebb (1946) has made a similar observation with regard to the recognition of "emotion" in chimpanzees. He notes that the attribution of "emotion" to these animals is not based on behavior alone, nor even on behavior in conjunction with a particular set of precipitating conditions. Rather, each animal has its idiosyncratic way of responding when "angry," "depressed," "fearful," and so on, and the identification of the response depends on a knowledge of such idiosyncrasies. The same is certainly even more true in the case of human beings.

Situational Cues

The relative weight given to situational cues as opposed to overt behavior (whether instrumental or expressive) is of considerable theoretical interest. We have seen, for example, how the object of anger involves a person's appraisal of the situation; and how the object, even more than the response, helps to define the emotion. The functional significance of anger also depends on an appropriate awareness of situational cues. If I believe that X makes John angry, then I may be hesitant about doing X, even if John does not show his anger.

In addition to rating the *absolute* importance of situational and behavioral cues, the results of which were presented in Table 10-6, targets in Study II also were asked to rate the *relative* importance of these two general classes of variables. For this purpose, a 7-point scale was provided. A -3 on the scale indicated that the initial impression of the other person's anger was based exclusively on situational cues; and a value of +3 indicated that the impression was based exclusively on the behavior of the angry person (expressive reactions, instrumental responses, etc.). If both types of cues were equally important, the subject was to mark 0, the midpoint of the scale.

The number of subjects marking each point on the scale is given below. In order to illustrate the meaning of the scale, examples of some of the open-ended responses that subjects gave for their ratings are also provided.

-3 (3 subjects) "I knew what would make him mad and I did it."
-2 (3 subjects) "I knew that parking my car in her place would make her angry, but I was not really thinking about it until she came along."
-1 (2 subjects) "When it happened I knew he would be mad and his body posture soon confirmed it."
 0 (20 subjects) "I could tell by her attitude and lack of responses [that she was angry] but I also knew that her anger was coming."

+1 (19 subjects)   "Even though I knew that the situation would make him angry I also didn't know how angry and if he actually was angry at me until I heard him yell and saw his reactions to my response."

+2 (16 subjects)   "From the situation I had an idea he might be angry but his responses proved my expectations to be correct."

+3 (17 subjects)   "I did not think that the situation would provoke anger. I just knew she was angry from her response."

Not all the explanations that subjects gave for their ratings were as clear-cut as the above examples might suggest. Nevertheless, the general trend of the data is clear. Most subjects found the behavior of the angry person more informative than knowledge of the precipitating incident. Only 10% of the subjects (8) placed greater weight on situational cues; 65% (52) placed greater weight on behavioral cues; and 25% (20) gave equal weight to both kinds of cues. The mean ratings for all subjects was +1.1.

The relative weight assigned to situational cues varied systematically as a function of the nature of the precipitating incident. Specifically, the mean rating on the above scale was 0.1 for those subjects who said that the precipitating incident was *voluntary and unjustified*. This was significantly ($p < .05$) lower than for any of the other three conditions (i.e., an avoidable accident, an unavoidable accident, or a justified act). The overall mean of the latter conditions—which did not differ among themselves—was 1.3. In other words, subjects who knew that they were acting unjustifiably tended to use this knowledge in inferring that the other person was angry. Still, even these subjects placed (on the average) equal or greater weight on the responses of the angry person.

The above results are not particularly surprising. A person may anticipate, on the basis of situational cues, that another will become angry; and yet it is not until the other person responds that the expectation is confirmed. Hence, response cues should typically be more important in the initial recognition of another's anger. Apropos of this, 44% of the targets indicated that the other person's anger was "somewhat" expected, and another 13% said that it was "very much" expected. Of course, the expectations of the target may influence whether, and at what point, another person's behavior is interpreted as anger. In extreme cases (e.g., a deliberate insult) the expectation may be so strong that nearly any change in the other person's behavior will be taken as a sign of anger.

This last point is of theoretical as well as practical interest. It means that anger may exert a controlling influence even when it is not expressed, or is only partially expressed. The mere expectation that one's own actions may elicit anger can be a powerful source of inhibition.

The Effects of the Other Person's Anger on the Target

Perhaps the most important aspects of any angry episode—at least from a functional point of view—are the reactions of the target. In Questionnaire B, four questions addressed this issue. The first question consisted of a list of nine possible reactions (e.g., defiance, indifference, an apology) which subjects were asked to rate on 3-point scales. The second question asked: "Regardless of how you reacted, how did you *feel* when you realized the person was angry?" Eight possible subjective experiences were listed. The third question asked subjects to rate eight additional responses and longer term changes in attitudes (e.g., gaining or losing respect for the angry person) that might have resulted from the episode. Finally, as in Questionnair A, subjects were asked to evaluate the overall beneficial and harmful effects of the episode.

The responses of subjects to the first question are presented in Table 10-7. The two most commonly reported reactions were "hurt feelings" and "surprise," each mentioned by more than 60% of the targets. An apology was also a common reaction, but so too was defiance. In general, subjects seemed to show a mixed and often ambivalent set of reactions as they attempted to come to terms with the other person's anger. As one person explained, "I was basically hurt, but I realized I was in the wrong. At first I was very defiant." Another commented, "I tried to justify my behavior before telling him I was sorry; I was somewhat nervous—didn't know what else to expect from him."

As may be recalled from Chapter 9, the subjects (angry persons) who participated in Study I also were asked to rate the reactions of the targets to their anger. Keeping in mind that different incidents are being described, a comparison of the reactions of targets as viewed by angry persons (Questionnaire A) and by targets (Questionnaire B) is of interest. The results of such a comparison are also presented in Table 10-7. From both the absolute values and the shift in relative rankings, it is

Table 10-7. Reactions of the Target as Reported by the Target (Study II) and by the Angry Person (Study I)

Reactions	Mean ratings[a] and percentages of subjects marking "somewhat" or "very much"		Significance of the differences between the means
	Targets ($n=80$)	Angry persons ($n=102$)	
Hurt feelings	.93 66%	.55 42%	$< .01$
Surprise	.91 63	.38 29	$< .01$
Apology or other sign of contrition	.85 58	.56 41	$< .05$
Defiance	.80 58	.62 46	ns
Anger or hostility	.61 49	.51 38	ns
Rejection	.48 39	.35 28	ns
Denial of responsibility	.48 36	.57 41	ns
Indifference or lack of emotion	.43 35	.62 44	$< .10$
Jokes, frivolity, or silliness	.39 33	.17 14	$< .01$
Other[b]			

[a] 0 = not at all; 1 = somewhat; 2 very much.
[b] Eighteen "other" reactions mentioned by the targets. The most frequent of these (by 5 subjects) was a discussion with the angry person. Angry persons who marked this category were more likely to see the target as negative or unresponsive (cf. Table 9-9).

clear that targets view themselves as more reactive (e.g., hurt) and forthcoming (e.g., apologetic) than do angry persons. Such differences in perception could well exacerbate an angry episode and hinder its resolution.

The subjects (targets) in Study II were also asked how they felt in response to the other person's anger, regardless of how they reacted. The most commonly experienced feelings were irritability and depression (reported by 76 and 66% of the targets, respectively). Over half of the targets also reported feeling ashamed, bewildered and/or anxious. On the positive side, about 30% of the targets reported feeling confident (self-assured), and approximately 15% actually felt good and/or relieved about the incident. These latter reactions primarily involved incidents in which the target believed that he or she was "standing up" to the angry person and refused to be intimidated. But on the whole it is quite clear that anger is a very unpleasant experience for the target, to be avoided if possible.

The immediate feelings and reactions of the target are of significance primarily to the extent that they foster changes in behavior and attitudes, changes that might help resolve the conflict and prevent recurrences in the future. Table 10-8 presents a list of eight possible changes, together with mean ratings and percentage of endorsement. Approximately 76% of the targets indicated that they came to realize their own faults as a result of the incident. That is hardly surprising, since anger is (if at all warranted) an imputation of blame. Somewhat more surprising is the fact that about 48% of the targets believed that their relationship with the angry person was *strengthened* because of the incident; by contrast, only 35% said that their relationship became cooler or more distant. (It might be noted, however, that a greater proportion of subjects who checked the latter item were more vehement in their response, marking "very much" rather than "somewhat.")

Table 10-8. Longer Term Responses or Changes Made by the Target as a Consequence of the Other Person's Anger (n = 80)

Response	Mean rating[a]	Percentage of persons marking "somewhat" or "very much"
You realized your own faults.	1.09	76
You felt your relationship with the angry person was strengthened.	.67	48
You realized your own strengths.	.66	50
You did something that was good for the angry person.	.59	39
Your relationship with the angry person became cooler or more distant as a result of this incident.	.55	35
You gained respect for the angry person.	.54	44
You did something that was for your own good.	.46	38
You lost respect for the angry person.	.34	29

[a] 0 = not at all; 1 = somewhat; 2 = very much.

About half of the targets also indicated that the incident helped them to realize their own strengths. At first, this might seem like a positive outcome. As will be discussed more fully below, however, this outcome was more likely to accompany episodes that were evaluated negatively overall.

Finally, in about 39% of the episodes the targets did something that they considered good for the angry person, and nearly as often they did something that was for their own good. Also, subjects more often gained respect for the angry person than they lost respect (in 44% as opposed to 29% of the episodes, respectively).

We shall return to a more detailed discussion of these results shortly. But first, it will simplify matters if we consider briefly the overall beneficial and harmful consequences of the incidents. As in Study I, the subjects who participated in Study II were asked:

> Everything considered (the nature of the precipitating incident, the other person's anger, your own reactions, and the long-term consequences), do you believe that this episode of anger was adaptive (beneficial)_____ or maladaptive (harmful) _____

The ratio of beneficial to harmful evaluations was 2.5:1; specifically, 54 subjects said that the incident was beneficial and 22 said it was harmful (4 said it was neither or both). Among the 102 angry persons completing Questionnaire A who informed the target of their anger, the corresponding ratio was 3.1:1. Although these ratios are not significantly different statistically, there is reason to believe that angry persons generally view the outcome of a typical angry episode as more beneficial than do targets. Anger is an unpleasant experience for both the angry person and the target; it is, however, more unpleasant for the latter. Also, anger is intimidating, and the target may respond in a conciliatory manner simply to avoid a scene, thus conveying to the angry person a false sense of "success."

Recognizing that the perspective of the target may be biased toward negative outcomes, it is particularly noteworthy that approximately 70% of the targets still evaluated the episodes as adaptive or beneficial. Let us consider some of the reasons for such favorable evaluations.

Four of the long-term outcomes listed in Table 10-8 showed statistically significant differences as a function of whether the episode was evaluated as beneficial or harmful. The outcome that most clearly distinguished between the overall evaluation of an episode was

(a) You felt your relationship with the angry person was strengthened. (Mean ratings = .87 vs. .18 for beneficial vs. harmful evaluations, respectively; $p < .01$.)

Two other outcomes also were associated with an overall beneficial evaluation, but to a lesser degree. These were

(b) You realized your own faults. (Mean ratings = 1.20 vs. .77, $p < .05$.)
(c) You gained respect for the angry person. (Mean ratings = .61 vs. .27, $p < .05$.)

One outcome showed a significant relationship in the opposite direction, that is, it was rated more highly by subjects who evaluated the incidents as harmful than by those who evaluated the incidents as beneficial. This "negative" outcome was

(d) You realized your own strengths. (Mean ratings = .95 vs. .52 for harmful vs. beneficial evaluations, respectively; $p < .05$.)

On a priori grounds, it would be expected that any beneficial or harmful outcomes of an angry episode would depend in part on the nature of the instigation and in part on the responses of the angry person. We will consider the nature of the instigation first. An "adequate provocation" in the everyday sense would involve either an *avoidable accident* or an *unjustified* act on the part of the instigator (target). It is primarily under these conditions that anger should have a beneficial effect. Data relevant to this issue are presented in Table 10-9.

Our concern for the moment is with the three outcomes associated with an overall beneficial evaluation of the incident. Two of these—a gain in respect for the angry person and a realization of one's own faults—show the predicted pattern. The results are, however, statistically significant only in the case of the former.

Surprisingly, the outcome that was regarded most beneficial, namely, a strengthening of the relationship with the angry person, did not vary systematically as a function of the precipitating incident. One reason for this rather anomalous result is suggested by the remarks of one subject who accepted full responsibility for instigating the episode. "No matter how forgiving both sides are, memories still exist and you don't forget that you [the instigator/target] did something harmful to a friend [the angry person]." In other words, the entire episode may be regarded as damaging to the relationship because of the lingering aftereffects of the original provocation. In a narrow sense, one could argue that the anger itself was beneficial in such instances if it helped prevent similar provocations in the future; nevertheless, it would have been better for the relationship had the entire incident, beginning with the provocation, never occurred.

A second reason for the apparent lack of association between the precipitating incident and the strengthening of a relationship is the converse of the above. As discussed earlier, the nature of the precipitating incident is often not fixed at the outset. Rather, it is subject to negotiation as the angry episode progresses. From their open-ended responses it is apparent that some of the targets considered their actions as "justified" even though they realized that the angry person would disagree. A few, in fact, even deliberately provoked the other person's anger in order to bring the disagreement into the open. If the episode helped to resolve the issue, then the relationship was considered strengthened, even though the other person's anger may still have seemed unwarranted from the target's point of view. Although such cases were not the norm, they were sufficient in number to help mask any association between the nature of the precipitating incident and a strengthening of the relationship between the target and the angry person.

Let us now consider the outcome that was most associated with an overall negative evaluation of the episode, namely, a realization by the target of his or her own strengths. Although this outcome is positive in and of itself, 68% of the targets who evaluated an episode as harmful mentioned this as one of the consequences, whereas only 41% of those who judged an episode as beneficial did so.

As might be expected, targets who said that they came to realize their own strengths also tended to regard the instigation as voluntary and justified (see Table

Table 10-9. Mean Ratings of Four Outcomes as a Function of the Nature of the Precipitating Incidents

Outcomes	Precipitating incident				Significance of the differences
	Avoidable accident (n=23)	Unavoidable accident (n=12)	Voluntary and justified act (n=28)	Voluntary and unjustified act (n=17)	
You gained respect for the angry person.	$.87_a$	$.33_b$	$.36_b$	$.52_a$	<.05
You realized your own faults.	1.21	1.00	.93	1.24	ns
Your relationship with the angry person was strengthened.	.83	.58	.79	.31	ns
You realized your own strengths.	$.57_a$	$.50_a$	1.04_b	$.29_a$	<.01

Note. The mean ratings are based on a 3-point scale (0 = not at all; 1 = somewhat; 2 = very much). For any given variable, the mean ratings with similar subscripts do not differ significantly from one another, using the Tukey α procedure.

10-9). In other words, these subjects saw themselves as defending their own actions against the presumably unwarranted anger of the other person.

It might be noted that several of the possible outcomes listed in Table 10-8 (viz., a cooling of the relationship with, and loss of respect for, the angry person) are more explicitly negative than the "harmful" outcome we have been discussing (i.e., realizing one's own strengths). Yet these outcomes did not differentiate between episodes that were evaluated as beneficial or harmful overall. The explanation may perhaps be found in the fact that the explicitly negative outcomes tended to be associated with incidents that involved acquaintances, strangers, or disliked others. Sixteen incidents fell into one or another of these categories, and in 12 (75%) of these incidents the target said that they either lost respect for the angry person, and/or that their relationship became more distant. By contrast, of the episodes in which the angry person was either a friend or loved one only 33% of the targets said that the relationship became cooler and/or that they lost respect for the angry person. These results strongly suggest that if the relationship between the target and the angry person is already distant or strained, then anger is likely to create further antagonisms, but such an outcome may not be regarded (by the target) as particularly harmful.

We will now consider briefly the relationship of perceived outcomes to the behavior of the angry person. For this purpose, the mean ratings of the four outcomes discussed above (see Table 10-9) were correlated with the four types of response of which the target was directly aware. The latter included direct verbal or symbolic aggression, the denial of some benefit, physical aggression or punishment, and talking the incident over without hostility (see Table 10-5). The largest correlation ($r = .40$, $p < .01$) was between a strengthening of the relationship and talking the incident over without hostility. All six of the correlations between the three beneficial outcomes and either physical or verbal aggression were negative (and three were statistically significant). In short, from the target's point of view, the more aggressive the behavior of the angry person, the less beneficial the outcome is liable to be considered.

Concluding Observations

The data in this chapter mainly serve to reinforce the picture of anger presented in Chapters 8 and 9. This is important, for it could be argued that the self-reports of angry persons cannot be trusted. For reasons of social desirability, angry persons might depict their anger as more reasonable and constructive than it actually is. However, when targets describe their experiences in a similar way, then confidence in the conclusions is greatly enhanced.

To recapitulate some of the major points of agreement, both angry persons and targets view an "adequate provocation" to anger as involving an unjustified act or an avoidable accident. Moreover, neither the angry persons nor the targets regard the typical episode of anger as malevolently motivated; and provided that the angry person does not become too aggressive, the outcome is generally evaluated by both as beneficial.

Within this general framework there is of course ample room for disagreement about particulars. Thus, angry persons are more likely than targets to view a provocation as unjustified (e.g., as a violation of some social norm). Also, angry persons tend to regard their own behavior as constructively motivated, whereas targets view the angry person as more selfishly (but not as more malevolently) motivated. Finally, angry persons see their own behavior as more controlled and less aggressive than targets see it.

It is tempting to ask, Which view is closer to the truth—that of the angry person or that of the target? In most instances this is not a very meaningful question. The typical episode of anger involves a conflict among close friends or loved ones. The anger is itself an attempt to clarify and resolve a source of disagreement. The surprising fact is how often the outcome of anger is evaluated as beneficial, whether from the point of view of the angry person or the target.

Not surprisingly, the beneficial effects of anger depend, in part, on the adequacy of the provocation and are inversely related to excesses in the response (e.g., too much aggression). That most episodes of anger are regarded as beneficial is perhaps the most important finding to emerge from Studies I and II, for it helps to resolve a paradox that has long plagued theories of anger. Anger is an unpleasant and distressing experience for both the angry person and the target; and, as we have seen in the case of Seneca (Chapter 4), anger has often been condemned as detrimental to the individual and to the commonweal. In view of all this negative reinforcement, why is anger such a prevalent response? The answer most commonly given to this question is that anger (conceptualized primarily in terms of physical aggression) was at one time biologically adaptive, but that it is no longer so. Like the vermiform appendix, which typically is benign but which sometimes becomes inflamed, anger is presumed to be a remnant of our biological heritage.

The results of the present studies provide support for a different explanation for the prevalence of anger; namely, anger continues to serve a function in the regulation of everyday affairs. In spite of the unpleasantness of the experience, most people feel that the final outcome of a typical angry episode is more beneficial than harmful. Thus, rather than likening anger to the vermiform appendix (a biological given), a better analogy might be to a medicine (a social product). A medicine may taste bad and have unpleasant side effects, but it nevertheless has generally beneficial effects if used appropriately.

Chapter 11

Differences Between Anger and Annoyance

In order to understand a phenomenon such as anger, it is often helpful to explore the similarities and differences between it and other closely related phenomena. That was the implicit rationale behind the discussion in Chapter 3 of cross-cultural variations in aggressive syndromes. The purpose of the present chapter is to contrast anger with a closely related emotion in our own culture, namely, annoyance. There is no special reason for selecting annoyance (as opposed, say, to contempt or jealousy) for this purpose. A little reflection suggests, however, that "annoyance" is the most common, as well as the most inclusive, term for relatively mild states similar to anger.

Many of the same situations that annoy us also occasion anger; and we often respond similarly when angry and annoyed. How, then, does anger differ from annoyance? We will attempt to answer this question in two ways. First, we will present empirical data from Study III, which was designed specifically to assess the differences between typical episodes of anger and annoyance. Second, on a more conceptual level, we will compare the differences between anger and annoyance, on the one hand, with the differences between knowledge and belief, on the other. At first, such a comparison might seem rather remote. However, the distinction between knowledge and belief has been the subject of analysis since antiquity, and some of the issues raised and resolutions proffered are directly relevant, in a logical sense, to our present concerns.

So as not to become immediately lost in a maze of data, it might be helpful at the outset to provide an overview of some of the major results. With regard to the empirical analysis, a typical episode of anger may differ from a typical episode of annoyance in any of the following ways. The episode of anger may (1) be more intense, (2) be elicited by a more serious incident, (3) be more likely to involve an attribution of blame, and (4) be experienced as more personally significant and relevant. Anger is also more likely (5) to involve interpersonal relationships, (6) to demand expression, and (7) to tax the normal coping resources of the individual. In addition, anger is more often (8) motivated by revenge, and (9) affected differently by the mood of the individual at the time of the provocation.

The above differences are of interest not simply because they help clarify the nature of anger, but also because they represent important variables in their own right. Take, for example, the matter of intensity. This is frequently regarded as a fundamental dimension of emotion. But what, exactly, do we mean by emotional intensity? And on what grounds are judgments of intensity based? Similar questions arise with regard to the other variables, as will be discussed following presentation of the data.

The foregoing ways in which anger *may* differ from annoyance are not sufficient to distinguish between these two emotional states. Consider again the dimension of intensity. Although anger is usually regarded as more intense than annoyance, the opposite sometimes occurs. Or consider the following facts: The behavior of someone who is angry may be indistinguishable from the behavior of a person who is only annoyed; moreover, the instigations to the two emotions are often the same (e.g., some appraised wrong). In such cases, the differences between anger and annoyance seem to lie in the network of social rules and obligations that lend each emotion its meaning, and not in the psychological state of the individual. But more of that later.

Study III. Empirical Analyses

Study III differs from Study I (one's own experience of anger) and Study II (experiencing another's anger) in method as well as purpose. In Studies I and II, subjects were asked to recall the most intense incident of anger that occurred during the past week. In Study III, by contrast, subjects were asked to keep a daily record of each instance of anger and annoyance for a period of 1 week. They then selected one instance of anger and one of annoyance on which to report in detail.

Subjects

The original goal was to have 50 subjects, 25 men and 25 women, complete the study. As a result of time and sampling constraints, however, the records of only 48 subjects were finally used for analysis. These were obtained as follows.

To maintain comparability with the student samples used in the previous studies, subjects were limited to unmarried native-born Americans 21 years of age or younger. During the course of a semester, 31 males and 27 females who met these criteria were recruited from introductory courses. Those who completed the study received $5.00 as well as some course credit.

Of those who volunteered, three males and one female did not complete the project. An additional four males did not keep their records accurately or completely, and their data had to be eliminated. This reduced the male sample to 24 subjects and the female sample to 26. To equalize the number of males and females, the data of two women were eliminated at random.

Methods

Potential subjects attended a small group meeting in which the nature of the study was described and instructions for completing the diary record and questionnaires were provided. The diary was to be kept for 7 consecutive days, but subjects were allowed some leeway with regard to the day on which they started. All of the records and questionnaires had to be completed and returned within 3 weeks.

The diary consisted of a specially prepared booklet containing two sheets for each day. The first sheet provided space for subjects to note briefly each incident of anger and annoyance that occurred during the day. Subjects were instructed to label clearly each incident as "anger," "annoyance," or "uncertain." On the second sheet, subjects described in more detail the most intense incident of anger (if any) and annoyance (if any) that occurred during the day. For each such incident they rated its intensity (on a 10-point scale) and described the target, the precipitating incident, any thoughts and feelings they had, their overt behavior, and the final outcome.

During the week of the diary, subjects were asked to set aside about a half hour each evening in which they could mentally go through the day, step by step, recalling each incident of anger and annoyance, and recording their experineces on the data sheets described above. The importance of distinguishing between anger and annoyance was emphasized. Specifically, subjects were instructed to label as annoyance only those incidents "in which you were clearly annoyed *but not angry*," and similarly, to label as anger "only those incidents in which you were clearly angry."

At the end of the week, subjects were asked to review the most intense incidents of anger and annoyance for each day. From these, they were to choose the single most intense incident for the week *that clearly represented anger* and the single most intense incident of *annoyance without anger*. Separate questionnaires were then completed, one for the incident of anger and the other for the incident of annoyance,

The two questionnaires were virtually indentical to that used in Study I (see Appendix A). Only minor changes were made at the beginning, in order to take into account the diary records (instead of the recall method used in Study I). The annoyance questionnaire was obtained simply by substituting the term *annoyance* for the term *anger* wherever relevant. To minimize carryover effects, the two questionnaires were completed on separate days. Half the subjects completed the annoyance questionnaire first, while the other half completed the anger questionnaire first.

At the end of the second questionnaire, subjects were asked to list up to three dimensions or features that helped them to distinguish anger from annoyance. These summary statements were to be based not only on the incidents described in the two questionnaires, but on the entire week's experiences as reported in the diary records. Content analyses were performed on these data in order to provide a framework for interpreting the more limited, but much more detailed, responses to the two questionnaires.

Finally, as a procedural check, the responses of subjects to the anger questionnaire were compared with the responses of the student subsample in Study I. The latter, it will be recalled, completed a comparable questionnaire, but without the

aid of a diary. There were no more statistically significant differences between the
two sets of data than would be expected on the basis of chance. This means that no
systematic differences were introduced by having subjects recall a recent incident of
anger (as in Study I) or by having subjects keep a diary record (as in Study III).
It also means that in presenting the results of Study III, we can focus primarily on
the differences between anger and annoyance. The relevant background data on the
everyday experience of anger are adequately represented in the previous chapters.

In presenting the results of this study, we shall follow the same sequence that
subjects did in collecting their data. That is, we shall summarize, first, the incidents
reported in the diary records; next, a detailed comparison will be made between the
two incidents described in the questionnaires; and third, content analysis is made of
the summary features or dimensions that subjects believed helped them to distinguish between anger and annoyance.

The Diary Records

For the week in which the diary record was kept, subjects reported 1,126 incidents
of annoyance and 348 incidents of anger. This means that, on the average, subjects
experienced 23.5 incidents of annoyance per week and 7.3 incidents of anger. In
addition, 62 incidents (4% of the total number of incidents recorded) were labeled
"uncertain." This figure is important, for it suggests that people are able, the vast
majority of the time, to distinguish between their own experiences of anger and
annoyance. Whether or not they can clearly state the basis for that distinction is
another matter, as we shall see below.

In their diaries, subjects only had to jot down a sentence or two regarding each
instance of anger and annoyance. These descriptions were too cursory to allow any
real comparative analysis. However, one bit of data is of potential interest. At the
end of the week, subjects were asked to indicate for each incident whether the primary object of the emotion was a person, an inanimate object, an instition, or
"something else." The results are presented in Table 11-1.

Approximately 70% of the anger incidents and 55% of the annoyance incidents
were directed at another person, a statistically significant difference ($p < .01$)
between the two emotional states. On the other hand, annoyance was more likely
than anger to be directed at inanimate objects, institutions, and/or something else
(e.g., states of affairs, such as hunger or being late for an appointment). All of these
differences, too, were statistically significant.

A Comparison of Specific Instances of Anger and Annoyance

As described earlier, subjects kept more detailed notes on the most intense incident
of anger that occurred each day (if any) and the most intense incident of annoyance. From these "most intense incidents." subjects selected one that "clearly illustrates *anger*" and one that "clearly illustrates *annoyance without anger*." Separate

Table 11-1. Proportion of Anger and Annoyance Incidents in Which the Primary Target was Another Person, an Inanimate Object, an Institution, or "Something Else"

Target	Emotional Reaction		Significance of the difference
	Anger	Annoyance	
Person	.70	.55	< .01
Inanimate object	.15	.22	< .01
Institution	.06	.11	< .05
Something else	.09	.13	< .05

Note. The significance of the differences was assessed by t tests, using both the raw proportions and an arc sine transformation. The significance levels reported in the table are based on the transformed data. The raw proportions yielded similar results, except in the case of the "something else" category, which failed to reach traditional levels of significance.

questionnaires were then completed for each incident. A comparison of the responses to the two questionnaires yielded the following results.

The Target of Anger and Annoyance

As indicated by the diary records, anger in general is more often directed at another person than is annoyance. However, among the more intense incidents described by subjects in the questionnaires, there were no significant differences between anger and annoyance in terms of the nature of the target. Of the 48 anger incidents, 79% were directed at another person; of the annoyance incidents, 77% were similarly directed.[1] Also, when the human targets were broken down by affectional and status relationships (e.g., a loved one or someone in authority), there were no statistically significant differences between the two kinds of episodes.

In comparing the anger and annoyance incidents on the remaining items in the questionnaires, two different sets of analyses were used. The first set of analyses was based on the data of all 48 subjects. However, since some variables are meaningful primarily when the target is a human being (e.g., the motive to gain revenge), a second set of analyses was performed on the data of those 28 subjects who became *both* angry and annoyed at another person. The results of the two sets of analyses were highly similar and, except where mentioned explicitly, only the results for the full sample are presented below. However, no differences between anger and annoyance are reported as statistically significant unless this was true of both the full and restricted samples.

---

[1] In another 10% of the cases subjects became angry or annoyed at themselves (five episodes each).

Intensity and Self-Control

Subjects were asked to rate the intensity of their experiences on a scale from 1 to 10. The mean rating for the anger incidents was 7.6 and that for the annoyance incidents was 7.3. The difference is not statistically significant. Thus, both the anger and annoyance incidents were rated as about equally intense, at least when considered within their own respective frames of reference. The frame of reference is important, for comparing the intensity of anger and annoyance may be like comparing the size of a cocker spaniel with that of a great dane—both may be "equally large" for their breed and yet differ greatly in size.

In order to compare the intensity of anger and annoyance, some criterion is needed that is relatively independent of the kind of emotion. The degree to which a person feels overcome or out of control is one such criterion. Indeed, as explained in earlier chapters, being overcome is part of what we mean by emotion.

As may be recalled from Chapter 8, ratings of self-control were obtained at two different points in the questionnaire, each time with reference to two different aspects of the emotional syndrome: (a) the inward experience, or thoughts and feelings of the subject; and (b) the outward expression, or what the subject said and did. There were highly significant differences between anger and annoyance on these scales (p's < .01). With regard to the combined score for inward experience, subjects rated themselves as more impulsive and out of control while angry than while annoyed (mean ratings = 6.4 and 5.3, respectively). With regard to outward expression, the corresponding ratings were 4.5 and 3.1.

Duration

Also related to the intensity of an episode is its duration. The median duration of the anger incidents was reported to the about 1 hour. The median duration of the annoyance incidents was less than ½ hour, a statistically significant difference (p < .01).

The Instigation

As discussed in earlier chapters, the typical instigation to anger is an event that is either voluntary and unjustified or, if accidental, at least avoidable. From the data presented in Table 11-2 it can be seen that the same is true for annoyance. It is also evident from these data that annoyance, but not anger, is often elicited by events that are appraised as either justified or unavoidable. In other words, the appraisals that accompany anger almost always involve an attribution of blame; annoyance is more variable in this respect.

There is no convenient statistical procedure for testing the significance of the differences depicted in Table 11-2. However, by combining the first two rows and the second two rows, a simple 2 X 2 table can be created that is both logically meaningful and easily analyzable. With this simplification the frequency of anger

Table 11-2. Frequency of Anger and Annoyance as a Function of the Nature of the Instigation

Instigation	Anger		Annoyance	
	Number	Percentage	Number	Percentage
Voluntary and unjustified	25	52	16	33
Potentially avoidable accident	20	42	17	35
Voluntary and justified	2	4	8	17
Unavoidable accident	1	2	7	15

and annoyance can be related to instigations that are "blameworthy" (e.g., unjustified acts and avoidable accidents) as opposed to instigations in which no one is at fault (i.e., justified acts and unavoidable accidents). A McNemar test (Siegel, 1956) of these combined data reveals a significant difference in appraisal depending upon whether the person was angry or annoyed ($p < .01$). Inspection of Table 11-2 indicates that this is due primarily to the greater frequency of anger when the instigation is appraised as voluntary and unjustified, and to the greater frequency of annoyance (in comparison to anger) when the instigation is either justified or unavoidable.

It is also evident from the data in Table 11-2 that although blameworthiness is almost a necessary condition for anger, it is by no means a sufficient condition. In many instances a person may only become annoyed, even though the precipitating incident is regarded as unjustified, or at least avoidable. To provoke anger, an event must generally be appraised as relatively serious and/or personally involving, as well as blameworthy. But more of that shortly.

Responses

When angry, subjects were more likely to engage in verbal aggression, and to do so more vehemently, than when annoyed ($p < .05$). Specifically, verbal aggression was either "somewhat" or "very much" (mostly the latter) involved in 50% of the angry incidents; by contrast it was involved (mostly "somewhat") in only 35% of the annoyance incidents.

The reverse trend was observed in the case of contrary reactions (i.e., behavior opposite to the expression of anger or annoyance). Only 10% of the subjects said that they engaged in contrary reactions when angry, but 42% did so when annoyed ($p < .01$).

A number of expressive reactions also occurred significantly more often, or more intensely, during anger than annoyance. These were flushing, crying (women only), and a shaky cracking voice (p's $< .01$).

Perhaps the major conclusion that can be drawn from these results is that anger is more likely to be expressed than is annoyance. This conclusion is supported by the fact that the target was twice as likely to know when the subject was angry than when he or she was annoyed (in 68% of the angry episodes vs. 32% of the annoyance episodes, counting only those episodes where the target was another person).

Motives

Only two motives distinguished anger from annoyance; namely, to get even for past wrongs and to gain revenge for the present incident. The first was involved "some-what" or "very much" in 46% of the anger incidents, but in only 19% of the annoyance incidents ($p < .01$). The corresponding values for the second motive (to gain revenge for the present incident) were 60% and 42% ($p < .05$). In general, it appears that anger places an emphasis on equity and retribution, whereas annoyance is a more automatic response to an irritating situation.

Outcomes

In terms of consequences, the incidents of both anger and annoyance were judged to be about equally beneficial. Specifically, 29 (60%) of the subjects said that their anger had been beneficial; a similar number—30—said that their annoyance had been beneficial. The reasons offered by subjects for the benficial outcomes were, however, different for the two emotions.

The majority of reasons offered by subjects can be divided into two broad categories. First, the episode may have altered the external circumstance, for example, by getting the instigator to change his or her ways and/or by increasing mutual understanding. Second, the person's own attitudes and behavior may have changed as a result of the episode, for example, through increased self-understanding.

With regard to the first category, 17 subjects said that their anger helped to change the situation for the better; only about half that many (9) said that their annoyance influenced the situation. This trend was reversed when it came to changing the person's own attitudes and behavior. Only 7 subjects said that their anger had such an effect, whereas annoyance was said to have increased self-understanding in 14 instances. This reversal in trend was not affected by the elimination of incidents that were directed at inanimate objects or at the self.

In short, although the outcomes of both anger and annoyance may be regarded as equally positive, the former is more likely to influence the external environment. Anger is a more action-oriented emotion than is annoyance.

About 30% of the anger and annoyance episodes were regarded as negative in outcome—as opposed to the 60% positive outcomes discussed above. (The remainder of the episodes—about 10% for each emotion—were regarded as neither positive nor negative, or as both.) The reasons offered by subjects for the harmful outcomes were difficult to classify and did not appear to differentiate between the two emotions.

The results reported thus far, based on analyses of the diary records and responses to the two questionnaires, are listed below. (This is the first of several lists that will be provided for purposes of comparison.)

List 1. Differences Between Anger and Annoyance Based on the Diary Records and Responses to the Questionnaires by Subjects in Study III

1. Anger is more likely than annoyance to be directed at another person (as opposed to an inanimate object, institution, etc.).
2. Anger occurs less frequently.
3. Anger lasts longer.
4. Anger is experienced as more difficult to control.
5. Anger is more likely than annoyance to be occasioned by an act that is appraised as unjustified; annoyance is more likely than anger to be occasioned by acts that are appraised as either justified or unavoidable.
6. Anger is more often accompanied by verbal aggression and/or expressive reactions, and less often by contrary reactions.
7. Anger is more often motivated by a desire to get even for past wrongs and/or to gain revenge for the present incident.
8. Anger is more likely than annoyance to effect a change in the situation.

Content Analyses of Subjects' Own Descriptions of the Differences Between Anger and Annoyance

At the end of the second questionnaire (either anger or annoyance, depending on the counterbalanced order), subjects were given the following instructions:

> You have now completed two detailed questionnaires on anger and annoyance, and you have compiled a diary record of all such incidents for an entire week. On the basis of these experiences, what do you believe are the main differences between anger and annoyance? If you can, list three dimensions or distinguishing features, indicating how anger differs from annoyance on each dimension.

Only half (24) of the subjects were able to list three features, as requested. The task was evidently not an easy one. Nevertheless, a total of 107 responses were obtained, and these were analyzed in the following manner. Three judges went through the enitre list and categorized the responses into relatively homogeneous groupings. For the initial sorting, the judges worked independently, each using his or her own intuitive judgment as to which items belonged together. When an item could be classified in more than one way, only the dominant theme was considered.

After the first sorting, the judges discussed the various categories they had developed and the process was repeated a second time. Following another interchange of ideas, still a third sorting was made. After the three sortings, 85 of the features listed had been placed in one of 10 categories by at least two of the three judges. The 10 categories, with sample responses to help clarify their meaning, are summarized in the following list.

List 2. Differences Between Anger and Annoyance Based on Content Analyses of the Distinguishing Features Mentioned by Subjects in Study III

1. Anger involves greater physical expression. (18 responses)

   "Anger usually causes you to want to show you are angry in some manner, sometimes verbally, sometimes physically, or perhaps even both."

   "Usually when I'm annoyed I keep it to myself unless it bugs me for a long time. When I'm angry I let it be known—passively (calmly) or violently."

2. Anger is more intense than annoyance. (17 responses)

   "Anger is like annoyance except it is much more intense."

   "Annoyance—the feeling is less vivid, less intense (though certainly it can be equally upsetting)."

3. Anger lasts longer. (12 responses)

   "For me, there is definitely a time factor involved. If something affects me just at a certain moment, it's usually annoyance. If it's a long-term affect (plans, feelings) it's usually anger."

   "Anger often lasts for a longer period of time. Annoyances go away as fast as they come."

4. Anger is caused by more serious incidents. (8 responses)

   "Annoyance occurs over trivial incidents; things one usually wouldn't think twice about (unless writing them down in a journal). Anger occurs over a major issue."

   "Anger is usually expressed over more crucial (important) things (determined by the individual) than is annoyance."

5. In anger the precipitating incident is taken personally. (8 responses)

   "Anger is more personalized than annoyance. To make me angry, the incident must be intense but also it must be directed at me."

   "Anger is something very personal to me. If anything endangers my personal life, the result is usually anger instead of annoyance."

6. Anger is more difficult to control. (6 responses)

   "I have more control over my feelings when annoyed than when angry."

   "Anger is an explosion of emotions while annoyance is controlled, restrained emotions."

7. Annoyance, if repeated or sustained, may lead to anger. (5 responses)

   "Being annoyed is being bothered somewhat yet not really being concerned about it, while anger is the 'last straw' of annoyance where emotions come into play."

"Anger comes at the point of maximum annoyance when you just can't take it any more."

8. Anger is less frequent than annoyance. (5 responses)

"Anger is a lot harder to arouse than annoyance. People get annoyed often, and angry less often."

"Annoyance occurs many times more than anger."

9. Anger is more often directed at people. (4 responses)

"Anger is mostly shown towards people, while annoyance can be both (people and inanimate objects)."

"In proportion I get more angry at people, and more annoyed at objects, weather, etc."

10. One's mood at the time helps determine the emotion. (3 responses)

"It depends on the mood of the person at the time, sometimes you're quicker to anger."

"One major difference depends on the particular mood you're in at the time of the incident."

Of the 22 items not classified, many were suggestive but vague (e.g., "My goals and motives for anger and annoyance are very different."). Other responses were clear enough, but rather idiosyncratic (e.g., "Once I build up a high enough level of anger, it stops bothering me."). In some instances, the response of one subject would be contradicted by that of another. For example, one subject noted that "anger is usually less constructive than annoyance," whereas another believed that "anger is better in that it is more likely to move one to change a situation, while annoyance is easier to put off and not deal with."

Supplementary Data from Study I

Before discussing the theoretical implications of the above results, one further set of analyses needs to be presented. In Study I, it may be recalled, subjects were asked to describe briefly the most intense incident of annoyance that occurred during the preceding week, the most intense incident of anger, and the difference between the two (see questionnaire items 2, 5, and 7 in Appendix A). The purpose of these preliminary items was to get subjects to focus specifically on an incident of anger. The results of Study I, as they pertain to the everyday experience of anger, have been presented in Chapters 8 and 9. Our present concern in only with the initial descriptions subjects gave of the anger and annoyance incidents, and the differences between the two.

The responses of the 160 subjects to the three items were analyzed in a manner similar to that described in the preceding section; that is, three sortings were made by three judges, with a discussion follwoing each step in order to help resolve disagreements. To be finally included within a given category, at least two of the three judges had to agree on the placement of an item.[2]

Fourteen categories were formed on the basis of the above procedures. These are listed below.[3] Verbatim responses from two subjects illustrate each category. The responses of 41 subjects (approximatley 25% of the total) could not be categorized because they were too vague, superficial, or idiosyncratic.

List 3. Differences Between Anger and Annoyance Based on Content Analyses of Supplementary Data from Study I

1. In anger the precipitating incident was perceived as unjustified or especially blameworthy. (14 responses)

   "In both. . . instances I felt I was being wronged. My daughter's [annoying behavior] was an act of thoughtlessness but the woman [who angered me] was trying to get away with something she knew wasn't right."

   "I felt the behavior [precipitating the anger incident] was inexcusable whereas in [the annoyance incident] I could understand it and let it go. I sometimes do similar things myself."

2. *The angry e₋isode involved a strong desire for some form of physical expression, often violent. (13 responses)

   "In anger I get violent and will fight, in an annoying incident I get very nervous and will not say very much."

   "Anger incident was different. . . I felt I would like to take her apart limb from limb. It was a more violence-provoking situation."

3. *The angry episode was precipitated by a more serious incident. (12 responses)

   "My annoyance was over something very temporary because I knew I wouldn't have to take orders from this woman for long, but my anger arose because such a seemingly large chunk of my life was going to be in a sense taken away from me."

   "The difference was the importance of the situation. The personal business couldn't have been taken care of any other time and is still not taken care of. The golf game was less important."

4. The events leading to anger involved greater frustration and/or disappointment. (11 responses)

---

[2] The judges (three graduate students) who made these categorizations were not the same as those who did the content analysis reported in the previous section (see List 2).

[3] Categories marked with an asterisk also appeared in List 2.

"In annoyance I tried to dismiss it [doing poorly on an examination] and said I'll try better the next time. I was really mad because my girlfriend couldn't come up [for a weekend visit]. We had planned it for a long time and I'm still mad about it."

"[I became both annoyed and angry] when my 11-month-old son kept spitting out his food when I was trying to feed him. I became very frustrated because he is just learning the meaning of 'no' and he was definitely testing me. . . . Usually I become angry when I am frustrated."

5. *The angry episode involved more intense feelings. (10 responses)

"Anger is worse than annoyance so I was more upset, had more sick feelings, intense feelings, than with annoyance."

"In the anger incident, I could really feel that I was angry, I was really upset. In the annoyance incident I was just irritated."

6. *The angry episode involved a human target. (9 responses)

"Anger dealt with a deliberate act by human beings. Annoyance dealt with bad luck."

"I was angry at a person and what he did to me and made me feel. The car [target of annoyance] can't choose whether or not it will annoy me but a person can."

7. In anger, there was a close personal relationship with the target (e.g., spouse, parent, friend). (9 responses)

"I care more about the person I got angry with than the girl that only annoyed me."

"One being my wife so I am apt to fly off the handle faster with her than with someone in a bar."

8. In the angry episode, there was a feeling of helplessness, an inability to cope with the situation. (8 responses)

"In the anger incident I felt helpless in my situation because at the time there was no way out ot it. I was frustrated and felt it deeply inside. In the annoying situation I just complained at my amazement for having missed the bus for the third time. I swore a little at myself and then thought what I should do next to get home."

"I was refused something in both cases, but could find no means of retaliation in the anger incident."

9. In the angry episode, the angry person was partly at fault for the precipitating incident. (7 responses)

"I was angry with myself and with something I had done that I was ashamed of, but in [the annoyance incident] somebody did something to me and when

I saw how immature he was I didn't care anymore. I could forget it. I was in control."

"I think I was mad because I felt it was something I screwed up myself."

10. *The angry episode occurred after repeated or prolonged aggravation. (6 responses)

"Anger incident was built up. . . . Wasn't a one-shot deal, it's onging but partly was 'the last straw.'"

"Anger was more of a smoldering type where it took time to settle in. Then I realized how upset it made me."

11. *In anger, the precipitating incident was more personal; that is, it was directed at, or affected directly, the self-interests of the angry person. (6 responses)

"Feel anger was a more personal incident while annoyance is nothing personal—just a general pain."

"One [anger] involved me while the other didn't. Anger was because of personal hurt while annoyance was more of a physical hurt."

12. The angry episode involved a loss of pride or self-esteem. (5 responses)

"The crushing of my male ego. . . ticked my anger off."

"My pride was at stake [in the anger incident] ."

13. *The anger lasted longer. (5 responses)

"Anger stayed with me a lot longer. I hurt more and a feeling of revenge came across my mind.The annoyance wasn't as deep and a lot easier to deal with."

"Anger was strong at the time and still is when I think of it. My annoyance has passed and I don't think about it."

14. *The person's mood or other extraneous factors contributed to the anger. (4 responses)

"I was behind in my work. My customers were waiting. No one seemed to notice or tried to help. . . . I had been sick off and on for a week, and my stomach felt very bad at the time."

"In anger incident I was suffering from an internal state of hunger. The annoyance was generated by the external events of losing money."

Only two of the dimensions that appeared earlier in List 2, based on content analysis of the data from Study III, do not appear in List 3. These are (a) that anger is more difficult to control and (b) that annoyance occurs more frequently. The first of these is mainly a variation on the theme that anger is more intense than annoyance, and/or that anger demands some kind of physical expression. The second dimension (i.e., the more frequent occurrence of annoyance) undoubtedly reflects the fact that subjects in Study III had maintained a diary of all instances of anger and annoyance for a week. The greater frequency of annoyance was thus more salient for these subjects.

On the other hand, List 3 does contain a number of dimensions (those not marked by an asterisk) that do not appear in List 2. In large part, these additional dimensions stem from the fact that subjects in Study I were contrasting specific incidents of anger and annoyance, and hence the resulting categories also tended to be more specific and numerous.

An Integrative Summary of the Differences Between Anger and Annoyance

We now have three lists of features that help to distinguish anger from annoyance. The first list is based on analyses of the diary records and the two questionnaires completed by subjects in Study III. The second list is based on a content analysis of the dimensions which these same subjects believed distinguished their experiences of anger from annoyance. The third list is based on a similar content analysis of data from Study I. We may now consolidate these lists, providing a simpler and more coherent account of the major differences between anger and annoyance. In particular, a typical episode of anger may differ from annoyance in one or more of the following nine ways.

1. Anger Is Typically More Intense Than Annoyance

One of the most frequently mentioned and intuitively obvious differences between anger and annoyance is that, on the average, anger is the more intense emotion. Indeed, some theorists have not bothered to distinguish anger from annoyance, assuming that the difference in only one of intensity (cf. Plutchik, 1980). It is therefore important to consider exactly what is meant by the intensity of an emotional experience.

The intensity of an emotion can be manifested in a variety of different ways; for example, the degree of physiological arousal, the vehemence of overt behavior, the duration of the experience, the extent to which a person thinks about or ruminates over the incident, and so forth. From a theoretical perspective, the aspect of intensity that has received the most attention is physiological arousal. The present data, being based on self-reports, do not provide much information with regard to this dimension. Nevertheless, a few observations can be made. The questionnaires on anger and annoyance did contain a section in which subjects were asked to rate a variety of expressive reactions and/or physiological symptoms. The most frequently rated item for both anger and annoyance was an increase in "general tension." However, there was no significant difference between the two emotions on this variable. During anger, 46% of the subjects said that they felt "very" tense, while almost the same percentage (42%) reported feeling similarly tense during annoyance. Considering the overlap in the distributions, it is obvious that persons often feel more tense during annoyance than during anger.

The physiological symptom that most distinguished anger from annoyance (in terms of self-reports) was "flushing or rise in temperature." Since this is a stereotypic way of describing anger (e.g., being "hot under the collar"), it is unclear how much weight should be given to this difference. Nevertheless, even on this variable, a few (8%) of the subjects reported feeling more flushed when annoyed than when angry. (Another 38% reported either no flushing on either occasion, or an equal amount of flushing on both occasions.)

Another criterion for the intensity of an emotion is the nature and vehemence of any overt responses (instrumental acts) that might be made. From List 1 it can be seen that anger is more often accompanied by verbal aggression, and less often by contrary reactions, than is annoyance. And from Lists 2 and 3 it appears that subjects often feel a strong desire to express their anger openly and vehemently. However, overt behavior is under the control of many variables other than intensity, as will be discussed more thoroughly below.

Still another aspect of the intensity of an emotion is the extent to which the person is preoccupied with thoughts about the incident. This perhaps accounts for the longer duration of anger, a feature noted in all three lists. Anger may continue to fester long after the immediate provocation has passed. Annoyance, by contrast, tends to cease with removal of the irritating stimulus, and it does not leave the individual with thoughts of revenge.

In short, the more intense an emotion, the more response elements—physiological, behavioral, and/or cognitive—are incorporated into the syndrome. Intense emotions tend to monopolize. Colloquially speaking, the more intense the emotion, the more an individual is "overcome." In Study III, the inability to control one's thoughts and feelings, as well as overt behavior, was one of the features that most distinguished anger from annoyance (see Lists 1 and 2). Yet, as discussed in previous chapters, the experience of being overcome is itself an interpretation of behavior, a product of reflective awareness. As such, it cannot be reduced in any simple way to a matter of physiological arousal, overt behavior, cognitive preoccupation, or whatever.

To summarize, anger is often (but not always) experienced as more intense than is annoyance. However, the concept of emotional intensity is vague and multifaceted. If intensity is identified too closely with any one of its indices (e.g., physiological arousal), then the assertion that anger is more intense than annoyance has too many exceptions to be very informative. On the other hand, if intensity is interpreted in its broadest sense; that is, as indicating the extent to which the person feels "overcome" or out of control, then we are left with the generalization that anger is more properly an emotion (passion) than is annoyance. But we are still left with the question of what is means to be angry instead of annoyed.

2. Anger Is Typically Elicited by More Serious Incidents Than Is Annoyance

In both Lists 2 and 3, the seriousness of the precipitating event is one of the most frequently mentioned features that distinguishes anger from annoyance. This feature is related to the intensity dimension discussed above. Other things being equal, more intense responses will be elicited by more serious incidents, and vice versa.

But other things are not always equal: Sometimes we do become upset over trivial matters, and at other times we remain calm in the face of serious provocation. The appraisal of an event as serious may thus contribute independently to the experience of a response as either anger or annoyance.

In what sense are provocations to anger more serious than incidents that lead to annoyance? A provocation can be serious in different ways (just as a response can be intense in different ways). Some subjects mentioned that their anger was occasioned by greater frustration, a loss of pride, repeated aggravations, and the like (see List 3, especially). As discussed in Chapter 8, however, such events *by themselves* are usually not sufficient to elicit anger. The event should also be unjustified, or at least avoidable. And that brings us to what is perhaps the most important distinction between anger and annoyance.

3. Anger Involves an Attribution of Blame; Annoyance Often Does Not

People may become either angry or annoyed at events they consider unjustified and/or avoidable. Anger, however, tends to be limited to such incidents, whereas annoyance can be directed at a completely "innocent" target. This was the difference most often mentioned by subjects in Study I (see List 3). These subjects often stated quite explicitly that in the angry episode they had been "wronged," "taken," "betrayed," or otherwise unfairly treated. The data from Study III are somewhat more ambiguous on this point. The comparison of the two questionnaires yielded results in the expected direction (see List 1). However, when subjects in Study III were asked to list three features that helped them to distinguish anger from annoyance, justification of the instigation did not emerge as a separate category. This is probably because the features listed by these subjects summarized a large number of incidents, and the implication of wrongdoing was often embedded in some more general characterization (e.g., the seriousness of the incident or its personal relevance—see List 2).

The attribution of blame inherent in anger can also involve the self. Thus, seven subjects in Study I (List 3) mentioned that a major difference between their anger and annoyance was that in the former they themselves were partly at fault for precipitating the incident. These subjects were angry, in part, at themselves, although they typically focused their anger on some external object or person. Such an externalization of anger is not the same as displaced aggression (which also commonly occurred); rather, it is more a matter of displaced blame.

In Chapters 4 and 5, on ethical and legal norms, we saw how anger is itself considered justified only if the provocation is unjustified and/or avoidable. Such norms not only help to regulate the expression of anger, they also help consitutue the emotion. Of course, there is some slippage between what should be and what actually is. Hence, people do sometimes become angry at frustrations, criticisms, and the like that are either unavoidable or quite warranted. In such instances, however, if the person *truly* admits and believes that the precipitating incident was unavoidable or warranted, then he cannot remain angry—annoyed and upset, perhaps, but not angry.

4. Anger Affects One Personally, but Not Necessarily Directly; Annoyance Affects One Directly, but Not Necessarily Personally

In anger, as opposed to annoyance, the precipitating incident tends to be taken personally, a feature noted in both Lists 2 and 3. However, an incident that is taken personally need not affect an individual directly. For example, a person might become quite angry at some perceived "wrong" (such as the killing of whales), even though the event has no direct effect on him as an individual. Contrast this with a typical incident of annoyance; for example, being awakened in a strange city by the sound of traffic. In annoyance, the precipitating incident must affect the person directly, or else it has no effect at all; it need not, however, be personally involving.

The above distinction is important not only because it illustrates one way in which provocations to anger may be more "serious" than incidents that elicit annoyance, but also because it illustrates the greater cognitive complexity of anger. Anything that disturbs us can become a source of annoyance, even simple sensory experiences such as an itch or aching tooth. Provocations to anger, by contrast, are liable to involve violations of deeply held convictions and values, or else pose a threat to one's sense of self (as in a loss of pride).

5. Anger Is an Interpersonal as Well as a Highly Personal Emotion

That anger is an interpersonal as well as a very personal emotion has been discussed in detail in previous chapters, and requires little additional elaboration here. The interpersonal nature of anger is manifested most starkly by the fact that the normative target of anger is another person; annoyance, by contrast, can be occasioned by a variety of animate and inanimate objects. But not all persons are equally likely to become the object of anger. An action that might lead to anger if done by a friend or loved one may lead to simple annoyance if done by a stranger.

There are a variety of reasons why a person is more likely to become angry at loved ones and friends, as opposed to strangers (see Chapter 8). But whatever the reasons, it is clear that anger is fundamentally an interpersonal emotion. Any theory of anger that does not make this fact a primary consideration is liable to be deficient in important respects.

6. Anger Involves a Strong Desire for Physical Expression

In List 3, the second most frequently mentioned difference between anger and annoyance is that anger seems to require physical expression; and in List 2, this is the most frequently mentioned difference. Moreover, comparisons of the two questionnaires (see List 1) indicates that subjects in Study III engaged in more verbal aggression and fewer contrary reactions when angry than when annoyed. There can thus be little doubt that one of the major features of anger, as opposed to annoyance, is a tendency to engage in direct action, often of an aggressive nature.[4]

---

[4] These remarks are not meant to place undue emphasis on the aggressive element in anger. The comparison is with annoyance. In an absolute sense neither anger nor annoyance is particularly aggressive, at least in ordinary circumstances (see Chapter 9).

The press for direct action during anger is undoubtedly related to the greater intensity of this emotion. However, the direction of the relationship is not entirely clear. In part, anger may be regarded as intense because it is accompanied by a strong desire for physical expression, or vice versa. But no matter: The expression of anger is of theoretical interest in its own right. Only if an emotion is openly expressed can it have any influence on the course of events. And anger, much more than annoyance, is a response to situations that require action. It is as though one cannot be *really* angry unless one wants to express it (although, of course, we often do inhibit our anger for a variety of reasons).

7. In Anger There Is an Inability to Cope in the Usual Way

Anger may involve a strong desire for physical expression, as discussed above; but frequently anger is also accompanied by feelings of helplessness or by a perceived inability to cope (see List 3). As discussed in Chapter 9, anger does not flourish in situations where response options are either too limited or too abundant. When no responses are viable, a threat that might otherwise lead to anger may instead be the occasion for fear or depression. On the other hand, if the individual can easily cope with the threat, then it may be dismissed as a minor nuisance or annoyance.

Anger is an escalated response. It occurs in situations where other attempts to cope have failed, or are not deemed likely to meet with success. This is perhaps one reason why skills training has proven to be an effective technique for helping people who have trouble controlling their anger (cf. Novaco, 1975).

8. Anger Is Motivated by a Desire for Revenge

Of the 11 motives listed in the questionnaires, only two distinguished between anger and annoyance at acceptable levels of statistical significance. These were (a) to get even for past wrongs and (b) to gain revenge for the present incident (see List 1). These results, as well as some of the other features already discussed, would seem to support Aristotle's definition of anger "as an impulse, accompanied by pain, to a conspicuous revenge for a conspicuous slight directed without justification towards what concerns oneself or towards what concerns one's friends." From the discussion in Chapter 4, however, it may be recalled that Lactantius criticized this definition; he argued instead that justified anger is not marked by vengeance for personal injuries, but rather is aroused "in order that discipline be preserved, morals corrected, and license suppressed." In other words, Lactantius viewed anger as more constructively motivated than did Aristotle.

At first it might seem that Aristotle has had the best of this argument. However, it must be noted that the present data are relevant only to a comparison of anger with annoyance, neither of which is malevolently motivated in ordinary circumstances.

The desire for retribution or revenge is not necessarily destructive, nor incompatible with the preservation of discipline and the correction of morals. In this respect, one might expect to find greater differences in motivation between anger and annoyance, on the one hand, and other aggressive syndromes, such as contempt and jealousy, on the other hand. Perhaps the most that can be said with regard to the difference in motivation between anger and annoyance is that the former is more involved with matters of equity and justice, whereas the latter is more concerned with the straightforward elimination of an irritating condition.

9. Whether a Person Experiences Anger or Annoyance May Depend on His or Her Mood at the Time of the Incident

This is the last feature mentioned in both Lists 2 and 3. In one sense, to say that the difference between anger and annoyance depends on one's mood seems to imply that there are no important differences between the two emotions. Yet a little reflection suggests that mood may affect anger and annoyance differently, and the difference is instructive.

A remark that is passed off as a joke on one occasion, or dismissed with a condescending attitude, may elicit an angry response on another occasion, and the only difference may indeed be one's mood at the time. It is important to note, however, that even when in a bad mood, a person typically has a *reason* for becoming angry; for example, the remark is perceived as insulting or inconsiderate. Annoyance, by contrast, does not really need a reason, only a cause. When ill, fatigued, or simply out of sorts, a person can be very annoyed by a minor nuisance, but the nuisance will not oridnarily lead to anger unless it is interpreted as inconsiderate and avoidable. In fact, knowing that one is in a bad mood may actually raise the threshold for anger, since responsibility for the upset is shifted from the instigating conditions to the person's own condition. "I shouldn't get angry about that. It's not his fault; I'm just in a bad mood." Such reasoning may be quite effective in short-circuiting anger, but it generally has little influence on annoyance (although, of course, it may influence the expression of annoyance).

In short, the appraisals that underlie anger are much more complex than those that underlie annoyance. This insulates anger, to a certain extent, from negative swings in mood. A person who becomes angry at something one day and not the next, simply as a function of mood, may be accused of being inconsistent in his or her beliefs, attitudes, and values. The person who becomes annoyed in a similar fashion may simply be regarded as moody or temperamental. The difference is important.

Summary

Taken together, the above nine features can be used to form an iterative definition of anger relative to annoyance. Specifically, anger is a relatively more *intense, interpersonal* emotion, and is more likely to involve an *attribution of blame* and a *desire for revenge.* Anger is typically provoked by an *incident regarded as serious* and/or *personally threatening*; and it is accompanied by a strong desire for *direct action,* this in spite of the fact that *normal coping resources may seem inadequate.* Moreover, since anger is cognitively and socially more complex than annoyance, it is *affected differently by changes in the mood* of the individual.

This definition summarizes the major features that help distinguish anger from annoyance. Yet, being based on averages, it is misleading in important respects.

No two experiences of anger and annoyance described by the subjects in the present study differed in all of the above ways. Indeed, for any pair of incidents, the normal relationship between anger and annoyance was often reversed on some—even a majority—of the "distinguishing" features. For example, some incidents of annoyance were more intense than the corresponding incidents of anger, were provoked by more serious incidents, and so on.

In a sense, then, the picture that we have drawn thus far exaggerates the differences between typical incidents of anger and annoyance. Yet it is also evident that people are generally quite able to distinguish between their experiences of anger and annoyance, even when differences in terms of the above-mentioned features are minimal and/or conflicting. This is illustrated by the fact that of the 1,536 episodes recorded by subjects in their diaries, 96% were classified as either anger or annoyance. In only 4% of the episodes did subjects indicate that they were "uncertain" about how to classify a response. This suggests that there are other differences between anger and annoyance, more fundamental perhaps than the ones discussed thus far. In order to uncover these differences, which are more social than psychological, we must take a closer look at the meaning of the concepts of anger and annoyance.

Conceptual Analyses

By way of background, it is instructive to consider briefly the distinction between another pair of concepts drawn from an entirely different domain of discourse. In the dialogue *Theaetetus*, Plato asked what the difference is between knowledge and true belief. The question has plagued philosophers ever since, and many of the answers that have been offered parallel those that might be offered for the distinction between anger and annoyance. Plato's answer, for example, was that knowledge and belief differ in terms of their objects (the immutable Forms as opposed to corruptible matter). Others have claimed that knowledge is really a species of belief— a particularly strong or "intense" belief, perhaps, or a belief "plus" something else (e.g., adequate proof). Still others have maintained that knowledge and belief represent different kinds of dispositions or capacities, such that the person who knows is disposed to respond differently than the person who only believes.

The above answers share a common feature; namely, they all focus on the individual. But knowledge is not simply a private affair; it also plays a role in social interaction. This point has been made most clearly by Austin (1946/1961), in a now classic paper dealing with knowledge of other minds.

Austin takes it for granted that a person may either know something or simply believe it. That is, there is no necessary difference in the objects of knowledge and belief (Plato notwithstanding). Similarly, a person may act in much the same way, based on either knowledge or belief. Perhaps, then, knowledge and belief reflect different modes of cognition. Austin rejects this possibility also. He observes that to say "I know" is not the same as "saying, 'I have performed a specially striking feat of cognition, superior, in the same scale as believing and being sure, even to being merely quite sure': for there *is* nothing in the scale superior to being quite sure" (p. 67).

Yet for Austin there is a big difference between knowledge and belief, one that we all intuitively *feel* when we make the statement "I know" as opposed to "I believe" or even "I am absolutely sure." To bring out this difference he compares statements of knowledge not with beliefs, but with promises.

> When I say, "I promise", a new plunge is taken: I have not merely an-
> nounced my intention, but, by using the formula (performing this ritual),
> I have bound myself to others, and staked my reputation, in a new way.
> Similarly, saying, "I know" is taking a new plunge. . . .When I say, "I
> know", I *give others my word*: I *give others my authority for saying* that
> "S is P." (p. 67)

Stated somewhat differently, a claim to knowledge is like a promissory note; it is a guarantee that what I say is true. By contrast, in stating a belief I hedge my bets. I cannot say, "I know that such-and-such is true, but I may be wrong." On the other hand, it is acceptable to say, "I strongly believe that such-and-such is true, but I may be wrong." Of course, I may in fact be mistaken when I claim knowledge, as when I assert a belief. The "price" I would have to pay for the mistake is, however, different in the two cases.

The originality of Austin's argument lies in the recognition that the difference between knowledge and belief is not just logical, nor even psychological; it is also sociological. That is, knowledge has a social use that cannot be "reduced" to a strictly psychological or logical level of analysis.

There are other locutions that are promissory in the same sense as knowledge. Consider the difference between loving and liking. One current theory (Berscheid & Walster, 1974) suggests that "love" is a label that we attach to a state of physiological arousal given certain environmental cues, for example, a moonlit night, an attractive partner. But such a theory does not explain why "love" is used as a label rather than, say, "like." Indeed, the young man who tells his sweetheart, "I love you" is probably more interested in influencing her state of arousal than he is in labeling his own. And in this respect, a statement such as "I like you a lot" would undoubtedly have far less impact. Why?

The difference is not simply that love is a more intense form of liking. We may like a friend as much as is reasonably possible and be willing to make great sacrifices for the person; yet liking is not loving. In case this assertion seems too dogmatic, consider the fact that we may love a person whom we do not particularly like. This is a common theme in romantic tragedies; and is sometimes also reported by young people with regard to their parents (Falkowski, 1975).

The difference between loving and liking seems to be largely one of commitment. Love, even more than knowledge, has a promissory quality. This is perhaps one reason why "love" and "knowledge" have so frequently been associated, for example, within the mystical tradition.

Now let us return to the problem of anger. Anger (as opposed to annoyance) has some of the same qualities as knowledge (as opposed to belief) and love (as opposed to liking). Anger is an indictment, and like knowledge, a claim of anger should not be made without warrant. Anger is also a promise, a commitment to action if things do not change. Notice, too, that in anger a person's reputation is placed on the line. People are known by the things that make them angry, and by the appropriateness of their follow-through.

Annoyance, by contrast, does not share the above qualities to any great extent. I may on occasion become annoyed at the same provocation that on another occasion might make me angry; but in the case of annoyance I do not choose to make a stand on the issue. There is no indictment in annoyance, and no commitment to action. Of course, if the provocation continues, or if circumstances change, annoyance may turn to anger. But, as will be explained more fully below, that is not so much a change in psychological state as it is a change in the rules of the game being played.

At this point, an objection might be raised. To say "I am angry" (or "I know," "I love you") is not the same as being angry (having knowledge, being in love). The first-person linguistic expression may indeed have promissory functions, but that does not mean the underlying state—anger, knowledge, or love per se—can be so characterized.

This objection would be valid if I were claiming that the meaning of the concept of anger is exhausted by the promissory use of the first-person locution "I am angry." However, the claim I want to make is more modest. It is simply that the promissory use of the concept of anger helps determine (and is, in turn, determined by) other aspects of the entire emotional syndrome. The relationship between an emotional concept and the remainder of an emotional syndrome is a dialectical one. This point was discussed in some detail in Chapter 1 (p. 23ff.) and in Chapter 3 (p. 64ff.); it need not be elaborated upon at this point. Suffice it to say that the promissory function of a statement such as "I am angry" helps reinforce—and is reinforced by—the differences between anger and annoyance noted earlier in this chapter.

The forgoing observations focus attention once again—but in a somewhat different way—on the social nature of anger. To borrow a phrase from Wittgenstein (1953), statements such as "I am angry" and "I am annoyed" belong to different language games. People can easily recognize when they are angry as opposed to annoyed, not only on the bases of their feelings and reactions, but also because they are following different rules. The person who is angry is playing a different "game" (rule-governed social transaction) than the person who is annoyed.

Concluding Observations

By the nature of their discipline, psychologists tend to view behavior on an individualistic basis, in isolation from the broader social context. When viewed in such a fashion, anger and annoyance tend to differ along a number of dimensions, such as intensity, seriousness, and personal involvement. But these differences are not in thesmselves crucial. Their significance lies in what they mean with respect to broader social considerations. In this respect, we have seen how the differences between anger and annoyance are in some respects analogous to the differences between knowledge and belief, and also between liking and loving. If we wished, we could carry the logic of the analogy even further afield. In Chapter 5, for example, we saw how the difference between murder and manslaughter is not just a matter of the thoughts, feelings, and behavior of the individual defendant. Rather, the distinction is made in large part on social considerations that transcend the individual (cf. the reasonable-man test).

Is it important to take into account such broader social considerations when analyzing a psychological phenomenon? For some purposes, perhaps not. But those purposes are very limited.

Chapter 12

Temporal Dimensions of Anger: An Exploration of Time and Emotion[1]

Bram M. Fridhandler and James R. Averill

The purpose of the present chapter is to clarify the theoretical and practical impor-tance of time with respect to anger in particular and emotion in general. The first half of the chapter is largely theoretical. A review of the treatment of time in tradi-tional theories of emotion suggests that in order to provide a coherent account of the temporal course of events in anger, we must reconceptualize emotional states as a type of psychological *disposition* organized into time-limited *episodes*. Some of the empirical bases for, and implications of, this reconceptualization are illus-trated in the second half of the chapter, which presents the results of a survey (Study IV in this series) designed to explore the temporal dimensions of anger. The focus of Study IV is primarily on the duration of anger and its correlates, and secondarily on the factors that help terminate an angry episode.

A Review of Theories

Rarely has the duration of emotions been singled out as a topic worthy of sustained attention and discussion in its own right. For the most part, the issue of duration has been made subsidiary to other theoretical assumptions, for example, those regarding the nature of emotional responses.

The Physiological Tradition

Virtually every theory has included physiological responses as important, if not essential, components of emotional behavior. For the moment, we will focus on those theories—relatively few in number—that define emotion consistently and

[1] This chapter is based on a Master's thesis by Bram M. Fridhandler. Thanks are due to Drs. Ronnie Janoff-Bulman and Richard Halgin for their assistance as members of the thesis committee, and to Mary Haake for comments on an earlier draft of the chapter. The work was partially supported by a University Fellowship awarded to Bram M. Fridhandler by the University of Massachusetts.

exclusively in physiological terms. Wenger (1950) is a good representative of this tradition. He defines emotion as "visceral action," and specifies further that

> emotion is activity and reactivity of the tissues and organs innervated by the autonomic nervous system. It may involve, but does not necessarily involve, skeletal muscular response or mental activity. (Wenger, Jones, & Jones, 1956, p. 343)

By way of clarity, this definition would seem to leave little to be desired, and Wenger is admirably consistent in applying it, to the point of counting exercise and sleep as emotions. There is, however, an ambiguity hidden in the definition which leads to conflicting implications regarding duration. The autonomic nervous system (ANS) is always active to some extent, and this must imply, on Wenger's definition of emotion, that one is always, from birth until death, in some sort of emotional state. Indeed, emotion has often been thought of in this way, that is, as a kind of background arousal, fluctuating in degree and perhaps in quality. However, we also commonly—perhaps more commonly—think of emotions as occurring in discrete episodes with a concrete beginning and end.

Any particular emotion is, according to Wenger, identifiable as a distinct (though temporally changing) pattern of autonomic activity. This implies that an emotion endures for as long as the distinct pattern persists. Leaving aside the question whether it is possible to relate patterns of physiological arousal to everyday emotions—a topic much in dispute (Schachter, 1971; Mandler, 1975)—we do not believe that such a view provides unequivocally for the duration of emotions. One would have to specify fairly precisely what demarcates one pattern of autonomic activity from another; in order to avoid an excessive degree of circularity, this would have to be accomplished more or less independently of the observed duration of emotions. This specification would be further complicated by the different temporal features of the two main components of physiological arousal during emotion: activity of the autonomic nervous system and of the endocrine system. Everything considered, it is highly unlikely that the duration of emotion, as generally recognized, bears any direct one-to-one relationship to temporal changes in physiological activity. Indeed, some of the research reviewed in Chapter 6 (e.g., on the transfer of arousal) would suggest otherwise.

Before leaving Wenger and the physiological tradition we will note another ambiguity in the treatment of time, the significance of which will become clear shortly. In the course of his treatment of emotion, Wenger (Wenger et al., 1956) vascillates between referring to emotion and "emotional change," and similarly between referring to ANS activity and *change* in ANS activity. From the context it is not always clear whether Wenger considers emotion to be visceral action in general or, more narrowly, a *change* in visceral acitvity; that is, it is not clear whether he considers emotions to be temporally open ended, on the one hand, or temporally bound and inherently brief, on the other.

Facial Feedback Theories

Since the time of Darwin (1872/1965) facial expressions have figured prominently in theories of emotion. Recently, a number of theorists have concluded that the face is even more important than the viscera for the experience of emotion (Ekman, 1977; Izard, 1971, 1977; Leventhal, 1974, 1980; Tomkins, 1962, 1963, 1981b). The following quotation from Izard (1977) will serve to illustrate this position:

> An internal or external event, as processed by the selectivity and organizing functions of relevant receptors changes the gradient of neural stimulation and the pattern of activity in the limbic system and sensory cortex. Impulses from either the cortex or from limbic structures (probably the thalamus) are directed to the hypothalamus, which plays a role in emotion differentiation, determining what facial expression will be effected. . . . Finally, the cortical integration of facial-expression feedback generates the subjective experience of emotion. . . . Facial feedback plays its role in emotion activation in a rapid reflexive fashion and *awareness of facial activity or facial feedback is actually our awareness of the subjective experience of a specific emotion.* One does not ordinarily become aware of the proprioceptive and cutaneous impulses (as such) created by frowning or smiling; rather one becomes aware of experiential anger or joy. (pp. 59, 60; emphasis added)

Drawing on studies demonstrating the cross-cultural recognizability of certain facial expressions (see Chapter 2, for a review), Izard concludes that for each of 10 "fundamental" emotions there exists an innate neurological template which produces a specific pattern of facial muscular activity in response to a preprogrammed set of eliciting conditions. The "proprioceptive and cutaneous" sensations resulting from this muscular activity are then integrated into the subjective experience of emotion.

Izard provides certain alternatives to this process for even fundamental emotions, and in response to an empirical challenge to the facial feedback hypothesis (Tourangeau & Ellsworth, 1979) he has deemphasized the facial expression still further (Izard, 1981). These qualifications notwithstanding, the tradition exemplified by Izard gives preeminent importance to the face in the experience of emotion.

What does such a position imply about the duration of emotions? At first blush one might suppose that since the patterning of facial activity to which these authors refer is typically rather brief—even "micromomentary"—then emotions, for them, must likewise typically last for only a matter of seconds. However, such a conclusion would thoroughly contradict our everyday conception and experience of emotion; and the theorists, accordingly, do not assert that emotions are typically this brief. Instead, they tend to maintain that facial expression is necessary for the *initiation* of emotion but not for the *sustaining* of emotion. For example, in introducing the first passage cited above, Izard (1977) states:

> Differential emotions theory postulates the continual presence of emotion in consciousness. Therefore, the following description of the emotion process applies to the activation and experiencing of a new emotion. (p. 59)

Izard (1981) again emphasizes this point in his reply to Tourangeau and Ellsworth:

> Even a properly stated facial feedback hypothesis would be concerned only with emotion activation, something that occupies only milliseconds in an emotion process that may last for a relatively long period of time and have substantial influences on cognitive and motor processes. (p. 351)

What, then, is this "relatively long period of time"? Izard does not say, and he provides little from which one might deduce it. In contrast with his detailed neuro-anatomical elaboration of the initiation of emotion, Izard provides virtually no account of what constitutes an emotion over the majority of its duration, beyond suggesting that it might reside in the "activity of the striate muscles of the body and the smooth muscles of the viscera" (1977, p. 60).[2]

Thus, as proved to be the case with Wenger and the physiological tradition, we may locate in Izard and the facial feedback tradition an ambiguity as to whether emotions are temporally bound and inherently brief or temporally open ended. In Wenger, this ambiguity emerged as an alternating emphasis on visceral activity and change in such activity; in Izard it emerges as a heavy theoretical reliance on an aspect of emotional response—facial expression—that, as Izard himself acknowledges, can account for only a very small proportion of the time course of a typical emotion.

Two-Factor Theory

The general features of Schachter's (1971) two-factor, or cognition-plus-arousal, theory, are well known. In brief, Schachter (1964) accounts for emotions with the assertion that

> given a state of physiological arousal for which an individual has no imme-diate explanation, he will "label" this state and describe his feelings in terms of the cognitions available to him. (p. 53)

The implications of this theory regarding the duration of emotions depends on whether one focuses on the arousal component or the cognitive component. If the former, the reasoning provided above in discussing physiological theories is applicable: The duration of emotions is determined by the functioning of the auto-nomic and related systems. The ambiguities inherent in such a thesis have already been discussed. On the other hand, if the focus is on the cognitive rather than on the physiological component, the implications for duration are open, for the cate-gory of "cognition" is left so unelaborated by Schachter that it would seem to impose no constraints whatever on the duration of emotion.

Overlapping, and perhaps determining, whether the focus in this realm is on arousal or cognition is the issue of whether one's concern is with emotional *exper-ience* or emotional *behavior*. Schachter would almost certainly hold that emotional

---

[2] It should be noted that Izard explicitly recognizes the problem that duration pre-sents for theories of emotion. "An emotion is still considered by many an intense experience of brief duration. Relatively little consideration has been given to the possibility that any particular emotion can linger over indefinite periods of time at varying levels of intensity" (Izard, 1979, p. 4). For the most part, however, Izard tends to conceptualize long-enduring emotional states as affective-cognitive inter-actions or structures, rather than as emotions per se. The difference in conceptuali-zation reflects an assumption about the proper unit of analysis for the study of emotion, an issue about which we shall have much to say in Chapter 14.

experience is contingent on arousal; once arousal fades, there can be no emotional experience. For emotional behavior, however—particularly if this is understood to include instrumental actions and social interactions as well as the more frequently emphasized expressive reactions—the issue is more complicated. As Zillmann (1978) has demonstrated, a stimulus condition may produce a predisposition to respond (e.g., to retaliate against a provocateur), even though the response itself may be separated by an extended period of time from the original situation (see Chapter 6, for a more detailed discussion of relevant research).

Psychoanalytic Theory

Psychoanalytic thought has developed into a set of distinct and competing schools. For our present purposes the American ego-psychology movement, led by Hartmann, Kris, Loewenstein, and Rapaport, is the most germane; it has for some decades exercised a wide influence on American analytic thought, and it has emphasized the refinement of Freud's metapsychological theory more than most other schools. Rapaport (1953) outlined the development and then-current status of the psychoanalytic theory of affects, and his paper remains one of the most important statements of the theory; in the present section we will draw on Rapaport's paper in order to say a few words about the temporal dimensions in the psychoanalytic theory of affects.

As presented by Rapaport, the psychoanalytic theory of affects, at least in its later phases, accepts the existence of emotions of a wide range of duration, from "momentary affect storms" to "continuous" states, such as anxiety or depression, which could presumably last for months. Affects can even be "frozen" into lifelong character traits. However, the theory does not provide the means to delineate specific *instances* or *episodes* of emotion, and thus does not provide an unambiguous theoretical account of the duration of emotional states.

In Freud's earliest theorizing (before *The Interpretation of Dreams*), affect was not distinguished from psychic energy in general; to be in an emotional state was to be in a high state of drive tension. In the second, "dynamic," phase of the theory (until about 1926), affect was seen as a *discharge* of psychic tension. More specifically, affect discharge served as a "safety valve" for drive tension when discharge through action was unavailable. In the final, "structural," phase of the theory, affect lost its function as a discharge of drive tension. According to the new formulation, affect could be "bound," by the strong, mature ego, at any rate, and used as a "signal" of internal or external danger.

In the second (dynamic) phase of the theory, the duration of an episode of affect was necessarily understood to be demarcated by the beginning and end of an unbroken active period of felt emotion; an emotion that was not discharging, not consciously felt, could have no status beyond that of sheer potential. By contrast, in the third (structural) phase, while the temporal dimensions become more ambiguous, emotions appear to be understood as temporally open ended. To pursue the issue further at this point would take us too far afield, since the conflict between the dynamic and structural conceptions of affect turns on some of the most arcane and controversial features of psychoanalytic metapsychology. Suffice it to say that certain difficulties in the ego-psychological psychoanalytic theory of affect have their origin, in part, in unresolved ambiguities about the temporal dimensions of emotion.[3]

Subjectivist Theories of Emotion

One of the most popular conceptions of emotion is in terms of subjective experience. At one time it was also common among psychologists to define emotions as feelings. What implications does such a definition have for the temporal dimensions of emotions? In addressing this issue we will concentrate on Richardson's (1918) extensive study of anger. Working within the introspectionist tradition, Richardson employed structured diary and interview techniques to study the "behavior of consciousness" during anger. In the context of such a relatively straightforward approach, one might anticipate that the question how long anger typically lasts would receive a simple and direct answer; unfortunately, it does not. Part of the difficulty is that Richardson's reporting, while rich in observations, does not include a great many quantitative details, and he does not divulge the typical duration of the incidents of anger reported by his subjects. In general, he seems to suggest that for the most part incidents lasted for a matter of minutes; in one of the few mentions of a specific time period, the discussion of a case lasting "over three quarters of an hour" implies that this was an unusually long duration among his sample of incidents (p. 35). However, more remains to be said regarding the duration of incidents of anger in Richardson's study, and here again we encounter an ambiguity which has appeared in some form in almost every perspective we have reviewed. At various points Richardson speaks of "re-appearances" of an "anger emotion" arising from the same "mental situation" (i.e., instigation); this is especially common, he observes, when the angry person has failed to devise a satisfying means of expressing his feelings. Though Richardson generally regards each "appearance" of anger as a discrete incident, one might—either as investigator or as angry subject—consider all appearances of an "anger emotion" deriving from the same instigation as constituting a *single* incident. In one case, Richardson himself does so: "The emotion may last for several days, *appearing at intervals*" (p. 58, emphasis added). Here, in Richardson's subjectivist framework, the ambiguity regarding whether emotions are inherently brief or temporally open ended emerges as a virtual contradiction: How are we to understand a single, unitary subjective experience which appears in consciousness only at intervals?

On Dispositions and Episodes

We have isolated a persistent ambiguity in the way traditional theories have dealt with the temporal dimensions of emotion; it is now time to specify the nature and source of this ambiguity more exactly. Each theory founders when it attempts to

---

[3] One major source of ambiguity centers on the notion of repressed emotion. This issue will be discussed in Chapter 13.

apply inherently momentary, dynamic, occurrent concepts to cover features of emotions which are clearly *extended* in time. That this is the source of the difficulty is perhaps clearest in the case of the facial feedback tradition, in which momentary— even micromomentary—facial expressions are closely identified with the emotion as a whole; similarly, Wenger at points identifies emotions with inherently brief changes in visceral activity. This conceptual confusion and its consequences are less clear in the subjectivist framework until one considers that in this framework emotions are identified with feelings, and feelings (or sensations, at any rate) are temporally bound, ordinarily brief, and "occurrent" (i.e., they are either simply present or simply absent). Schachter's two-factor theory, by virtue of its emphasis on perceived physiological arousal, also assumes a close link between emotions and the occurrence of feelings. Finally, the introduction of notions such as "affect charges" or "repressed feelings," as found in some versions of psychoanalytic theory, simply drives the phenomena underground, so to speak, without changing the occurrent nature of the presumed events.

In each of the above cases, we are faced with one variety of what Ryle (1949) called a category mistake—the joint application of subtly incompatible concepts, concepts which belong to different logical categories, leading to untenable and incoherent conclusions. In the present section, we will argue that emotional concepts refer to a type of psychological disposition, and not to specific occurrences or events, such as physiological or expressive reactions, feelings, drive discharges, or whatever. We will further argue that emotional dispositions differ from other psychological dispositions (e.g., traits and sentiments) in a number of ways; most important, emotions are organized into temporally bound *episodes*. By distinguishing emotions from occurrent reactions, and emotional episodes from longer term dispositions, we may overcome much of the conceptual confusion that has stood in the way of a proper understanding of the temporal dimensions of emotion.

Emotional Dispositions

Dispositions may be physical properties of objects as well as psychological properties of people. They usually do not refer to any single behavior of the object or person, nor, exactly, to a *set* of behaviors. Rather, they refer to the fact that an object or person will behave in certain ways in some given set of circumstances. Formally, dispositions are expressible in one or a number of conditional sentences— "If x, then y," where x is a set of circumstances and y is some behavior. (For a more detailed presentation of the logic of dispositional concepts in the philsophy of mind, see Ryle, 1949, and in the philosophy of science, Pap, 1962.)

A simple and straightforward example of a psychological disposition is the conditioned reflex. To say that an organism has been conditioned is not to claim that it is ceaselessly making the conditioned response, only that (with some specifiable degree of probability) it *will* make that response when presented with the conditioned stimulus. No one is likely to observe the organism at rest and ask, "Where's the reflex?"; the reflex is in a different logical category than are the responses by which it is manifested.

To further clarify the nature of psychological dispositions, let us consider the concept of a personality trait. The dispositional character of traits is well recognized; indeed, we often use the terms *trait* and *disposition* almost synonymously. A trait refers to a set of regularities of response to circumstances. When we call a person compassionate, for example, we mean that he or she may be expected to express sympathy and offer assistance when confronted by suffering. We do *not* mean that the person is constantly performing compassionate acts, only that he or she is "disposed" to do so when the situation demands it and conditions are reasonably favorable. Thus, although the trait is manifested in the occurrence of compassionate acts, it is not reducible to them; the trait does not come into and pass out of existence with each compassionate act; the trait is in another logical category. (It is, in a sense, an abstraction from the more concrete acts of compassion.)

In the area of emotion, psychologists are well accustomed to making a distinction between personality traits, on the one hand, and emotional states, on the other. With respect to anxiety, Spielberger (1966) has drawn this distinction as follows:

> Anxiety as a personality trait (A-trait) would seem to imply a motive or acquired behavioral disposition that predisposes an individual to perceive a wide range of objectively nondangerous circumstances as threatening, and to respond to these with A-state [anxiety state] reactions. (p. 17)

We agree with the kind of distinction made by Spielberger and others. We would however, carry the logic of the argument even further. Like traits, reflexes, and many other psychological phenomena, *emotional states are dispositional in nature.* Here we have the conceptual solution to the conflict between the fact that the component responses of emotions are occurrences which are temporally bound and inherently brief, whereas emotions are temporally open ended—that is, potentially more enduring than any component response. The emotional state is a disposition which is manifested by, or constituted of, the occurrent component responses; however, the state—as a disposition to respond—is in a different logical category. The absence of any given response at a particular moment—or the absence of any relevant response whatever— does not invalidate a claim for the presence of an emotional state, any more than the absence of compassionate acts at a given moment invalidates an attribution of the trait of compassion or the absence of a conditioned response invalidates a claim that an organism has been conditioned.

To this point we have discussed the dispositional character of emotional states in the context of temporal dimensions, and especially in relation to the quandary presented by emotions that outlast any component response. It is equally important to recognize that continuous, uninterrupted emotional states are also dispositional. As discussed in Chapter 1, neither emotions as a class nor specific emotions such as anger depend on any one response or any one type of response. Rather, emotions consist of patterns (syndromes) of co-occurring responses no single element of which is absolutely essential to the whole. From a constructivist point of view, the various elements of a given emotional syndrome are formed into a coherent whole by socially based principles of organization. When viewed as external to the individual, these principles are the rules that define the emotional role; when viewed as internal to the individual, they are the cognitive constructs or schemata that underlie appropriate emotional response to situations. Rarely, if ever, are all the responses contained in the schema for a particular emotion manifested in a given instance; to be in the emotional state is merely to be *disposed* to make the relevant responses. Thus, a proper comprehension of the syndromelike nature of emotions depends on a recognition that emotional states, of whatever duration and regardless of whether they are continuous or intermittent, are dispositions.

Emotional Episodes

We need to specify further the character of emotional states. So far we have only specified their logical type; now we must differentiate emotional states from other types of dispositions, of which there are many. Part of what distinguishes emotional states from other dispositions is that they are relatively brief, lasting from between a few minutes, or possibly seconds, to several days or weeks (with the exception of a few emotions, such as grief, which can last for some months). However, duration is not the only characteristic that distinguishes emotional states from other psychological dispositions. We need a formal concept to serve as an organizing framework for the defining features of emotional states; in the present section, we advance the concept of an episode to meet this need.

The concept of an episode has recently been the subject of extended analysis by Harré (1972; Harré & Secord, 1972). According to Harré, episodic concepts impose order on social interactions in the form of, among other things, a shared comprehension of beginnings, middles, and ends, as well as a shared interpretive framework for understanding the significance of actions. Harré takes as prototypic examples of formal episodes such events as marriage ceremonies; but many of the same considerations apply to less formal episodes, including states of emotion. The latter, too, are coherent social interactions based on a shared conceptual framework or normative structure.

The study of episodes consists of the explication of the "normative logic" that helps to structure behavior into meaningful units. In the remainder of this section we will attempt, in a preliminary fashion, to elucidate the normative logic for demarcating an angry episode, for delineating what belongs to an angry episode and what does not. This logic forms the basis of the temporal structure of the episode.

Probably the foremost criterion for demarcating an episode of anger is the requirement that all elements of the anger, regardless of their separation in time, must refer in some fairly direct way to a single intentional object. As discussed in earlier chapters, the object of anger can be divided into three interrelated aspects: the instigation, the target, and the aim or objective of the response. Let us consider each aspect in turn.

First, an anger episode must be centered around a single set of instigating conditions. It is always fair to ask an angry person what he or she is angry about; if we ask twice at different times and receive unrelated answers, we must conclude that we are observing two distinct episodes (unless we believe one of the answers was a dissimulation). This points up the possibility of engaging in a dispute about the instigation on which an angry response is based, which would by the same token be a dispute about what *episode* the angry response belongs to. Suppose someone becomes angry at us for a trifling offense the day after we angered them with a more serious one. We might say, "You're not angry about this, you're still angry about what happened yesterday." Even if the angry person denied this, the matter need not end there, for we might respond, "Nonsense, you've never gotten angry about this before, you *must* still be angry about yesterday." (In such a dispute, both parties would probably apply other aspects of their shared comprehension of anger, such as those aspects concerning duration and termination.)

Here, we must distinguish between the instigation, as an aspect of the object, and the cause of an emotion. We have seen that the instigation to anger is usually an action of some person which unjustifiably or unfairly inflicts some kind of harm on the angry person. (Of course, neither the unfairness nor the harm need be objectively present, only subjectively so.) A *cause* of an emotion is any condition or event without which the emotion would not have occurred. The relevance of this distinction to the present discussion is this: A given episode of anger can have only one instigation, but it can have any number of causes.

Second, an anger episode must be directed at a single target. This target is closely connected with the single set of instigating conditions; specifically, the target of an episode is whoever is responsible for the instigation, as perceived (or, possibly, misperceived) by the angry person. Thus, the target could comprise more than one person. One exception to the rule that anger should have a single target seems possible. It may be that one sometimes discovers one was mistaken in the attribution of responsibility—that is, that the person responsible for the instigation is someone other than the one who was originally blamed. In such cases it seems sensible to hold that the episode is still under way—that no new episode has been constituted—but that now the episode has a new target. In any event, an episode may have only one target at a time.

The third and final aspect of the requirement that an episode have a single intentional object is that a given episode must have a more or less unitary *aim*; that is, an objective that would, if obtained, bring the anger episode to an end. Examples of such aims would be an apology from the person who is the target of the anger, or an attempt on the part of that person to set right the damage he or she had done. Just as it is always fair to ask an angry person what he or she is angry about, we can also ask what would "satisfy" his or her anger and bring it to an end. If the angry person can say little or nothing about what would bring his or her anger to an end, or is exerting no effort toward this end even when circumstances are favorable—or if we make a presumably satisfying response without the angry person's anger thereby being brought to an end—we will wonder whether there is more involved than a simple description of a coherent single episode of anger would encompass.

Here it is necessary to make another logical distinction. Just as we must distinguish between the instigation and the cause(s) of an episode of anger, we must distinguish between the aim of the episode, on the one hand, and the variety of events or conditions which would terminate the episode, on the other. The latter might be called "termination conditions." They would include the aim, but would also include many other events and circumstances, any one of which might suffice to *cause* the episode to come to an end. Some examples might be the occurrence of some positive event for the angry person, a serious misfortune befalling the target, or the passage of a long period of time. Any one of these events might terminate an angry episode without having been any part of the angry person's aim.

Apart from the requirement for a single intentional object, there is a second set of criteria for demarcating an episode. In the absence of major obstacles, anger should be evidenced whenever possible or appropriate, for example, in all consecutive direct encounters between the angry person and the target, and perhaps even in all direct or indirect encounters, so to speak, with other aspects of the intentional obejct—for example, reminders of the instigation. This second criterion is somewhat looser than the first; that is, it is not as closely linked, in a logical sense, to the unity of an episode as is the intentional object. However, the importance of behavioral criteria for the unity of an episode can be seen in the legal treatment of crimes of passion. As was discussed in Chapter 5, in order for a charge of murder to be mitigated to voluntary manslaughter, the homicide must have been committed "in the heat of passion" and with "insufficient cooling time." This means, among other things, that the response to the instigation could not have been interrupted or too long delayed, especially for the conduct of "business" unrelated to the instigation. In everyday affairs, too, it is reasonable to assume that the consistent appearance of relevant responses is one way of establishing the unity and internal consistency of an angry episode.

To sum up, then, a single episode of anger is demarcated by a single intentional object—instigation, target, and aim—and continuity of responses over time or (possibly) consistency of appearance on consecutive relevant occasions.

For Harré, shared episodic concepts underlie and structure everyday social interactions. We maintain that our everyday concept of anger is episodic in this sense; and in the present section we have described some of the logical criteria for demarcating angry episodes. Let us turn now to some empirical data.

Study IV. On the Duration of Anger

Study IV was undertaken to explore the issue of duration and to gather additional data on the everyday experience of anger. These new data will not be used to "test" the preceding theoretical argument in any straightforward sense; the relationship between theory and data is, in this case, different than the relationship that customarily obtains in psychological research. In the usual psychological study, hypotheses are ostensibly deduced from previous theory and research and tested against the new data. In the preceding discussion, considerable emphasis has been placed on certain conceptual points, that is, on the dispositional and episodic nature of emotional states. These points do not depend in any strict sense on the data to be presented; they are already embedded in our ordinary language. The data do, however, illustrate in a systematic way the empirical basis for the conceptual points, and they provide the foundations for further theorizing.

Methods and Procedures

Subjects were 235 students enrolled in psychology courses (primarily introductory courses) at the University of Massachusetts. No restrictions were placed on the age or sex of the subjects. Ages thus ranged from 18 to 48 (mean = 20.6); 75 of the subjects were men and 160 were women. All testing was done in group sessions (about 15 subjects per group, on the average). As in Studies I and II of this series, subjects were asked to recall the most intense episode of anger during the preceding week, or the most recent episode prior to that. It was also emphasized that the experience should be one of anger and not of annoyance or irritation. The questionnaire used to describe the angry episode was patterned after that used in Studies I and III (see Appendix A). However, a number of major modifications were made, including the following:

1. In Questionnaire A subjects were asked how long their anger lasted "when it first occurred." For reasons that will be discussed more fully below, this question proved to be ambiguous. (This is why we did not devote a great deal of attention to the variable of duration in the presentation of the results of the previous studies.) On the basis of the concept of an episode described above, subjects in Study IV were asked to indicate the time interval from the point at which they first became angry about the particular incident to the point when they no longer felt angry at the target over the specific instigating conditions.
2. In previous studies the nature of the target was left open, but Study IV was restricted to incidents between loved ones, friends, and acquaintances.
3. Items were added to the questionnaire in order to assess variables that might influence the duration of anger. These included a wide range of contextual variables (e.g., related to the opportunity to express one's anger at the time); the history of the instigation (e.g., how often it had happened in the past); the nature of the relationship between the angry person and the target (e.g., the intimacy of the relationship and the likelihood of futher contact); and so forth. Special attention also was devoted to factors that might help terminate an angry episode. These terminating factors will be described at appropriate places in the presentation of the results. For now, suffice it to say that the items were constructed on the basis of subjects' responses in the "motives" and "responses" sections of Questionnaire A.
4. In order to keep the questionnaire a reasonable length, some items contained in Questionnaire A had to be dropped (e.g., the items related to motives and to responses that the subject only "felt like" doing).
5. Finally, many items from Questionnaire A were reworded. For example, with regard to the category of angry responses, the seven most frequently endorsed items from Questionnaire A were incorporated directly into the present questionnaire. However, one response item—"verbal or symbolic aggression"—was broken down into three more specific categories. Also, three new items were added in order to assess responses specific to relatively long-term episodes of anger (e.g., planning for a confrontation). Similar changes were made with respect to the instigations, and so on . These changes were designed not only to provide more complete information relevant to the duration of anger, but also to provide a check on potential biases introduced by the specific wording of the questionnaires.

To present all of the results and discussion of Study IV would be both tedious and unnecessary. Therefore, we will concentrate only on those data that bear directly on the issue of duration and its correlates, and/or that supplement the results presented in previous chapters.

Duration

Subjects were asked to indicate the duration of their anger from the time they first became angry in the episode, or first "realized" they were angry, to the time they stopped feeling angry. The results are presented in Figure 12-1, together with corresponding data from Studies I and II. In those earlier studies the time distribution was clearly bimodal, with episodes typically lasting less than 10 minutes or more than 1 day. By contrast, the time distribution in the present study was more nearly normal, with both the mean and the median duration being 1 to 2 hours. However, in this study, as in Study I, the most frequently mentioned (modal) duration was "more than 1 day."[4]

The discrepancies between the studies are probably due to two factors. In Studies I and II subjects were asked, "How long did your [the other person's] anger last *when it first occurred?*" (italics added). The question proved to be somewhat ambiguous. Since longer lasting episodes of anger may consist of a series of discrete periods of angry reactions, some subjects whose anger was relatively lengthy (Study I), or who were the targets of long-term anger (Study II), may have reported the duration of only the initial period of angry feelings or interaction. (That was actually the intent of the question.) But many subjects evidently reported the entire episode, and hence the bimodal distribution. In Study IV this ambiguity was removed, and all subjects were asked to report the duration of the episode from the beginning until they were no longer angry about the incident.

The second possible source of discrepancy is that in the present study subjects were asked to describe only incidents of anger that involved persons they knew well. In the earlier studies, incidents involving strangers and nonhuman targets were included. Anger at loved ones, friends, or acquaintances may last longer than anger at strangers or at inanimate objects.

But the major importance of the data presented in Figure 12-1 is not the differences between the studies; it is the similarities. The data clearly indicate that angry episodes may vary greatly in duration, and that many endure for a day or more.

Continuity in Time

Subjects were asked whether their anger consisted of a single uninterrupted train of thoughts and feelings, or whether it consisted of a series of periods of angry feelings and/or interactions concerning the incident, separated by periods during which the

---

[4] Actually, in Study IV (only) the upper end of the duration scale was broken down into more categories; thus in Figure 12-1 "more than 1 day" includes "2-3 days," "4 days -1 week," and "more than 1 week" for Study IV. When the results are considered employing this more differentiated scale, the distribution appears essentially normal.

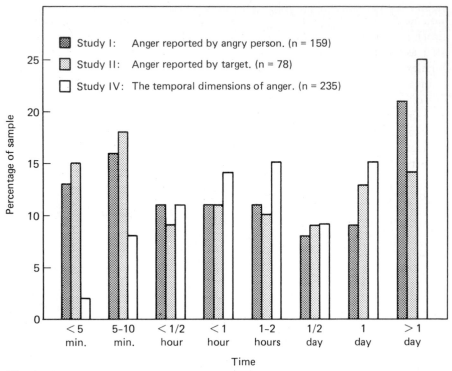

Fig. 12-1. Duration of anger in Studies I, II, and IV.

anger was not on their minds. Twenty-three percent of the subjects said that their anger was "uninterrupted from start to finish"; whereas 12% indicated that their anger consisted of "six or more" discrete periods. The modal number of periods of angry thoughts and feelings during an episode was three (mentioned by 29% of the subjects). Not surprisingly, the longer the duration of an angry episode, the more it tended to be broken up into discrete periods ($r = .52, p < .01$).

In an absolute sense, the above figures must be interpreted with some caution. Particularly in the case of longer episodes, subjects seemed to have had a difficult time distinguishing subperiods of active feelings. Or perhaps it would be more correct to say that the delineation of subperiods is relative to the duration of the episode. Longer episodes tended to be broken into subperiods—usually three or four—which presumably could in turn be broken into even smaller units. Our concern, however, is not with the precise numbers involved. Qualitatively, the conclusion is clear enough; namely, an angry episode as *ordinarily conceived* is a disposition to respond, a disposition that may or may not be manifested continuously throughout the episode.

Correlates of Duration

Although an attempt was made to assess a number of background factors (including the nature of the relationship between the angry person and the target, prior occurrences of similar instigations by the target, and features of the prevailing situation at the time of the instigation that might have inhibited the expression of anger), none of these proved to have a significant correlation with the duration of anger as reported by subjects. This lack of relationship is undoubtedly due to the complex nature of the relationships involved, a complexity that cannot be made manifest by the correlational techniques appropriate for use in the present study. This discussion will therefore focus on three categories of variables which show a more simple and direct relationship with duration; namely, the instigating conditions, the expression of emotion, and terminating factors. But before getting to these variables, a few words must be said about the relationship between the duration and intensity of angry episodes.

Intensity. There was a highly significant correlation ($r = .44, p < .01$) between the rated intensity of an episode and its duration. What is responsible for this relationship? It might be supposed that intensity is a causal factor, that is, that the more intensely anger is aroused (at the outset, presumably), the longer it takes to "dissipate." However, on the view of anger and other emotions on which the present study is based, this explanation is unsatisfying. First, the notion of anger dissipating depends, at least in part, on a concept of emotions as automatic, quasi-physiological processes, rather than normatively based, self-interpretive constructions. Second, that anger is a syndrome of related responses and not a single response or type of response means that the intensity of an episode is not a simple, singular feature, but rather a complex *integration* of a variety of features, as judged by the angry person (see Chapter 11 for a more detailed discussion of this point).

Thus, it does not seem to be the case that intensity causes duration. The relationship seems to be more the reverse; duration may be one of the features of an episode that is (often) subsumed in a judgment of its intensity. That is, duration is partly "constitutive" of intensity. In any case, in order to help distinguish issues of duration and intensity, we will present the results of most of the following analyses in two forms: the simple correlations of duration with other variables, and the corresponding correlations with covariance due to intensity partialled out.

Instigations. Subjects were provided with a list of instigations and were asked to rate the extent to which each was involved in their anger. The most frequently endorsed instigation (rated as "somewhat" or "very much" involved by 87% of the subjects) was the following:

> An action which was not in keeping with the kind of relationship you have or would like to have with this person, or with what you expect from this person.

This was also the only instigation to show a significant correlation with duration ($r = .29, p < .01$). The correlation was only slightly reduced when intensity was partialled out (partial $r = .26$)

The other two most frequently cited instigations were these:

> Something which got in the way of something you were doing or planned to do, interfering with some ongoing or planned activity [cited by 66% of the subjects].

A criticism of you, complaint or an insult. Anything someone said to you which implied a bad opinion of you or something you had done [cited by 57% of the subjects].

These two instigations, together with the one discussed above, were also the three most frequently cited instigations in Study I, even though the wording of the items differed. In Study I, however, frustration was the most frequently mentioned of the three, whereas a violation of personal expectations ranked third. The change in ordering is probably due to the fact that the present study was limited to angry incidents among persons involved in ongoing relationships.

As far as the duration of anger is concerned, perhaps the major point to note is that incidents occasioned by simple frustration tended to be of shorter duration than incidents occasioned by either the violation of personal expectations or criticisms $(p < .05)$.

Responses. The correlations between duration and the specific angry responses listed in the questionnaire are presented in Table 12-1. Before discussing these data, it is important to note a pertinent ambiguity in the interpretation of the subjects' ratings of their actions and behaviors during the episode. Subjects were instructed to rate the "degree" to which they made each of the responses at any time during their anger. While to some extent they probably rated the *absolute* amount of time they spent performing each response and/or the sheer vigor of the response during this episode (relative to other times they had engaged in the behavior or to the typical vigor of similar responses in other people), it is also likely that to some extent they were rating the amount of time spent on each response *relative* to the intensity of the episode, which would include, in addition to its duration (see above), the vigor of the other responses. Thus, these ratings may reflect an *emphasis* or *predominance* of a response as much as or more than they indicate the simple "degree" to which the action was performed or the behavior engaged in.

In general, the data presented in Table 12-1 suggest that indirect, nonverbal means of expressing anger and indirect means of coping with anger (i.e., means which do not involve a direct confrontation with the target) tend to increase and/or become more predominant as the duration of the episode increases, whereas direct verbal expression either does not increase or does not become more predominant with an increase in duration.

Consider for a moment the first group of items listed in Table 12-1. These five items refer to the direct expression of anger, whether aggressive or nonaggressive, actual or planned. None of these items is correlated with duration after intensity has been partialled out. By contrast, most of the items that suggest an indirect expression of anger, avoidant responses, and/or telling a thrid party show a mild relationship with duration, even when intensity is held constant.

Needless to say, no causal relationships can be inferred with certainty from these data. In fact, the generally positive correlations between duration and responses may have a trivial explanation: The longer an episode lasts, the more responses can be made, especially indirect ones. However, the pattern of correlations here is at least consistent with the following supposition: It may be that when people become angry they first attempt to express their anger directly to the target; if such

Table 12-1. Mean Ratings and Correlations of Responses During Anger with Duration of the Episode

Responses	Mean ratings[a]	r	Partial r[b]
Direct expression to target			
Scolding the offender, accusing him or her of wrongdoing	1.00	-.04	-.11
Thinking about and planning a confrontation; imagining ways to express your anger or resolve the incident	1.00	.21**	.11
Emphatically pointing to the damage done by the offender; pointing out the hurt he or she inflicted on you or the problems he or she caused you	.96	.15*	.08
Talking the event over with the offender without exhibiting hostility	.76	-.06	-.05
Making nasty remarks, calling the offender names, generally expressing bad feelings or ill will toward the offender	.60	.17*	.06
Indirect expression to target or others			
Showing your displeasure by withdrawing from the situation, wanting to be alone, or giving the target of your anger the cold shoulder	.89	.20**	.15*
Denial or removal of some benefit customarily enjoyed by the offender	.67	.25**	.16*
Crying, coming to tears over the incident	.37	.24**	.09
Avoidant responses			
Trying to talk yourself out of feeling angry	.87	-.03	-.03
Engaging in calming activities (e.g., going for a walk, watching TV)	.86	.13*	.14*
Trying not to think of the incident, avoiding thoughts of the offender and what he or she did	.68	.20**	.19**
Telling a third party			
Talking the incident over with a neutral uninvolved third party, with no intent to harm the offender	.98	.36**	.33**
Telling a third party in order to get back at the offender, or to have the offender punished	.25	.24**	.19**

[a] 0 = not at all; 1 = somewhat; 2 = very much.
[b] Intensity of anger partialled out.
*$p < .05$.
**$p < .01$.

expression is not possible or fails to bring about a satisfying result (a topic to which we will return shortly), the angry person may then resort to indirect expression, the involvement of a third party, or avoiding thoughts of the incident altogether.

Having advanced this hypothesis (which is also consistent with the results of Study I reported in Chapter 9) we must, on the other hand, point to a number of facts that illustrate the complexity of the relationship between the expression of anger and its duration. First, 59% of the subjects in the present study indicated that they were unable to express their anger immediately, for example, because the target was not present or the situation was inappropriate. There was, however, only a very modest relationship between the ability to express one's anger immediately and the duration of the episode ($r_{pbis} = .14$, $p < .05$). Moreover, even this modest relationship tended to disappear when the nature of the instigation was held constant.

Second, 28% of the subjects said that they did not express their anger to the instigator at any point during the episode. There was no statistically significant difference in the duration of anger between these subjects and those who did make their anger known at some point.

Finally, there was no correlation ($r = -.01$) between duration and whether or not the overall consequences of an episode were judged (on a 7-point scale) as harmful or beneficial. (The majority of subjects rated the episodes as either neutral—22%— or to some degree beneficial—54%.)

Thus, the safest conclusion to draw at this point is that there is no simple and direct relationship between duration and either the direct expression of anger (whether at the outset of the episode or later) or the overall benefits of the episode; nevertheless, indirect and avoidant types of responses do tend to predominate more in longer episodes, and this may be because they are resorted to when more direct methods fail.

Events Leading to the Termination of Anger

One is prompted by a consideration of duration to devote more attention to the termination of anger than has traditionally been the case. While the duration of a given episode of anger has a large and varied number of determinants, the limiting factor (the "effective cause" of duration, in a certain sense) is the set of events responsible for bringing the episode to an end. In the present study these terminating events were assessed in three ways. First, all subjects were provided with a list of 10 events that, on the basis of the results of previous studies, were believed important in bringing anger to an end. Subjects were asked to rate the extent to which each event occurred at any time during the episode ("not at all," "somewhat," or "very much"), and these ratings were correlated with the duration of the episode. Second, subjects whose anger lasted more than 1 hour were asked to rate the same list of 10 events, but now only with regard to their occurrence during the first hour (or the first half hour for those subjects whose anger lasted only an hour). This allowed a comparison between the same events as they occurred in episodes that terminated within an hour, and as they occurred (or failed to occur) during the first hour of longer lasting episodes. The third way of assessing terminating factors was to ask subjects to rate directly the events that brought their anger to an end and to choose the single event that contributed most to the termination of their anger.

Table 12-2 presents the results of the first analysis. Of the 10 events (possible outcomes, for the most part) that might have occurred at any time during the episode, the occurrence of 5 was significantly correlated with duration. These 5 events, although they may have contributed to an episode's termination, were nevertheless associated primarily with episodes of long duration. Two of the events had to do with a change in attitude toward the target (i.e., attributing the instigation to the target's shortcomings, and losing regard for the instigator). The other three items involved the agreement and/or support of a third party, events that would have reinforced the subject's view that his or her anger was justified. We will discuss the implications of these results shortly. But first, let us consider the results of the second type of analysis described above, that is, a comparison between the 10 events listed in Table 12-2 as (1) they occurred in episodes that terminated within an hour, and (2) they occurred during the first hour of episodes that continued to endure for a longer period.

A discriminant analysis was used to make the above comparison. This type of analysis assesses the degree to which it is possible to predict, from events occurring within the first hour, whether or not an episode was terminated at that point. The group of terminated episodes was composed of the 84 subjects whose anger lasted less than 1 hour. The group of nonterminated episodes was composed of 146 of the subjects whose anger lasted 1 hour or more. (The remaining five subjects reporting episodes of 1 hour or more neglected to rate the first-hour events.)

The first-hour ratings of the events were able to discriminate between terminated and nonterminated episodes to a degree which was statistically significant (Wilk's lambda = .82, chi-square = 45.3, df = 10, p < .01). Of the 230 cases, 157 (68%) were correctly classified by the discriminant function; 101 (out of 146) were correctly classifed as nonterminated, and 56 (out of 84) were correctly classified as terminated.

A stepwise regression procedure was employed to determine which of the events were associated with termination. Five of the 10 showed a statistically significant association. Three of the five showed a *positive* relationship with termination (i.e., they tended to be rated higher in the terminated episodes than in the nonterminated episodes):

Learn Needs—"The offender learned about your personal needs and desires, and/ or you felt that his or her respect for these needs and desires was increased." Take Back—"The offender 'took back' what it was that made you angry, or tried to undo the damage that was done." No Repeat—"The offender told you that 'it won't happen again,' that he or she wouldn't repeat the action which made you angry, or gave you other reason to believe that the action would not be repeated."

The remaining two events showed a *negative* relationship with termination (i.e., they tended to be rated higher in the nonterminated episodes than in the terminated episodes):

Table 12-2. Mean Ratings and Correlations of Events During Anger with Duration of the Episode

Events	Mean ratings[a]	r	Partial r[b]
You realized that what the offender did or said that made you angry had more to do with his or her problems or shortcomings than with anything about you.	1.24	.22**	.17**
Your determination to change the situation which led to the action which angered you was increased, or your confidence that you could do so was increased.	1.02	.07	.06
One or more people (apart from the offender) agreed with you that you had been treated badly or wrongly, and/or that you had a right to be angry.	1.00	.37**	.27**
The offender learned about your personal needs and desires, and/or you felt that his or her respect for these needs and desires was increased.	.91	.01	-.02
You felt that you had less need or affection for the offender than you had thought.	.60	.24**	.14*
The offender (i.e., the person you were angry at) "took back" what it was that made you angry, or tried to undo the damage that was done.	.60	.03	.00
The offender became angry or hostile toward you.	.57	.03	-.01
The offender told you that "it won't happen again," that he or she wouldn't repeat the action which made you angry, or gave you other reason to believe that the action would not be repeated.	.49	.01	-.07
Your image with one or more people (apart from the offender) was improved, and/or misconceptions which may have arisen in the other peoples' eyes as a result of the action which angered you were corrected or prevented.	.42	.21**	.15*
One or more people (apart from the offender) agreed to help you improve the situation and/or prevent the action which angered you from being repeated.	.41	.33**	.25**

[a] 0 = not at all; 1 = somewhat; 2 = very much.
[b] Intensity of anger partialled out.
*$p < .05$.
**$p < .01$.

Less Affection—"you felt that you had less need or affection for the offender then you had thought."

Others' Help—"One or more people (apart from the offender) agreed to help you improve the situation and/or prevent the action which angered you from being repeated."

The three events with a positive association with termination show a substantial degree of multicollinearity; that is, each is correlated with the other two (r's range from .46 to .59), and therefore their predictive power is confounded. "Learn Needs" showed the highest simple correlation with termination (r_{pbis} = .29), and it is the only one of the three that makes a statistically significant contribution to prediction when the other two events are also included in the equation.

The two events with a negative association with termination are correlated with each other (r = .27). "Others' Help" makes a significant contribution to prediction only if it is included before "Less Affection."

The results of the two analyses described thus far complement each other. Both suggest that the support of a third party is associated with anger of long duration (presumably because such support would not be forthcoming unless the anger were justified and/or because such support is sought only after other coping strategies have failed). Both analyses also suggest that an important factor in bringing anger to an end is a cooling of the relationship with the instigator. (How long that cooling typically lasts cannot, of course, be inferred from these data.) The first analysis further emphasizes the importance of third-party support in anger of long duration, and of the angry person's reappraisal of the target in such instances. The second (discriminant) analysis, by contrast, highlights the importance of the target's own behavior (e.g., recognizing the needs of the angry person) in quickly resolving an angry episode.

The third type of analysis designed to investigate the termination of anger involved the subjects' own assessment of the factors they believed most important in bringing their anger to an end. From a list of 12 factors, subjects chose the one they considered the most important; in addition, they rated the degree to which each factor was involved in the termination of their anger. Ten of the factors listed were the same as those presented in Table 12-2. Two additional items—which refer not so much to outcomes as to activities on the part of the subject that might directly influence the termination of anger—were also included. Finally, subjects were allowed to describe in their own words any other factors they believed might have contributed to the termination of their anger. The present discussion will be limited to the six most frequently cited factors; over 75% of the subjects considered one or another of these six as the *most* important factor in bringing their anger to an end.

1. *You realized that what the offender did or said that made you angry had more to do with his or her problems or shortcomings than with anything about you.* This item was rated as the single most important terminating factor by 22% of the subjects, and as "somewhat" or "very much" involved in the termination by 73% of the subjects.

A person may attribute shortcomings to another with compassion (a kind of pitying response) or with denigration. Either way would tend to reduce anger by placing the instigation in a different light. In the present study, a few subjects did indicate that they reevaluated the blameworthiness of the instigation in light of the target's frailties—a more or less compassionate, if condescending, judgment. However, subjects' written comments suggest that they more often had in mind a denigration of the target, a reduction of that person's stature, or a low estimate of his or her character.

It is in some respects puzzling that denigration of the target should be such a frequent element in the termination of anger. Denigration seems itself to be an angry response, and, moreover, one that might prolong rather than resolve a conflict. Indeed, the analysis described earlier (see Table 12-2) suggests that this kind of event is more associated with long-term than with short-term anger.

It may be that many of the subjects who rated this event as the most important element in the termination of their anger were describing a shift in their self-interpretation from an emotional schema to an *attitudinal* one, such that the transitory nature of the negative judgments of anger has *ostensibly* been exchanged for the more established nature of an attitudinal judgment. (This ostensible shift in the nature of the judgment might play a part in the subjects' self-interpretations without constituting a genuine change; it is a separate question whether a lasting lowering of esteem had indeed occurred.) This interpretation of the subjects' reports seems especially plausible in those instances where the target is obdurate, where he or she does not offer a conciliatory response to the subjects' anger. The subject would in effect be saying that there is no point in being angry, and would be blaming the target for this unsatisfying state of affairs.

2. *You discovered, or were convinced, that your anger was unfounded or unjustified; that is, you found out that the event was not really one which should make someone angry, or you realized for some other reason that you had no right to be angry.* This kind of reappraisal was cited as the most important terminating factor by 13% of the subjects, and as at least somewhat involved in the termination of their anger by 40% of the subjects. It might also be noted that this is one of the new items added to the list of terminating factors; that is, it does not appear in Table 12-2. A separate analysis indicated that this item was negatively correlated with duration ($r = -.19$, $p < .01$); that is, a benign reinterpretation tended to be associated with episodes of shorter duration.

From a social-constructivist point of view, all terminations of anger episodes involve some reappraisal of the appropriateness of anger or, more precisely, a shift of self-interpretation out of the anger schema and into some other schema, most probably a nonemotional one. What makes the simple reevaluation presently under discussion unique is that it is not occasioned by any readily identifiable change in the stance of the target person or any other aspect of the situation. It is as if the angry person for some reason decides that, on reconsideration, the adoption of the angry role in the prevailing circumstances is untenable, indefensible, or for some other reason undesirable, and wishes to withdraw his or her commitment to that role. (In many cases, of course, such a reappraisal is quite appropriate; as discussed in Chapter 6, a person's anger is often caused, in part, by factors other than a normatively appropriate instigation.)

3. *The offender learned about your personal needs and desires, and/or you felt that his or her respect for these needs and desires was increased.* Twenty-six subjects (11%) considered this the most important factor in the termination of their anger, and 70% said that it was at least "somewhat" involved. In the discriminant analysis reported earlier, the occurrence of this event within 1 hour of the instigation of an anger episode was the single strongest predictor of termination within the hour. Two closely related events which were also associated with the termination of some episodes may be mentioned here. The target's "taking back" the offending action or trying to undo the damage he or she had done was endorsed by 14 subjects (6%) as the most important factor in termination, while 12 subjects (5%) said that the target's offering assurances that the offending action would not be repeated was the most important element. In the discriminant analysis both of these events emerged as ones associated with an early termination, but their association, in both cases, was largely confounded with that of the target's learning the subject's needs, with which they are both highly correlated.

It is not surprising that direct conciliatory responses from the target—an attempt to undo the damage or an assurance that the offending action will not be repeated— can be effective in terminating anger and are sometimes cited by the angry person as the most important factor in the termination. What is perhaps somewhat surprising is that the more general, perhaps less explicit, acknowledgment of the angry person's personal needs emerges as a more important factor. Partly this is to be accounted for by the fact that it is a considerably more common occurrence than either of the more specific conciliatory responses, but this fact does not account entirely for the greater frequency of its endorsement as the most important termination factor, since in 19 of the 26 cases in which it was cited as most important, the subject reported that one or both of the more specific responses had occurred at least somewhat; moreover, it does not account for the stronger association between this general acknowledgment and termination observed in the discriminant analysis. It would appear that an acknowledgment of the validity of one's needs and desires (specific to the instigation and/or in general) often counts as a satisfying response to anger. As we shall see below, this is true even when the acknowledgment comes from an uninvolved third party.

4. *Your determination to change the situation which led to the action which angered you was increased, or your confidence that you could do so was increased.* This item was not correlated with the duration of anger, nor did it help discriminate between short-term and long-term angry episodes (see Table 12-2). Nevertheless, it was cited by 10% of the subjects as being the most important factor in terminating their anger, and it was mentioned as "somewhat" or "very much" involved by 71% of the subjects.

A determination to change the situation can occur soon after the instigation, or it may take some time for an adequate coping strategy to develop. But once a plan of action has been settled upon, the episode tends to be brought to a close, at least as far as anger per se is concerned. As described in the last chapter, anger does not thrive in situations that are either too poor or too rich in response options. But there is undoubtedly more involved in the termination of anger than the mere availability of an adequate response. Determination to change a situation implies a deliberate, well-thought-out plan of action, and these features are incompatible with the emotional role as ordinarily conceived.

5. *You engaged in calming activities, like going for a walk, trying not to think about it, and so on.* Calming activities were cited as the most important factor in the termination of their anger by 10% of the subjects; 62% said such activities were "somewhat" or "very much" involved in bringing their anger to an end. This item was not among the events listed in Table 12-2, and it did not form part of the discriminant analysis between short-term and long-term episodes. However, a very similar item was included in the list of responses discussed in the previous section (see Table 12-1). From that discussion it may be recalled that calming activities showed a slight, but nevertheless statistically significant, correlation with duration ($r = .13$).

From a traditional point of view, the terminating influence of calming activities would seem to be unproblematical, since that view tends to regard anger as consisting of, or at least fully dependent on, physical agitation. However, from a constructivist point of view, anger involves a self-interpretation of a syndrome of responses which may (or may not) include physical agitation. On such a constructivist view, a reduction in physical agitation does not constitute, or bring about in an unmediated way, a reduction in anger.

That the reduction of physical agitation cannot always be directly responsible for the cessation of anger, even in cases where calming activities are considered the most important element in termination, is made obvious by the fact that among the 23 subjects citing calming activities as the most important termination factor, 14 (61%) reported episodes which lasted longer than 1 hour. In the case of episodes of relatively long duration, it is unreasonable to assume that a reduction in physical agitation was directly responsible for a termination of anger. It seems implausible that in such cases the angry person's agitation remained at a constant high level throughout the hour or more of the episode, only to be reduced by means of deliberate calming activities. An alternative account, consistent with a constructivist view, is that calming activities are effective primarily when they are part of a deliberate effort to end anger, and thus form an element of self-interpretation.

6. *One or more people (apart from the offender) agreed with you that you had been treated badly or wrongly, and/or that you had a right to be angry.* According to 9% of the subjects, this was the most important factor in bringing their anger to an end, and 56% said that it was at least "somewhat" involved in the termination of their anger. As was discussed earlier (see Table 12-2), this factor also tended to be associated with episodes of long duration.

We have already noted how acknowledgment by the target of the angry person's needs and desires may help to resolve an episode quickly (see item 3 above). Evidently, if such an acknowledgment is not forthcoming from the target, then confirmation by a third party that the angry person is in the right may serve as a partial substitute. This is not particularly surprising, since third-party support may bolster one's self-esteem and confidence; and, as we have seen, such support may also contribute to the denigration of the target by the angry person.

Before leaving this topic, it is perhaps worth recalling the distinction made earlier between *aims* and *terminating conditions*. The aim (objective) of a person's anger is what the person is seeking as a satisfaction to his or her anger, while the terminating conditions subsume all events which are capable of bringing the episode to a close. Fulfillment of the aim would be one terminating condition, assuming that the anger was "in good faith"; that is, that no ulterior motives were involved. Certain of the terminating factors we have been discussing could not sensibly constitute aims: Attribution of the offending action to the target's shortcomings (item 1), reevaluation of the instigation (item 2), increased determination to change the situation (item 4), calming activities (item 5), and a third party's support (item 6) would fall within this category. On the other hand, conciliatory responses on the part of the target—for example, an acknowledgment of the angry person's needs and desires (item 3)—could easily constitute one of the more common aims of anger.

It is somewhat surprising that the kind of event that might fulfill an aim was not more frequently cited as the chief terminating factor. However, 60% of the subjects said that the target's acknowledgment of their needs and desires was at least "somewhat" involved in the termination of their anger; moreover, 54% rated the overall outcome of the episode as beneficial, while only 24% rated it as harmful (with 22% neutral). These figures suggest that some aims were being met, at least in the majority of episodes.

In our discussion of the relationship between modes of responses and duration, we noted that the pattern of correlations was compatible with the hypothesis that people tend first to express their anger directly to the target, and proceed to the other common angry responses only if direct expression fails to achieve a satisfying result. We may now state this hypothesis more precisely: When people become angry at someone they know personally, they attempt to realize the *aim* of their anger. Such aims generally center on an accommodation on the part of the target to the needs and desires of the angry person. (Recall here that the discriminant analysis indicated that such an accommodation by the target was the factor most responsible for bringing an angry episode to a rapid conclusion.) When the aim proves impossible to accomplish, the anger may then endure until the person reevaluates the instigator and/or the instigation, or settles upon a plan of action to change the situation. Other common bases for the termination of anger when the aim proves unobtainable include calming activities and gaining the support of a third party.

Concluding Observations

In a sense, the major conclusion to be drawn from our exploration of time and emotion is also the most simple and the most obvious, but nevertheless one that has frequently been ignored in traditional theories of emotion. That conclusion is, namely, that emotions endure in time, and that no response (as ordinarily conceived) need be manifested continuously throughout the period from beginning to end. Largely because of a confusion between occurrent and dispositional concepts, most theories of emotion have difficulty accommodating this basic fact. Recognizing that emotions are dispositional (and, by the same token, that the notion of "state" is conceptually confused and inadequate as it is currently applied in theories of emotion) opens the way to a more adequate consideration of the temporal dimensions of emotion.

Most social occasions or events are associated with temporal expectations. In many cases, these temporal expectancies are among the rules (social norms) that help constitute the event. Consider a sporting event, such as a football game. The rules of football stipulate that a game should last no longer than 60 minutes of actual playing time. In other sports, such as baseball, the temporal boundaries of a game are not so clearly demarcated; duration depends rather on the outcomes of the actions of the players. But even a baseball game, if it lasts too long, may be called on account of time.

The emotions, too, we have argued, are played according to rules; and some of these rules have to do specifically with time. Certain emotions, such as fright, are expected (under normal conditions) to last only a short time; whereas other emotions, such as grief, may last for months or even years. If an emotion lasts too long, or not long enough, we may search for "hidden causes," or even redefine the syndrome. Thus, the fright that lasts too long is not *just* fright, and the grief that is over too quickly is not *real* grief.

That there are definite expectations (social norms) regarding the time course of anger is evident from our discussion of the law of homicide (Chapter 5). As will be recalled, a homicide can be judged a crime of passion only if "insufficient cooling time" has elapsed between the provocation and the act. Insufficient cooling time, it is also relevant to note, is subject to the reasonable-man test; that is, the criteria for duration are based on community standards and not on the psychological state of the defendant.

It is also possible to discern the impact of norms governing the duration of anger in the results of Study IV. Although the major element in these norms concerns how long an episode may last and still be considered a single episode of anger, there may also be some limit to how short an episode may be. Thus, very few subjects (2%) reported episodes lasting less than 5 minutes. While there are several probable contributions to this lower limit (including the fact that subjects were asked to report the most intense incident during the previous week), it may also be that an episode of under 5 minutes duration simply tends to be too short to qualify as genuine anger. With regard to episodes of longer duration, only 10% of the subjects reported that their anger lasted more than 3 days, which seems to suggest an upper limit.

Perhaps of greater interest than the upper and lower limits evident in subjects' reports is that 63% of the subjects indicated that the incident that made them angry had not been completely resolved, even though their anger was presumably over. That is, in order to conform to the normative upper limit of duration, a person may bring his or her anger to a close before the issue is resolved. This may be accomplished in a number of different ways. In many cases, the episode may simply be "forgotten." Where there is an occasion to provide an account of the termination of the episode, the angry person may offer a variety of accounts, such as that the anger dissipated, that it was transformed into a sentiment (e.g., dislike for the instigator), that the original episode ended but a new one has been kindled by recalling the instigation, and so on.

The 17th century poet and moralist Francis Quarles (1880) offered the following observation:

> Anger may repast with thee for an houre, but not for a night: The continuance of anger is Hatred, the continuance of Hatred turns Malice. That anger is not warrantable, which hath seen two Sunnes. (Cent. II, Cap. LX)

The data from Study IV suggest somewhat greater leeway in the duration of anger than Quarles would condone. Yet this maxim is of interest for two reasons. First as a maxim, it exemplifies the *normative* limits on the acceptable duration of anger; and second, it also makes explicit the relationship between duration and other more structural features of the emotion.

In the present chapter,we have tried to accommodate the temporal organization of emotional behavior by suggesting that emotional states be conceptualized as short-term dispositions; and we have introduced the notion of an episode to distinguish emotional states from longer-term dispositions (e.g., an angry episode from hatred or malice). Specifically, the duration of an emotional episode over a period of time is the persistence of a disposition over that period of time. In some episodes of emotion (generally briefer ones) the disposition is coterminous with a particular response or with a series of temporally overlapping responses; in other episodes (usually longer lasting ones) there are periods during which *no* relevant response is present. Not only does the recognition of the dispositional character of emotions make possible a noncontradictory conceptually coherent account of longer lasting noncontinuous episodes, it also aids our comprehension of the independence of emotion from any one response or type of response. To be in an emotional state does not imply that one necessarily makes any given component response of the emotional syndromes, only that one is disposed to make such responses. Emotional states are episodic dispositions.

Chapter 13

Differences Between Men and Women in the Everyday Experience of Anger

W. Douglas Frost and James R. Averill

Stereotypically, women have been regarded as more emotional than men. Presumably, men learn that "big boys don't cry" and tend to inhibit the spontaneous expression of emotion (except in special restricted circumstances, e.g., at sports events). But there is an important exception to this stereotype. In the case of anger, women are thought to be less, not more, emotional than men.

Two kinds of argument have been advanced to support the notion that women are less prone to anger than men. The more traditional argument is biological; that is, men are "by nature" the more aggressive members of the species, and hence are more liable to become angry when provoked. The alternative argument reaches the same conclusion by a different route; namely, that men and women have the same potential (biologically speaking) for aggressiveness, but that society encourages such behavior in men while discouraging it in women. The most ardent proponents of this point of view are feminists. In the words of Bardwick (1979): "Women are not entitled to anger. Anger, except in some girlish tantrum, is unfeminine. Direct, bold, eyeball-to-eyeball, confronting, dominating, resisting, insisting anger has been traditionally forbidden to women" (p. 48).

In the present chapter we will examine the evidence relevant to possible sex differences in the everyday experience of anger, and the implications of biological and feminist arguments for an understanding of anger, when these arguments are evaluated in terms of the empirical evidence.

We shall proceed as follows. First, we will review in some detail the biological and feminist arguments, which imply that there are marked differences in the way men and women experience and/or express their anger. Second, the data from Studies I-IV, the main results of which were presented in previous chapters, will be examined for possible sex differences. To anticipate briefly, no *major* differences were observed. Third, evidence from other sources—self-report data, experimental research, and clinical observations—will be reviewed. This evidence also provides little support for the existence of marked sex differences in the everyday experience of anger. Finally, the theoretical implications of these findings will be discussed.

One additional point needs to be made by way of introduction. In previous chapters, we have emphasized that anger should not be identified too closely with aggression. The results of the analyses presented below will reinforce this view. Nevertheless, the distinction between anger and aggression is often hard to maintain, especially when presenting the views of others. As we shall see, much of the evidence for sex differences in anger comes from studies on aggression. This is true of the human as well as the animal research. To complicate matters even further, a third variable is often introduced into the argument, namely, dominance. Very briefly, aggression is viewed as a means of establishing and maintaining a position of dominance. On the basis of this assumption and the close identification of anger with aggression, the conclusion is drawn that, given a difference in dominance between individuals or groups, differences in anger must also exist. The conclusion seems plausible, but it is based on questionable assumptions.

Let us turn now to the details of the biological and feminist arguments, keeping in mind the frequent conflation of dominance, aggression, and anger.

The Biological Argument

One of the best established facts in behavioral biology is that the males of most mammalian species are more aggressive than the females; and, moreover, that this difference is dependent on the male hormone testosterone (see Moyer, 1976, for a review of relevant research). This fact alone provides strong presumptive evidence for sex differences in human aggressiveness. However, cross-species comparisons must be made with caution. Even among the apes (the "highest" of the nonhuman primates), there are marked differences in the degree of sexual dimorphism related to aggression. The female gibbon, for example, is about as aggressive as the male. For this reason, and because of the exigencies of space, we will limit our review to a few observations on man's nearest primate relative, the chimpanzee, and to cross-cultural comparisons among humans.

Anger and Aggression in the Chimpanzee

For reasons discussed in earlier chapters, the attribution of anger to infrahuman animals is largely metaphorical. However, chimpanzees seem capable of self-awareness (Gallup, 1977), and at least some of the rudiments of language (Rumbaugh, 1976; but see also Terrace, Petitto, Sanders, & Bever, 1979); it would therefore be wrong, perhaps, to deny to them the rudiments of anger also. According to Hebb (1972), the chimpanzee displays "the full picture of human anger in its three main forms: anger, sulking and the temper tantrum" (p. 202).

Hebb's (1972) comments on "anger" in the chimpanzee are based on observations made on captive animals at the Yerkes Laboratory in Florida (cf. Hebb, 1946). He does not make any particular note of sex differences, possibly because he was not looking for such differences and possibly because they were not evident in that situation. It should also be noted, however, that Hebb distinguishes three forms of anger: "anger, sulking and the temper tantrum." Presumably by "anger" in the narrow sense, he means aggression. That, at least, is what most observers have meant when they speak of "anger" in the chimpanzee.

Only in the last several decades have detailed observations been made on the behavior of chimpanzees in their natural habitat; and there, sex differences in anger/aggression have frequently been noted. Some of the best of these observations have been made at the Gombe Research Center in Tanzania under the leadership of Jane van Lawick-Goodall. A variety of different investigators have been involved, and the present discussion is based on reports by Buirski, Plutchik, and Kellerman (1978), Bygott (1979), and Hamburg, Hamburg, and Barchas (1975).

According to Hamburg et al. (1975), there are striking similarities between the threat and attack patterns of chimpanzees and human beings, especially in respect to the behavior of children and adolescents. Both species seem to be well skilled in various techniques of bluff and intimidation, as well as in direct attack. With regard to sex differences, Hamburg et al. note that young male chimpanzees are more active and aggressive, and engage in more rough-and-tumble play, than do young females. These differences are evident from a very early age, and become especially pronounced during the transition from adolescence to adulthood.

The adolescent male chimpanzee undergoes a growth spurt at about the age of 8 years. This is followed in a few months by an increase in the frequency and vigor of aggressive behavior, often directed toward females other than his mother. By the age of 10, the young male is able to dominate many females who, a few years earlier, were dominant over him. During the final years of adolescence, he gradually begins to threaten and attack lower ranking males, until he himself is accommodated into the adult male hierarchy.

The pattern of development in the female chimpanzee takes a somewhat different course. As a juvenile, she spends a large portion of her time in association with her mother, and she seems fascinated by small infants. Following an adolescent growth spurt, there is an increase in the young female's sexual behavior, analogous to the increase in aggressive behavior on the part of the male. (Needless to say, these sex differences are relative, not absolute. Adolescent males and females both show an increase in aggressive and sexual behavior, but in differing degrees.)

According to Bygott (1979), when female chimpanzees have aggressive encounters, it is more likely to be with a male than with another female; moreover, the females almost invariably end up being subordinate to the males. When female chimpanzees do aggress against one another, the outcome is more likely to be inconclusive than when two males, or a male and a female, engage in a fight. Bygott concludes that dominance-subordinate relationships are either not as important or not as clearly defined among female chimpanzees as among males.

Within the male hierarchy there is a rough correlation between the rank of a chimpanzee and its aggressiveness (Buirski et al., 1978). The relationship is far from perfect, however. Once a hierarchy is established, the most dominant animals are seldom attacked and hence tend to be involved in fewer aggressive encounters. Still, the potential is there. In this connection, it is worth recalling the studies by Delgado (1967, 1970) described in Chapter 2. Direct stimulation of the brain was more likely to lead to aggression when a monkey (*Macaca mulatta*) was high in a dominance hierarchy than when it was low.

Overall, the existence of a dominance hierarchy tends to inhibit aggression among chimpanzees within a troop. The most likely targets of attack (after a hierarchy has been established) are acquaintances who have been separated for a period, or strangers. As Bygott (1979) notes, "Male chimpanzees, perhaps more than males of any other primate species, have developed the ability to spend long periods in peaceful proximity to one another, to take collective action against intruders, and even to cooperate in the hunting of mammalian prey" (p. 426).

Two questions are raised by the above considerations. First, what is the relationship between dominance and "anger" in the chimpanzee? And second, to what extent can we generalize from chimpanzee to human behavior? With regard to the first question, it must be emphasized again that the attribution of anger to animals is largely metaphorical. But it is a metaphor that is taken seriously by many theorists. With specific reference to anger and dominance, Plutchik (1980) argues that

> anger and fear are emotions that act to deal with the problem of hierarchies. Consistent with this interpretation is the evidence that organisms high in a hierarchy tend to be bossy and irritable, and those at lower levels tend to have anxiety. (pp. 146-147)

And as we shall see shortly, a close link has also been postulated between human anger and (male) dominance, regardless of whether that dominance is biological or social in origin.

With regard to the second question raised above, we have already emphasized the need for caution when generalizing from one species to another, even when those species are as closely related as are chimpanzees and human beings. To reinforce this point, consider the fact that in the chimpanzee, female sexual behavior is closely tied to the estrous cycle; in the human, it is not. Has human aggressive behavior been correspondingly "freed" from biological constraints, so that women may be as aggressive as men, or conversely? Only research on the human level can answer this question.

Cross-Cultural Comparisons

Rohner (1976) examined the ethnographic records of 101 societies in order to determine the universality of gender differences in human aggression. For 14 societies it was possible to obtain separate ratings of aggressiveness for boys and girls (up to the age of about 6, or as long afterward as the parent-child relationship remained constant). For 31 societies it was possible to assess gender differences in adult aggression. The results are as follows.

In the 14 societies where it was possible to compare young boys and girls, the boys were rated as more aggressive in 10 (71%). In the remaining four societies both sexes were rated as equally aggressive. In spite of the small size of the sample (14 societies), and possible biases in the original ethnographic accounts, these data strongly support the notion that in humans, as in most other primate species, young males are more aggressive than are young females. However, an important qualification must be added. The differences between the societies studied by Rohner were much greater than the differences between the sexes within any given society. For example, the girls in one society might be rated as less aggressive than the boys in that same society, and yet as more aggressive than the boys in another society. Across all 14 societies the correlation coefficient between the rated aggressiveness of boys and girls was .88, which means that cultural influences were more important than biological influences in determining the general level of aggressiveness of either sex.

The importance of cultural influences is also apparent in the ratings obtained by Rohner for adult aggression. On the basis of animal research, some of it reviewed above, one would expect sex differences in aggression to be more pronounced among adults than among children. During adolescence, boys typically outdistance girls in both size and strength; and in adolescent boys, as in the males of most mammalian species, there is a correlation between aggression and circulating levels of the male hormone testosterone (cf. Olweus, Mattsson, Schalling, & Lööw, 1980).[1]

Among humans, acts of violence are primarily a male prerogative, as would be expected on the basis of the above considerations. However, when "normal" aggression within a society is examined, sex differences largely disappear. Thus, among the 31 societies for which Rohner was able to obtain separate ratings for men and women, the sexes were rated as equally aggressive in 20; men were rated as more aggressive in 6 societies and the women as more aggressive in 5 societies. Moreover, in societies where ratings were available for both children and adults, the men were generally rated as less aggressive than the boys and the women as more aggressive than the girls. In other words, for certain kinds of aggression, at least, socialization seems to foster a convergence between men and women. The importance of this fact will become apparent later in this chapter when we discuss possible sex differences in anger within our own society.

It would, of course, be hazardous to base conclusions on a single set of analyses. However, the conclusions reached by Rohner are in general agreement with the results of other cross-cultural studies of aggression (e.g., Omark, Omark, & Edelman, 1973; Rosenblatt & Cunningham, 1976; Whiting & Edwards, 1973). Since much of the earlier research on this issue has been reviewed in depth by Maccoby and Jacklin (1974), there is no need to go into additional detail here. Suffice it to say that Maccoby and Jacklin present a brief for the case that men are more aggressive than women; and that the difference is, at least in part, of biological origin.

---

[1] Studies relating circulating levels of testosterone to aggressive behavior have yielded mixed results (cf. Ehrenkrantz, Bliss, & Sheard, 1974; Monti, Brown, & Corriveau, 1977). The positive findings reported by Olweus et al. (1980) involved self-reported physical and verbal aggression, mainly in response to provocation or threat, among adolescent boys in Sweden. Pubertal stage, body build, and antisocial behavior did not appear to be mediating variables. Nevertheless, circulating levels of testosterone during adolescence or adulthood are probably not a particularly important determinant of male aggressiveness. Of greater importance would be the sensitivity of neural structures to whatever levels of testosterone might be present. The sensitivity and/or organization of neural structures related to aggressive behavior, as to sexual behavior, is influenced by testosterone during fetal development.

The above conclusion does not mean (nor do Maccoby and Jacklin in any way imply) that sociocultural influences are unimportant in determining sex differences in human aggression. Indeed, even if we reject the validity and/or relevance of the biological argument, a case can still be made that men are more prone to anger or aggression than are women.

The Feminist Argument

The resurgence of feminism in the last decade has served to focus attention on the way women experience and express their anger. Numerous feminists have argued that women living in a male-oriented society have had to suppress their anger, that the legitimacy of their anger has been denied, and that their physical and mental health has suffered as a result. Harriet Lerner (1977), for example, declares that, "In contrast [to men], women have been denied the forthright expression of even healthy and realistic anger. . . . All our definitions of 'femininity' have perpetuated the myth that the truly feminine woman is devoid of anger and aggressiveness, especially toward men and children" (p. 5). Adrienne Rich (1976) makes a similar point in her highly regarded book, *Of Woman Born*. She quotes a 19th-century "male expert" on mothering as follows:

> Let a mother feel grieved, and manifest her grief when her child does wrong; let her, with calmness and reflection, use discipline which the case requires; *but never let her manifest irritated feeling, or give utterance to an angry expression.* (p. 28, italics added)

Rich also notes that "as a young mother, I remember feeling guilt that my explosions of anger were a 'bad example' for my children, as if they, too should be taught that 'temper' is a defect of character having nothing to do with what happens in the world outside one's flaming skin" (p. 29). Others argue that women in contemporary American society are supposed to be emotional but that being emotional does not include being angry: "Both women and children are expected to show emotion, 'allowed' to cry (though made to feel guilty for it), expected to lower eyes and head before authority; display of anger is prohibited" (Henley, 1977, p. 14).

Until very recently the major social roles assigned to women have been those of wife and mother. Feminists have argued that these roles are so constituted that women's anger is not tolerated. As Adrienne Rich (1976) has noted, it is the mother "who carries the major share of childbearing, and who also absorbs the frustrations and rage her husband may bring home from work (often in the form of domestic violence). Her own anger becomes illegitimate, since her job is to provide him with the compassion and comfort he needs at home in order to return daily to the factory or mine pits" (p. 37).

The severe consequences of the apparent societal proscription of female anger are attested to by other authors as well. Phyllis Chesler (1971) suggests that "Both psychotherapy and marriage enable women to express and defuse their anger by experiencing it as a form of emotional illness, by translating it into hysteria, frigidity, chronic depression, phobias, and the like. . . . Open expressions of rage are too dangerous and too ineffective for the isolated and economically dependent woman" (pp. 373-374).[2]

In a similar vein, Friday (1977) describes how women, whose main source of self-esteem and identity is their role as wife and mother, are unable to allow themselves to be angry in an open, direct fashion. She quotes psychotherapist Sonya Friedman as follows: "The more I talk to a woman the more anger I uncover. All the depression, the going to sleep early, not having energy, the fact that it's three in the afternoon and she is still sitting around in her housecoat—all of these are various forms of anger" (p. 405). Friday describes women who project their anger onto their husbands, getting him to express the anger that she feels but cannot allow herself; and women who, instead of using their husbands to express their anger, turn it inward. "We feel we are failures, become insomniacs, compulsive housekeepers, victims of obsessive ideas of aging, death. One very frequent face this inner fear and anger wears is that of the controlling woman" (p. 417).

This point of view is echoed by Lerner (1977), who writes, "So powerful are the prohibitions against the direct expression of anger in women, that women frequently turn their anger into self-destructive symptoms, or vent it in a poorly controlled manner that makes it easy for others to write them off" (p. 6).

The emphasis that feminists place on male dominance as a factor in the inhibition and distortion of a woman's anger would seem to make their argument congruent with the biological argument reviewed above (in that the latter also emphasizes the importance of male dominance). It hardly needs saying, however, that the congruence is rather superficial. To the feminist, male dominance is a consequence of socioeconomic factors. Any biological differences in aggressive tendences that might exist between the sexes are regarded as of trivial importance (if they are acknowledged to exist at all). Thus, one goal of feminism is to encourage women to express effectively the anger they *really* feel. Appropriately harnessed and directed, anger is viewed as a "tool for growth." The theme "anger is changing our lives" is often voiced at feminist rallies and support groups. For example, Glennon cites the following description of anger as it occurs in an informal feminist theater workshop:

> One woman becomes angry and pounds the floor and then suddenly another hears her and recognizes it and then all the women are angry. From an inarticulate moaning and pounding comes an angry fury as they rise together chanting "No! No! No!—No more shame." (anonymous, cited by Glennon, 1979, p. 83)

Whether one favors the biological or the feminist argument, or some combination of the two, the implication is clear: Women do not experience anger as frequently, intensely, and/or in the same manner as do men. But is that really the case? On the basis of evidence that will be presented below, the answer to this question is a qualified no. (This answer has already been foreshadowed by the findings of Rohner, reviewed above, that men and women do not differ in aggressiveness as much as do young boys and girls.)

---

[2] By permission of Basic Books, Inc., Publishers. © 1971 by Basic Books, Inc., New York, New York.

To adumbrate briefly the discussion to come, we note that sex differences in the everyday experience of anger do not appear to be nearly as great as either the biological or the feminist arguments would seem to imply. This conclusion, if correct, is of considerable theoretical interest. On the one hand, it suggests that anger—as opposed to aggression in general—is relatively independent of man's biological heritage. In this regard, the feminists would seem to have the better part of the argument. On the other hand, the feminist assertion that women are inhibited in, and tend to distort, their experience of anger must be viewed with caution. This assertion is less a statement of fact than it is a condemnation of conditions which (from a feminist perspective) should arouse anger in any reasonable person.

We will return to these issues later in the chapter. But first, let us examine the evidence.

Sex Differences in the Self-Reported Experience of Anger

In the preceding chapters we presented the results of four studies. Study I (Chapters 8 and 9) concerned a person's own experience of anger, as reported by two samples of subjects, 80 university students and 80 community residents. Study II (Chapter 10) explored the experience of a person upon being the target of another's anger. This study was based on the self-reports of 80 university students. Study III (Chapter 11) contrasted everyday experiences of anger and annoyance, based on the reports of 48 university students. In each of these studies, half of the subjects were male and half were female. Of the 235 subjects—university students—who participated in Study IV (on the temporal dimensions of anger—Chapter 12), 160 were women and 75 were men. We will now compare the responses of the men and women who participated in these four studies.

Study I. A Person's Own Experience of Anger

The results for Study I were analyzed in several ways. When a group of related items, such as instigations, responses, or motives were involved, multivariate analyses of variance were performed. For example, the linear combination of the 11 motives listed in the questionnaire was treated as a dependent variable in a single analysis, with sex of the subject as the independent variable. A variety of two-way and three-way analyses also were performed in which the subjects were broken into subgroups depending upon the nature of the target and the instigation.

Surprisingly few reliable differences due to sex of the subject were observed. Both the women and men who participated in this study seemed to experience anger in much the same way. Indeed, the number of statistically "significant" differences that were obtained did not greatly exceed what might be expected on the basis of chance (sampling error).[3] It is, of course, difficult to argue from negative find-

---

[3] If all of the items on the questionnaire were independent of one another, one would expect fewer than five significant differences on the basis of chance alone. Of course, the items are not independent. Hence, if there is a significant difference on

ings. Therefore, we will present the results from Study I in considerable detail, noting all of the variables that seemed to suggest a reliable difference between the sexes. Only in that way can the reader obtain an unbiased picture of possible sex differences (or lack of differences) in the everyday experience of anger. But before examining sex differences on the part of the angry person, we will consider briefly the differential liability of men and women to become targets of anger.

Anger as a function of the sex of the target. One of the most frequently reported findings in both experimental and field research is that men are more often the target of anger and/or aggression than are women. (The evidence on which this conclusion is based will be reviewed later in this chapter.) A similar result was obtained in the present study. In 48% of the episodes the target was male, and in 30% of the episodes the target was female. (In the remaining 22% of the episodes, the target was a group of people, an institution, an inanimate object, etc.)

Although these results are consistent with prior research, a major qualification must be added before any broad generalizations are drawn. As Table 13-1 shows, the sex of the target differs markedly as a function of the relationship between the angry person and the target.

When the target was a loved one, there was a statistically significant interaction between the sex of the subject and the sex of the target, with men becoming angry at women and women becoming angry at men. This pattern is hardly surprising, since the loved ones were, for the most part, spouses and sweethearts. (In a few instances, parents, siblings, or especially dear friends were included in this category.)

By contrast, same-sexed dyads were most common when the angry episodes involved someone who was well known and liked. In these cases, men become angry at other men more often than at women, and vice versa for the women.

The preponderance of male over female targets occurred primarily in the "acquaintance" and "stranger" categories. In these two categories combined, the ratio of male to female targets was 4.6:1, and it did not matter whether the angry person was a man or a woman.

Finally, when the relationship was close but negative (i.e., the target was well known and disliked), the situation is ambiguous. Men tended to outnumber women as targets in this category, but the ratio is small and the number of episodes are too few to draw any conclusions.

In summary, the oft-reported finding that men are more likely than women to be the target of anger depends very much on the relationship between the persons involved. It is primarily when the target is not well known (an acquaintance or stranger) that men are viewed as more provocative than women. Later in this section, we will discuss differences in the response of the angry person as a function of the sex of the target and of the relationship between the angry person and the target. But first, we will consider the "main effects" due to the sex of the subject,

---

one item, whether by chance or a real difference in the population, other related items would also tend toward significance. This makes it impossible to say what the "true" error rate is, but it is probably somewhat greater than the traditional .05 level.

Table 13-1. The incidence of anger as a function of the sex of the subject, the sex of the target, and the relationship between the subject and the target.

			Relationship and sex of target							
Sex of Subject	loved one[a]		know well and like[b]		know well and dislike		acquaintance		stranger	
	M	F	M	F	M	F	M	F	M	F
M	0	12	11	4	4	1	14	3	6	1
F	15	7	4	9	2	3	8	4	8	0
Total	15	19	15	13	6	4	22	7	14	1

Note. N = 116 incidents. The table does not include incidents in which the target was a child, or in which the sex of the target was ambiguous (e.g., becuase two or more persons were involved).
[a]X^2 (1 df.) = 12.00, p < .01
[b]X^2 (1 df.) = 3.51, p = .06

that is, the ways in which men and women differed in their anger regardless of the nature of the target.

Anger as a function of the sex of the angry person. In comparing the angry experiences of the male and female subjects, two sets of analyses were performed. One set was based on the entire sample of subjects (n=160). The other set was based on the subsample of subjects (n=126) who reported that the target of their anger involved, at least secondarily, another adult. The results of both sets of analyses were very similar. Therefore, unless otherwise mentioned, all of the figures reported below are for the entire sample.

To begin with, the episodes of anger described by the women were rated as more intense than the episodes described by the men (a mean rating of 7.4 vs. 6.8 on a 10-point scale, $p < .05$). Also, the women were more likely to report that their anger was greater than the incident called for ($p < .05$).

A multivariate analysis of variance of the responses subjects "felt like doing" yielded a statistically significant F ratio ($p < .05$). Univariate analyses indicated that this result was due to sex differences on two variables. The women, more often than the men, reported that they felt like talking the incident over with the instigator ($p < .01$) and/or with a neutral third party ($p < .01$). In terms of responses actually made, the multivariate F ratio did not reach statistical significance for the full sample ($p < .25$) or the subsample ($p < .10$). However, univariate analyses suggest that the women were more likely than the men to talk the incident over with a third party ($p < .01$ in both samples) and to deny some benefit customarily enjoyed by the instigator ($p < .10$, full sample; $p < .05$, adult targets only).

In terms of absolute values, the largest difference among all the response variables, whether felt or actually done, involved the desire to talk the incident over with the instigator. Specifically, 62% of the women said that they "somewhat" or "very much" felt like responding in this fashion; 40% of the men said the same thing.

The most striking differences between the two sexes were observed in the area of expressive reactions, where the multivariate F ratio was significant beyond the .01 level of confidence. In terms of specific reactions, the women reported crying more often than the men ($p < .01$), responding with a shaky, cracking voice ($p < .05$), and experiencing greater tension ($p < .05$). Of these three variables, crying was by far the most important. Thirty (38%) of the women reported that they cried, at least "somewhat"; six (8%) of the men did so. The tendency of women to cry during an argument has frequently been noted in the popular literature, and it apparently begins at a relative early age. For example, in an analysis of 200 quarrels among preschool children, Dawe (1934) found that girls cried in 36% of the incidents, whereas boys cried in only 20% of the incidents.

No other univariate or multivariate analysis revealed any significant main effect due to the sex of the subject. That is, there were no differences between the men and the women in the perceived nature of the instigation, motives, cognitive reinterpretations, outcomes, and so forth.

Considering the large number of items on which men and women could have differed, the above results lend only modest support to the notion that women and men differ markedly in their everyday experience of anger. A possible objection might be raised to this conclusion, however. Perhaps the questionnaire was simply too insensitive to detect differences between the sexes. To test this possibility, a series of two-way analyses of variance (or, where more appropriate, χ^2 tests) was conducted. The sex of subject represented one independent variable; the population from which the subjects were drawn—student versus community resident—represented the other factor. Separate analyses were performed on most of the items in the questionnaire, provided that the assumptions of the statistical test being used were not grossly violated (e.g., because an item was endorsed by too few subjects). Of the 87 tests performed, only 9 yielded a significant main effect for sex of subject All 9 of these variables have been discussed above. By contrast, students differed from community residents on 19 variables. (These latter differences were discussed in Chapters 8 and 9, where the main results for Study I were presented.) In other words, twice as many differences were observed between students and community residents as between men and women. This suggests that the questionnaire itself was not particularly insensitive to group differences; but rather that the differences between the sexes were not particularly great.[4]

Another possible objection might be raised at this point. Perhaps the sex differences in anger are too complex to appear as simple main effects in analyses such as those reported above. For example, men and women may vary in their experience of anger, but only with respect to some targets and certain kinds of instigations. To test this possibility, subjects were divided into groups depending upon the nature of

---

[4] There were no more "significant" interactions between sex of subject and sample (students vs. community residents) than would be expected on the basis of chance (using a .05 error rate as a rough approximation). Therefore, only the "main effects" for sex and sample have been presented.

the target and the justification of the instigation. Different combinations of two-way and three-way analyses were then performed, with sex of the subject as one factor and the grouping variables (sex of the target, relationship with the target, etc.) as the other factors.

For the most part, we can dispense with the results of these analyses rather quickly. As far as the instigation is concerned, it did not matter whether the precipitating incident was interpreted as accidental or as voluntary, as justified or as unjustified; the men and women responded similarly. The same is true with regard to the relationship between the angry person and the target. Men and women responded alike whether the target was a loved one, friend, acquaintance, or whatever.

Multivariate and univariate analyses did reveal a few statistically significant interactions between the sex of the subject and the sex of the target. For example, when responding to a target of the opposite sex, subjects reported a greater loss of behavioral control while angry, and feelings of depression and shame following the episode. The subjects also reported that targets of the opposite sex tended to react with greater hostility and rejection than did targets of the same sex.

Interactions of the above type were for the most part not replicated in Study III (counting as a "replication" simply the same direction of response, regardless of the level of statistical significance). Nevertheless, there is a conceptual issue here that deserves brief mention. Even if the above interactions were reliable, their implications for the issue of sex differences in anger would still be moot. Consider the fact that women reported feeling more depressed and ashamed after becoming angry with a man than with another woman. This might be taken as support for the feminist argument that women are oppressed by men, and hence cannot express themselves freely. However, the interaction effects indicate that men felt the *same* way after becoming angry with a woman.

Of course, one need not stop with the investigation of two-way interactions. As described earlier, the sex of the target varies systematically as a function of the relationship between the angry person and the target. That is, when the target is a loved one, men tend to become angry with women, and women with men; when the target is someone well known and liked, men tend to become angry with men, and women with women; and when the target is an acquaintance or stranger, both men and women tend to become angry with men. It is reasonable to assume that interactions between sex of the subject and sex of the target might also vary as a function of the relationship between the angry person and the target.

Because of the small number of subjects in some of the cells (see Table 13-1), it was not possible to disentangle with any confidence the relative contributions of the target's sex from his or her relationship with the angry person. Where feasible, separate two-way analyses (sex of subject by sex of target) were performed for different categories of relationships (e.g., friends, acquaintances). To increase the number of subjects per cell, categories were also combined in various ways (e.g., loved ones and friends vs. acquaintances and strangers), and three-way analyses were performed (sex of subject by sex of target by type of relationship). The results of these analyses were inconclusive. Suffice it to say that there was little indication of three-way interaction effects in the present set of data.

To summarize briefly, a number of simple main effects due to the sex of the subject were observed. The women rated their anger as more intense and out of proportion to the precipitating incident than did men. The women also were more likely to talk the incident over with the instigator or with a neutral party, and to deny some benefit customarily enjoyed by the instigator. Finally, the women experienced greater tension, cried, and responded with a shaky, cracking voice more often than did the men. On the other hand, men were more often the targets of anger than were women, especially when the persons involved were only acquaintances or strangers. A few interactions between the sex of the subject and the sex of the target were observed, but these do not provide unambiguous support for sex differences in the everyday experience of anger.

Study II. Experiencing Another Person's Anger

In Study II, the most marked difference between male and female subjects (targets) was in how they reacted upon realizing that the other person was angry (e.g., with indifference, hurt feelings, defiance, anger). On this set of variables, the multivariate F ratio was highly significant ($p < .01$), primarily because of two items. Over 80% of the women reacted at least "somewhat" with hurt feelings, whereas only 50% of the men did so ($p < .01$). On the other hand, men were more likely than women to deny responsibility for instigating the incident (45% vs. 28%, $p < .05$).

A multivariate analysis of variance of the precipitating incidents listed in the questionnaire (frustration, loss of self-esteem, violation of social norms, etc.) also indicated a significant difference ($p < .01$) due to the sex of the subject/target. The difference was due primarily to one item: 78% of the women said that the instigation involved a violation of an expectation or wish on the part of the angry person; 68% of the men said the same thing. The major difference on this item was not the percentage endorsement, but the extremity of the ratings. Most of the women said that such a violation was "very much" a factor in precipitating the incident; the majority of the men said that it was only "somewhat" involved.

Finally, more women (75%) than men (48%) believed that the other person's anger was of greater intensity than the incident called for ($p < .01$). This may reflect the above-noted fact that women viewed the other person's anger as idiosyncratic, that is, as based on expectations or wishes that are not widely shared by others. But something else may be involved. In Study I, it will be recalled, the women indicated that their *own* anger was disproportionate to the precipitating incident. This suggests that women may have a general bias against the display of anger, whether by themselves or by others.

In short, when they realized that they were the target of another's anger, the women—more often than the men—reacted with hurt feelings, whereas the men—more often than the women—reacted with defiance. The women also were more convinced that the precipitating incident (typically something they had done) violated a personal expectation or wish on the part of the angry person; and they believed that the angry person's response was out of proportion of the precipitating incident. This pattern is consistent with the feminine stereotype. Still, at the risk of belaboring the obvious, it must again be noted that the observed differences were few, considering the large number of variables that could have proven significant (see the questionnaire for Study II, Appendix B). One of the problems with stereotypes is that it is all too easy to "see" confirming evidence in almost any pattern of results.

Study III. Differences Between Anger and Annoyance

The number of statistically significant interactions between sex of the subject and type of emotional experience (anger vs. annoyance) were negligible. We will therefore focus only on sex differences in response to the anger questionnaire. This provides the opportunity to cross-validate some of the findings of Study I, since essentially the same questionnaire was used in both studies (see Appendix A). But before getting to that, it will be recalled that the subjects in Study III (24 men and 24 women) were asked to keep a daily record of all their experiences of anger and annoyance for a 1-week period. On the average, the men recorded 7.7 episodes of anger per week, and the women recorded 6.8. The difference did not begin to approach statistical significance. (In Study I, it might be noted, the women reported becoming angry more often than the men. There too, however, the difference was minor.) Finally, no reliable sex differences were observed in the frequency of anger as a function of the nature of the target (a person, institution, inanimate object, or "something else").

As in Studies I and II, most of the data collected in Study III concerned the most intense incident of anger experienced during the week. The remainder of this discussion will concern these most intense incidents. In order to save space and to avoid capitalizing on chance findings, we will mention only those variables that were found to be significant in Study I.

In Study I women rated their anger as significantly more intense ($p < .05$) than did the men. In Study III the results were also significant ($p < .01$), but in the opposite direction (a mean rating of 8.3 for men and 6.2 for women). This illustrates the importance of cross-validation and the need for caution against the hasty interpretation of "significant" findings. Of the two studies, the results of Study I are probably the more valid, being based on a larger and more varied sample of subjects. Nevertheless, for both the frequency and the intensity of anger, the safest conclusion would seem to be "no difference" attributable to the sex of the subject.

Of the other main effects that were found to be significant in Study I, the results of Study III were *in the same direction*. For example, there was some consistency across studies in the tendency for women to respond in nonaggressive ways (e.g., talking things over, or denying some benefit customarily enjoyed by the instigator).[5]

---

[5] That women were more likely than men to engage in these "nonaggressive" ways does not necessarily mean that the women were any less aggressive. In neither Study I nor III were there any statistically significant sex differences on the questionnaire items related to verbal or physical aggression, whether directed at the target or displaced on some other object. And of course the denial of some benefit

However, in Study III the differences between the sexes were generally trivial in magnitude. The major exception to this generalization was crying. In Study III 29% of the women reported that they cried at least "somewhat"; only 8% of the men did so. These percentages approximate those obtained in Study I.

Study IV. The Temporal Dimensions of Anger

In this study we also find little indication of major differences between men and women in the everyday experience of anger. The most marked difference again had to do with crying: 34% of the women reported that they cried while angry, whereas only 9% of the men did so. We will have more to say about this variable shortly. Women also reported, to a greater extent than did men, that they were angered by an action on the part of the instigator that was "not in keeping with the kind of relationship you have or would like to have with this person, or with what you expect from this person." Specifically, 91% of the women indicated that this factor was "somewhat" or "very much" involved in their anger, compared with 79% of the men. The difference, although not great, is statistically significant ($p < .05$). Interpersonal relationships evidently were of greater concern to, or presented greater problems for, this sample of women students than for the men.

One other set of data is noteworthy. There were no statistically significant differences between the men and women in terms of the intensity or duration of their anger. However, there was a difference in the way these two variables were related. For the men, the correlation between intensity and duration was only moderate ($r = .20$), whereas among the women the correlation was quite substantial ($r = .54$). The difference between these two correlations is statistically significant ($p < .01$). A similar difference was observed in Study I (where the correlation was .29 for men and .44 for women) and in Study III (.09 and .37, respectively). What could this mean?

One possibility is that when a woman becomes intensely angry, she tends to inhibit expression of her anger, thus prolonging the episode. (For a discussion of the relationship between duration and inhibition of anger, see Chapter 12.) Because there are few data to support such a possibility, we prefer a somewhat different explanation. As discussed in Chapter 11, judgments of intensity are based on a complex array of factors (e.g., the degree of physiological arousal, overt behavior, thoughts about the instigation, and duration). From the correlations presented above, it appears that women give more weight to duration when judging intensity than do men. This may be a consequence of the cultural stereotype that men are more "aggressive" than women, and presumably more forthright and active in the expression of anger. The results that we have reviewed thus far in this chapter (and other research that will be reviewed in subsequent sections) suggest that this stereo-

---

may itself be considered a form of aggression. The open-ended responses to the questionnaires do suggest that when aggressive, women tend to be less brazen than men. However, the present data lend little support to the notion that women are unable to express their anger in an open and forceful way.

type is greatly exaggerated. But exaggerated or not, it could have an impact on the way men and women interpret their anger. Specifically, men may place greater emphasis on their behavior, as opposed to the duration of an episode, when making judgments about intensity. Women, on the other hand, appear to place less emphasis on behavior and more on the amount of time involved.

Let us return now to the issue of crying. On the basis of previous studies it was (correctly) predicted that a good proportion of the women in Study IV would report having cried while angry. A number of items were therefore included in the questionnaire to assess when during the course of an episode crying was most likely; what meaning it had for the person involved; and its perceived influence on the target. Since two few men reported crying to allow meaningful comparisons between the sexes, we will present only the data for the women.[6]

Of the 55 women who reported crying, 36% did so primarily or only near the beginning of the episode, 45% primarily or only in the middle, and the remainder near the end. Responding to an adjective checklist designed to assess the meaning of their crying, the majority of women said that it was a sign of frustration (78%), sadness (64%), and/or helplessness (55%). Few regarded their crying as a sign of resignation (15%), relief (9%), self-assertion (4%), defiance (4%), and/or attack (2%).

About half of the women who cried (45%), did so in the presence of the person at whom they were angry; 38% cried only when alone. (The remaining 17% reported crying only in the presence of some person other than the target.) A comparison was made between the women who cried in the presence of the target and those who only cried alone. The former were more likely to report that they had a more intimate relationship with the target; had gotten angry at the target previously for the same offense; had made it clear to the target on more than one occasion that the offense was not to be repeated; and pointed out to the target the hurt that he or she had caused. Women who cried alone, on the other hand, were more likely to report that the incident involved simple frustration (e.g., as opposed to a violation of relational expectancies), and that one or more people had agreed to help improve the situation. (All differences were statistically significant at the $p < .05$ level.)

As far as the impact of the subject's crying on the instigator is concerned, the 25 women who cried in the target's presence reported that the target responded by comforting her (12), by apologizing for the incident (11), and/or by stopping and listening better (8). Five or fewer targets reportedly left the subject by herself, laughed at her, ignored her, or became angry at her for crying. From these data, it appears that crying is an effective means of eliciting sympathy, even during anger, and of underscoring the seriousness of the incident. However, the fact that about 80% of the women reported crying near the beginning or middle of an episode, rather than near the end; suggests that crying, by itself, is usually not sufficient to bring an episode to a close.

---

[6] In this doctoral dissertation, Cornelius (1981) investigated the occasions for "sad" and "happy" weeping. He also found that women weep more frequently than men; but when men do weep, it is for much the same reasons and to much the same effect as when women weep.

A final set of analyses were performed comparing the responses of all the women who cried with those who did not. The results of these analyses need not be described in any detail. Very briefly, crying tended to occur in episodes that were more serious, involved close relationships, and were difficult to resolve.

Summary

The results of Studies I-IV suggest that women are more likely than men to cry when angry, to feel hurt when they are the target of another's anger, and perhaps to be more affected by disturbances in interpersonal relationships. Women also tend to place greater emphasis on duration when judging the intensity of an episode, and to be less overtly aggressive in the expression of their anger. This last conclusion is based, in part, on the fact that women more often talked the incident over, either with the instigator or with a neutral third party, and/or denied some benefit customarily enjoyed by the instigator. However, this conclusion is also based on a general impression gained from the questionnaire as a whole, that is, the open-ended responses as well as the forced-choice items.

Still, when all the data are considered, it is remarkable that the observed sex differences were so few in number and (with the exception of crying) small in magnitude. As far as the everyday experience of anger is concerned, men and women are far more similar than dissimilar.

Perhaps the failure to observe greater differences between men and women in the present series of studies is attributable to the fact that, except for the diary records in Study III, subjects were asked to focus on the most intense episode of anger that they experienced during the week. This may have resulted in selective recall and a blurring of subtle differences between the sexes. More importantly, because of the manner in which the task was defined for the subjects, the episodes described were most likely ones in which the subjects experienced relatively little conflict over the nature of their feelings. That is, they felt that their anger was "reasonable," if not always justified. This is an advantage when it comes to identifying the general norms of anger. It may be a disadvantage, however, when individual and group differences in anger are of interest.

In the next section we will supplement the present results with a review of other research findings. As will be seen, most of the evidence points in the same direction, namely, that the differences between men and women in the everyday experience of anger are not as great as might be expected from either the biological or the feminist perspective.

A Brief Review of Research on Sex Differences in Anger and Aggression

We will first summarize the results of several previously published studies that have used questionnaires or self-report data to explore possible sex differences in anger. Experimental research relevant to the issue will then be examined; and finally, the clinical literature will be reviewed briefly.

Self-Report Data

In previous chapters a number of studies were described that used the controlled diary method (Anastasi et al., 1948; Gates, 1926; Meltzer, 1933). One of these (Meltzer) involved a direct comparison between men and women (35 male and 58 female students at Oregon State College). For the most part, differences between the sexes were minor. The men did report becoming angry more often than did the women: 5.9 vs. 4.0 incidents per week, respectively. Based on the standard deviations provided by Meltzer, this difference is statistically significant. However, the men also were more likely than the women to become angry at "things" as opposed to persons (45% vs. 20%). As far as human targets were concerned, both the men and the women became angry about equally often. In terms of responses and aftereffects, the men and women also were basically similar, although the men did report that they felt like doing physical injury to the offender more often than did the women.

A more recent study relevant to sex differences in anger has been reported by Allen and Haccoun (1976). These authors designed an "Emotionality Survey" consisting of four categories: responsiveness, expressiveness, attitudes (orientation), and situations. Additional distinctions were drawn within each category. For example, intensity and frequency of affect were distinguished within the category of responsiveness; direct and indirect expression within the category of expressiveness; and attitudes toward one's own feelings and attitudes toward the expression of emotion by others within the category of attitudes. For the categories of responsiveness, expressiveness, and attitudes, an overall score was obtained, as well as scores on the various subdimensions.

Subjects (61 male and 61 female undergraduates) rated their usual experience of anger, fear, joy, and sadness on the above survey. This study thus allows a comparison of possible sex differences in anger with sex differences in other emotions.

With regard to the category of *responsiveness*, no sex differences were observed in the frequency with which the various emotions were experienced. The women did report a greater intensity of affect in the case of fear, joy, and sadness, but *not in the case of anger*. The overall responsiveness score, which took into account both intensity and frequency, showed a significant difference only for fear and sadness.

With regard to the category of *expressiveness*, the women reported being significantly more expressive (overall score) for each emotion. The difference was greatest in the case of fear and *least in the case of anger*. In terms of direct expression, men appeared to express more joy and sadness to female targets and more fear and anger to male targets; women appeared to express more of each emotion to male targets. In terms of indirect expression women exceeded men most for fear and sadness and least for joy and anger.

With regard to overall *attitudes* or orientation toward the various emotions, men and women differed only with respect to joy, the women being more positive toward the expression of joy. No sex difference was observed regarding orientation toward one's own feelings. Analysis of data relevant to orientation toward another's expression of emotion revealed that both sexes preferred the expression of positive emotion from the opposite sex, and that both men and women reported a more positive attitude toward fears expressed by women than by men.

When describing the *situations* that led to their emotional experiences, women reported more of an interpersonal basis for their emotions than did men. The overall differences between the sexes were small, however. Both men and women reported more of an interpersonal basis for anger (72% of the usable protocols) than for the other emotions (e.g., 51% for sadness).

Allen and Haccoun (1976) suggest that the functional significance of various emotions differs for men and women. Whether this is so remains to be seen. For our present concerns, the important thing is that greater sex differences were observed in fear and sadness than in anger. Allen and Haccoun note that this result is somewhat surprising, since anger supposedly is associated with strength and power (male attributes) and men are generally more aggressive than women.

One last self-report study may be cited. Balswick and Avertt (1977) asked a sample of 263 male and 260 female undergraduates to rate how often they expressed 16 different emotions. For purposes of analysis these emotions were combined into four broad affective dimensions or "scales." For example, ratings of anger, hate, resentment, and rage were combined into a "hate scale." A "love scale," "happiness scale," and "sadness scale" were derived from the remaining 12 emotions. Balswick and Avertt found that women were significantly more expressive of feelings of love, happiness, and sadness than were men; however, no sex differences were found on the hate scale. These results support the findings of Allen and Haccoun (1976) reported above.

Experimental Research

Of the literally hundreds of laboratory studies on aggression that have been conducted over the last several decades, most have involved male subjects only. Whether due to chivalry or chauvinism on the part of investigators (most of whom have been male), this lopsidedness reflects the general cultural attitude that anger and aggression are primarily male problems. Fortunately, however, enough studies involving both men and women have been conducted so that some tentative conclusions regarding sex differences can be drawn. The bulk of this research has been reviewed by Frodi, Macaulay, and Thome (1977). The present discussion draws heavily on their analysis.

Frodi et al. divide the studies under review into two broad categories, depending upon whether subjects were provoked or unprovoked. A subject was considered provoked if he or she was "deliberately angered or hurt" as part of the experimental manipulation. In the unprovoked category Frodi et al. included studies that involved reactions to frustrations or arousal unconnected with the target, modeling, conformity to experimental demands to hurt another, and studies of general levels of hostility or aggressiveness.

Clear-cut sex differences were observed in studies of unprovoked aggression, with men being more aggressive than women. However, Frodi et al. report that these differences were much diminished—although not entirely eliminated—in studies where subjects were provoked to anger. For example, in 26 studies involving direct verbal aggression on the part of angered subjects, 16 found no statistically significant differences between men and women, 9 found men to be more aggressive, and 1 found women to be more aggressive. In 13 studies involving direct physical aggression (delivery of electric shock, for the most part), 6 found no sex differences, and 3 found men to be more aggressive in some aspect or phase of the study but not in others. In only 4 studies was there a significant overall sex difference, with men being more aggressive than women.

After taking into account possible confounding factors, Frodi et al. conclude that "studies of direct physical (but not violent) aggression do not reliably show angered men to be more aggressive than angered women" (p. 639). Similarly, they conclude that "angered adult women have not been shown to be reliably more or less verbally aggressive than men" (p. 640). These conclusions are perhaps the most important for our purposes, but they necessarily oversimplify a very complex issue, as will become evident below.

Frodi et al. consider a number of factors that might account for sex differences in aggression in nonangry situations, and the reduction in such differences when subjects are angered. One possibility they do not consider is that sex differences in general aggressiveness may be of biological origin. But neither do they deny this possibility. They focus instead on social factors that could exaggerate or minimize whatever biological differences might exist. Among the factors they consider, the most important (in terms of available evidence) are justification for aggression, response inhibition, mode of response, sex of the target, the nature of the instigation, gender role orientation, and observer effects. We will discuss each of these factors briefly, updating Frodi et al.'s review where relevant.

Justification. When Frodi et al. examined as a set those studies in which no sex differences were observed, most had one characteristic in common, namely, an aggressive response was justified. The justification could take various forms. For example, punishment delivered to a target might be excused as being helpful (e.g., in a learning task), or as a contribution to scientific research (e.g., in a study of stress). Needless to say, a provocation to anger also serves as a form of justification. Subjects who are angry tend to perceive the provocateur as deserving punishment. Indeed, if sufficiently provoked, a person may not even consider retaliation to be a form of aggression. Thus, to the extent that a provocation justifies retaliation on the part of both men and women, sex differences in aggression should be—and apparently are—minimized.

Response inhibition. Assuming that aggression is justified in a given situation, the response may still be inhibited for a variety of reasons, such as fear of retaliation by, or empathy with the target. Some theorists (e.g., Bandura, 1973) have argued that a low level of aggressiveness among women can be attributed to such an inhibition of performance rather than to any lack of ability to aggress. Frodi et al. review a fair amount of evidence that lends some support to this hypothesis. For example, women tend to find aggression more anxiety provoking and distasteful than do men, and women are also more likely to empathize with the target of aggression. The evidence is not unequivocal, however, and differences within the sexes on such variables as guilt and anxiety over aggression are far greater than differences between the sexes. Moreover, other variables within the situation (such as justification) can often override any inhibitory tendencies that might exist.

A lack of unequivocal evidence is not, however, the only problem with the hypothesis that possible sex differences in anger and/or aggression can be accounted for in terms of response inhibition rather than ability factors. There is also a knotty conceptual issue involved. Women do not have the same ability as men to engage in strenuous physical combat. No one denies that. However, the type of aggression observed in most angry encounters is well within the capability of both men and women. A woman, for example, is just as able as a man to give a verbal rebuke, or to press a button to deliver an electric shock (a common response in most laboratory studies). Does this mean that women are as able as men to aggress in most circumstances? Not necessarily. The concept of ability as used in this context is ambiguous. It can refer not only to the capability to respond, but also to the desire ("I just *couldn't* do a thing like that"). Thus, although a woman might have the capability to respond aggressively, she might not have the desire; and in the absence of desire, there is no need to inhibit behavior.[7]

If women have a relatively low ability to aggress in a motivational sense, then one might expect that they would also show anxiety, guilt, and other signs of distress in situations where they are nevertheless expected to aggress. Hence much of the same evidence that is used to support a response-inhibition hypothesis could also be taken as support for a lack-of-ability (desire) hypothesis.

We mention these two hypotheses, and the difficulty in distinguishing between them, because they overlap with the feminist and biological arguments outlined in the introduction to this chapter. That is, the feminists believe that women are inhibiting (even repressing) their aggressiveness, whereas those favoring a biological position argue that women do not have the same ability (desire) to respond as do men. Actually, the whole issue may be rather moot, at least as far as anger is concerned. From the evidence reviewed thus far, it appears that women typically overcome whatever disinclination they might have against the expression of anger,

---

[7] The terminology we are using here is somewhat arbitrary, for there are no words in ordinary language that convey our meaning exactly. Therefore, an example from a different area might help to clarify the distinction we are making between the two senses of ability, that is, as capability and as desire. Few people in our culture drink urine. This is not because of a lack of capability, since the same responses are involved in drinking urine as in drinking water. People are unable to drink urine because they find such an act abhorrent, that is, they lack the desire. When there is a lack of desire, there is obviously no need to invoke a mechanism such as response inhibition to explain the absence of a response (urine drinking, in this case). Under conditions of extreme water deprivation, a person may turn to urine as a substitute, albeit with considerable distress (Lucas, 1969). In such a case, it could also be said that the person overcame his or her inhibitions. But that is a rather loose way of speaking; it means nothing more than that the person did something that, in another context, would be found distasteful.

regardless of whether that disinclination is due to response inhibition or to a lack of ability (desire) to respond.

Mode of response. Anger can, of course, be expressed in a great variety of ways. It is possible that women, as a result of either ability or inhibitory factors, might express their anger differently than men, but not less frequently or intensely. For example, the results of Studies I-IV, described earlier, suggest that women may prefer less aggressive modes of response. Frodi et al. also review evidence, based largely on field studies, that women may shy away from physical aggression, and that they may also try to avoid face-to-face verbal aggression. Unfortunately, there is little experimental research that would either confirm or refute these observations. This is because most laboratory studies have not provided subjects with a choice of response. Rather, the subject is given the option only of aggressing or not aggressing in the manner prescribed by the experimental procedures.

An experiment by Shope, Hendrick, and Geen (1978) is an exception to the above generalization. These investigators varied the sex of the subject, the type of aggression available to the subject (physical vs. verbal), the sex of the experimenter, and the sex of the target. They found that women who had been provoked became verbally more aggressive, but did not increase their use of physical punishment (shock), in comparison with women who were not provoked. By contrast, men administered both verbal and physical punishment following provocation. These results support the notion that women are less prone than men to engage in physical aggression if other forms of punishment are available to them.

To complicate matters, however, Shope et al. also found that both the sex of the target and the sex of the experimenter had an impact on the subjects' behavior, and that the impact differed depending upon whether the subject was male or female. We shall have more to say about target and observer effects below. For the moment, suffice it to say that higher-order interactions between mode of response, sex of subject, sex of target, and sex of observer make any generalization extremely difficult.

Perhaps the safest conclusion to draw is that, other things being equal and given a choice, women are less likely than men to engage in direct physical (and perhaps verbal) aggression. Any differences in response tendencies do not appear to be great, however. And things are seldom equal, nor is a choice always possible.

Sex of the target. In a majority of the studies reviewed Frodi et al., where sex of the target was a factor in the design, both men and women behaved more aggressively toward men than toward women. In their review of sex differences in aggression, Maccoby and Jacklin (1974) conclude that males of most infrahuman animals —and among humans, male children as well as adults—are more likely than females to be the target of aggression. Baron (1977) also considers the preponderance of male targets to be one of the best established findings in aggression research.

Even if it were true that men are more often the target of aggression than women, the relevance of this fact for sex differences in anger is unclear. As the above-cited study by Shope et al. (1978) suggests, sex of the target may interact with mode of response and with other variables in an angry situation. For the sake of simplicity we will limit the present discussion to "main effects." Is it true in the case of anger, as opposed to certain other forms of aggressive behavior, that a man is more likely to be the target than a woman?

The results of Study I presented earlier indicate that the preponderance of male targets occurs primarily when the persons involved in an angry episode are strangers or mere acquaintances. This is, of course, the situation in most laboratory studies of anger and aggression. In everyday affairs, by contrast, most episodes of anger involve disputes between friends and loved ones. In episodes of this type, the nature of the relationship dictates the target. The sex of the target per se thus does not appear to be a major determinant of anger in most circumstances, although it may influence the course of the interaction in complex ways.

Nature of the provocation. In their review of the experimental literature, Frodi et al. (1977) speculate that "there may be some categorical differences in what makes women and men angry, and beyond that, differences in the outcome of arousal that depend on what the provoked person is attending to" (p. 654). At the time of their review, there was little experimental evidence that bore upon these issues. In order to gather additional information, Frodi (1977b, 1978) therefore conducted several studies of her own. The first of these consisted of a survey to determine whether there are differences between men and women in what constitutes a provocation to anger. She asked 60 male and 70 female college students to describe what was the most anger-provoking behavior a same- and an opposite-sex peer could display toward them. These descriptions were sorted into categories by independent judges. Frodi found that women were most angered by condescending treatment (e.g., when another person acts superior), regardless of the sex of the provoker. Men, on the other hand, were more angered by physical and verbal aggression (e.g., being shoved or yelled at) on the part of another male and by a condescending attitude on the part of a female.

No one doubts that on a specific level, men and women may find different things provocative. What a woman finds condescending is not necessarily what a man finds condescending. From Frodi's data, however, it appears that both sexes find condescension *qua* condescension (with its implied threat to self-esteem) as equally provocative, at least when the provocateur is a woman. The primary "difference" observed by Frodi is that men reported being more angered by physical and verbal aggression on the part of another male. Does this represent a major sex difference? Probably not. As noted in the above discussion of the sex of the target, a man is more likely than a woman to be attacked by a stranger or a mere acquaintance. But this kind of provocation is relatively rare in everyday affairs. Moreover, there is little reason to believe that if a woman were attacked, physically or verbally, she would feel less anger than a man.

In spite of the above qualification, there is an important methodological point in Frodi's study. Experiments that present men and women with *precisely* the same provocation may obtain sex differences, not because men and women differ in their anger, but because the specific provocation was less effective for one sex than the other.

In a second study, Frodi (1978) provoked male and female subjects in a "sex-appropriate" fashion (verbal aggression for males and condescension for females).

The provocateur was always of the same sex as the subject. Subjects were then provided an opportunity to administer aversive sounds to the provocateur as a function of his or her performance on the learning task. (No sounds were actually received, since the provocateur was a confederate of the experimenter, but this was unknown to the subject.) The subjects' responses were measured in terms of physiological reactivity, intensity of aversive sounds administered, mood and attitude questionnaires, and "stream of consciousness" reports (cf. Antrobus et al., 1966). It was found that given sex-appropriate provocation, women and men became equally angry, showed parallel increases in physiological arousal, and displayed equal amounts of aggressive behavior.

Examination of subjects' "stream of consciousness" reports, however, provided some indication that the male and female subjects adopted different strategies for coping with their anger. Half of the women and men were asked to write down their thoughts and feelings (stream of consciousness) following their interaction with the provocateur. It was found that men tended to preoccupy themselves with thoughts of anger or "stirring themselves up"; whereas women tended to preoccupy themselves with nonaggressive thoughts. Furthermore, the men who had to verbalize their thoughts in the stream of consciousness condition rated themselves as more angry, displayed more negativity toward their partner, and became behaviorally more aggressive than the corresponding women. Similar results were not found for angered subjects who did not have to verbalize their thoughts.

This study suggests that, when angered, women may have fewer aggressive tendencies (at least in fantasy) than do men. This is consistent with the findings discussed above in connection with sex differences in preferred modes of response. It is noteworthy, however, that Frodi did not observe any sex differences in the expression of anger (self-reports, aggressive behavior, etc.) except when the men were induced to ruminate on their thoughts and feelings by the stream of consciousness procedure.

Sex role orientation. Another variable that might mediate possible sex differences in anger and aggression is, according to Frodi et al. (1977), "some kind of sex role variable" (p. 653). They note, however, that the research on this issue is inconclusive, in part because the notion of gender or sex role is itself ill defined (cf. Pedhazur & Tetenbaum, 1979). A study by Hoppe (1979) will serve to illustrate some of the problems in this area of research.

Hoppe (1979) divided male and female subjects into four groups depending upon whether their role orientation was predominately masculine, feminine, androgynous (a mixture of masculine and feminine characteristics), or undifferentiated (a relative lack of either masculine or feminine characteristics). The Bem (1974) Sex Role Inventory was used as the basis for classification. The experiment consisted of a competitive reaction time task in which subjects could aggress (deliver electric shock) against a male or female opponent under conditions of increasing provocation. It was found that male subjects with a masculine orientation aggressed more than any of the other groups, regardless of the degree of provocation or the sex of the opponent. Female subjects with a masculine orientation also showed a high level of aggression, but only against male opponents.

Finally, there was *no* interaction between sex of the subject, sex role orientation, or sex of the target, on the one hand, and degree of provocation, on the other hand. That is, when provoked, all subjects tended to retaliate to some extent, and the various subgroups kept their relative positions with respect to one another as the degree of provocation increased.

Several features of Hoppe's study deserve brief comment. The first thing to note is that the Bem Sex Role Inventory used by Hoppe defines the masculine role largely in terms of such characteristics as dominance, assertiveness, and strength. This is true of other sex role inventories as well. It is thus hardly surprising that persons who are rated high on masculinity also tend to be aggressive. Stated differently, the finding that persons with a masculine role orientation are more aggressive than individuals with other orientations may simply be an artifact of the way the masculine role is typically defined.

This raises another question. What exactly constitutes a masculine or a feminine role? Men and women enter into many roles during their lifetimes; some of these may be sex linked (e.g., policeman, nurse) and others may be neutral with regard to sex (e.g., poet, tennis player). Moreover, the sex linkage of a role may change with changing social attitudes. Male nurses and female police are no longer oddities. But is there a feminine or a masculine role per se? Most analyses of gender role emphasize temperamental characteristics—whether biological or social in origin— that are more common among persons of one sex as opposed to the other (e.g., nurturance in the case of women and aggressiveness in the case of men). To call such characteristics "roles" is questionable. Unfortunately, to pursue this further is beyond the scope of the present chapter. Suffice it to say that we agree with Hoppe's conclusion that simply knowing the biological sex of a person is of little use in predicting aggressive tendencies, at least in most situations.

Observer effects. The final variable that we will consider is the influence exerted by the presence of others. Frodi et al. (1977) suggested that conformity to sex role expectancies might be enhanced by the presence of onlookers. A similar suggestion has been made by Caplan (1979), who goes so far as to maintain that the presence of adult observers may account for most of the reported findings that young boys are more aggressive than young girls. Such differences tend to be diminished, according to Caplan, when children do not realize that they are being observed.

The presence and presumed attitudes of others has an undeniable effect on the display of anger and aggression. It has been demonstrated, for example, that the presence of an observer can either decrease (Baron, 1971) or enhance (Borden, 1975) the aggressiveness of male subjects in a provocative situation, the effect being dependent upon the values conveyed by the observer. A similar effect has been noted for female subjects (Richardson, Bernstein, & Taylor, 1979).

As important as observer effects are, however, there has been no demonstration (nor is there any reason to believe) that onlookers *in general* expect women to inhibit their responses when provoked and expect men to respond aggressively. There are situations, of course, in which social norms condoning and condemning angry behavior apply differently to men and women. Thus, observer effects might interact differentially with other variables (e.g., sex of the target, mode of response, or nature of the instigation), depending upon the sex of the angry person. Such complex interactions have, in fact, been observed in the laboratory (Shope et al., 1978), and they are undoubtedly commonplace in everyday affairs.

Summary. The experimental research that we have reviewed in this section supports the notion that men tend to be more aggressive than women but that this difference is greatly diminished ("muddied" might be a better term) under conditions of adequate provocation. This does not mean that men and women respond alike in all situations simply because they are angry. It does mean, however, that blanket assertions to the effect that women are less prone to anger, or have greater difficulty in expressing anger, receive little support from experimental research.

Clinical Observations

Self-report data, such as that reviewed earlier, and experimental research, such as that discussed above, have been criticized as "superficial"—self-reports because they are subject to conscious and unconscious dissimulation, and experimental research because it takes place in an artificial laboratory context. If women, as compared to men, are truly "suffering" from an inability to experience and/or express anger, the difference might be more in evidence in clinical observations. It is not possible here to offer a thorough review of the clinical literature relevant to possible sex differences in anger and aggression. However, through selected examples we can convey what we believe to be an accurate picture of the kinds of observations that are typical. This task is made easier by the fact that clinical discussions of possible sex differences in anger and aggression are most conspicuous by their absence.

Before proceeding further, it should be noted that in the clinical literature, as in the experimental literature, anger is typically subsumed under the general heading of aggression. Indeed, the two terms are often used almost interchangeably, with "anger" denoting the affective side of aggressive behavior. By now it should hardly bear repeating that anger and aggression cannot be related in any simple one-to-one fashion. Many of the aggressive tendencies which bring clients into therapy undoubtedly have little to do with anger, except in the most extended sense. Nevertheless, most therapists would probably agree with Rothenberg's (1971) assertion that "as clinicians we devote a considerable portion of our thinking and practice to unearthing, clarifying, and tracing the permutations of anger in our patients. . . . We interpret the presence of anger, we confront anger, we draw anger, we tranquilize anger, and we help the working through of anger" (p. 454).

We will begin this brief review of the clinical literature with some observations on psychoanalysis. As is well known, psychoanalysis places great emphasis on both sex and aggression as fundamental aspects of the human psyche. Surely here, if anywhere, we should find documentation regarding sex differences in anger and/or aggression. That is not the case.

Freud's own ideas about the existence and importance of sex differences in aggression underwent several changes during the course of his lifetime (Stepansky, 1977). In his early work he seemed to feel that males are by nature more aggressive than females and that this difference has some consequences insofar as the etiology of certain forms of psychopathology are concerned. However, in his later work he made it clear that although sex differences in aggression do exist, such differences are generally of little consequence. In writing about psychosexual development, for example, Freud (1933/1965) notes that "undoubtedly the material is different to start with in boys and girls. . . . A little girl is as a rule less aggressive, defiant and self-sufficient. . . . These sexual differences are not, however, of great consequence: They can be outweighed by individual variations" (p. 117). Freud goes on to note that although sex differences might have been expected, "Analysis of children's play has shown our women analysts that the aggressive impulses of little girls leave nothing to be desired in the way of abundance and violence. With their entry into the phallic phase the differences between the sexes are completely eclipsed by their agreements" (p. 118).

Turning to more recent developments, the 27th International Psycho-Analytic Congress, held in 1971, had as its theme the topic of aggression. Commenting on this congress, Anna Freud (1972) noted that a useful survey of relevant publications had been produced; she complained, however, that the papers presented and the discussions held at the congress consisted largely of repetitions and reassertions of opinions originally expressed by Freud and his immediate followers. Rangell (1972) voiced a similar concern. Of greater importance for our present discussion is that *none* of the presentations at the Congress dealt with possible sex differences in anger or aggression.

The 27th International Psycho-Analytic Congress was not anomalous in its disregard of possible sex differences in anger or aggression. Consider Erich Fromm's book *The Anatomy of Human Destructiveness* (1973). Fromm intended this to be the first volume of a comprehensive work on psychoanalytic theory. And although the book is devoted largely to the topic of human aggression, Fromm does not deal in any significant way with possible sex differences. (He does, however, devote considerable space to the interconnections between sexual and aggressive "drives," e.g., as in sadism.)

Clinical case studies of anger and aggression also shed little light on possible sex differences. A few recent examples will illustrate the kinds of observations that are common. Winer (1978) has described a female patient with multiple personalities. He attributes this condition to the patient's inability to express rage at her parents. This is not, however, presented as an example of *female* difficulties with anger, but rather as a *case* in which anger is a problem. Similarly, Eichler (1976) reports on the psychoanalytic treatment of a woman diagnosed as having a hysterical character and special problems with aggression. He provides a detailed description of the genesis and various manifestations of this woman's "aggressive impulses." There is no suggestion, however, that this patient's problems with her aggressive impulses have anything to do with the fact that she is *female*. In this and other such cases, what seems most evident is a fear on the part of the patients that their anger will destroy or antagonize a loved one such that they themselves will be destroyed.

Numerous studies could also be cited which attempt to link "repressed" anger to specific clinical syndromes, such as depression. Within psychoanalytic theory, depression is understood as a manifestation of anger directed inward against the self rather than outward against the target of one's anger. Moreover, in Europe and North America at least, depression is much more frequent among women than men (the ratio being about 2:1). Might not this sex difference in depression be taken as evidence for a sex difference in anger also?

Although many psychiatrists still adhere to some version of Freud's anger-turned-inward theory of depression, other theories have been proposed which do not impute any particular role to anger (e.g., Beck, 1967; Lewinsohn, 1974; Seligman, 1975). And even in the psychoanalytic literature, there is little discussion linking sex differences in depression to sex differences in anger *as the latter might be manifested outside of the depressive context*. Therefore, unless one wants to run the risk of a circular argument, the evidence on depression does little to clarify possible sex differences in anger.

We do not wish to imply that sex differences in anger and aggression have gone entirely unnoticed by psychoanalytically oriented clinicians. To take one recent example, Symonds (1976) specifically examines the psychodynamics of aggression in women. He points out that in his clinical experience, men and women describe anger in different terms. Women, to a much greater extent than men, use the word "hurt," and such phrases as "hurt feelings" or "afraid to hurt their feelings," as equivalents of anger, resentment, or even rage. (This is consistent with the results of Study II presented above.) Symonds suggested that when provoked, women often respond with "horizontal aggression"; that is, women attempt to make their antagonist feel guilty. Men, by contrast, tend to engage in "vertical aggression"; that is, they respond more forcefully and with more self-assertion. Symonds emphasizes that what he describes is "the aggression of dependency and not a sex-linked trait" (p. 202); but he also notes that because of the "pressures of society and family values" women are more likely than men to be dependent in a way that results in the more frequent utilization of horizontal rather than vertical aggression. Furthermore he suggests that the individual who employs horizontal aggression, even if she does so effectively, is left feeling powerless and helpless.

The feminist movement is also beginning to have an impact on the way psychoanalysts view possible sex differences in anger and aggression. For example, a panel discussion on anger/aggression in men and women was held at the 1979 meeting of the American Academy of Psychoanalysis. According to one of the participants, Teresa Bernadez-Bonesatti, denial of anger is a major cause of the many dysfunctional behaviors that presumably trouble American women today.

We shall return to the feminist argument shortly. But first, let us consider a different genre of clinical literature. In recent years a number of psychologists and psychiatrists have written self-help books aimed at the general public. Some sample titles are *The Angry Book* (Rubin, 1969), *Creative Aggression* (Bach & Goldberg, 1974), *How to Get Angry Without Feeling Guilty* (Bry, 1977), and *How to Live With and Without Anger* (Ellis, 1977). The authors of these books do not represent any single theoretical persuasion. They do, however, share the conviction that angry feelings are natural, that such feelings can and should be expressed (in appropriate ways), and furthermore, that it is very unhealthy not to express angry feelings when they arise. With all this emphasis on the "healthy" expression of anger, one would expect some discussion of sex differences in either the ability to express anger or the style of expression, if women were indeed inhibiting their anger. However, the implicit assumption in these works seems to be that both women and men have similar problems with anger. Both have difficulty being angry and both suffer deleterious consequences when they fail to express angry feelings.

This perspective is adhered to even in discussions of conflicts between men and women, such as occur in marriage. Bach and Goldberg (1974), for example, make it clear that while there are some individual differences in the way anger and aggression are manifested, such differences are largely independent of the individual's sex. In a book advising persons on "how to fight fair in love and marriage" (*The Intimate Enemy*), Bach and Wyden (1968) note that "the psychological differences between the sexes have been exaggerated in our culture, especially male and female reactions toward hostility" (p. 89). Bach and Wyden do note three stereotypic differences in male-female fight styles:

1. males tend to listen passively with seemingly bottomless patience, only to explode at a later time;
2. women tend to be overly patient with noncommunicative males of the "strong, silent type";
3. women tend to use tears as a fight tactic.

Despite such "minor variations," Bach and Wyden believe that there are no intrinsic differences between male and female fight styles. Indeed, they assert as a fact that "male and female fight styles are largely interchangeable" (p. 92) and that the masculinity-femininity issue is a red herring. Bach and Wyden (1968) end their discussion of male-female fight styles by noting that "a genuinely angry woman is little different from a genuinely angry man, and the sooner husbands and wives accept this psychological truth, the better they will be able to level with each other for constructive intimate warfare" (p. 94).

Before concluding this brief review of clinical observations, we need to mention one additional set of facts. Even a superficial reading of the clinical literature discloses that more women than men are in therapy for problems stemming from a lack of aggressiveness or assertiveness. For example, all of the case studies described earlier involved women. On the other hand, when the problem is excessive aggression or violence, the patient is more likely to be a man than a woman (e.g., Kaufmann & Wagner, 1972; Novaco, 1976, 1977; Rimm, de Groot, Boord, Reiman, & Dillow, 1971). The implications of this difference are, however, unclear.

The first thing to note is that women are grossly overrepresented in psychotherapy, for reasons (e.g., economic, social) that have little to do with the actual incidence of psychopathology (Chesler, 1972). Hence, case studies involving women will also be overrepresented in the clinical literature, for many kinds of disorders, not just those involving the denial of anger. It is doubtful that the differential incidence of unexpressed anger on the part of women, as evidenced in clinical case studies, is due *entirely* to the fact that more women than men undergo psychotherapy. However, if men were in therapy in equal numbers to women, then unexpressed anger would undoubtedly be a common finding among men also.

And what about the fact that men are more likely than women to have problems with aggressive outbursts or violence? As the previous review of experimental and other research indicates, men may be more aggressive than women in nonangry situations, or in situations where aggression is unjustified. One might expect this difference to be even more marked in clinical populations. The mere fact that a person is in need of psychotherapy indicates that his (or her[8]) behavior is not considered justified by community standards.

To the extent that psychotherapy helps people to adjust to their social environment, a leveling process seems to be occurring with respect to sex differences in aggression. Persons who suffer from outbursts of violence (mostly men, perhaps) are taught how to control their temper, for example, by making more benign appraisals of threatening situations and by coping in nonaggressive ways. Conversely, people who are overly inhibited (mostly women, perhaps) are taught how to be more assertive. The implicit assumption seems to be that there *should* be no real or important differences between men and women in the way that they respond to provocation.[9] This assumption is reflected in the clinical literature, where emphasis is clearly on anger as a human problem, and not as a special problem for either men or women. In everyday affairs, as opposed to the therapist's office, it appears that socialization has been largely successful in reducing, if not eliminating, major differences between men and women in the incidence of anger and its expression. Even among those whose problems with anger and aggression have brought them into therapy, sex differences have not been sufficiently evident to elicit much comment or discussion.

Summary

When the results of Studies I-IV are considered in light of the self-report data, experimental research, and clinical observations reviewed in this section, a rather consistent picture emerges. Men tend to be more aggressive than women in non-

---

[8] Men are not the only ones who have problems with hyperaggressiveness. For example, in Lundsgaarde's (1977) study of homicides in Houston, the results of which were described in Chapter 5, more women killed their husbands or lovers than men killed their wives or lovers. Mothers are also as likely—if not more likely—than fathers to use severe or abusive violence on their children (Strauss, Gelles, & Steinmetz, 1980). On a less violent level, Rickles (1971) has described what he calls an "Angry Woman Syndrome," the symptoms of which include "periodic outbursts of unprovoked anger, marital maladjustment, serious suicide attempts, proneness to abuse of alcohol and drugs, a morbidly critical attitude to people, and a contrary excessive need to excell in all endeavors, with an intense need for neatness and punctuality" (p. 91).

[9] This view of the therapeutic process would seem to be diametrically opposed to one presented by Chesler (1972), who regards traditional psychotherapy as a patriarchal institution that helps keep women dependent. Chesler is concerned, however, with broader issues than just sex differences in anger, and hence the opposition may not be as great as it appears.

angry situations. This difference in aggressiveness may carry over into clinical disorders, where men may have more problems controlling aggression and women expressing it. But whatever differences between the sexes might exist in the capacity for aggression, few differences are observed in the everyday experience of anger. Women become angry as frequently and as intensely as men, for much the same reasons, and with about the same effectiveness. There is some indication that when angry, women may respond with less physical aggression than men, preferring instead to talk things over. In ordinary circumstances, however, men also are not particularly aggressive when angry. And when punishment seems called for, it can take such a wide variety of forms (e.g., a verbal retort, or the denial of some benefit) that women have ample means for expressing their anger. Perhaps the most consistent finding from a variety of sources is that women are more likely to feel hurt and cry when engaged in an angry encounter. Some might argue that feeling hurt and crying are only the surface manifestations of much more fundamental differences (cf. the horizontal anger described by Symonds). Still, when all the evidence is considered, the similarities between men and women are far more striking than the differences.

Implications

We have dwelt at length on possible sex differences in anger not because we believe that such differences (or lack thereof) are of great interest in their own right, but rather because the issue helps to clarify the nature of anger in general. In what follows we will discuss the implications of the present findings for the biological and feminist arguments outlined at the beginning of the chapter. Sandwiched between these arguments will be a brief discussion of the problem of "repressed" or unexpressed anger.

Implications for the Biological Argument

For those who believe that men are by nature (genetic predisposition) more aggressive than women, there is ample evidence to support their argument. Among most higher primates, including chimpanzees, males are more aggressive than females. Among humans, young boys in nearly all cultures are more aggressive than young girls; war is largely a male prerogative, especially direct physical combat; men are the perpetrators of most violent crimes; men participate in, and enjoy watching, aggressive sports more than do women; and finally, laboratory studies most often find men to be more aggressive in nonangry contexts.

By contrast, the evidence reviewed above also suggests that men and women do *not* differ markedly in their everyday experience of anger. From this it would seem to follow that anger is not very closely related to aggression in a biological sense. A corollary would be that anger is a product of social rather than biological evolution.

From a constructivist view of emotion, such as that outlined in Chapter 1, there is little reason to expect marked sex differences in anger. Of course, one could argue (as the feminists have) that even from a social perspective there should be— and are—marked sex differences in the experience of anger. We shall consider the implications of the present findings for the feminist argument below. For now it suffices to note that the norms of anger per se do not call for marked sex differences in the experience and/or expression of anger.

Young girls, just as much as young boys, are taught the differences between right and wrong (as defined by their society), and they are encouraged to redress wrongs to the best of their abilities. Moreover, society provides the means for redressing most wrongs, means that are well within the capabilities of both sexes (e.g., verbal aggression, denial of benefits, talking things over). Under what conditions, then, would one expect women to be less able to express their anger than men? Primarily in situations that call for direct physical aggression, a rare occurrence for either sex.

It should go without saying that for both social and personal reasons, men and women often differ in what they consider to be wrong, and hence on an "adequate provocation" for anger. In our own culture at the present time, for example, a negative comment about one's appearance is liable to be considered more provocative by a woman than by a man. However, on a broader level of analysis (e.g., in terms of responding to a provocation, regardless of its specific nature), it appears that both men and women are provoked about equally often, and that they respond in a roughly comparable manner.

The fact that on a specific level of analysis men may find some things provocative and women other things may reflect important differences in role expectations, sexual stereotypes, status relationships, and so forth. Moreover, as a society changes, behavior that was once considered provocative may subsequently be viewed as justified, and vice versa. Such currently is the state of affairs with regard to the norms that help define "proper" masculine and feminine behavior in Western societies. Consequently, there is currently much debate about what men and women *should* be angry at. We will have more to say about this issue below, when we consider the implications of the present findings for the feminist argument. For the moment, suffice it to note that a lack of major sex differences in the everyday experience of anger can be accounted for more parsimoniously from a social rather than a biological perspective.

The Problem of Repressed Anger

At several points in this chapter we have noted how repressed anger has been postulated as an etiological factor in a wide variety of disorders. The notion is that anger, if left unexpressed, may find outlet in unusual ways, including behavioral and psychosomatic disorders. A variety of mechanisms have been proposed to explain the vicissitudes of repressed anger, the hydraulic model of classical psychoanalysis being perhaps the most familiar. It is not our intention to review and criticize these various formulations. Our goal is much more modest. We wish only to point out some of the pitfalls and conceptual confusions that often plague discussions of repressed anger.

Earlier, we quoted the psychotherapist Sonya Friedman to the effect that "all the depression, the going to sleep early, not having energy, the fact that it's three in the afternoon and she is still sitting around in her housecoat—all these are various forms of anger." Certainly, there are times when sitting around in a housecoat at three in the afternoon might be regarded as a sign of anger. Such an inference might be warranted, for example, if it were demonstrated that (a) the woman considered the role of a housewife to be unfulfilling, or even demeaning; (b) she believed that, except for her husband, she would not have to remain at home; and (c) she knew that sitting around all day in a housecoat irritated and embarrassed her husband. Of course, the woman might not be able to articulate these attitudes clearly, or she might not recognize the link between them, in which case it would be appropriate to speak of her anger as "repressed" or "unconscious." The argument for repressed anger would be strengthened even further if in this instance it also could be shown that the woman did not behave in a similar fashion when her husband was away on trips, and hence would not be aware of her behavior; or if she engaged in other bothersome behavior (e.g., going to sleep early) when she was not able to sit around all day in her housecoat.

There are few limits on the way anger can be expressed, and the capacity of people (including an angry person) for self-deception is truly great. This makes it easy to interpret many reactions as signs of anger, even when the person involved denies that he or she is angry. But too often the interpretation is not based on careful analysis or sound evidence of the kind illustrated above.

For example, a woman might sit around in a housecoat at three in the afternoon *simply* because she is depressed, and lacks energy, and not because she is angry. Unless one is already committed to the anger-turned-inward hypothesis of depression it must be admitted that a person may appraise a situation as depressing without ever becoming angry. Depression is as legitimate an emotion in its own right as is anger.

Pursuing the above example even further, if the depressed housewife could be convinced that she is being wrongly "oppressed," and that she has the power to change the situation and lead a more autonomous life, then she might well become angry. In the current argot, her consciousness would have been raised. This does not mean that some repressive barrier has been lifted, so that years of submerged anger can now well up from the depths of her unconscious. It simply means that she has learned to appraise her situation differently, so that what formerly made her depressed now makes her angry. And the more severe her former depression, the more wronged she is now likely to feel, and hence the more angry.

Finally, the obvious also deserves mention because it is so often overlooked. A woman who sits around in a housecoat until three in the afternoon may do so because she finds it comfortable. She may be angry, depressed, or perfectly contented with her situation, quite independently of her choice of clothes and behavior on a given afternoon.

Observations similar to the above could be made with regard to a wide range of psychosomatic complaints that are often attributed to repressed anger, and they apply to men as well as to women. Ulcers are a case in point. The stereotypic young (typically male) executive may find himself frustrated by a boss who blocks his advancement; and because of constitutional factors, or past conditioning, he may respond to the frustration with increased gastrointestinal activity, leading to an ulcer. After talking to an outside observer (a psychiatrist, perhaps), the young executive may come to view the behavior of his boss as unreasonable and unjustified; and becoming angry, he may take action to change the situation, or to seek another job, after which the ulcer may undergo remission. Does this mean that the young executive was really angry all along, that his anger was repressed, and that being repressed it caused the ulcer? Not necessarily. Ulcers, no less than housecoats in the afternoon, can sometimes be a symptom of repressed anger. More commonly, however, ulcers are the result of less differentiated psychophysiological stress reactions. Ulcers may occur independently of, or concurrently with, a wide variety of emotional syndromes, including anger, depression, or even the excitement of closing a new business deal.

In short, one must be cautious about overinterpreting a response. It is a fallacy to conclude that because *I* would be angry in a situation, *you* must also be angry, whether or not you realize it. A related fallacy is to conclude that what makes me angry *now*, must also have made me angry at some *earlier point in time*, even though I did not realize it. Such fallacious inferences are often made to appear valid by an unsubstantiated appeal to notions such as "repression" and "false consciousness."

Implications for the Feminist Argument

According to the feminist argument, women do not become angry enough, and when they do become angry, they often express it in roundabout and ineffective ways. The research we have reviewed in this chapter offers little support for such a contention. What, then, are we to make of the feminist argument?

In addressing this issue, it is important to recognize that the feminist argument is not open to confirmation or refutation in the usual sense. It is an ideological argument, a social critique that asserts what *should* be (from the feminist perspective) and not what *is*. When viewed in this light, the failure of nonfeminists (whether therapists or the typical woman in the street) to note any particular problems with anger is neither surprising nor particularly relevant.

The feminist perspective shifts responsibility for many of the problems experienced by women from the individual to society; and it shifts an understanding of these problems from an explanation in terms of the natural stresses and strains of everyday life, which some individuals may handle better than others but to which all must adjust, to an explanation in terms of the presumed exploitation and domination of women by men. From this perspective, then, the difficulties faced by women are not natural, are not necessary, but rather reflect a system of exploitation perpetuated by men at the expense of women, not just as individuals but as a class.

The feminist argument is thus less concerned with women's anger per se than with the condition of women within society. The argument that women are greatly inhibited in their anger is clearly an overgeneralization. Women can and do become angry as readily as men, and they are able to express their anger as effectively. But from the feminist perspective, women are not becoming angry at the right kinds of things.

Hochshild (1979) has made a distinction between "feeling rules" and "framing rules" that is helpful in clarifying the nature of the feminist argument. Feeling rules are internalized social norms that help constitute particular emotional experiences —what it feels like to be in love, to grieve, to stand in reverence, to be angry, and so forth. Framing rules, on the other hand, help to specify the proper occasions for experiencing a particular emotion, but they do not affect the nature of the experience per se. During a period of ideological transition, either or both kinds of rules may be transformed. If feeling rules are transformed, then new emotions may be experienced. Religious conversions, for example, may be accompanied by new emotions that help validate the adopted ideology. Similarly, when moving to a new culture, it may be necessary to acquire different emotional experiences. A transformation in framing rules, by contrast, is not nearly so radical (psychologically speaking). It involves a redefinition of situations, so that traditional feelings can be experienced in new contexts. According to Hochschild (1979):

> The feminist movement brings with it a new set of rules for framing the work and family life of men and women: the same balance of priorities in work and family now ideally applies to men as to women. This carries with it implications for feelings. A women can now as legitimately (as a man) become angry (rather than simply upset or disappointed) over abuses at work, since her heart is supposed to be in that work and she has the right to hope, as much as a man would, for advancements. . . . "Old-fashioned" feelings are now as subject to new chidings and cajolings as are "old-fashioned" perspectives on the same array of situations. (p. 567)[10]

In other words, the feminist argument is actually quite conservative as far as the feeling rules for anger per se are concerned. It could not be otherwise. As traditionally conceived, anger is a potent force for social change. If one's anger is accepted as legitimate, then the onus is focused on the instigator, which in the case of ideological arguments is typically a class of individuals or institutions. Also, as we have seen in previous chapters, the feeling rules for anger are action oriented. A person cannot be angry and not want to do something about the situation. That is one reason why social movements often try to arouse anger in their followers, or to convince them that they really have been angry all along, if only they would recognize the fact.

Concluding Observations

In this chapter we have examined the evidence for sex differences in the everyday experience of anger, and have found it wanting. Men and women become angry about equally often, for much the same reasons, and with about equal effect. The differences that do exist between the sexes are few in number and small in magnitude when compared with individual differences within each sex.

This conclusion is inconsistent with both the biological and feminist arguments presented at the outset of this chapter. It is, however, consistent with the notion, adumbrated in Chapter 1, that anger is a social construction, a transitory social role, so to speak. As a transitory social role, anger is equally accessible to both men and

---

[10] Copyright © 1979 by The University of Chicago. Reprinted by permission.

women, even though the manner in which any particular person fulfills the role is, of course, dependent upon his or her personal characteristics (which would include any sex-linked differences in temperament and style).

To avoid misunderstanding, some limitations must also be placed on the above conclusion. It should hardly bear repeating that we are concerned here with possible sex differences in anger, and not with aggression in general. Neither are we concerned with conflict in general. For example, men and women may experience marital conflict in ways that are linked to their respective roles as husbands and wives. Important as such differences may be, they are somewhat removed from the present chapter's focus on anger. Finally, with respect to the feminist argument, nothing that we have said contradicts or affirms the assertion that women *should* be more angry at certain situations than they appear to be. That is a social-political assertion which must be assessed on its own merits. We have raised the question of possible sex differences in anger not to engage in debate about contemporary social issues, but to see what could be learned *about anger* by examining how two different types of social actors (men and women) experience and express it.

Chapter 14

Epilogue

Much material related to anger and aggression, and to emotion in general, has been presented in the previous chapters. Yet, much has been left unsaid. In this, the final chapter, we will tie together some loose ends, address some potential criticisms, and discuss several issues—such as the development of anger, and abnormal (nonnormative) angry reactions—that have only been touched upon briefly in previous chapters.

A Summary Definition of Anger

To begin the chapter, it might be helpful to have before us a concise definition of anger, a definition that would summarize some of the salient features of the preceding analyses. Accordingly, anger may be defined as a *conflictive emotion* that, on the biological level, *is related to aggressive systems and, even more important, to the capacities for cooperative social living, symbolization, and reflective self-awareness*; that, on the psychological level, *is aimed at the correction of some appraised wrong*; and that, on the sociocultural level, *functions to uphold accepted standards of conduct.* Let us consider briefly the four key (italicized) elements of this definition.[1]

---

[1] Elsewhere (Averill, 1979) I defined anger as "a socially constituted response which helps regulate interpersonal relations through the threat of retaliation for perceived wrongs, and which is interpreted as a passion rather than as an action so as not to violate the general cultural proscription against deliberately harming another" (p. 71). That definition and the one offered here differ in detail and emphasis, but they are fundamentally congruent. Also, in Chapter 11 a brief iterative definition was offered which highlights the differences between anger and annoyance.

Anger Is a Conflictive Emotion

When treated in a strictly formal or abstract manner, that is, without regard to the individuals involved, emotions can be conceptualized as socially constituted syndromes or as transitory social roles. On a less abstract level, the person who is in a particular emotional state, such as anger, may be said to be disposed to respond in a manner consistent with the syndrome. In this respect, emotions can also be conceptualized as relatively short-term psychological dispositions to respond in particular ways, and to interpret those responses as emotional (i.e., as passions rather than as actions). The above ways of conceptualizing emotions have been throroughly discussed in previous chapters (especially Chapters 1 and 12). Further discussion or review at this point would be largely redundant. There are, however, several issues that deserve elaboration. The most important of these issues has to do with the nature of the social rules or norms that help constitute emotional syndromes in general and anger in particular. We will have much to say about this issue shortly. Our immediate concerns are more limited, namely, the nature of anger as a *conflictive* emotion.

Conflict has sometimes been considered the *sine qua non* of emotional behavior. In textbooks, it is even common to classify a whole tradition of speculation under the heading "Conflict Theories of Emotion." However, rather than calssifying theories of emotion in this manner, it would seem more appropriate to classify the emotions themselves; for surely conflict plays a more important role in some emotions than in others.

As discussed in Chapter 1, conflictive emotions can be distinguished from impulsive emotions (straightforward inclinations and aversions) and from transcendental emotional states (which involve a breakdown in ego boundaries). The historical roots of the distinctions among these three classes of emotion have also been discussed (Chapter 4). Needless to say, the distinctions are not absolute. A typical angry episode may involve impulsive and transcendental, as well as conflictive, aspects. But for the moment, our concern is with the latter.

Any complex system of behavior, whether at the biological, psychological, or social level of analysis, is apt to involve conflicting elements or subsystems. When conflict exists, new forms of behavior may arise, be reinforced, and eventually achieve functional autonomy. For example, on the biological level, the proximity of a potential mate may elicit conflicting tendencies to approach (even attack) and flee. A compromise pattern of responses may ensue. In certain circumstances, such compromise reactions may have functional significance (e.g., as signals); and through natural selection, they may be preserved, perhaps as part of the courtship display of the species. (See Hinde, 1970, Chap. 16, for numerous illustrations of this process.) On the psychological or intrapsychic level, competing demands on the individual may also result in compromise reactions that, in addition to their symbolic significance, produce some secondary gain. The Freudian theory of hysterical (conversion) reactions is based on such a process. And so it is, also, with respect to social systems. No society is so simple that its various subsystems intermesh without potential conflict. Conflictive emotions, as here conceived, are symbolically transformed compromise reactions that help meet conflicting demands within the social system, and/or between society, on the one hand, and incompatible biological or psychological impulses on the other.

Campbell (1975) has commented on the possible conflict between biological and social systems in the case of anger. According to Campbell, practices that are condemned as sinful or immoral often represent biological impulses that run counter to the requirements for social living. And, he notes, "rage and anger are omnipresent in sin lists, perhaps in part as evidence of the need for [social] system curbing of vertebrate territoriality" (p. 1119).

A similar argument could be made with reference to conflict between social and psychological systems of behavior. Anger is often motivated by a desire for personal gain or aggrandizement. That, too, is subject to condemnation as "sinful." However, the major conflict with respect to anger would seem to lie within the social system itself. One indication of this is the fact that the *failure* to become angry upon adequate provocation has often been considered as sinful as the tendency to become angry for selfish ends (whether biologically or psychologically determined).

The conflicting social norms that help constitute anger are most apparent in historical teachings (Chapter 4) and in legal practices (Chapter 5). To recapitulate briefly, these norms involve an injunction, on the one hand, to retaliate forcefully against perceived injustice and wrongdoing, and on the other hand, to settle disputes in a forgiving and reasoned way. The conflict between these competing norms may be resolved by interpreting the resulting behavior as a passion rather than as an action, thus absolving the angry person of responsiblity for his or her acts. Such an interpretation is particularly likely when the discouraged response (e.g., aggression) is exhibited following an "adequate" provocation.

The conflictive aspect of anger is less apparent at the level of everyday experience than it is from a broad social perspective. This is to be expected, since the resolution of a conflict need not itself be experienced as conflictual. Also, since most everyday episodes of anger do not involve a great deal of aggression or other untoward responses, there is little reason for the individual to experience conflict. But in spite of these qualifications, the conflicting norms that help give anger its meaning are seldom completely absent or hidden. One indication of this fact is the ambivalence with which most people regard anger. Anger is a negative experience, and it is widely condemned. Yet, as we have seen, the outcome of a typical angry episode is generally viewed as positive.

Although anger illustrates some of the salient features of conflictive emotions, this aspect of our definition should not be overemphasized. Anger is a complex phenomenon. An adequate definition must take into account additional features at the biological, psychological, and sociocultural levels of analysis.

On the Biological Level, Anger Is Related to Aggressive Systems and to the Capacities for Cooperative Social Living, Symbolization, and Reflective Self-Awareness

At many points throughout this volume I have commented on the relationship between anger and aggression and on the tendency among psychologists to conflate these two phenomena, so that our understanding of each is diminshed. The research reported in previous chapters provides ample testimony to the fact that anger cannot be equated with aggression, or with a motive or drive toward aggression. This fact does not mean, however, that biologically based aggressive elements do not form part of the anger syndrome (see Chapter 2). Nor does it mean that the close conceptual link between anger and aggression is a figment of psychologists' imagination. As we will see later in this chapter, there is a sense in which aggression is a prototypic feature of anger, even though anger is not a particularly aggressive syndrome.

Of course, even if we take aggression as a prototypic feature of anger, not all aggression is biologically based. And, conversely, there are nonaggressive aspects of anger that are, at least indirectly, of biological origin. The latter deserve more attention than they have traditionally recieved in theories of anger. These nonaggressive aspects are related to the capacities for cooperative social living, symbolization, and reflective self-awareness.

Many animal species are social, but humans are social in a unique—or almost unique—way. Human sociality is based on custom, that is, on rules. Humans are *by nature* rule-following animals. The rules themselves are not biologically given; but the tendency to formulate and to follow rules is; and so, too, we may presume, is the tendency to become "upset" when accepted (internalized) rules are broken. Anger is one form such upset may take.

The ability to formulate and to follow rules presumes, of course, a capacity for symbolic thought, and the related capacity for reflective self-awareness (i.e., to monitor one's own behavior in accordance with rules). Anger is, as we have seen, a highly symbolic activity, not only in terms of the appraisals on which it is based and its most common modes of expression, but also in the way it is related to the self (as a passion rather than as an action). These characteristics are as definitive of anger as is aggression; and they are based on capacities that are as deeply rooted in our biological heritage.

On the Psychological Level, Anger Is Aimed at the Correction of Some Perceived Wrong

In Chapter 1 we emphasized that the object of an emotion is one of its most defining characteristics, and that the object typically encompasses three aspects—the instigation, the target, and the aim or objective. The definition we have offered for anger encompasses, on the psychological level, two of these three aspects; namely, the instigation (some appraised wrong) and the aim (correction of the wrong). The target is implicit in this definition, that is, it is another human being or, by extension, some other entity (the self, an institution) that can be held responsible or blameworthy.

The above features of anger have been so repeatedly discussed in previous chapters that they hardly deserve further mention at this point. Nevertheless, to avoid misunderstanding, it should be emphasized that the notions of "appraised wrong" and "correction" must be interpreted rather broadly in this context. The appraised wrong need not involve deliberate misconduct, but only an event for which the target can be held responsible (e.g., because of negligence). Similarly, the correction of the appraised wrong can take many forms, from a restored sense of equity on the part of the angry person to a more or less permenent change in behavior on the part of the target. The important thing to note in this respect is that the aim of anger is not simply the infliction of pain or injury on the target, as in the case of cruelty or wanton violence. When aggression does occur during anger, it is more a means to an end than it is an end in itself.

Perhaps at this point it is also worth reemphasizing the distinction between the object and the causes of anger. In Chapter 6 we discussed a number of conditions (e.g., frustration, physiological arousal, aggressive cues) that may help explain the occurrence of anger on any particular occasion. Such causal variables have sometimes been incorporated into definitions of anger. That would be acceptable if there were a sufficiently close connection between the presumed cause and appraised instigation. For the most part, however, the relevant connection (e.g., between frustration and some perceived wrong) is only incidental and highly tenuous. Hence, definitions of anger that incorporate presumed causal mechanisms have not met with great success or widespread acceptance.

Similar considerations apply to the aims of anger and potential terminating factors (see Chapter 12). As just described, the aim of anger is the correction (broadly conceived) of some perceived wrong. In many instances, the factors that are causally important in bringing an angry episode to a close have little connection with this aim. Just as the occurrence of a frustrating event unrelated to the appraised instigation may help trigger an angry outburst, so too the occurrence of a happy event unrelated to the aim may help terminate an episode.

On the Sociocultural Level, Anger Functions to Uphold Accepted Standards of Conduct

The general cultural directive for anger might be paraphrased as follows:

> You should avoid becoming angry. However, under certain conditions, for example, A, B, or C, a reasonable person cannot help but be angry. If under such conditions you respond in manner X, Y, or Z, then your behavior will be interpreted as a passion, and you will not be held responsible.

This general directive encompasses the conflicting norms which simultaneously discourage and encourage angry behavior, as well as the means for resolving the conflict (i.e., by interpreting the response as a passion). The variables A, B, and C stand for adequate provocations, and X, Y, Z represent acceptable responses. The instantiation of these variables depends on such factors as the age, sex, and social status of the individuals involved; the specific setting in which the episode occurs (e.g., a barroom or a formal banquet); alternative means for resolving the dispute; and so forth.

Since the general cultural directive for anger can be instantiated in so many different ways, it is not possible to define anger precisely in terms of the relevant variables. However, it is possible to give a functional definition of anger on the sociocultural level. Specifically, it is here postulated that anger has evolved and is maintained within the social system because it serves to uphold accepted standards of conduct.

It is important to distinguish the functions of anger on a sociocultural level from the aims of anger on a psychological level. The aim of a person who becomes angry is usually not to uphold some social standard. However, as we saw in Chapter 8, the typical instigation to anger involves the violation of social norms, either directly or indirectly: directly when the insitgation is some breach of etiquette or widely shared standard of conduct; and indirectly when the instigation is a violation of some expectation idiosyncratic to the angry individual, but which is perceived as unwarranted, unjustified, and unfair. In the long run, the correction of such appraised wrongs should have the net effect of helping to regulate interpersonal relationships by encouraging potential targets to conform to socially accepted standards of conduct.

In the remainder of this chapter we will explore some of the ramifications of the above definition of anger. Although our specific focus will be on anger, a major concern will be with the implications of the present analysis for the study of emotion in general.

Rules, Norms, and the Appropriate Unit of Analysis for the Study of Emotion

The definition of anger offered in the preceding section goes beyond our ordinary concept of anger. Yet the same phenomena are denoted by each. This raises a question regarding the proper unit of analysis for the study of emotion. Should our scientific concepts refer to the same phenomena as our ordinary concepts, or should we, for the sake of precision, restrict the former to some more limited range of phenomena (e.g., physiological reactions, cognitive processes)? Much depends, theoretically speaking, on how this question is answered. But before getting to that, we need to clarify the use of the terms *rules* and *norms* as they apply to emotions such as anger.

Rules and Norms of Anger

For our purposes a rule may be defined as a precept or standard that helps guide behavior. By implication, rules are social in origin and prescriptive (or proscriptive) in nature. That is, they indicate how people may—or should—behave in particular situations. The existence of rules can often be inferred from statistical regularities (which is one reason why so much space has been devoted in previous chapters to a presentation of "normative" data on the everyday experience of anger). However, the failure of people to behave in a particular way does not necessarily invalidate a rule *qua* precept. Thus, the fact that people sometimes become angry at legitimate restrictions and unavoidable accidents does not invalidate the rule that anger should only be directed at events that are either unjustified or at least avoidable.

Social norms represent a subclass of rules. Hence what is true of rules is also true of norms. The reverse is not necessarily true; but for our purposes, the differences between rules and norms are not crucial.[2] In the present discussion, therefore, I will generally speak only of rules, except where common usage makes *norm* a stylistically more appropriate term.

Rules, as they relate to emotional syndromes, can be classified in a variety of different ways. For example, Table 14-1 presents a partial list of the rules of anger, divided into the four overlapping classes discussed in Chapter 1, namely: rules of appraisal, which specify the appropriate objects (instigations/targets/aims) of an emotion; rules of behavior, which pertain to the way an emotion is expressed; rules of prognostication, which have to do with the temporal course of an emotion and its suitable outcomes; and rules of attribution, which determine how emotional behavior is causally interpreted, especially with respect to the self.

The rules listed in Table 14-1 are based on analyses reported in previous chapters, although they are not meant as a summary of those analyses. The list is too incomplete for that. Primarily, the list provides a basis for further discussion. Six points, in particular, deserve brief mention.

1. Perhaps the first thing to note is how difficult it can sometimes be to distinguish between a rule and a mere statistical regularity. Take, for example, the fact that anger is more often directed at persons who are well known than at strangers; and that when the target is a stranger, anger is more often directed at a man than at a woman. (See rules I.B.1.c and d.) These are statistical regularities that can be accounted for, in large part, by nonnormative factors (e.g., the likelihood of provocation, confidence in making a response). However, rules related to politeness, civility, and chivalry (to the extent that it is not completely dead) are also involved. The person who becomes angry at a stranger, and especially at a strange woman, is liable to be considered boorish unless the provocation is particularly blatant.

As a second and even more problematical example of the distinction between a rule and a mere statistical regularity, consider the rule (II.B.1.a) that "an angry person should be sufficiently involved in the emotional role to display an appropriate level of physiological arousal." That anger typically involves a certain degree of arousal can be explained without reference to social norms—but perhaps not completely. Note that there is a certain "oughtness" about physiological arousal during anger, as indicated by our suspicion of the person who responds in a cold and deliberate manner (cf. Descartes's condemnation of the person who becomes pale rather than flushed while angry, presumably because the former is more brooding and cunning). In this respect, consider also the legal criterion that in order for a homicide to be mitigated from murder to manslughter, it must have been committed in "the heat of passion." There are, of course, a variety of direct and indirect ways in which a person can stoke the fires of passion. That is not our present concern. It suffices to note that emotional rules pertain not

---

[2] If social rules were arranged on a continuum from those that are merely practical or procedural to those that are value laden, norms would tend toward the latter end of the distribution. Compare, for example, the rules found in a cookbook with those found in a book of etiquette, or the rules (grammar) of a dialect with those of standard speech.

Table 14-1. A Partial List of the Rules and Norms Related to Anger
_____

I. Rules of appraisal
  A. With respect to the instigation
    1. Prescriptive
      a. A person has the right (duty) to become angry at intentional wrong-doing, including an affront to one's honor, freedom, property, or other rights.
      b. A person has the right (duty) to become angry at the unintentional misdeeds of certain others if those misdeeds are due to negligence, carelessness, oversight, and so forth.
    2. Proscriptive
      a. A person should not become angry at events which are beyond his or her influence.
      b. A person should not become angry at events which can be remedied in more standard ways.
  B. With respect to the target
    1. Prescriptive
      a. Anger should be directed only at persons, and by extension, other entities (the self, human institutions) that can be held responsible for their actions.
      b. Anger is more appropriately directed at a peer or subordinate than at a superior.
      c. Anger is more appropriately directed at someone who is well known than at a stranger or mere acquaintance.
      d. Among strangers, anger is more appropriately directed at men than at women.
    2. Proscriptive
      a. Anger should not be directed at persons who cannot be held responsible for their actions (e.g., because of age or ignorance).
      b. Anger should not be directed at persons who cannot profit from the experience (e.g., because of infirmity).
  C. With respect to the aim or objective
    1. Prescriptive
      a. The aim of anger should be to correct the situation, restore equity, and/or prevent recurrences, not to inflict pain or injury on the target.
    2. Proscriptive
      a. Anger should not be used as a tool to achieve selfish ends.
II. Rules of behavior
  A. With respect to overt behavior
    1. Prescriptive
      a. The response should be proportional to the instigation.
      b. The response should be open and direct (so that the target knows who is angry and why).
      c. The response, even when it involves physical aggression, should conform to community standards of appropriateness (which may vary as a function of the target, the angry person, the setting, etc.).
    2. Proscriptive
      a. The response should not exceed what is necessary to correct the situation, for example, to prevent the instigation from happening again, or to restore equity.

Table 14-1. (continued)

        b. The response should not unfairly or unnecessarily take advantage of the target (e.g., through public humiliation, or "hitting a man when he is down").

  B. With respect to physiological arousal

    1. Prescriptive

        a. Depending on the circumstances, an angry person should be sufficiently involved in the emotional role to display an appropriate level of physiological arousal, that is, to be "in the heat of passion."

  C. With respect to subjective experience

    1. Prescriptive

        a. Anger should be spontaneous and not deliberate.

        b. Anger should involve commitment and resolve.

III.   Rules of prognostication

  A. With respect to the sequence of events

    1. Prescriptive

        a. Anger should begin with an explanation of the harm done, and only if that fails should it escalate to the denial of some benefit, verbal aggression, and—as a last resort—physical aggression.

        b. Anger should proceed without interruption, as far as opportunity permits.

  B. With respect to duration

    1. Prescriptive

        a. Anger should terminate whenever the target apologizes, offers restitution, or gives assurance that the instigation will not be repeated.

    2. Proscriptive

        a. Anger should not last more than a few hours or days, at most. (If the situation has not been resolved during that period, action may still be taken, but it will not be interpreted as anger.)

IV.   Rules of attribution

  A. With respect to events

    1. Prescriptive

        a. There should be a causal connection between the target, the insitgation, and the angry response.

    2. Proscriptive

        a. Anger should not be displaced on an innocent thrid party, nor directed at the target for reasons other than the instigation.

  B. With respect to the self

    1. Prescriptive

        a. An angry response may, and sometimes should, be dissociated from the self-as-agent (i.e., interpreted as a passion rather than as an action).

    2. Proscriptive

        a. An angry person should not be held completely responsible for his or her behavior.

---

only to the appraisal of objects and overt responses, but also to the presumably more "involuntary" aspects of the syndrome, including physiological change. (For further discussion of this issue, see Chapter 1, on *Involvement in Emotional Roles*.)

326 · 342 of 418

2. Many of the rules listed in Table 14-1 relate to the functions of anger. The relationship is direct in the case of the rule (I.C.l.a) that "the aim of anger should be to correct the situation, restore equity, and/or prevent recurrences." It is more indirect in the case of the rule (I.A.2.a) that "a person should not become angry at events which are beyond his or her influence." Needless to say, we all do sometimes become angry at events over which we have little influence (e.g., acts of government). Are such episodes exceptions to the rule? Not necessarily. Anger can be largely expressive and still serve a function. For example, the anger may demonstrate to significant others a commitment to shared values, thus keeping alive the possibility for future action. Even anger that is never expressed openly may serve to reaffirm a person's own sense of values and self-worth. (Incidentally, this may account for some of the cathartic effects of anger.) It is important to note, however, that such expressive and individual effects of anger are derivative. Private anger, like private speech, is ultimately social in origin.

3. It is also evident that the rules listed in Table 14-1 are not independent. Some of the rules can be derived from others: and many could be derived from rules that have little to do with anger per se. To illustrate this point, norms of civility toward strangers may proscribe a too ready display of anger, but only incidentally. This fact (i.e., that many rules of anger represent specific applications of more general rules) has important implications. For one thing, it means that an emotion such as anger is embedded in an entire network of rules that govern social relations, and hence that anger cannot be understood in isolation. For another thing, it means that the development of anger, which depends on the acquisition of the relevant rules, is an integral part of the broader process of socialization. Different principles are not needed to explain emotional development than are needed to explain the development of other kinds of social behavior. But more of that shortly.

4. Social rules and norms can be distinguished along a number of dimensions, such as generality and flexibility. This fact is also illustrated by the rules presented in Table 14-1, which are for the most part quite general and highly flexible. For example, what counts as an appraised wrong (see rule I.A.l.a) may vary as a function of the respective statuses, rights, and obligations of the persons involved, as well as of the context in which the incident occurs. We have also seen how the nature of an appraised wrong may be subject to renegotiation as an episode proceeds. In these respects, the rules of anger are not like the rules that govern formal social episodes, such as wedding ceremonies and sporting events. Rather, the rules of anger are general guidelines, within which a great deal of improvisasation is allowed.

5. Most of the rules presented in Table 14-1 are rather self-evident. This transparency is a result, in part, of the generality of the rules as stated. The application of the rules, however, is not so clear-cut, as is evidenced by the difficulty so many people seem to have in managing their anger. But more of that shortly. Of more immediate concern is the fact that the rules of anger *should* be self-evident for anyone well socialized into the culture. One does not "discover" rules of this type, as one might discover a new chemical element or a distant star. If we did not already know the rules at least implicitly, and conform our behavior

to them, they could not be considered rules in the relevant sense. Thus, rather than a discovery, the rules of anger as presented in Table 14-1 offer a challenge: How are they related to behavior?

6. This last question brings us to an issue that is central to a constructivist view of emotion. Some of the rules presented in Table 14-1 are *constitutive* of anger, whereas others are primarily *regulative*. Take, for example, the rule (I.A.1.a) that one has the right (duty) to correct intentional wrongdoing on the part of certain others. This rule helps constitute a response as anger (as opposed, say, to envy); it is part of what we mean by anger. On the other hand, the rule (I.B. 1.d) that among strangers anger is more appropriately directed at men than at women serves primarily to regulate behavior with respect to a given class of potential targets.

The distinction between constitutive and regulative rules was introduced by Searle (1969) in connection with language (speech acts). The rules of grammar do not simply regulate the way people speak (e.g., loudly or softly, depending on the circumstances); rather, they establish the possibility for speech in the first place. Pearce and Cronen (1980) have elaborated upon this distinction within the broader context of social episodes. According to Pearce and Cronen's formulation, regulative rules specify what actions should be taken within a given context; constitutive rules, on the other hand, place the actions within a hierarchy of meaning, so that the episode "counts as" something (e.g., an episode of anger). In this connection, we might also recall the distinction made by Hochschild (1979) between "feeling rules" and "framing rules." As we discussed in Chapter 13, feeling rules are constitutive of the experience in question. Framing rules, by contrast, are primarily regulative; they determine the appropriate occasions for the emotion.[3]

All theorists have recognized that emotional behavior is subject to regulation by social rules and norms. But most have stopped there, assuming that emotions per se somehow preexist (e.g., are innate), and hence are subject *only* to regulation. Tomkins (1981a) has expressed this assumption in the following way:

> Because the free expression of innate affect is extremely contagous, all societies exercise substantial control over the free expression of affect, particularly of the sound of the cry of affect. As a consequence there is a universal confusion of the experience of backed-up affect with that of *biologically and psychologically authentic innate affect.* (p. 324, italics added)

By contrast, the present (constructivist) view of emotion assumes that at least some of the rules that help regulate affective experience are also constitutive. The validity of this assumption depends in part on what we choose as the proper unit of analysis for the study of emotion. Therefore, let us turn to that issue.

---

[3] Actually, what Hochschild (1979) has called framing rules (i.e., "rules according to which we ascribe definitions or meanings to situations" —p. 566) are closer to what I have called rules of appraisal. Rules of appraisal can be constitutive of feelings as well as regulative, although Hochschild emphasizes the latter function in her analysis.

The Unit of Analysis

When, in the above quotation, Tomkins (1981a) speaks of "biologically and psychologically innate affect," he is not referring to the complex syndromes denoted by everyday emotional concepts. He recognizes that such "affect complexes" may indeed be constituted, in part, by social rules and norms; but it is critical, Tomkins warns us, "that such complexes not be confused with the very restricted number of biologically primary affects" (p. 326). Although he is not entirely consistent on this point, Tomkins would evidently like to restrict the concept of emotion not only to a limited number of primary affects, but also to certain elements of these primary affects—particularly facial expressions and their underlying neural circuitry. Referring to my own constructivist view of emotion, Tomkins (1981a) makes the following observation:

> Averill (1980[a]) suggests that "an emotion may be defined as a socially constituted syndrome which is interpreted as a passion rather than an action. . .but there is no single subset of responses which is an essential characteristic of anger or of any other emotion" (p. 146). It is extraordinary that this can be asserted despite the overwhelming evidence of the universality of facial expressions across cultures, among neonates, and even the blind. (Tomkins, 1981 a, p. 319)

The suggestion that emotions are social constructions seems extraordinary to Tomkins largely because he has chosen to restrict the meaning of emotional concepts to a rather limited range of phenomena. Admittedly, there is ample scientific precendence for such a restriction. Everyday emotional concepts do refer to complex states of affiars. For the sake of precision, it is therefore tempting to focus attention on simpler and presumably more basic phenomena. But is that really a remedy for the confusion that seems to plague the study of emotion? There are reasons for doubt; and because of the importance of the issue, these reasons deserve brief mention.

To begin with, it should be noted that emotional concepts can be restricted in either or both of two ways: First, only a limited number of emotions may be recognized as truly authentic (however authenticity is defined); and second, only certain aspects of behavior may be considered truly representative of emotion (e.g., physiological arousal, expressive reactions). Logically, these two ways of restricting emotional concepts are quite distinct, and they raise somewhat different issues. In practice, however, many authors combine both appraoches. Thus, Tomkins suggests that there are only a few "authentic innate affects" (of which anger is one); and, moreover, that certain processes—primarily, but not only, biologically based facial expressions—are uniquely associated with these primary emotions.[4]

---

[4] I do not mean to single Tomkins out for criticism. However, over the years his rich and varied writings on the topic of emotion (e.g., Tomkins, 1962, 1963, 1970, 1980) have been very influential (cf. Ekman, Friesen, & Ellsworth, 1972; Izard, 1977). Moreover, others not so directly influenced by him have advocated positions that are in important respects similar, particularly with regard to the issue of "basic"

Let us consider, first, the assumption that certain processes are uniquely emotional. The proposed processes vary from one theroist to another. However, among theorists who adopt this approach, it is generally assumed that the relevant processes are biologically innate. Socially constituted elements are treated as dross, pollutants of the pure emotional metal. But even if it were possible to refine, through abstraction, the emotional metal in pure form, its very purity might decrease rather than enhance its value. An emotion is inherently a mixture of diverse elements. For analytical purposes, it may be useful to separate the elements, and to try to understand the way they combine; but none of the elements contains the properties of the whole. To imply otherwise is to invite confusion, as when in the above quotation Tomkins implies that what is true of one class of elements (certain facial expressions) is also true of an entire emotional syndrome (anger).

From a constructivist point of view, emotions are responses of the whole person, and the proper unit of analysis is respresented by the natural categories of emotion as reflected in our ordinary language. It is certainly appropriate and desirable to investigate the physiological mechanisms underlying emotion, but appropriate physiological concepts are available for that purpose. The same is true with respect to underlying psychological and sociological processes. Such "sub-personal" processes (to borrow a phrase from Dennett, 1978) are not themselves emotional.

Now let us turn to the suggestion that emotional concepts, in their strictest sense, be limited to a few "authentic innate affects." Such a suggestion leaves in theoretical limbo a wide range of emotional syndromes that are more clearly social in nature. Guilt, pride, hope, envy, reverence, and nostalgia are a few examples. The precise list is not important, for it could always be claimed that any particular emotion is innate (at least in some of its "essential" features—cf. the preceding argument), or else that it is compounded from presumably more basic, innate affects. At some point, however the postulated number of innate emotions must come to an end, and among the emotions that are excluded will be some that many people would regard as truly authentic, and yet as fundamentally social in origin. And if it is legitimate, even necessary, to approach some emotions from a social-constructivist point of view, then why not begin with such an approach and see where it leads, even in the case of so-called primary or basic emotions? That is what I have attempted to do in this volume, using anger as a paradigm case.

But regardless of how one begins, any theory of emotion must in the end relate to the kinds of phenomena, no matter how complex, that are recognized as emotions in ordinary language. Therefore, if we redefine our terms at the outset, so that they apply to only a few basic emotions or are limited to certain subpersonal processes, we are still left with the task of relating their new (restricted) meanings to their common (everyday) meanings. In the meantime, the dual usage of the same

---

(biologically innate) emotions and the importance of expressive reactions (cf. Leventhal, 1980; Plutchik, 1980). In spite of the present criticisms, there also is much in the work of these various theorists with which I agree. Special mention might be made of Tomkins' recent (1979) elaboration of "script theory" and Leventhal's (1980) research on schematic and conceptual processing during emotion.

term in both a restricted and an everyday sense can lead to greater, not less, confusion.

Natural Categories of Emotion

The above comments assume that everyday emotional concepts are—or can be—scientifically useful. This has not been a very fashionable notion, but fashions are subject to change. Much recent research in cognitive psychology and anthropology has been devoted to an analysis of natural categories, as reflected in the way people order and conceptualize the world about them (for reviews, see Rosch & Lloyd, 1978; Mervis & Rosch, 1981). The primary thrust of this research has to do with information processing. However, the findings have implications for a wider range of theoretical issues. Neisser (1979), for example, has reopened the question "What is intelligence?" beginning with an analysis of the everyday concept of intelligence. Similar analyses have been made of other personality characteristics (Cantor & Mischel, 1979). Therefore, let us review briefly some of the features of natural categories, with special reference to categories of emotion.

Natural categories form hierarchical systems or taxonomies, with three levels of abstraction being common. This is best illustrated by example. The concept "chair" represents a basic-level category which is subordinate to the more inclusive category "furniture" and superordinate to the more specific category "kitchen chair." Basic-level categories tend to be more readily named, recognized, and used than categories at either a higher or lower level of abstraction.

Emotional categories also form taxonomies, with categories like anger, fear, and hope representing the basic level. However, our primary concern at the momemt is not with taxonomies but with the internal structure of natural categories. In formal systems, such as logic, all members of a category may be presumed to share certain essential features. Since the time of Aristotle, it has been common to assume that objects in the natural world also fall into categories on the basis of shared essential attributes. This essentialist doctrine proved to be a major handicap in the development of scientific theory, especially in the biological sciences (Mayr, 1972). But the appeal of essentialism is not only strong, it can also be quite subtle. Even theorists who explicitly reject essentialism in its more blatant form may sometimes have recourse to essentialist arguments (cf. the preceding quotation by Tomkins).

Essentialism is not a feature of the natural world. As Rosch (1978) has pointed out, the members of a natural category are woven together by overlapping threads—constellations of attributes that tend to covary without any particular attribute being essential to the whole. This is, of course, not a new observation. Wittgenstein (1953) made much the same point when he spoke of "family resemblances" among members of a category. A more novel feature of Rosch's analysis is the way she treats representativeness. Not all attributes are equally important in determining membership in a category—some are more *prototypic* than others. For example, prototypic attributes of a chair include a comfortable seat, a back, legs, and a size appropriate for one person. Objects that have these attributes are easily recognized as chairs. But none of these attributes is essential to "chairness." Thus, beanbag chairs may be very comfortable, but they have no legs or back in an ordinary sense. The lack of essential attributes also means that natural categories tend to be indeterminant at the boundaries. Chairs and couches and stools form distinct categories if only prototypic features are considered; but this does not preclude the existence of couchlike chairs and chairlike stools.

The category of chair can be used to illustrate another feature of natural categories. Some prototypic attributes of chairs represent modal or typical properties. For example, most chairs have legs and backs. However, some prototypic attributes represent maximal or idealized properties that may be only approximated under ordinary conditions. Thus, a "real" chair is a truly comfortable chair.

Now let us apply some of the above considerations to the analysis of emotional categories, particularly anger. Perhaps the first thing to note is that our definition of anger as a syndrome is consistent with the nonessentialist nature of most natural (and many scientific) categories. Second, there are many boundary conditions that are difficult to classify as anger, for example, as opposed to annoyance or jealousy or envy or hatred. Third, anger is a basic-level category, but in a conceptual and not a biological sense. As a basic-level category, anger may subsume more specific varieties (such as the constructive, malevolent, and fractious anger discussed in Chapter 9); and, looking upward in the hierarchy, we find that anger may be subsumed under one or more superordinate categories (such as "conflictive emotion").

What are the prototypic attributes of anger? To a certain extent, these are specified by the modal responses of subjects to the questionnaires described in the previous chapters. For example, an episode would be easily recognized as anger if it were instigated by some unjustified act on the part of the target; if it involved some form of retaliation, or at least an attempt to resolve the situation; and it if were accompanied by general tension or arousal. However, there are other prototypic attributes of anger that appear to have little basis in everyday experience. One of these attributes is aggression; another is the experience of passivity. These are maximal or idealized attributes which help define the category, but which are seldom actualized in practice.

This view of aggression as an idealized (but not necessarily valued) attribute of anger places some old controversies in a new light. Because of the close conceptual link between anger and aggression, psychologists have often assumed that if aggression is not exhibited during an angry episode, the aggressive impulse must have been inhibited, transformed, or displaced; or else the claim may be made that the episode is not representative of "true" anger. (This is analogous to saying that an uncomfortable chair has had its comfort displaced; or else that the chair is not a real chair.) As an idealized attribute of anger, aggression need not be present in order to serve a function. As discussed in Chapter 9, it is the *possibility* of aggression, not aggression itself, that lends anger its force. Indeed, the actual occurrence of aggression might even be taken as a sign that anger has failed its objective; for as we saw in Chapter 10, the more aggressive the response, the less beneficial the outcome is likely to be.[5]

---

[5] We have also seen how, in courts of law and in everyday affairs, if a response is *too* aggressive or dramatic, that is, if it is disproportional to the insitgation, then a claim of anger may be disallowed. One can overshoot the mark, even in the case of idealized attributes.

Similar considerations apply to the experience of passivity during anger. This, too, is an idealized attribute, one that is seldom realized (or sought after) in actual practice, but yet which helps lend the syndrome its meaning *qua* emotion.

The notion of prototypic attributes (whether typical or idealized) is also relevant to our previous analysis of the rules of anger. Instead of speaking of the attributes of the members of a natural category, we could just as well have spoken of the rules that people use to categorize (conceptualize) objects. And when the object in question is a human artifact (such as a chair) or human behavior (such as anger), then some of the relevant rules are constitutive of the attributes to which they pertain.

If we take as our unit of analysis natural categories of emotion, as reflected in our ordinary language, does this have any implications for research as well as theory? I believe so. It means, among other things, that one of the major goals of research should be to uncover the prototypic attributes of various emotions; to determine the constitutive and regulative rules that pertain to these attributes; and to clarify the existential bases and functional significance of the attributes, for example, in relation to broader biological, psychological, and social systems of behavior.[6] There are also implications for the study of emotional development and for our understanding of abnormal emotional reactions, as will be described next.

The Development of Anger in Children

There are three major traditions with respect to emotional development. The *nativist* tradition assumes a limited number of innate basic emotions, and accounts for development largely in terms of stimulus substitution and response elaboration (e.g., as a consequence of classical conditioning). By contrast, the *sociological* tradition assumes that the child is basically open to the world at birth, but that such openness quickly becomes preempted by custom (e.g., through the internalization of norms and rules). Finally, the *social-learning* tradition emphasizes the direct and vicarious reinforcement of emotional responses, the modeling of behavior, and the conditions in the immediate environment that maintain a given response.

Each of the above traditions contains important insights and limitations. The nativist tradition recognizes that humans are not born into this world as blank slates upon which can be written any scenario. But by identifying emotions too closely with biological systems of behavior, nativist theories tend to limit and misdirect inquiry. The socialization tradition correctly emphasizes the importance of social rules in the constitution of emotional syndromes, but it is vague on the mechanisms of internalization. The social-learning tradition attempts to remedy this deficiency, with its emphasis on reinforcement and modeling, but the analyses are often superficial.

---

[6] This is not to deny the importance of, nor necessity for research into the mechanisms underlying emotions. However, as was discussed earlier, such mechanisms or part-processes are not themselves "emotional."

The truth of the matter is that we know very little about the development of emotion in children. One illustration of this state of ignorance is the fact that Bridges's (1932) figure depicting the differentiation of various emotions from a background of general arousal still graces many of our introductory textbooks. Few theorists have much confidence in the conclusions reached by Bridges, but textbook writers—even more than nature—abhor a vacuum.

A good deal of information has recently been collected on expressive reactions in infants and young children (e.g., Izard & Buechler, 1979). Also, at least as far as aggressive behavior is concerned, there are numberous observational studies dating back to the 1930's (e.g., Goodenough, 1931). However, as Hartup (1974) has noted, most of the research on childhood aggression has not been informed by developmental theory. Neither has it been guided by emotional theory. Indeed, the development of anger, as opposed to the development of aggression, has seldom even been discussed.

Perhaps the greatest lack is the paucity of research on emotional development during the crucial years from 2 to 5. This is the period during which children rapidly learn to categorize—and in many respects to construct—their world. Language is an important aspect of this process. By the time children are 5 years old they already have a reasonably good grasp of many basic-level emotional concepts (Barden, Zelko, Duncan, & Masters, 1980). This is no mean feat, considering the complexity of most emotional concepts. But what, precisely, is being learned during this crucial period of emotional development? In view of the dearth of relevant data, not to mention the lack of agreement among developmental theorists, it would be presumptuous of me even to attempt to answer this question. Nevertheless, a few general observations can be made with regard to the nature of the problem.

As far an anger is concerned, most relevant research has focused on the acquisition of aggressive responses. From a constructivist point of view, however, what is learned during emotional development is not a specific kind of response, but rather the rules that help constitute and regulate behavior. Perhaps an analogy with the acquisition of language will help to clarify this point. When children learn a language, they do not simply learn specific speech acts. More important, they learn a set of rules (the grammar of the language) by which new responses can be generated indefinitely. The mechanisms by which such learning occurs are not well understood. But then neither do we understand the mechansims by which classical or instrumental conditioning occurs. And if we must choose an analogue for human emotional development, I believe a child learning to speak would provide a better model than a dog salivating or a rat pressing a lever. I would go even further: The acquisition of language provides more than just an analogue for emotional development. As discussed earlier in this chapter (see also Chapter 3), there is a close relationship between the meaning of emotional concepts, on the one hand, and the experience and expression of emotion on the other. It follows that emotional development is intimately related to conceptual development and to the acquisition of language.

A brief digression might be useful at this point, in order to further illustrate the distinction between the learning of specific responses and the acquisition of rules. Much recent research on the development of aggression (and, by implication, of anger) has focused on the role of television as a socializing agent, and in particular on the tendency of children to imitate the aggressive acts they see portrayed. Spokesmen for the broadcast industry point out by way of rebuttal that the perpetrators of unjustified violence are usually punished. Even if the punishment is itself highly aggressive, the message, presumably, is that aggression does not pay. In terms of content, it might also be noted, contemporary television shows are not more violent than the myths, fairy tales, and morality plays of earlier generations.

In the above dispute, the representatives of the broadcast industry may be correct in principle but wrong in fact. Certainly there is an important difference between a gratuitous act of violence in the pursuit of selfish ends and a superficially similar act committed in the pursuit of some prosocial or altruistic goal (e.g., in connection with the prevention of a crime). Critics of television sometimes ignore this distinction, confusing the medium with the message. This, however, should be little comfort to the broadcast industry, for evidence suggests that children may be subject to the same confusion (Liebert & Poulos, 1976). Young children, especially, may not be able to follow the "moral" of a fast-paced television program; the primary lesson that may be learned is that aggression is an acceptable or standard way or solving disputes. In this respect, television cannot be compared with fairy tales and other "violent" childrens' stories. The latter are typically read to children, and the comprehension of the child can be monitored as the story progresses.

The above considerations raise a further question: By what means are the rules of anger conveyed to young children? Television models are one way, but probably a minor way, even in our own society. To address this question in its most general form, we must return for a moment to our earlier discussion of natural categories. It will be recalled that some members of a category are more *prototypic* than others, that is, they are better exemplars of the rules that help consitute the category. Research has demonstrated that prototypic exemplars are learned more readily and at an earlier age than are other members of a category (for a review, see Mervis & Rosch, 1981). Expanding upon this notion, we may say that emotional prototypes are embedded in "paradigm scenarios" through which the child is introduced to and learns the attributes and rules that determine the various emotional categories.

The phrase *paradigm scenario* is borrowed from de Sousa (1980), who also used it in connection with emotional development. It is a particularly apt phrase from a social-constructivist point of view. The concept of a scenario highlights the role properties of emotional syndromes. But even more important is that the concept of a paradigm—made familiar to psychologists through the work of Kuhn (1970) in the philosophy of science—emphasizes not only the prototypicality of the event, but also its importance for the acquisition of new ways of thinking and behaving.

A brief review of Kuhn's analysis of scientific paradigms may be useful at this point. Accroding to Kuhn (1970), a scientific paradigm consists of a limited set of concrete achievements, for example, as presented in standard textbooks and laboratory exercises. By studying these paradigm cases and working out closely related problems on their own, students of science acquire an intuitive grasp of what constitutes a problem, how that problem might be attacked, and the kind of outcome that might be accepted as a solution to the problem. In short, by working through paradigm cases, preferably under the tutelage of a seasoned investigator, the novice scientist is socialized into the ways of a discipline.

Similar considerations apply to emotional development; through paradigm scenarios the child is socialized into the emotional life of his or her culture. A paradigm scenario may be an event in the life of the child (e.g., punishment for some transgression, a death in the family, receipt of a highly prized gift). But scenarios can also be experienced vicariously, for example, through stories told at the dinner table or read in books. In any case, under the tutelage of parents and other role models, and through practice (children play at being angry and sad, just as they play at being doctors and teachers), the child learns the rules that help constitute various emotional syndromes. The hallmark of a well-socialized child is not only that his behavior conforms to the appropriate rules; even more important is that his feelings also conform.

Anger Gone Awry

Throughout this volume the positive aspects of anger have been emphasized. This is for two reasons. First, one of the orienting assumptions behind a constructivist view is that emotional syndromes are maintained within the social system because they serve a function. But whatever the heuristic value of this assumption, it cannot be accepted on a priori grounds alone. In Chapter 3, for example, we noted how syndromes such as running amok and envy may be socially constituted, but only as by-products of other social processes. That does not appear to be the case with respect to anger, which brings me to the second reason for emphasizing the positive aspects of this emotion. The data suggest that anger does, in fact, serve a function. For example, as we saw in Chapter 10, even targets agree that the typical episode of anger is more often beneficial than harmful; and on a broader social level, anger is often encouraged by groups seeking to uphold or secure their rights (cf. the feminist argument discussed in Chapter 13).

Still, whatever good anger may serve, it does so at considerable cost, both individually and socially. Seneca overstated the case when he called this "the most hideous and frenzied of all the emotions." However, it would be an even greater mistake to gloss over the untold acts of meanness, cruelty, and violence that have been committed in the name of anger. In the present section, therefore, we will consider briefly some of the ways in which anger may go awry. Nonnormative or abnormal angry reactions can occur for any of three broad classes of reasons: (a) inadequate socialization; (b) the influence of extraneous variables, and (c) unmanageable stress.

Inadequate Socialization

Earlier in this chapter we distinguished between two kinds of rules, constitutive and regulative. There are two corresponding ways in which socialization can be inadequate, and the result is a person who is either "neurotic" or "delinquent" with respect to anger.

Constitutive abnormalities. A person who has not acquired the constitutive rules of anger will show behaviors that can best be described as neurotic. Consider the following observations by Adler (1964):

> In the investigation of a neurotic style of life we must always suspect an oppenent, and note who suffers most because of the patient's condition. Usually this is a member of the family, and sometimes a person of the other sex, though there are cases in which the illness is an attack upon society as a whole. There is always this element of concealed accusation in neurosis, the patient feeling as though he were deprived of his *right*—i.e., of the center of attention—and wanting to fix the responsibility and balme upon someone. By such hidden vengeance and accusation, by excluding social activity whilst fighting against persons and rules, the problem-child and the neurotic find some relief from their dissatisfaction. (p. 81)

The person who exhibits the above pattern of behavior might be described as angry, *but only in a very extended sense.* Such a person believes that his rights are being violated, places blame on someone else, and seeks vengeance. The general cultural directive for anger is thus fulfilled. However, nearly every constitutive rule that helps instantiate this prescription is misconstrued. The "right" of the person that is violated (being the center of attention) is no right in an ordinary sense; the blame for the presumed violation is displaced on an inappropriate target (perhaps a spouse, or someone else in a close relationship); and vengeance is exacted in an idiosyncratic and devious way (the neurotic symptoms).

As we have noted, not all the attributes of anger are equally prototypic. The greatest disturbances appear when the norms that constitute prototypic attributes are internalized imporperly, so that the object of anger is egregiously misconstrued; inappropriate responses are made (either the anger is expressed too violently, or is not expressed at all); or the passionate element is overemphasized (the person acts in a hysterical fashion, whether violent or not, and refuses to accept any responsibility for his behavior while angry).

Regulative abnormalities. Inappropriate behavior, expecially of a violent nature, may also result from a failure of an individual to internalize appropriate regulative rules. Of course, what is considered "appropriate" in this sense depends on the group making the valuation, namely, the dominant culture. Subgroups within the culture, while sharing many of the norms and values that help constitute anger, may nevertheless regulate their behavior differently, forming what Wolfgang and Ferracuti (1967) have called a subculture of violence. Within this subculture behavior is regulated by rules that do not discourage, and often condone, a violent response to acknowledged cues.

Wolfgang and Ferracuti (1967) take as exemplars of the subculture of violence such groups as the *vendetta barbaricina* in Sardinia and the *mafioso* in Sicily. However, their general thesis—that much violence is regulated by subcultural norms and values—can be readily extended to less organized groups, particularly inner-city gangs in impoverished neighborhoods. To illustrate this point, Wolfgang (1979) cites the following statistics: Of nearly 10,000 boys born in Philadelphia in 1945, about 35% had at least one contact with the police for delinquent behavior by the age of 18. However, 52% of all delinquencies, and an even higher percentage of violent crime, were comitted by a relatively small number of chronic offenders (6.3% of the entire birth cohort). These chronic or hard-core delinquents epitomize what Wolfgang considers to be the subculture of violence as it is represented among the youth in contemporary American cities.

Many of the violent crimes (e.g., robberies and rapes) committed by the chronic offenders in Wolfgang's sample had nothing to do with anger. However, the statistics do illustrate how violence has become part of the life-style for this group, an accepted way of solving interpersonal problems. Moreover, even clearly criminal acts committed by members of this subculture are sometimes "excused" by well-intentioned (if not well-guided) critics as manifestations of anger (e.g., against society). As discussed in Chapter 6, anger is often used as a post hoc rationalization for almost any kind of violence, regardless of the actual instigation or aim.

Before leaving this topic, we should perhaps reiterate that the distinction between constitutive and regulative norms is relative and not absolute. Most constitutive norms help to regulate behavior; and conversely, most regulative rules are to some degree constitutive. It follows that the distinction between neurotic and delinquent behavior is also relative. Nevertheless, it is important to distinguish between these two ways in which anger can go awry through improper socialization. Depending on where along the continuum the problem lies, the experiences of the individuals may differ greatly, and so too must any attempt at intervention.

Extraneous Causal Variables

A second general way in which anger may go awry has little to do with inadequate socialization; it has to do, rather, with the influence of extraneous variables of the types discussed in Chapter 6, for example, miscellaneous frustrations, uninterpreted physiological arousal, aggressive cues in the situation, audience effects, and ulterior motives on the part of the individual. (To the extent that ulterior motives become habitual and distort the objectives of anger, this last factor could also be counted as an instance of inadequate socialization). We might also include within the category of extraneous varibles some of the physiological abnormalities—hormonal imbalance, brain lesions—discussed in Chapter 2.

Consider the following hypothetical case. A man is frustrated at work because he cannot complete a project as anticipated, due to an unavoidable delay in securing needed material. While driving home from work in heavy traffic, he is involved in a near accident. Although outwardly calm by the time he arrives home, he retains a residue of physiological arousal. The man has promised to take his son to a school function that evening, and would very much like to get out of it. He goes to his son's room, where the boy is playing a war game, with a variety of toy weapons lying around the room. The man becomes quite angry at his son, ostensibly because the boy has not done certain chores; and as punishment he refuses the boy permission to leave the house that evening.

If asked why he was angry, the man in this anecdote could correctly reply that he was angry at his son for failing to do household chores as requested. But obviously the anger was overdetermined. In view of the antecedent and concurrent conditions, it is likely that the man would have found a reason to become angry at his son even if all the chores had been performed.

Incidents such as the above are commonplace. Fortunately, most are also trivial. But it is easy to see how the concatenation of extraneous variables can so lower the threshold for anger that even a minor instigation can trigger a violent outburst. Undoubtedly, many episodes of child abuse, spouse beating, and even attacks on strangers can be attributed to the effects of extraneous variables. Indeed, in view of the ubiquity of the frustrations and so forth that one encounters in everyday affairs, it is somewhat surprising that aggression is not more common than it is. In this respect, it should be noted that the norms of anger serve to restrain as well as to encourage aggressive acts. That is, an attack—if it is to count as anger—must be in response to an *adequate* provocation, and it should not exceed the provocation in intensity. Extraneous causal variables are most likely to lead to violence among persons who have also experienced inadequate socialization, that is, who are either neurotic or delinquent in the senses discussed earlier.

Unmanageable Stress

The kinds of extraneous causal variables discussed above are, by themselves, commonplace and relatively benign. Not all variables are so innocuous. Psychiatric and legal files are replete with cases of persons who, after being subjected to severe trauma or psychological stress, have reacted in a violent rage. These are instances in which anger—if the reaction can still be called by that name—is truly a "short madness."

The stressfulness of a situation depends on two sets of factors—the nature of the threat and the resources of the individual to cope with the threat. Since it is a rather unusual occurrence for a situation to be so stressful (objectively speaking) as to occasion a violent outburst in a normal individual, let us consider briefly some of the ways in which coping resources may be inadequate. Two of the most common sources of an inability to cope are low intelligence and a lack of social (especially verbal) skills. A third source is less obvious and, from a psychological point of view, more interesting.

Megargee (1966) has proposed that persons who engage in assaultive behavior can be divided into at least two distinct personality types, the undercontrolled and the overcontrolled. The undercontrolled type has a minimum of internal inhibitions against aggression. When provoked, such an individual may cope by becoming verbally or physically aggressive, but within limits. In many ways, the undercontrolled individual is like the person who has been inadequatley socialized with respect to the regulative rules of anger, as discussed above. By contrast, the overcontrolled type of individual is characterized by strong internal inhibitions against aggression. If such an individual experiences sufficient stress, usually from an ongoing frustration or provocation that seems inescapable, the inhibitions against aggression may eventually be overwhelmed and a violent outburst may ensue.

In a test of the above (undercontrolled/overcontrolled) typology, Megargee (1966) compared a group of juveniles arrested for extremely violent acts (homicides, assaults with a deadly weapon, brutal beatings) with a group of more moderately aggressive offenders, and with several groups of juveniles detained either for non-violent offenses against property or for unruliness. In comparsion with the other groups, the boys who committed extremely violent acts were more likely to be first offenders, to have had more stable educational histories, to be more responsible and achievement oriented, and to be less aggressive generally. Similar findings have been reported by Blackburn (1968, 1971), who found extremely assaultive psychiatric offenders to be more controlled, introverted, conforming, and less hostile than moderatively assaultive offenders.

In defining anger as a conflictive emotion, we called attention to the competing demands placed on the individual both to refrain from aggressive acts and yet to defend one's rights. The overcontrolled individual has internalized both sets of norms in a rigid and uncompromising fashion. As a result, anger—which is itself a way of coping—cannot be expressed in a moderated and adaptive fashion. Rather, the individual exhibits an outward veneer of calm and conformity until the stress of provocation overwhelms the prohibitions against aggression, and vengeance is wreaked in a cataclysm of violence.

Concluding Observations

I have argued (a) that anger is a social construction, and (b) that anger often goes awry, causing great misery and misfortune. It would seem to follow from the first of these propositions that anger *could* be eliminated, and from the second that perhaps anger *should* be eliminated. But would it be possible and/or desirable to eliminate anger?

As we have seen, anger has been a central feature of Western civilization for over 2,500 years—from the time of Plato and Aristotle, and undoubtedly much earlier. Moreover, if the concept of anger is interpreted broadly enough (i.e., in a generic rather than a specific sense), then an emotional syndrome akin to anger probably exists in all human societies. This suggests that it would be very difficult, if not impossible, to eliminate anger completely.

There are groups in which anger, even in its most generic sense, appears to be rare. For example, Briggs (1970) reports that among the Utku, a small group of Canadian Eskimos, "threre are no situations that justify *ningaq* [angry] feelings or behavior, no people, Utku or others, toward whom it is permissible to express them" (p. 333). *Ningaq,* which can only be loosely translated as anger, refers to aggressive tendencies. The term is seldom used in the first person (i.e., to refer to one's own thoughts and feelings), but primarily in reference to others. Even angry thoughts are believed by the Utku to have the power to harm, and are strongly discouraged. When frustrated by events, including the actions of others, an Utku is more likely to experience amusement (*tiphi*) or—less appropriately—depression (*hujuujaq*) than anger.

At first, the way the Utku have institutionalized responses to frustration and provocation might seem superior to the way anger has become institutionalized in our own society. And in some respects, their way is superior. However, several qualifications should be kept in mind. The number of Utkus varies from about 20 to 35 individuals, and they are the sole inhabitants of an area of about 35,000 square miles. Considering the smallness of the group and the harshness of the environment, it is imperative that social conflict be kept at a minimum. Anything resembling anger, at least in its more aggressive aspects, is therefore discouraged; but so too is any deviation from established custom that might provoke anger. One might also ask, when a provocation does occur, is amusement and/or depression a more appropriate response than anger? In some contexts, perhaps, but surely not in all—at least not in our own society, and presumably not even among the Utku.

In sum, it is easy to condemn anger because of its excesses. It is also easy to praise anger, to "let it all hang out" in the name of some self-righteous adventure. It is much more difficult to maintain a balanced perspective, to understand anger in both its positive and negative aspects, and to behave accordingly. In this respect, I can think of no better way to conclude an analysis of anger than with the words of Aristotle:

> Anyone can get angry—that is easy;. . .but to do this to the right person, to the right extent, at the right time, with the right motive, and in the right way, that is not for everyone nor is it easy; wherefore goodness is both rare and laudable and noble (*Nicomachean Ethics*, 1109a25).

Questionnaire A, Used in Studies I and III for the Description of the Subject's Own Experience of Anger

A. Try to recall the number of times you became annoyed and/or angry during the past week. Also think of the differences between the situations in which you became annoyed as opposed to those in which you became angry. (For example, you may be greatly annoyed by an aching tooth, but not necessarily angry; and, of course, you may become annoyed at another person without being angry.) In addition to the more intense experiences of annoyance and anger, be sure to include the minor everyday incidents—perhaps when a driver cut in front of you on the highway, the children did not pick up their room, the car stalled at an intersection, or the like.

1. How often during the last week did you become annoyed, irritated, or aggravated (but *not* angry)?

    _____ not at all during the week
    _____ 1 to 2 times during the week
    _____ 3 to 5 times during the week
    _____ about 1 time each day
    _____ about 2 times each day
    _____ about 3 times each day
    _____ about 4 to 5 times each day
    _____ about 6 to 10 times each day
    _____ more than 10 times each day

2. Briefly describe the *most* annoying of the above experiences. (If you did not become annoyed at all during the past week, describe the most recent incident that you can remember.)

    _____

    _____

    _____

    _____

3. How intense was your annoyance in the incident described above? (Circle appropriate number)

$\underline{1\ :\ 2\ :\ 3\ :\ 4\ :\ 5\ :\ 6\ :\ 7\ :\ 8\ :\ 9\ :\ 10}$

very   very intense;
mild   as annoyed as most
                                                               people ever become

4. How often during the last week did you become angry?

_____ not at all during the week
_____ 1 to 2 times during the week
_____ 3 to 5 times during the week
_____ about 2 times each day
_____ about 3 times each day
_____ about 4 to 5 times each day
_____ about 6 to 10 times each day
_____ more than 10 times each day

5. Briefly describe the most angry of these experiences (even if that experience now seems rather unimportant, trivial, or even silly). Or, if you did not become angry at all during the week, describe the most recent incident that you can remember.

_____

_____

_____

_____

6. How intense was your anger in the incident described above?

$\underline{1\ :\ 2\ :\ 3\ :\ 4\ :\ 5\ :\ 6\ :\ 7\ :\ 8\ :\ 9\ :\ 10}$

very   very intense;
mild   as angry as most
                                                               people ever become

7. What features do you think were present in the anger incident (#5) that were not present in the annoying incident (#2);

_____

_____

_____

_____

PLEASE NOTE: THE REMAINDER OF THIS QUESTIONNAIRE CONCERNS *ONLY* THE EXPERIENCE OF ANGER WHICH YOU DESCRIBED IN RESPONSE TO QUESTION 5: THAT IS, THE MOST INTENSE EXPERIENCE DURING THE PAST WEEK (OR THE MOST RECENT EX-

PERIENCE BEFORE THAT). BEFORE PROCEEDING FURTHER, THINK CAREFULLY ABOUT THAT EXPERIENCE AND TRY TO RE-LIVE IT AS IT HAPPENED AT THE TIME.

B. Sometimes persons report being "overwhelmed" or "overcome" by anger.

In the present instance:

8. How able were you to control the outward expression of your anger; that is, what you did and said?

1 : 2 : 3 : 4 : 5 : 6 : 7 : 8 : 9 : 10

I was in complete control of my actions

I was completely overcome; I couldn't help acting the way I did

9. How able were you to control the inward experience of your anger; that is, what you thought and felt?

1 : 2 : 3 : 4 : 5 : 6 : 7 : 8 : 9 : 10

I was in complete control of my thoughts and feelings

I was completely overcome; I couldn't help thinking and feeling the way I did

C. The following questions concern the object or target of your anger; that is, the person or thing at which you became angry.

10. The primary object of your anger was: (If there was more than one object, indicate the most important with the number "1", the next most important with the number "2", etc.)

_____ an adult human
_____ a child
_____ an animal
_____ an inanimate object or thing
_____ an informal group (e.g., a crowd, social gathering, gang of teenagers, etc.)
_____ a specific institution (e.g., governmental or state agency, or business organization)
_____ society or "things in general"
_____ other (Specify): _____

11. If one of the objects of your anger was a person, was that person male _____ or female _____?

12. Was he or she: (Check only 1)

_____ a loved one
_____ someone you know well and like
_____ someone you know well and dislike

_____ an acquaintance (anyone with whom you occasionally interact, but whom you do not know well, e.g., business colleague, boss, neighbor, pupil, etc.)

_____ a stranger

13. Was he or she: (Check only 1)

_____ someone who had authority over you
(e.g., employer, parent, teacher, policeman, etc.)

_____ someone over whom you had authority
(e.g., employee, child, student, etc.)

_____ an equal or peer
(e.g., colleague, neighbor, spouse, room-mate, etc.)

14. In your own words, briefly describe the object or target of your anger, adding any further information that might be relevant to the experience.

_____

_____

_____

D. Often when we become angry, we make an immediate judgment about the incident or event that made us angry: Was it accidental or voluntary? Was it justified or unjustified? and so forth. In answering the following questions, think carefully about what you thought *at the time of your anger*, even though your opinions may since have changed.

15. Which of the following categories best describes the incident which angered you?

(Read through *all* the items and then select the *one* that is most appropriate. As the examples illustrate, a wide variety of incidents may fit into any category.)

_____ Potentially avoidable accident or event: the result of negligence, carelessness, lack of foresight.

(examples: A stranger, not looking where he was going, backed into your car; A friend away on a long trip didn't write because he/she had forgotten your address; Your spouse forgot to let the dog out overnight and the dog chewed the furniture.)

_____ Unavoidable accident or event: it could not have been foreseen or was beyond anyone's control.

(examples: One of the children became ill just as you were about to leave on vacation; The tube of your television set burned out while you were watching a favorite program; A heavy branch fell on your new car during a storm.)

_____ Voluntary and justified: the instigator knew what he was doing and had a right to do it.

(examples: A policeman gave you a ticket when you were going 50 m.p.h. in a 35 m.p.h. zone; Your boss corrected you for doing a sloppy job when you had been careless and haphazard about your work.)

_____ Voluntary and unjustified: the instigator knew what he was doing, but he had no right to do it.

(examples: A policeman gave you a ticket for going through a yellow light even though you could not have stopped on time; Your child ate a pan of brownies right before dinner; Your spouse refused to help you with the chores.)

Please describe in your own words the relevant aspects of the incident, indicating why it fits into the category which you checked. (If it does not fit into any, explain.)

_____

_____

_____

16. At the time of your anger, did you believe that the event or action that made you angry was directed specifically at you or at another?

at you _____ at another _____ at both you and others _____ at no one _____

17. At the time, did you believe that the object of your anger (if a person) was intending to do harm or damage?

No _____ Yes _____ Not applicable _____

[*Note*.—Responses to items 16 and 17 proved to be ambiguous, and hence they were not analyzed.]

E.   The following is a list of factors which may have been involved in the event which angered you. Read the entire list. Then, for each item, circle the number 0, +1, or +2 in the right-hand column according to the following scale:

$$0 = \text{not at all involved in what angered you}$$
$$+1 = \text{somewhat involved in what angered you}$$
$$+2 = \text{very much involved in what angered you}$$

Did the incident in any way involve	not at all	some-what	very much
18. Possible or actual physical injury and/or pain?	0	+1	+2
(examples: you tripped, fell, or otherwise hurt yourself; your child was injured at school; a car just missed you)			
19. Possible or actual property damage?	0	+1	+2
(examples: accidental or deliberate breakage; lost			

	not at all	some- what	very much

or stolen property; equipment malfunction;
vandalism)

20. Frustration or the interruption of some ongoing or
    planned activity?   0   +1   +2

    (examples: interference with relaxation, work, sleep,
    etc.; failure to receive an expected benefit; being
    hindered by rules and regulations)

21. An event, action, or attitude which resulted in a loss
    of personal pride, self-esteem, or sense of personal
    worth?   0   +1   +2

    (examples: correction or criticism of you, your family,
    your religion, your political beliefs, etc.; rejection by
    someone you like or respect? an insult or slight)

22. Violation of socially accepted ways of behaving or
    widely shared rules of conduct?   0   +1   +2

    (examples: criminal acts; civil disobedience; breaches
    of etiquette, such as bad manners or rudeness; unfair,
    irrational, or unethical behavior)

23. Violation of expectations and wishes which are
    important to you but which may not be widely
    shared by others?   0   +1   +2

    (examples: someone disregards one of your pet
    likes or dislikes; your spouse or child does not act
    in line with your expectations; you don't like a
    neighbor's life-style)

24. In your own words, briefly describe the most important factor involved in
    what made you angry. (Your description should help clarify your responses to
    the above items.)

    _____

    _____

    _____

F. The general context of your anger.

25. How would you describe your mood just prior to the incident?

    good _____   bad _____   other (specify) _____

26. Everything considered, do you think that this incident was very typical _____,

somewhat typical ____, or not at all typical ____, of what generally makes *you* angry? (Check one)

27. Everything considered, do you think that this incident was very typical ____, somewhat typical ____, or not at all typical ____, of what makes *people in general* angry? (Check one)

28. Do you think that your anger was less intense than ____, proportional to ____, or more intense than ____, what the incident called for? (Check one)

29. How long did your anger last when it first occurred? (Check the most appropriate time interval)

_____ less than 5 minutes
_____ 5-10 minutes
_____ less than ½ hour
_____ less than 1 hour
_____ 1-2 hours
_____ ½ day
_____ 1 day
_____ more than 1 day

30. Do you still get angry when you think about the incident? No ____ Yes ____

31. How many days ago did the incident occur? _____

G. The following are a number of things you may have done, or felt like doing, when you became angry. For each item, circle the number 0, +1, or +2 in the column labeled "Actually did", and also in the column labeled "Felt like doing", according to the following scale:

$$0 = \text{not at all involved in your anger}$$
$$+1 = \text{somewhat involved in your anger}$$
$$+2 = \text{very much involved in your anger}$$

The following examples of "verbal or symbolic aggression" illustrate how you might mark these scales.

	Actually did	Felt like doing

Example 1

You didn't say anything, although you felt like making a very nasty remark.   ⓪ +1 +2   0 +1 ⊕2

Example 2

You said something very nasty, just as you felt like doing.   0 +1 ⊕2   0 +1 ⊕2

Example 3

You impulsively said something very nasty, although you felt like making a more mild remark.   0 +1 ⊕2   0 ⊕1 +2

Before making your ratings, read through all the items (#32-42) on the list. Then, for *each* item, circle the appropriate numbers in the "Actually did" column *and* in the "Felt like doing" column.

	Actually did			Felt like doing		
32. Physical aggression or punishment directed at the offender (examples: hitting, spanking, shoving)	0	+1	+2	0	+1	+2
33. Denial or removal of some benefit customarily enjoyed by the offender (examples: withdrawing the children's allowance; refusing to go out with the offender; not speaking; withdrawing affection)	0	+1	+2	0	+1	+2
34. Engaging in activities opposite to the expression of anger (examples: being extra friendly to the instigator; "turning the other cheek"; joking with the instigator)	0	+1	+2	0	+1	+2
35. Verbal or symbolic aggression or punishment directed at the offender (examples: yelling, scolding, making a nasty remark; shaking your fist or making an obscene gesture; slamming a door in the offender's face)	0	+1	+2	0	+1	+2
36. Talking the incident over with the offender *without* exhibiting hostility (examples: calmly explaining the reasons for your anger)	0	+1	+2	0	+1	+2
37. Aggression, harm, or damage to someone or something important to the offender (examples: destroying an object liked by the offender; refusing to cooperate on a joint project; threatening harm to yourself or someone else in order to get back at the offender)	0	+1	+2	0	+1	+2
38. Telling a third party in order to get back at the offender, or to have the offender punished (examples: informing the boss about a co-worker who has been goofing off; telling a mutual friend about the shortcomings of the offender; writing an anonymous letter to the editor)	0	+1	+2	0	+1	+2
39. Engaging in calming activities (examples: going for a walk; taking a shower; watching television)	0	+1	+2	0	+1	+2

	Actually did	Felt like doing

40. Taking your anger out on some *person* other than the offender; that is, aggression (physical, verbal, or otherwise) toward an individual who was *not* involved in the instigation (examples: taking it out on your spouse when you're really angry at your boss; snapping at the grocery clerk when you just had an argument with a friend)   0   +1   +2   0   +1   +2

41. Taking your anger out on, or attacking, some *non-human object or thing* not related to the instigation (examples: yelling at the dog when you carelessly hit your finger with a hammer; kicking the curb when your car won't start)   0   +1   +2   0   +1   +2

42. Talking the incident over with a neutral, uninvolved third party, with no intent to harm the offender or make him/her look bad (examples: discussing the incident with a trustworthy friend; talking to your clergyman about the incident)   0   +1   +2   0   +1   +2

43. In your own words, briefly describe the most important things you actually did while angry. (Your description should help clarify your responses in the first column of the preceding list.)

_____

_____

_____

44. In your own words, also describe what you most felt like doing. (Your description should help clarify your responses in the second column of the preceding list.)

_____

_____

_____

45. Considering what you actually did, how would you describe your behavior while angry? (Circle the appropriate number)

Self-controlled;   Uncontrolled;
Deliberate   1 : 2 : 3 : 4 : 5 : 6 : 7 : 8 : 9 : 10   Impulsive

46. Considering what you felt like doing, how would you describe your thoughts and feelings while angry? (Circle the appropriate number)

Self-controlled: Uncontrolled;
Deliberate   1 : 2 : 3 : 4 : 5 : 6 : 7 : 8 : 9 : 10   Impulsive

H. During your anger, did you exhibit or experience any of the following expressive reactions and/or physiological symptoms? (Circle appropriate number)

		not at all	some- what	very much
47.	Flushing or rise in temperature	0	+1	+2
48.	Nervous laughter	0	+1	+2
49.	Crying	0	+1	+2
50.	Restlessness	0	+1	+2
51.	General tension	0	+1	+2
52.	Shaky, cracking voice	0	+1	+2
53.	Frowning	0	+1	+2
54.	Other (specify) _____	0	+1	+2

I. After becoming angry, we sometimes have "second thoughts" about the incident that angered us. For example, we may decide that the incident was actually laughable rather than enraging; that it was unimportant or unworthy of our attention; that the person who angered us didn't really mean any harm; and so forth. Check whichever of the following reinterpretations (if any) you may have made in the present incident.

_____   55. You reinterpreted the event humorously
               (e.g., thinking, "it really was funny")

_____   56. You decided the incident was less important than you originally thought
               (e.g., thinking, "it didn't really matter much")

_____   57. You minimized the importance of the person who made you angry
               (e.g., thinking, "I don't care what he/she says anyway")

_____   58. You reinterpreted the motives or guilt of the person who angered you
               (e.g., thinking "it wasn't really his/her fault," or "he/she was only trying to do what was best for me")

_____   59. You reinterpreted your own motives, guilt, or role in the incident
               (e.g., thinking, "I deserved it," or "it was partly my fault")

_____   60. You made some other reinterpretation (Please describe) _____
               _____
               _____

_____   61. You made *no* reinterpretations

J.   Sometimes when we become angry, we may simply want to get back to the person or thing that angered us. Often, however, additional motives are involved in our anger. For example, we may become angry at a child for running into the street in order to protect him from injury; or we may become angry in order to get someone to help us out with some work. Although such motives are quite common, *we typically are not fully aware of them at the time of our anger*. It may only be in looking back and thinking carefully about the incident that we may come to realize all that was involved in our anger.

Read through the following list of possible motives (items 62-72), and then, beginning with the first item (62), indicate by circling the appropriate number whether such a motive was involved in your anger. Be sure to mark *each* item, using the following scale:

$$0 = \text{not at all involved in your anger}$$
$$+1 = \text{somewhat involved in your anger}$$
$$+2 = \text{very much involved in your anger}$$

In becoming angry, did you wish:	not at all	some- what	very much
62. To get even for past "wrongs" by the instigator?	0	+1	+2

(examples: You became angry at a friend for being 10 minutes late when you really were upset because he/she had forgotten your birthday. The instigator had been bothering you for a long time and this was simply "the last straw".)

63. To get back at, or gain revenge on, the instigator for the present incident?	0	+1	+2

(examples: You simply wanted to get back at the instigator for what he/she/it did to you on *this* occasion. You wanted the instigator to feel the same way you felt.)

64. To get out of doing something for the instigator?	0	+1	+2

(examples: You had promised to help with some work, but no longer wanted to; therefore, you got angry over some minor incident and used your anger as an excuse for not helping. You got angry so that you wouldn't have to go out with the instigator.)

65. To get the instigator to do something for you?	0	+1	+2

(examples: You got angry, hoping that if a friend felt "guilty" or "intimidated", then he/she might agree to do something you wanted in order to make amends.)

66. To bring about a change in the behavior of the instigator primarily for his or her own good?	0	+1	+2

(examples: You got angry at a friend for dwadling,

	not at all	some- what	very much

knowing that he/she needed to finish some work.
You became angry at your child for running into the
street, in order to teach him/her not to do so.)

67. To bring about a change in the behavior of the insti-
    gator primarily for your own good?   0   +1   +2

    (examples: By getting angry at a relatively minor
    incident, you hoped the instigator would not bother
    you again in the future. Your spouse had a habit
    which you did not like and you wanted him/her to
    change.)

68. To break off a relationship with the instigator?   0   +1   +2

    (examples: You wished to end a friendship, and you
    therefore became angry in order to have an excuse
    for not seeing the person again.)

69. To strengthen a relationship with the instigator?   0   +1   +2

    (examples: You hoped to increase communication
    and end conflict. You wished to increase under-
    standing between yourself and the instigator.)

70. To assert your authority or independence, or to
    improve your image?   0   +1   +2

    (examples: You used your anger to increase your
    self-esteem or maintain prestige, to gain respect, or
    to support your opinions.)

71. To express your general dislike for the instigator?   0   +1   +2

    (examples: You simply did not care for the insti-
    gator, so you seized the opportunity to vent your
    feelings when he/she/it did something "wrong".)

72. To "let off steam" over miscellaneous frustrations
    of the day which had nothing to do with the pres-
    ent incident?   0   +1   +2

    (examples: You got angry over a relatively minor
    incident because you were upset from lots of little
    things that had gone wrong during the day.)

73. In your own words, briefly describe any motives or goals involved in your
    anger, even if you were not aware of such motives at the time. (Your descrip-

tion should help clarify your responses to the above items.)

_____

_____

_____

_____

K. The general context of your response.

74. Briefly describe any aspects of the situation which might have influenced how
    you expressed your anger, e.g., the social and physical surroundings at the time,
    the ability of the other person to retaliate, etc.

_____

_____

_____

_____

75. Everything considered, do you think that your responses in this instance were
    very typical _____, somewhat typical _____, or not at all typical _____ of how
    you generally respond when angry? (Check one)

76. Everything considered, do you think that your responses in this instance were
    very typical _____, somewhat typical _____, or not at all typical _____, of how
    other people generally respond when angry? (Check one)

L. How did the instigator (object or target) respond to your expression of anger?

77. _____   The instigator was an inanimate object and hence could not respond.

78. _____   The instigator did not know that you were angry.

79. _____   The instigator knew that you were angry and responded with:
                (Circle the appropriate number following each item)

		not at all	some-what	very much
a.	Indifference or lack of concern	0	+1	+2
b.	Hurt feelings	0	+1	+2
c.	Defiance	0	+1	+2
d.	Anger or hostility	0	+1	+2
e.	Jokes, frivolity, or silliness	0	+1	+2
f.	Apology or other sign of contrition	0	+1	+2
g.	Rejection	0	+1	+2
h.	Denial of responsibility	0	+1	+2

	not at all	some- what	very much
i. Surprise	0	+1	+2
j. Other (specify) _____	0	+1	+2

M. How did you feel about your own anger after your initial (first) response? (Circle the appropriate number following each item)

	not at all	some- what	very much
80. good, pleased, glad	0	+1	+2
81. irritable, hostile, aggravated	0	+1	+2
82. triumphant, confident, dominant	0	+1	+2
83. depressed, unhappy, gloomy	0	+1	+2
84. ashamed, embarrassed, guilty	0	+1	+2
85. relieved, calm, satisfied	0	+1	+2
86. anxious, jittery, nervous	0	+1	+2
87. Other (specify) _____	0	+1	+2

N. Overall evaluation of your anger.

88. Everything considered (the nature of the instigation, your responses to it, the consequences of your anger, etc.), do you believe that this episode of anger was adaptive (beneficial) _____ or maladaptive (harmful) _____ ?

Please explain: _____

_____

_____

_____

*   *   *

Questionnaire B, Used in Study II for the Description of the Subject's Experiences as the Target of Another Person's Anger

A. Think about some recent incidents of annoyance and anger. Also think of the differences between the situations which lead to annoyance as opposed to those which lead to anger. (For example, a person may become greatly annoyed by an aching tooth, but not necessarily angry; and, of course, one may become annoyed at another person without being angry.) In addition to the more intense incidents of annoyance and anger, be sure to think about the minor everyday incidents—perhaps when a driver cut in front of someone on the highway, the children did not pick up their room, a car stalled at an intersection, or the like.

* * * *

Having thought about the differences between annoyance and anger in a general way, now try to recall the number of times you believe someone became annoyed and/or angry *at you* during the *past week*. The persons may not have expressed their annoyance or anger; that is not important. *We are interested only in your beliefs or impressions at the time of the incidents.*

1. How often during the last week did you feel that someone became annoyed, irritated, or aggravated at you (but *not* angry)?

    _____ not at all during the week
    _____ 1 to 2 times during the week
    _____ 3 to 5 times during the week
    _____ about 1 time each day
    _____ about 2 times each day
    _____ about 3 times each day
    _____ about 4 to 5 times each day
    _____ about 6 to 10 times each day
    _____ more than 10 times each day

2. Briefly describe the incident which you believed at the time involved the most annoyance on the part of another person. (If you felt that no one became annoyed with you, then describe the *most recent* incident you can remember.)

    _____

    _____

_____

_____

3. How intense was that person's annoyance in the incident described above? (Circle appropriate number)

<u>1 : 2 : 3 : 4 : 5 : 6 : 7 : 8 : 9 : 10</u>
very   very intense; as annoyed
mild   as most people ever become

4. How often during the last week did you feel that someone became angry at you?

_____ not at all during the week
_____ 1 to 2 times during the week
_____ 3 to 5 times during the week
_____ about 1 time each day
_____ about 2 times each day
_____ about 3 times each day
_____ about 4 to 5 times each day
_____ about 6 to 10 times each day
_____ more than 10 times each day

5. Briefly describe the incident which you believe involved the most anger on the part of another person. That is, pick the incident during the last week in which, at the time it occurred, you felt the most anger was being directed at you, even though that incident may now seem rather unimportant, trivial, or even silly. (If you felt that no one became angry at you within the last week, describe the *most recent* incident you can remember, no matter how mild that incident was.)

_____

_____

_____

_____

6. How intense was the person's anger in the incident described above? (Circle appropriate number)

<u>1 : 2 : 3 : 4 : 5 : 6 : 7 : 8 : 9 : 10</u>
very   very intense; as angry as
mild   most people ever become

7. What features do you think were present in the anger incident (#5) that were not present in the annoying incident (#2)?

_____

_____

_____

_____

PLEASE NOTE: THE REMAINDER OF THIS QUESTIONNAIRE CON-
CERNS ONLY THE INCIDENT OF ANGER WHICH YOU DESCRIBED
IN RESPONSE TO QUESTION #5; THAT IS, THE MOST INTENSE
INCIDENT DURING THE PAST WEEK (OR THE MOST RECENT EX-
PERIENCE BEFORE THAT). BEFORE PROCEEDING FURTHER,
THINK CAREFULLY ABOUT THAT INCIDENT AND TRY TO RE-LIVE
IT AS IT HAPPENED AT THE TIME.

B. The following questions concern the person whom you felt was angry at you.

8. Was the person male _____ or female _____ ?

9. Was he or she: (check only 1)

_____ a loved one
_____ someone you know well and like
_____ someone you know well and dislike
_____ an acquaintance (anyone with whom you occasionally interact, but whom you do not know well, e.g., business colleague, boss, neighbor, pupil, etc.)
_____ a stranger

10. Was he or she: (check only 1)

_____ someone who had authority over you
(e.g., employer, parent, teacher, policeman, etc.)
_____ someone over whom you had authority
(e.g., employee, child, student, etc.)
_____ an equal or peer
(e.g., colleague, neighbor, spouse, room-mate, etc.)

11. In your own words, briefly describe the person who became angry at you, adding any further information that might be relevant to the incident.

_____

_____

_____

_____

12. At the time of the person's anger, did you believe that the event or action that made the person angry was the result of: (Check the most important)

_____ something you yourself had done
_____ something someone associated with you had done
(i.e., your child, best friend, room-mate, etc.)
_____ something that happened which had nothing to do with you

13. Did you realize beforehand that what was happening would make the person angry?

_____ yes _____ no

14. Briefly describe any other aspects of the situation that may have contributed to this person's anger, e.g., illness, other people present, that person's mood at the time, what that person was doing at the time, and the like.

_____

_____

_____

_____

C.   In answering the following questions, think carefully about the incident that made the person become angry at you. An accident may have happened for which the angry person held you responsible, or you may have justifiably criticized the person for something he had done wrong, or a policeman may have given him a ticket and he took it out on you. Base your answers on your view of the precipitating incident *at the time it occurred*, even though your opinions may since have changed.

15. Which of the following categories best describes the incident which angered the other person?

(Read through *all* the items and then select the *one* that is most appropriate. As the examples illustrate, a wide variety of incidents may fit into any category.)

   a. _____ Potentially avoidable accident or event: the result of negligence, carelessness, lack of foresight.

   (examples: When not looking, you, or someone else, had backed into the angry person's car; when away on a long trip, you didn't write because you had forgotten the person's address; someone forgot to let the dog out overnight and the dog chewed the slippers of the person who became angry.)

   b. _____ Unavoidable accident or event: it could not have been foreseen, or was beyond anyone's control.

   (examples: The person became angry when you had to cancel a date because of illness; the tube of the television set burned out while the person was watching a favorite program, and he became angry at you.)

   c. _____ Voluntary and justified: you, or whoever instigated (caused) the anger, knew what you were doing and had a right to do it.

   (examples: You were supervising a task and rightly corrected the person who became angry for doing a sloppy job; a policeman gave the person a ticket for going 50 m.p.h. in a 35 m.p.h. zone, and he/she became angry at you.)

   d. _____ Voluntary and unjustified: You, or whoever instigated (caused) the anger, knew what you were doing but had no right to do it.

(examples: You had refused to do your share on a joint project, and the person became angry; your child had deliberately thrown a stone at the angry person's dog; you had eaten the last piece of cheesecake that the angry person had been saving for later.)

Please describe in your own words the relevant aspects of the incident, indicating why it fits into the category you checked. (If it does not fit into any category, explain.)

_____

_____

_____

D. The following is a list of factors which may have been involved in the event which angered the person. Read the entire list. Then, for each item, circle the number 0, +1, or +2 in the right-hand column according to the following scale:

$$0 = \text{not at all involved in what angered the person}$$
$$+1 = \text{somewhat involved in what angered the person}$$
$$+2 = \text{very much involved in what angered the person}$$

Did the incident in any way involve:	not at all	some-what	very much
16. Possible or actual physical injury and/or pain? (examples: the angry person had tripped, fallen, or otherwise hurt himself; his or her child had been injured at school; a car had just missed the person)	0	+1	+2
17. Possible or actual property damage? (examples: something belonging to the angry person had been accidentally or deliberately damaged, lost, stolen, or caused to malfunction)	0	+1	+2
18. Frustration or interruption of some ongoing or planned activity? (examples: the angry person's relaxation, work, or sleep had been interfered with; he/she had failed to receive an expected benefit; he/she had been hindered by rules and regulations)	0	+1	+2
19. An event, action, or attitude which resulted in a loss of personal pride, self-esteem, or sense of personal worth? (examples: the angry person had been corrected or criticized; his/her religion or beliefs had been questioned; he/she had been insulted, slighted, or rejected)	0	+1	+2

	not at all	some- what	very much
20. Violation of socially accepted ways of behaving or widely shared rules of conduct? (examples: the angry person had been the recipi- ent of, or had witnessed, bad manners, rudeness, irrational or unethical behavior, or unlawful actions)	0	+1	+2
21. Violation of expectations or wishes which were important to the person who became angry, but which may not be widely shared by others? (examples: one of the angry person's pet likes or dislikes had been disregarded; you or someone else had not acted in line with the angry person's expec- tations; he/she did not like your lifestyle)	0	+1	+2

22. In your own words, briefly describe the most important factors involved in what made the other person angry. (Your description should help clarify your responses to the above items.)

_____

_____

_____

E.   The general context of the other person's anger.

23. Everything considered, do you think that this incident was very typical ____, somewhat typical ____, or not at all typical ____ of what makes *people in general* angry? (Check one)

24. Do you think that the person's anger was less intense than ____, proportional to ____, or more intense than ____ the incident called for? (Check one)

25. How long did the other person's anger last when it first occurred? (Check the most appropriate time interval)

_____ less than 5 minutes
_____ 5-10 minutes
_____ less than ½ hour
_____ less than 1 hour
_____ 1-2 hours
_____ ½ day
_____ 1 day
_____ more than 1 day

26. How many days ago did the incident occur? _____

F. The following are a number of ways that people may act when they become angry. Read through all the items (27-37) carefully. Then, for *each* item, circle the appropriate number according to the following scale:

> 0 = not at all involved in the person's anger
> +1 = somewhat involved in the person's anger
> +2 = very much involved in the person's anger
> ? = don't know whether or not involved in the person's anger

Did the person:	not at all	some-what	very much	don't know
27. Physically aggress against or punish you? (examples: The angry person hit, spanked, or shoved you).	0	+1	+2	?
28. Deny or remove some benefit customarily enjoyed by you? (examples: The angry person refused to go with you; would not speak to you; withdrew affection).	0	+1	+2	?
29. Engage in activities opposite to the expression of anger? (examples: The angry person acted extra friendly to you; "turned the other cheek"; joked with you).	0	+1	+2	?
30. Verbally or symbolically aggress against or punish you? (examples: The angry person yelled, scolded, or made a nasty remark to you? shook his/her fist or made an obscene gesture; slammed a door in your face).	0	+1	+2	?
31. Talk the incident over with you *without* exhibiting hostility? (example: The angry person calmly explained the reasons for his/her anger).	0	+1	+2	?
32. Aggress against, harm, or damage someone or something important to you? (examples: The angry person destroyed one of your favorite objects; refused to cooperate on a joint project; threatened harm to him/herself in order to get back at you).	0	+1	+2	?
33. Tell a third party in order to get back at you, or have you punished? (examples: The angry person informed the boss that you had been goofing off; he/she told a mutual friend about your shortcomings).	0	+1	+2	?

	not at all	some- what	very much	don't know

34. Engage in calming activities? (examples: the angry   0   +1   +2   ?
    person went for a walk, took a shower, watched
    television).

35. Take his/her anger out on some *person* other than   0   +1   +2   ?
    you; that is, aggress against (physically, verbally,
    or otherwise) an individual *not* involved in the
    instigation? (examples: The angry person took
    his/her anger out on a spouse or coworker;
    snapped at the clerk when having an argument
    with you)

36. Take his/her anger out on some *non-human*   0   +1   +2   ?
    object or thing not related to the instigation?
    (examples: The angry person yelled at the dog
    while angry at you; kicked the chair while arguing
    with you).

37. Talk the incident over with a neutral, uninvolved   0   +1   +2   ?
    third party, with no intent to harm you or make
    you look bad? (examples: The angry person dis-
    cussed the incident with a trustworthy friend or
    counsellor).

38. In your own words, briefly describe the most important things the person did
    while angry. (Your description should help clarify your responses to the pre-
    ceding items.)

    _____

    _____

    _____

    _____

39. Considering what the person did, how would you describe his/her behavior
    while angry? (Circle the appropriate number.)

    self-controlled;   1 : 2 : 3 : 4 : 5 : 6 : 7 : 8 : 9 : 10   uncontrolled;
    deliberate   impulsive

G. Sometimes when a person becomes angry, he/she may simply want to get back
at us. Often, however, additional motives are involved in anger. For example, a parent may become angry at a child for running into the street in order to protect the
child from injury, or a friend may become angry at us in order to get us to help him
with some work. Although such motives are quite common, *the angry person typically is not fully aware of them at the time*. It may only be in looking back and

thinking carefully about the incident that we may come to realize all that was involved in an incident of anger.

Read through the following list of possible motives (items 40-50) and then, beginning with the first item (40), indicate by circling the appropriate number whether you believe such a motive was involved in the other person's anger. Be sure to mark *each* item, using the following scale:

$$0 = \text{not at all involved in the person's anger}$$
$$+1 = \text{somewhat involved in the person's anger}$$
$$+2 = \text{very much involved in the person's anger}$$
$$? = \text{don't know whether involved in the person's anger}$$

In becoming angry do you believe the person wished:	not at all	some-what	very much	don't know
40. To get even with you for past "wrongs?" (examples: The person became angry at you for being 10 minutes late when he/she was really upset because you had broken a promise. You had been bothering the person for a long time and this was simply "the last straw.")	0	+1	+2	?
41. To get back at you, or gain revenge for the present incident? (examples: The angry person simply wanted to get back at you for what you did on *this* occasion. The person wanted you to feel the same way he/she felt.)	0	+1	+2	?
42. To get out of doing something for you? (examples: The person had promised to help with some work, but he no longer wanted to; therefore, he got angry over some minor incident and used his anger as an excuse for not helping you. The person got angry so that he/she wouldn't have to go out with you.)	0	+1	+2	?
43. To get you to do something for him/her? (examples: The person got angry, hoping that if you felt "guilty" or "intimidated", then you might agree to do something in order to make amends.)	0	+1	+2	?
44. To bring about a change in your behavior primarily for your own good? (examples: The person got angry at you for dawdling, knowing that you needed to finish some work for your own benefit. The	0	+1	+2	?

	not at all	some- what	very much	don't know

person wanted to prevent you from doing something he/she considered dangerous or harmful.)

45. To bring about a change in your behavior for his or her own good?
(examples: By getting angry at a relatively minor incident, the person hoped you would not bother him again in the future. You had a habit which the person did not like and wanted you to change.)

| 0 | +1 | +2 | ? |

46. To break off a relationship with you?
(examples: The person wished to end a friendship or romance, and therefore became angry in order to have an excuse for not seeing you again.)

| 0 | +1 | +2 | ? |

47. To strengthen a relationship with you?
(examples: By becoming angry, the person hoped to increase communication and end conflict. The person wished to increase understanding with you.)

| 0 | +1 | +2 | ? |

48. To assert authority or independence, or to improve his/her self-image?
(examples: The person used his anger to increase self-esteem or maintain prestige, gain respect, or support his opinions.)

| 0 | +1 | +2 | ? |

49. To express general dislike for you?
(examples: The person simply did not care for you so he seized the opportunity to vent his feelings when you did something "wrong.")

| 0 | +1 | +2 | ? |

50. To "let off steam" over miscellaneous frustrations of the day which had nothing to do with the present incident?
(examples: The person got angry over a relatively minor incident because he/she was upset from lots of little things that had gone wrong during the day.)

| 0 | +1 | +2 | ? |

51. In your own words, briefly describe any motives or goals you think may have been involved in the other person's anger. (Your description should help clarify your responses to the above items.)

_____

_____

_____

_____

H. The following questions deal with *your own* impressions of, and reactions to, the other person's anger.

52. Did the other person's anger come as a surprise to you, or did you expect that it would occur?

_____ Not at all expected
_____ Somewhat expected
_____ Very much expected

53. Sometimes, when someone becomes angry at us, we sense their anger through subtle cues, and/or our knowledge of the circumstances, long before they show it or declare it in any outright manner. Which of the following were involved in your initial impression that the other person was angry? *Mark as many items as are appropriate* according to the following scale:

$$0 = \text{not at all involved}$$
$$+1 = \text{somewhat involved in your initial impression of the other person's anger}$$
$$+2 = \text{very much involved in your initial impression of the other person's anger}$$

You *first* sensed that the other person may have been angry:

	not at all	some- what	very much
a) from the person's expressive reactions			
1) facial expressions	0	+1	+2
2) body posture or gestures	0	+1	+2
3) tone of voice	0	+1	+2
b) from the precipitating incident, i.e., you knew something had happened which would make this person angry	0	+1	+2
c) from the way the person acted			
1) the person became withdrawn or non-communicative	0	+1	+2
2) the person became physically aggressive	0	+1	+2
d) from the content of what he/she said (example: the person told you he was angry, or made a nasty remark)	0	+1	+2

Please explain, adding any other cues that may have been important to your first impression that the other person may have been angry.

_____

_____

_____

54. On the following scale, indicate the *relative* importance that situational as opposed to personal cues played in your initial impression of the other person's
anger. For example, a value of "–3" indicates that you relied exclusively on
situational factors (the precipitating incident), and a value of "+3" indicates
that you relied exclusively on personal cues (the responses of the individual);
a "–1" would indicate that both types of cues were important, but situational
cues slightly more so; and a "0" would indicate that both kinds of cues were
equally important.

	–3	–2	–1	0	+1	+2	+3	

situational factors   both kinds of   personal factors
(i.e., the precipitating   cues were   (i.e., the person's
event provided the   equally   responses provided
most important   important   the most
cues)   important cues)

55. Please explain why you chose the number you did on the above scale.

_____

_____

_____

56. How did you react when you realized that the other person was angry?

You reacted with:

	not at all	some-what	very much
a. Indifference or lack of concern	0	+1	+2
b. Hurt feelings	0	+1	+2
c. Defiance	0	+1	+2
d. Anger or hostility	0	+1	+2
e. Jokes, frivolity, or silliness	0	+1	+2
f. Apology or other sign of contrition	0	+1	+2
g. Rejection	0	+1	+2
h. Denial of responsibility	0	+1	+2
i. Surprise	0	+1	+2
j. Other (specify) _____	0	+1	+2

57. Regardless of how you reacted, how did you *feel* when you realized the person
was angry?

a. good, pleased, glad	0	+1	+2
b. irritable, hostile, aggravated	0	+1	+2
c. confident, dominant, self-assured	0	+1	+2
d. depressed, unhappy, gloomy	0	+1	+2
e. ashamed, embarrassed, guilty	0	+1	+2

	not at all	some-what	very much
f. relieved, calm, satisfied	0	+1	+2
g. anxious, jittery, nervous	0	+1	+2
h. bewildered, confused, perplexed	0	+1	+2
i. other (specify)	0	+1	+2

58. Describe any other ways you reacted or felt about the other person's anger.

_____

_____

_____

_____

59. Everything considered, do you think that your responses in this instance were very typical ____, somewhat typical ____, or not at all typical ____ of how *you* generally respond when someone becomes angry at you?

60. Everything considered, do you think that your responses in this instance were very typical ____, somewhat typical ____, or not at all typical ____ of how *other people* generally respond when someone becomes angry at them?

J. In addition to the reactions mentioned in the previous question, you may have done a variety of things as a result of the person's anger. Read through the following list of possible responses (items 61-68) and circle the appropriate number in the right-hand column according to the following scale:

$$0 = \text{not at all}$$
$$+1 = \text{somewhat}$$
$$+2 = \text{very much}$$

As a result of the person's anger:	not at all	some-what	very much
61. You did something that was for your own good. (examples: You finally did the work that you had long been putting off; You stopped acting in a way that was potentially harmful to you.)	0	+1	+2
62. You did something that was for the good of the angry person. (examples: You took the person out to the movies, or prepared a special dinner; You let the person do something that he or she especially wanted to do; You let the person out of doing something he didn't want to do.)	0	+1	+2
63. You gained respect for the angry person. (examples: The person rightfully stood up for	0	+1	+2

	not at all	some- what	very much

what he or she believed in; You no longer take
the person's ideas for granted.)

64. You lost respect for the angry person.   0   +1   +2
   (examples: You decided the person was basically
   petty, and you no longer respect him or her as
   much as you did in the past.)

65. You realized your own faults.   0   +1   +2
   (examples: You became aware of some of your
   own shortcomings, and how they affect others.)

66. You realized your own strengths.   0   +1   +2
   (examples: The person's anger made you even
   more convinced that you were right; You
   became aware of your ability to stand up for
   your convictions.)

67. You felt your relationship with the angry   0   +1   +2
   person was strengthened.
   (examples: Greater communication and
   understanding was established between you
   and the angry person.)

68. Your relationship with the angry person   0   +1   +2
   became cooler or more distant as a result
   of this incident.
   (examples: This person's anger made you
   realize that it was no longer possible for your
   relationship to continue as it had in the past.)

69. Describe any other things you may have done or ways you may have changed
   as a consequence of the other person's anger.

   _____

   _____

   _____

K. Overall evaluation of the incident.

70. Everything considered (the nature of the precipitating incident, the other person's anger, your own reactions, and the long-term consequences), do you
   believe that this episode of anger was adaptive (beneficial) _____ or maladaptive
   (harmful) _____ ?

Please explain:_____

_____

_____

_____

* * *

References

Adler, A. *Understanding human nature*. New York: Fawcett World Library, 1954.

Adler, A. *Problems of neurosis*. New York: Harper Torchbooks, 1964.

Aida, Y. [*The structure of consciousness among the Japanese.*] Tokyo: Kodansha, 1970.

Allen, J. G., & Haccoun, D. M. Sex differences in emotionality: A multidimensional approach. *Human Relations*, 1976, *29*, 711-722.

Anastasi, A., Cohen, N., & Spatz, D. A study of fear and anger in college students through the controlled diary method. *Journal of Genetic Psychology*, 1948, *73*, 243-249.

Antrobus, J. S., Singer, J. L., & Greenberg, S. Studies in the stream of consciousness: Experimental enhancement and suppression of spontaneous cognitive processes. *Perceptual and Motor Skills*, 1966, *23*, 399-417.

Aquinas, T. *Summa Theologiae* (60 vols., Blackfriars). New York: McGraw-Hill, 1964.

Ardrey, R. *The hunting hypothesis*. New York: Atheneum, 1976.

Aristotle, *The basic works of* . . . (R. McKeon, Ed.; Oxford translation). New York: Random House, 1941.

Arnold, M. B., & Gasson, J. A. Feelings and emotions as dynamic factors in personality integration. In M. B. Arnold (Ed.), *The nature of emotion*. Harmondsworth: Penguin Books, 1968.

Atkinson, J. W. *An introduction to motivation*. Princeton, N.J.: Van Nostrand, 1964.

Augustine. *The city of God* (Vol. 7). Cambridge, Mass.: Harvard University Press, 1966.

Austin, J. L. Other minds. In J. L. Austin, *Philosophical papers*. London: Oxford University Press, 1961. (Originally published, 1946.)

Averill, J. R. An analysis of psychophysiological symbolism and its influence on theories of emotion. *Journal for the Theory of Social Behavior*, 1974, *4*, 147-190.

Averill, J. R. A semantic atlas of emotional concepts. JSAS *Catalog of Selected Documents in Psychology*, 1975, *5*, 330. (Ms. No. 421)

Averill, J. R. Anger. In H. Howe & R. Dienstbier (Eds.), *Nebraska Symposium on Motivation 1978* (Vol. 26). Lincoln: University of Nebraska Press, 1979.

Averill, J. R. A constructivist view of emotion. In R. Plutchik & H. Kellerman (Eds.), *Theories of emotion*. New York: Academic Press, 1980. (a)

Averill, J. R. On the paucity of positive emotions. In K. R. Blankstein, P. Pliner, & J. Polivy (Eds.), *Assessment and modification of emotional behavior*. New York: Plenum Press, 1980. (b)

Averill, J. R., Opton, E. M., Jr., & Lazarus, R. S. Cross-cultural studies of psychophysiological responses during stress and emotion. *International Journal of Psychology*, 1969, *4*, 83-102.

Bach, G. R., & Goldberg, H. *Creative aggression*. Garden City, N.Y.: Doubleday, 1974.

Bach, G. R., & Wyden, P. *The intimate enemy*. New York: Aron Books, 1968.

Balswick, J., & Avertt, C. P. Differences in expressiveness: Gender, interpersonal orientation, and perceived parental expressiveness as contributing factors. *Journal of Marriage and the Family*, 1977, *39*, 121-128.

Bandura, A. *Aggression: A social learning analysis*. Englewood Cliffs, N.J.: Prentice-Hall, 1973.

Barden, R. C., Zelko, F. A., Duncan, S. W., & Masters, J. C. Children's consensual knowledge about the experiential determinants of emotion. *Journal of Personality and Social Psychology*, 1980, *39*, 968-976.

Bardwick, J. M. *In transition*. New York: Holt, Rinehart & Winston, 1979.

Barker, R. G., Dembo, T., & Lewin, K. Frustration and aggression: A study of young children. *University of Iowa Studies in Child Welfare*, 1941, *18*, No. 1.

Baron, R. A. Aggression as a function of audience presence and prior anger arousal. *Journal of Experimental Social Psychology*, 1971, *7*, 515-523.

Baron, R. A. The aggression inhibiting influence of sexual arousal. *Journal of Personality and Social Psychology*, 1974, *30*, 318-322.

Baron, R. A. *Human aggression*. New York: Plenum Press, 1977.

Baron, R. A., & Bell, P. A. Sexual arousal and aggression by males: Effects of type of erotic stimuli and prior provocation. *Journal of Personality and Social Psychology*, 1977, *35*, 79-87.

Beach, F. A. Cross-species comparisons and the human heritage. *Archives of Sexual Behavior*, 1976, *5*, 469-485.

Beck, A. T. *Depression: Clinical, experimental, and theoretical aspects*. New York: Harper & Row, 1967.

Beecher, H. K. *Measurement of subjective responses*. New York: Oxford University Press, 1959.

Beigel, H. G. Romantic love. *American Sociological Review*, 1951, *16*, 327-335.

Bem, S. The measurement of psychological androgyny. *Journal of Consulting and Clinical Psychology*, 1974, *42*, 155-162.

Berkowitz, L. *Aggression: A social psychological analysis*. New York: McGraw-Hill, 1962.

Berkowitz, L. The contagion of violence: An S-R mediational analysis of some effects of observed aggression. In W. J. Arnold & M. M. Page (Eds.), *Nebraska Symposium on Motivation 1971* (Vol. 19). Lincoln: University of Nebraska Press, 1972.

Berkowitz, L. Some determinants of impulsive aggression: Role of mediated associations with reinforcements for aggression. *Psychological Review*, 1974, *81*, 165-176.

Berkowitz, L., & Geen, R. G. Film violence and the cue properties of avaialable targets. *Journal of Personality and Social Psychology*, 1966, *3*, 525-530.

Berkowitz, L., & LePage, A. Weapons as aggression-eliciting stimuli. *Journal of Personality and Social Psychology*, 1967, 7, 202-207.

Berlin, B., Breedlove, D. E., & Raven, P. H. General principles of classification and nomenclature in folk biology. *American Anthropologist*, 1973, *75*, 214-242.

Berscheid, E., & Walster, E. A little bit about love. In T. L. Huston (Ed.), *Foundations of interpersonal attraction*. New York: Academic Press, 1974.

Bigelow, R. The evolution of cooperation, aggression, and self-control. In J. K. Cole & D. D. Jensen (Eds.), *Nebraska Symposium on Motivation 1972* (Vol. 20). Lincoln: University of Nebraska Press, 1973.

Birdwhistell, R. L. *Kinesics and context*. Philadelphia: University of Pennsylvania Press, 1970.

Blackburn, R. Personality in relation to extreme aggression in psychiatric offenders. *British Journal of Psychiatry*, 1968, *114*, 821-828.

Blackburn, R. Personality types among abnormal homicides. *British Journal of Criminology*, 1971, *11*, 14-31.

Bloch, M. *Feudal society*. Chicago: University of Chicago Press, 1961.

Bohannan, P. Theories of homicide and suicide. In P. Bohannan (Ed.), *African homicide and suicide*. Princeton, N.J.: Princeton University Press, 1960.

Borden, R. J. Witnessed aggression: Influence of an observer's sex and values on aggressive responding. *Journal of Personality and Social Psychology*, 1975, *31*, 567-573.

Bossuat, R. *Drouart La Vache, traducteur d'André le chapelain*. Paris: Champion, 1926.

Boucher, J. D. *Emotion and culture project: Lexicon and taxonomy report*. Honolulu: East-West Center, 1980.

Bradley, D. R., Bradley, T. D., McGrath, S. G., & Cutcomb, S. D. Type I error rate of the chi-square test of independence in RXC tables that have small expected frequencies. *Psychological Bulletin*, 1979, *86*, 1290-1297.

Bridges, K. M. B. A genetic theory of the emotions. *Journal of Genetic Psychology*, 1932, *37*, 504-527.

Briggs, J. L. *Never in anger*. Cambridge, Mass.: Harvard University Press, 1970.

Brown, J. S., & Farber, I. E. Emotions conceptualized as intervening variables—with suggestions toward a theory of frustration. *Psychological Bulletin*, 1951, *48*, 465-495.

Brown, R. C., & Tedeschi, J. T. Determinants of perceived aggression. *Journal of Social Psychology*, 1976, *100*, 77-87.

Bry, A. *How to get angry without feeling guilty*. New York: New American Library, 1977.

Bryant, J., & Zillmann, D. Effect of intensification of annoyance through unrelated residual excitation on substantially delayed hostile behavior. *Journal of Experimental Social Psychology*, 1979, *15*, 470-480.

Buck, C. D. *A dictionary of selected synonyms in the principal Indo-European languages*. Chicago: University of Chicago Press, 1949.

Buckland, W. W. *A textbook of Roman law* (3rd ed.). Cambridge: Cambridge University Press, 1966.

Buirski, P., Plutchik, R., & Kellerman, H. Sex differences, dominance, and personality in the chimpanzee. *Animal Behavior*, 1978, *26*, 123-129.

Burnstein, E., & Worchel, P. Arbitrariness of frustration and its consequences for aggression in a social situation. *Journal of Personality*, 1962, *30*, 528-540.

Buss, A. H. *The psychology of aggression*. New York: Wiley, 1961.

Buss, A. H. Instrumentality of aggression, feedback, and frustration as determinants of physical aggression. *Journal of Personality and Social Psychology*, 1966, *3*, 153-162.

Buss, A. H., Booker, A., & Buss, E. Firing a weapon and aggression. *Journal of Personality and Social Psychology*, 1972, *22*, 296-302.

Bygott, J. D. Agonistic behavior, dominance, and social structure in wild chimpanzees of the Gombe National Park. In D. A. Hamburg & E. R. McCown (Eds.), *The great apes*. Menlo Park, Calif.: Benjamin/Cummings, 1979.

Camp, B. W. Verbal mediation in young aggressive boys. *Journal of Abnormal Psychology*, 1977, *86*, 145-153.

Campbell, D. T. On the conflicts between psychology and moral traditions. *American Psychologist*, 1975, *30*, 1103-1126.

Cannon, W. B. *Bodily changes in pain, hunger, fear, and rage* (2nd ed.). New York: Appleton, 1929.

Cannon, W. B. "Voodoo" death. *American Anthropologist*, 1942, *44*, 169-181.

Cantor, N., & Mischel, W. Prototypes in person perception. In L. Berkowitz (Ed.), *Advances in experimental social psychology* (Vol. 12). New York: Academic Press, 1979.

Capellanus, A. *The art of courtly love*. New York: Columbia University Press, 1941. (Originally written ca. 1185.)

Caplan, P. J. Beyond the box score: A boundary condition for sex differences in aggression and achievement striving. In B. A. Maher (Ed.), *Progress in experimental personality research* (Vol. 9). New York: Academic Press, 1979.

Chamberlain, A. F. On the words for "anger" in certain languages. A study in linguistic psychology. *American Journal of Psychology*, 1895, *6*, 585-592.

Chein, I. *The science of behavior and the image of man*. New York: Basic Books, 1972.

Cheng, L. Y. Discussion [of "A comparison of amok and other homicide in Laos" by J. Westermeyer]. *American Journal of Psychiatry*, 1972, *129*, 708-709.

Chesler, P. *Women and madness*. Garden City, N.Y.: Doubleday, 1972.

Chesler, P. Patient and patriarch: Women in the psychotherapeutic relationship. In

V. Gornick & B. K. Moran (Eds.), *Women in sexist society*. New York: Basic Books, 1971.

Clarke, W. C. Temporary madness as theatre: Wild-man behavior in New Guinea. *Oceania*, 1973, *43*, 198-214.

Cohen, A. Social norms, arbitrariness of frustration, and status of the agent of frustration in the frustration-aggression hypothesis. *Journal of Abnormal and Social Psychology*, 1955, *51*, 222-226.

Commonwealth v. *McCusker*, Pa., 292 A2d, 286 (Supreme Court of Pennsylvania, 1972).

Cornelius, R. R. *Weeping as social interaction: The interpersonal logic of the moist eye*. Unpublished doctoral dissertation, University of Massachusetts, Amherst, 1981.

Cullen, E. Adapatations in the kittiwake to cliff-nesting. *Ibis*, 1957, *99*, 275-302.

D'Agostino, R. B. A second look at analysis of variance on dichotomous data. *Journal of Educational Measurement*, 1971, *8*, 327-333.

Darwin, C. *The expression of the emotions in man and animals*. Chicago: University of Chicago Press, 1965. (Originally published, 1872.)

Davitz, J. R. *The language of emotion*. New York: Academic Press, 1969.

Dawe, H. C. An analysis of 200 quarrels of preschool children. *Child Development*, 1934, *5*, 139-157.

Deikman, A. J. Deautomatization and the mystic experience. *Psychiatry*, 1966, *29*, 324-338.

Delgado, J. M. R. Social rank and radio-stimulated aggressiveness in monkeys. *Journal of Nervous and Mental Disease*, 1967, *144*, 383-390.

Delgado, J. M. R. Modulation of emotions by cerebral radio stimulation. In P. Black (Ed.), *Physiological correlates of emotion*. New York: Academic Press, 1970.

Delgado, J. M. R., & Mir, D. Fragmental organization of emotional behavior in the monkey brain. *Annals of the New York Academy of Sciences*, 1969, *159*, 731-751.

Dennett, D. C. *Brainstorms*. Montgomery, Vt.: Bradford Books, 1978.

de Rougemont, D. *Love in the Western world*. New York: Harcourt Brace & World, 1940.

Descartes, R. The passions of the soul. In E. S. Haldane & G. R. T. Ross (trans.), *The philosophical works of Descartes* (Vol. 1). Cambridge: Cambridge University Press, 1968. (Originally written, 1649.)

de Sousa, R. The rationality of emotions. In A. O. Rorty (Ed.), *Explaining emotions*. Berkeley: University of California Press, 1980.

Dewey, J. The reflex arc concept in psychology. *Psychological Review*, 1896, *3*, 357-370.

Dienstbier, R. A. Emotion-attribution theory: Establishing roots and exploring future perspectives. In H. E. Howe, Jr. & R. A. Dienstbier (Eds.), *Nebraska Symposium on Motivation 1978* (Vol. 26). Lincoln: University of Nebraska Press, 1979.

Diogenes Laertius. *Lives of eminent philosophers* (Vol. 2). New York: G. P. Putnam's Sons, 1925.

Doi, T. *The anatomy of dependence*. Tokyo: Kodansha International, 1973.

Dollard, J., Doob, L., Miller, N., Mowrer, O., & Sears, R. *Frustration and aggression*. New Haven, Yale University Press, 1939.

Donnerstein, E. Aggressive erotica and violence against women. *Journal of Personality and Social Psychology*, 1980, *39*, 269-277.

Donnerstein, E., & Berkowitz, L. Victim reactions in aggressive erotic films as a factor in violence against women. *Journal of Personality and Social Psychology*, 1981, *41*, 710-724.

Doob, A. N., & Gross, A. E. Status of frustrator as an inhibitor of horn-honking responses. *Journal of Social Psychology*, 1968, *76*, 213-218.

Drye v. *State*, 184 S.W.2d,10 (Supreme Court of Tennessee, 1944).

Edmunds, G., & Kendrick, D. C. *The measurement of human aggressiveness*. Chichester: Ellis Horwood Ltd., 1980.

Ehrenkrantz, J., Bliss, E., & Sheard, M. H. Plasma testosterone: Correlation with aggressive behavior and social dominance in man. *Psychosomatic Medicine*, 1974, *36*, 469-475.

Eichler, M. The psychoanalytic treatment of an hysterical character with special emphasis on problems of aggression. *International Journal of Psychoanalysis*, 1976, *57*, 37-44.

Ekman, P. Biological and cultural contributions to body and facial movement. In J. Blacking (Ed.), *The anthropology of the body*. New York: Academic Press, 1977.

Ekman, P., & Friesen, W. V. Constants across cultures in the face and emotion. *Journal of Personality and Social Psychology*, 1971, *17*, 124-129.

Ekman, P., & Friesen, W. V. *Unmasking the face*. Englewood Cliffs, N.J.: Prentice-Hall, 1975.

Ekman, P., Friesen, W. V., & Ellsworth, P. *Emotion in the human face*. Elmsford, N.Y.: Pergamon, 1972.

Ekman, P., & Oster, H. Facial expressions of emotion. *Annual Review of Psychology*, 1979, *30*, 527-554.

Elliott, F. A. Neurological aspects of antisocial behavior. In W. H. Reid (Ed.), *The psychopath*. New York: Brunner/Mazel, 1978.

Ellis, A. *How to live with and without anger*. New York: Reader's Digest Press, 1977.

Ellsworth, P. C., & Tourangeau, R. On our failure to disconfirm what nobody ever said. *Journal of Personality and Social Psychology*, 1981, *40*, 363-369.

Esper, E. A. *A history of psychology*. Philadelphia: Saunders, 1964.

Falkowski, J. J. *The development of the concept of love*. Unpublished doctoral dissertation, University of Massachusetts, Amherst, 1975.

Fawl, C. L. Disturbances experienced by children in their natural habitats. In R. G. Barker (Ed.), *The stream of behavior*. New York: Appleton-Century-Crofts, 1963.

FBI Uniform Crime Reports. Washington, D.C.: U.S. Department of Justice, 1980.

Fortenbaugh, W. W. *Aristotle on emotion*. London: Duckworth, 1975.

Fraczek, A., & Macaulay, J. R. Some personality factors in reaction to aggressive stimuli. *Journal of Personality*, 1971, *39*, 163-177.

Frankenhaeuser, M. Psychoneuroendocrine approaches to the study of emotion as related to stress and coping. In H. E. Howe & R. A. Dienstbier (Eds.), *Nebraska Symposium on Motivation 1978* (Vol. 26). Lincoln: University of Nebraska Press, 1979.

Freud, A. Comments on aggression. *International Journal of Psychoanalysis*, 1972, *53*, 163-171.

Freud, S. *A general introduction to psychoanalysis* (G. S. Hall, trans.). New York: Boni and Liveright, 1920.

Freud, S. *New introductory lectures on psycho-analysis*. In J. Strachey (Ed. and trans.), *Standard Edition* (Vol. 22). New York: Norton, 1965. (Originally published, 1933.)

Friday, N. *My mother/my self*. New York: Delacorte Press, 1977.

Frodi, A. The effect of exposure to weapons on aggressive behavior from a cross-cultural perspective. *International Journal of Psychology*, 1975, *10*, 283-292.

Frodi, A. Sexual arousal, situational restrictiveness, and aggressive behavior. *Journal of Research in Personality*, 1977, *11*, 48-58. (a)

Frodi, A. Sex differences in perception of a provocation. *Perceptual and Motor Skills*, 1977, *44*, 113-114. (b)

Frodi, A. Experiential and physiological responses associated with anger and aggression in women and men. *Journal of Research in Personality*, 1978, *12*, 335-349.

Frodi, A. M., & Lamb, M. E. Infants at risk for child abuse. *Infant Mental Health Journal*, 1980, *1*, 240-247.

Frodi, A., Macaulay, J., & Thome, P. R. Are women always less aggressive than men? A review of the experimental literature. *Psychological Bulletin*, 1977, *84*, 634-660.

Frois-Wittmann, J. The judgment of facial expression. *Journal of Experimental Psychology*, 1930, *13*, 113-151.

Fromm, E. *The anatomy of human destructiveness*. New York: Holt, Rinehart & Winston, 1973.

Funkenstein, D. H. Norepinephrine-like and epinephrine-like substances in relation to human behavior. *Journal of Mental Diseases*, 1956, *124*, 58-68.

Gagnon, J. H. Scripts and the coordination of sexual conduct. In J. K. Cole and R. Dienstbier (Eds.), *Nebraska Symposium on Motivation 1973* (Vol. 21). Lincoln: University of Nebraska Press, 1974.

Gallup, G. G., Jr. Self-recognition in primates: A comparative approach to the bidirectional properties of consciousness. *American Psychologist*, 1977, *32*, 329-338.

Gantt, W. H. Principles of nervous breakdown: Schizokinesis and autokinesis. *Annals of the New York Academy of Sciences*, 1953, *56*, 143-163.

Gates, G. S. An observational study of anger. *Journal of Experimental Psychology*, 1926, *9*, 325-331.

Geen, R. G. Effects of frustration, attack, and prior training in aggressiveness upon aggressive behavior. *Journal of Personality and Social Psychology*, 1968, *9*, 316-321.

Geen, R. G., & Berkowitz, L. Name-mediated aggressive cue properties. *Journal of Personality*, 1966, *34*, 456-465.

Geen, R. G., & Stonner, D. The meaning of observed violence: Effects on arousal and aggressive behavior. *Journal of Research in Personality*, 1974, *8*, 55-63.

Gendin, S. Insanity and criminal responsibility. *American Philosophical Quarterly*, 1973, *10*, 99-110.

Gentry, W. D. Effects of frustration, attack, and prior aggressive training on overt aggression and vascular processes. *Journal of Personality and Social Psychology*, 1970, *16*, 718-725.

Gibson, E. *Homicide in England and Wales: 1967-1971*. London: Her Majesty's Stationery Office, 1975.

Gibson, J. J. *The ecological approach to perception*. Boston: Houghton-Mifflin, 1979.

Gil, D. G. *Violence against children: Physical child abuse in the United States*. Cambridge, Mass.: Harvard University Press, 1973.

Given, J. B. *Society and homicide in Thirteenth-century England*. Stanford, Calif.: Stanford University Press, 1977.

Glass, G. V., Peckham, P. D., & Sanders, J. R. Consequences of failure to meet assumptions underlying the fixed effects analysis of variance and covariance. *Review of Educational Research*, 1972, *42*, 237-288.

Glennon, L. M. *Women and dualism*. New York: Longman, 1979.

Goldstein, A. S. *The insanity defense*. New Haven: Yale University Press, 1967.

Goldstein, J. H. *Aggression and crimes of violence*. New York: Oxford University Press, 1975.

Good News Bible. New York: American Bible Society, 1976.

Goodenough, F. L. *Anger in young children*. Minneapolis: University of Minnesota Press, 1931.

Gosling, J. C. Emotion and object. *Philosophical Review*, 1965, *74*, 486-503.

Guttmacher, M. S., & Weihofen, H. *Psychiatry and the law*. New York: W. W. Norton, 1952.

Hager, J. C., & Ekman, P. Methodological problems in Tourangeau and Ellsworth's study of facial expression and experience of emotion. *Journal of Personality and Social Psychology*, 1981, *40*, 358-362.

Hall, G. S. A study of anger. *American Journal of Psychology*, 1899, *10*, 516-591.

Hamburg, D. A., Hamburg, B. A., & Barchas, J. D. Anger and depression in perspective of behavioral biology. L. Levi (Ed.), *Emotions: Their parameters and measurement*. New York: Raven Press, 1975.

Hamilton, E., & Cairns, H. (Eds.). *The collected dialogues of Plato*. New York: Pantheon Books, 1961.

Hardisty, J. H. Mental illness: A legal fiction. *Washington Law Review*, 1973, *48*, 735-762.

Harré, R. The analysis of episodes. In J. Israel & H. Tajfel (Eds.), *The context of social psychology: A critical assessment*. New York: Academic Press, 1972.

Harré, R., & Secord, P. F. *The explanation of social behavior*. Totowa, N.J.: Rowman and Littlefield, 1972.

Harris, M. B. Mediators between frustration and aggression in a field experiment. *Journal of Experimental Social Psychology*, 1974, *10*, 561-571.

Hartup, W. W. Aggression in childhood: Developmental perspectives. *American Psychologist*, 1974, *29*, 336-341.

Hebb, D. O. Emotion in man and animal: An analysis of the intuitive processes of recognition. *Psychological Review*, 1946, *53*, 88-106.

Hebb, D. O. *Textbook of psychology* (3rd ed.). Philadelphia: Saunders, 1972.

Henley, N. M. *Body politics*. Englewood Cliffs, N.J.: Prentice-Hall, 1977.

Henry, J. The linguistic expression of emotion. *American Anthropologist*, 1936, *38*, 250-257.

Hinde, R. A. *Animal behavior* (2nd ed.). New York: McGraw-Hill, 1970.

Hochschild, A. R. Emotion work, feeling rules, and social structure. *American Journal of Sociology*, 1979, *85*, 551-575.

Hoppe, C. M. Interpersonal aggression as a function of subjects' sex, subjects' sex role identification, opponents' sex and degree of provocation. *Journal of Personality*, 1979, *47*, 317-329.

Hull, C. L. *A behavior system: An introduction to behavior theory concerning the individual organism*. New Haven: Yale University Press, 1952.

Ishida, E. The culture of love and hate. In T. S. Lebra & W. P. Lebra (Eds.), *Japanese culture and behavior: Selected readings*. Honolulu: University Press of Hawaii, 1974.

Izard, C. E. Cross-cultural research findings on development in recognition of facial behavior. *Proceedings of the 76th Annual Convention of the American Psychological Association*, 1968, *3*, 727. (Summary)

Izard, C. E. *The face of emotion*. New York: Appleton-Century-Crofts, 1971.

Izard, C. E. *Human emotions*. New York: Plenum Press, 1977.

Izard, C. E. Emotions in personality and psychopathology: An introduction. In C. E. Izard (Ed.), *Emotions in personality and psychopathology*. New York: Plenum Press, 1979.

Izard, C. E. Differential emotions theory and the facial feedback hypothesis of emotion activation: Comments on Tourangeau and Ellsworth's "The role of facial response in the experience of emotion." *Journal of Personality and Social Psychology*, 1981, *40*, 350-354.

Izard, C. E., & Buechler, S. Emotion expressions and personality integration in infancy. In C. E. Izard (Ed.), *Emotions in personality and psychopathology*. New York: Plenum Press, 1979.

James, W. *Principles of psychology* (Vol. 2). Henry Holt, 1890.

Katkin, E. S., Blascovich, J., & Goldband, S. Empirical assessment of visceral self-perception: Individual and sex differences in the acquisition of heartbeat discrimination. *Journal of Personality and Social Psychology*, 1981, *40*, 1095-1101.

Kaufmann, L., & Wagner, B. Barb: A systematic treatment technology for temper control disorders. *Behavior Therapy*, 1972, *3*, 84-90.

Kaye, J. M. The early history of murder and manslaughter. *Law Quarterly Review*, 1967, *83*, 365-395 (part I), 569-601 (part II).

Kelly, G. A. *The psychology of personal constructs* (2 vols.). New York: Norton, 1955.

Kenny, A. *Action, emotion and will*. London: Humanities Press, 1963.

King, H. E. Psychological effects of excitation in the limbic system. In D. E. Sheer (Ed.), *Electrical stimulation of the brain*. Austin: University of Texas Press, 1961.

Koch, K. F. On "possession" behavior in New Guinea. *Journal of the Polynesian Society*, 1968, *77*, 135-146.

Konečni, V. J. The mediation of aggressive behavior: Arousal level versus anger and cognitive labeling. *Journal of Personality and Social Psychology*, 1975, *32*, 706-712.

Kuhn, T. S. *The structure of scientific revolutions* (2nd ed.). Chicago: University of Chicago Press, 1970.

Kunkel, W. *An introduction to Roman legal and constitutional history*. Oxford: The Clarendon Press, 1966.

Kurath, H. *The semantic sources of the words for the emotions in Sanskrit, Greek, Latin, and the Germanic languages*. Menasha, Wis.: George Banta Publishing Company, 1921.

LaBarre, W. The cultural basis of emotions and gestures. *Journal of Personality*, 1947, *16*, 48-68.

Lactantius. *The wrath of God*. In R. J. Deferrari (Editorial Director), *The fathers of the church* (Vol. 54, *Lactantius: Minor works*). Washington, D.C.: Catholic University of America Press, 1965. (Originally written, 313-314.)

Laird, J. D. Self-attribution of emotion: The effects of expressive behavior on the quality of emotional experience. *Journal of Personality and Social Psychology*, 1974, *29*, 475-486.

Langness, L. L. Hysterical psychosis in the New Guinea highlands: A Bena Bena example. *Psychiatry*, 1965, *28*, 258-277.

La Rochefoucauld. *Maxims* (L. Tancock, trans.). Hammondsworth: Penguin Books, 1959. (Originally published, 1665.)

Lazarus, R. S., & Launier, R. Stress-related transactions between persons and environment. In L. A. Pervin & M. Lewis (Eds.), *Perspectives in interactional psychology*. New York: Plenum, 1978.

Lebra, T. S. *Japanese patterns of behavior*. Honolulu: University Press of Hawaii, 1976.

Leeper, R. W. The motivational and perceptual properties of emotions as indicating their fundamental character and role. In M. B. Arnold (Ed.), *Feelings and emotions: The Loyola symposium*. New York: Academic Press, 1970.

Lerner, H. The taboos against female anger. *Menninger Perspective*, 1977, Winter, 5-11. (Also published in *Cosmopolitan*, 1979, November, 331-333.)

Leventhal, H. Emotions: A basic problem for social psychology. In C. Nemeth (Ed.), *Social psychology: Classic and contemporary integrations*. Chicago: Rand McNally, 1974.

Leventhal, H. Toward a comprehensive theory of emotion. In L. Berkowitz (Ed.), *Advances in experimental social psychology* (Vol. 13). New York: Academic Press, 1980.

Lewinsohn, P. M. Clinical and theoretical aspects of depression. In K. S. Calhoon,

H. E. Adams, & K. M. Mitchell (Eds.), *Innovative methods in psychopathology*. New York: Wiley, 1974.

Liebert, R. M., & Poulos, R. W. Television as a moral teacher. In T. Lickona (Ed.), *Moral development and behavior*. New York: Holt, Rinehart & Winston, 1976.

Linsky, A. Stimulating responses to mailed questionnaires. *Public Opinion Quarterly*, 1975, *39*, 82-101.

Linton, R. *The study of man*. New York: Appleton, 1936.

Lorenz, K. Kant's doctine of the a priori in the light of contemporary biology. *General Systems Yearbook*, 1962, *7*, 23-35.

Lubek, I. A brief social psychological analysis of research on aggression in social psychology. In A. R. Buss (Ed.), *Psychology in social context*. New York: Irvington, 1979.

Lucas, R. A. *Men in crisis*. New York: Basic Books, 1969.

Lundsgaarde, H. P. *Murder in space city*. New York: Oxford University Press, 1977.

Lunney, G. H. Using analysis of variance with a dichotomous dependent variable: An empirical study. *Journal of Educational Measurement*, 1970, *7*, 263-269.

Luria, A. R. *The working brain*. New York: Basic Books, 1973.

Lyons, W. *Emotion*. Cambridge: Cambridge University Press, 1980.

Maccoby, E. E., & Jacklin, C. N. *The psychology of sex differences*. Stanford, Calif.: Stanford University Press, 1974.

MacDowell, D. M. *The law in classical Athens*. Ithaca, N.Y.: Cornell University Press, 1978.

McDougall, W. *Outline of psychology*. New York: Scribner's, 1923.

McDougall, W. *An introduction to social psychology* (23rd ed.). London: Methuen, 1936.

McFarland, R. A. Heart rate perception and heart rate control. *Psychophysiology*, 1975, *12*, 402-405.

McKellar, P. The emotion of anger in the expression of human aggressiveness. *British Journal of Psychology*, 1949, *39*, 148-155.

McKellar, P. Provocation to anger and the development of attitudes of hostility. *British Journal of Psychology*, 1950, *40*, 104-114.

McKeon, R. (Ed.). *The basic works of Aristotle*. New York: Random House, 1941.

Mandler, G. *Mind and emotion*. New York: Wiley, 1975.

Mandler, G. Emotion. In E. Hearst (Ed.), *The first century of experimental psychology*. Hillsdale, N.J.: Erlbaum, 1979.

Mark, V. H., & Ervin, F. R. *Violence and the brain*. New York: Harper & Row, 1970.

Marshall, G. D., & Zimbardo, P. G. Affective consequences of inadequately explained physiological arousal. *Journal of Personality and Social Psychology*, 1979, *37*, 970-988.

Marx, K., & Engels, F. *The German ideology*. New York: International Publishers, 1939. (Originally written, 1845-1846.)

Maslach, C. Negative emotional biasing of unexplained arousal. *Journal of Personality and Social Psychology*, 1979, *37*, 953-969.

Mayr, E. The nature of the Darwinian revolution. *Science*, 1972, *176*, 981-989.

Megargee, E. I. Undercontrolled and overcontrolled personality types in extreme antisocial aggression. *Psychological Monographs*, 1966, *80* (3, Whole No. 611).

Meichenbaum, D., & Novaco, R. W. Stress innoculation: A preventive approach. In C. Spielberger & I. Sarason (Eds.), *Stress and anxiety* (Vol. 5). New York: Halstead Press, 1978.

Meltzer, H. Students' adjustments in anger. *Journal of Social Psychology*, 1933, *4*, 285-309.

Melzack, R., & Casey, K. L. The affective dimension of pain. In M. B. Arnold (Ed.), *Feelings and emotions.* New York: Academic Press, 1970.

Menninger, K. Regulatory devices of the ego under major stress. *International Journal of Psychoanalysis*, 1954, *35*, 412-420.

Mervis, C. B., & Rosch, E. Categorization of natural objects. *Annual Review of Psychology*, 1981, *32*, 89-115.

Milgram, S. *Obedience to authority.* New York: Harper & Row, 1974.

Minami, H. *Psychology of the Japanese people* (A. R. Ikona, trans.). Toronto: University of Toronto Press, 1971. (Originally published, 1953, University of Tokyo Press, Tokyo, Japan.)

Model penal code. In *Uniform laws annotated*, Vol. 10. St. Paul, Minn.: West Publishing Co., 1974. (Originally published by the American Law Institute, 1962.)

Monti, P. M., Brown, W. A., & Corriveau, D. D. Testosterone and components of aggressive and sexual behavior in man. *American Journal of Psychiatry*, 1977, *134*, 692-694.

Morse, S. J. Law and mental health professionals: The limits of expertise. *Professional Psychology*, 1978, *9*, 389-399.

Moyer, K. E. *The psychobiology of aggression.* New York: Harper & Row, 1976.

Murphy, H. B. M. History and the evolution of syndromes: The striking case of *Latah* and *Amok*. In M. Hammer, K. Salzinger, & S. Sutton (Eds.), *Psychopathology: Contributions from the social, behavioral, and biological sciences.* New York: Wiley, 1973.

Nagel, E. *Teleology revisited and other essays in the history and philosophy of science.* New York: Columbia University Press, 1979.

Neisser, U. The concept of intelligence. In R. J. Sternberg & D. K. Detterman (Eds.), *Human intelligence: Perspectives on its theory and measurement.* Norwood, N.J.: Ablex, 1979.

Newcomb, T. M. *Social psychology.* New York: Dryden Press, 1950.

Newman, P. L. "Wild man" behaviors in a New Guinea highlands community. *American Anthropologist*, 1964, *66*, 1-19.

Neitzsche, F. W. *Joyful wisdom.* New York: Ungar, 1960. (Originally published, 1882.)

Nisbett, R. E., Borgida, E., Crandall, R., & Reed, H. Popular induction: Information is not always informative. In J. Carroll & J. Payne (Eds.), *Cognitive and social behavior.* Potomac, Md.: Lawrence Erlbaum Associates, 1976.

Nisbett, R. E., & Valins, S. Perceiving the causes of one's own behavior. In E. E. Jones et al. (Eds.), *Attribution: Perceiving the causes of behavior.* New York: General Learning Press, 1971.

Nisbett, R. E., & Wilson, T. D. Telling more than we can know: Verbal reports on mental processes. *Psychological Review*, 1977, *84*, 231-259.

Nolan, J. W. Texas rejects M'Naghten. *Houston Law Review*, 1974, *11*, 946-959.

Novaco, R. W. *Anger control: The development and evaluation of an experimental treatment*. Lexington, Mass.: Lexington Books/D. C. Heath, 1975.

Novaco, R. W. Treatment of chronic anger through cognitive and relaxation controls. *Journal of Consulting and Clinical Psychology*, 1976, *44*, 681.

Novaco, R. W. Stress innoculation: A cognitive therapy for anger and its application to a case of depression. *Journal of Consulting and Clinical Psychology*, 1977, *45*, 600-608.

Novaco, R. W. The cognitive regulation of anger and stress. In P. C. Kendall & S. D. Hollon (Eds.), *Cognitive-behavioral interventions: Theory, research, and procedures*. New York: Academic Press, 1979.

Olweus, D. Stability of aggressive reaction patterns in males: A review. *Psychological Bulletin*, 1979, *86*, 852-875.

Olweus, D., Mattsson, Å., Schalling, D., & Lööw, H. Testosterone, aggression, physical and personality dimensions in normal adolescent males. *Psychosomatic Medicine*, 1980, *42*, 253-269.

Omark, D. R., Omark, M., & Edelman, M. *Dominance hierarchies in young children*. Presented to International Congress of Anthropological and Ethnological Sciences, Chicago, 1973.

Onians, R. B. *The origins of European thought about the body, the mind, the soul, the world, time, and fate*. Cambridge: Cambridge University Press, 1951.

Osgood, C. E. Dimensionality of the semantic space for communication via facial expressions. *Scandinavian Journal of Psychology*, 1966, *7*, 1-30.

Page, M. M., & Scheidt, R. J. The elusive weapons effect: Demand awareness, evaluation apprehension, and slightly sophisticated subjects. *Journal of Personality and Social Psychology*, 1971, *20*, 304-318.

Pap, A. *An introduction to the philosophy of science*. New York: Free Press, 1962.

Parke, R. D., & Collmer, C. W. Child abuse: An interdisciplinary analysis. In E. M. Hetherington (Ed.), *Review of child development research* (Vol. 5). Chicago: University of Chicago Press, 1975.

Parry, J. J. Introduction [to A. Capellanus, *The art of courtly love*]. New York: Columbia University Press, 1941.

Parsons, T. *The social system*. New York: Free Press, 1951.

Pastore, N. The role of arbitrariness in the frustration-aggression hypothesis. *Journal of Abnormal and Social Psychology*, 1952, *47*, 728-731.

Pearce, W. B., & Cronen, V. E. *Communication, action, and meaning: The creation of social realities*. New York: Praeger, 1980.

Pedhazur, E. J., & Tetenbaum, T. J. Bem Sex Role Inventory: A theoretical and methodological critique. *Journal of Personality and Social Psychology*, 1979, *37*, 1699-1712.

Penfield, W. *The mystery of the mind*. Princeton, N.J.: Princeton University Press, 1975.

Penfield, W., & Roberts, L. *Speech and brain mechanisms*. New York: Atheneum, 1966.

People v. *Lewis*, 123 N.Y.S.2d, 81 (Supreme Court, Appellate Division, 1953).

Pepitone, A. Toward a normative and comparative biocultural social psychology. *Journal of Personality and Social Psychology*, 1976, *34*, 641-653.

Perkins, R. M. The law of homicide. *Journal of Criminal Law and Criminology*, 1946, *36*, 391-454.

Plato. *Collected dialogues of . . .* (Edith Hamilton & H. Cairns, Eds.). New York: Bollingen Foundation, 1961.

Plutchik, R. *Emotion: A psychoevolutionary synthesis*. New York: Harper & Row, 1980.

Pribram, K. H. *Languages of the brain*. Englewood Cliffs, N.J.: Prentice-Hall, 1971.

Quarles, F. *Enchyridion*. In A. B. Grosart (Ed.), *The complete works in prose and verse of Fransis Quarles*. Edinburgh: Edinburgh University Press, 1980.

Rangell, L. Aggression, Oedipus, and historical perspective. *International Journal of Psychoanalysis*, 1953, *34*, 177-198.

Rapaport, D. On the psycho-analytic theory of affects. *International Journal of Psychoanalysis*, 1953, *34*, 177-198.

Reischauer, E. O. *Japan: Past and present* (3rd ed.). New York: Knopf, 1964.

Rich, A. *Of woman born: Motherhood as experience and institution*. New York: Norton, 1976.

Rich, M. C. Verbal reports and mental structures. *Journal for the Theory of Social Behavior*, 1979, *9*, 29-37.

Richardson, D. C., Bernstein, S., & Taylor, S. P. The effect of situational contingencies on female retaliative behavior. *Journal of Personality and Social Psychology*, 1979, *37*, 2044-2048.

Richardson, F. *The psychology and pedagogy of anger*. Baltimore: Warwick & York, 1918.

Rickles, N. A. The angry woman syndrome. *Archives of General Psychiatry*, 1971, *24*, 91-94.

Rimm, D. C., de Groot, J. C., Boord, P., Reiman, J., & Dillow, P. W. Systematic desensitization of an anger response. *Behaviour Research and Therapy*, 1971, *9*, 273-280.

Rohner, R. P. Sex differences in aggression: Phylogenetic and enculturation perspectives. *Ethos*, 1976, *4*, 57-72.

Rosch, E. Principles of categorization. In E. Rosch & B. B. Lloyd (Eds.), *Cognition and categorization*. Hillsdale, N.J.: Erlbaum, 1978.

Rosch, E., & Lloyd, B. B. (Eds.), *Cognition and categorization*. Hillsdale, N.J.: Erlbaum, 1978.

Rosenbaum, M. E., & DeCharms, R. Direct and vicarious reduction of hostilities. *Journal of Abnormal and Social Psychology*, 1960, *60*, 105-111.

Rosenblatt, P. C., & Cunningham, M. R. Sex differences in cross cultural perspective. In B. B. Lloyd & A. Archer (Eds.), *Exploring sex differences*. New York: Academic Press, 1976.

Ross, L. The intuitive psychologist and his shortcomings: Distortions in the attribution process. In L. Berkowitz (Ed.), *Advances in experimental social psychology* (Vol. 10). New York: Academic Press, 1977.

Rossi, P. H., Waite, E., Bose, C. E., & Berk, R. E. The seriousness of crimes: Normative structure and individual differences. *American Sociological Review*, 1974, *39*, 224-237.

Rothenberg, A. On anger. *American Journal of Psychiatry*, 1971, *128*, 454-460.

Rozin, P. The evolution of intelligence and access to the cognitive unconscious. In J. M. Sprague & A. N. Epstein (Eds.), *Progress in psychobiology and physiological psychology* (Vol. 6). New York: Academic Press, 1976.

Rubin, T. *The angry book*. New York: Macmillan, 1969.

Rule, B. G., & Hewitt, L. S. Effects of thwarting on cardiac response and physical aggression. *Journal of Personality and Social Psychology*, 1971, *19*, 181-187.

Rumbaugh, D. M. (Ed.). *Language learning by a chimpanzee: The LANA project.* New York: Academic Press, 1976.

Russell, B. *A history of western philosophy*. New York: Simon & Schuster, 1945.

Russell, J. A. A circumplex model of affect. *Journal of Personality and Social Psychology*, 1980, *39*, 1161-1178.

Ryle, G. *The concept of mind*. London: Hutchinson, 1949.

Sabini, J. P., & Silver, M. The social construction of envy. *Journal for the Theory of Social Behavior*, 1978, *8*, 313-332.

Salisbury, R. F. Possession in the New Guinea highlands. *International Journal of Social Psychiatry*, 1968, *14*, 85-94.

Sartre, J. P. *The emotions: Outline of a theory*. (B. Frechtman, trans.). New York: Philosophical Library, 1948.

Sartre, J. P. *The transcendence of the ego*. (F. Williams & R. Kirkpatrick, trans.). New York: Farrar, Straus, & Giroux, 1957.

Sayre, F. B. Mens rea. *Harvard Law Review*, 1932, *45*, 974-1026.

Schachter, J. Pain, fear, and anger in hypertensives and normotensives. *Psychosomatic medicine*, 1957, *19*, 17-29.

Schachter, S. The interaction of cognitive and physiological determinants of emotional state. In L. Berkowitz (Ed.), *Advances in experimental social psychology* (Vol. 1). New York: Academic Press, 1964.

Schachter, S. *Emotion, obesity, and crime*. New York: Academic Press, 1971.

Schachter, S., & Singer, J. E. Cognitive, social, and physiological determinants of emotional state. *Psychological Review*, 1962, *69*, 379-399.

Schafer, R. *A new language for psychoanalysis*. New Haven: Yale University Press, 1976.

Scherer, K. R. Nonlinguistic vocal indicators of emotion and psychopathology. In C. E. Izard (Ed.), *Emotions in personality and psychopathology*. New York: Plenum, 1979.

Schmidt, K., Hill, L., & Guthrie, G. Running amok. *International Journal of Social Psychiatry*, 1977, *23/24*, 264-274.

Schoeck, H. *Envy: A theory of social behavior*. New York: Harcourt, Brace & World, 1969.

Schwartz, R. D. Moral order and sociology of law: Trends, problems, and prospects. In R. H. Turner, J. Coleman, & R. C. Fox (Eds.), *Annual review of sociology* (Vol. 4). Palo Alto, Calif.: Annual Reviews, Inc., 1978.

Scott, J. P. The emotional basis of social behavior. *Annals of the New York Academy of Sciences*, 1969, *159*, 777-790.

Scruton, R. Emotion, practical knowledge and common culture. In A. O. Rorty (Ed.), *Explaining emotions*. Berkeley: University of California Press, 1980.

Searle, J. R. *Speech acts: An essay in the philosophy of language*. Cambridge: Cambridge University Press, 1969.

Segall, A. The sick role concept: Understanding illness behavior. *Journal of Health and Social Behavior*, 1976, *17*, 162-169.

Seligman, M. E. P. *Helplessness: On depression, development, and death*. San Francisco: Freeman, 1975.

Seneca. *On anger*. In J. W. Basore (trans.), *Moral essays*. Cambridge, Mass.: Harvard University Press, 1963. (Originally written, ca. A.D. 40-50.)

Shalgi, M. Aristotle's concept of responsibility and its reflection in Roman jurisprudence. *Israel Law Review*, 1971, *6*, 39-64.

Shope, G. L., Hendrick, T. E., & Geen, R. G. Physical/verbal aggression: Sex differences in style. *Journal of Personality*, 1978, *46*, 23-42.

Siegel, S. The relationship of hostility to authoritarianism. *Journal of Abnormal and Social Psychology*, 1956, *52*, 368-372.

Simon, W. The social, the erotic, and the sensual: The complexities of sexual scripts. In J. K. Cole & R. Dienstbier (Eds.), *Nebraska Symposium on Motivation 1973* (Vol. 21). Lincoln: University of Nebraska Press, 1974.

Skinner, B. F. *Science and human behavior*. New York: Macmillan, 1953.

Skinner, B. F. *Beyond freedom and dignity*. New York: Knopf, 1971.

Smith, E. R., & Miller, F. D. Limits on perception of cognitive processes: A reply to Nisbett and Wilson. *Psychological Review*, 1978, *85*, 355-362.

Solomon, R. C. *The passions*. Garden City, N.Y.: Doubleday (Anchor Press), 1976.

Spanos, N. P., & Hewitt, E. C. The hidden observer in hypnotic analgesia: Discovery or experimental creation? *Journal of Personality and Social Psychology*, 1980, *39*, 1201-1214.

Spielberger, C. D. Theory and research on anxiety. In C. D. Spielberger (Ed.), *Anxiety and behavior*. New York: Academic Press, 1966.

State v. Guido, N.J. 191 A.2d 45 (Supreme Court of New Jersey, 1963).

State v. Remus, No. 29969 (Ohio Com. Pleas, 1927); also, *Ex parte Remus*, 162 N.E. (Supreme Court of Ohio, 1928).

Stepansky, P. E. *A history of aggression in Freud*. New York: International Universities Press, 1977.

Strauss, M. A., Gelles, R. J., & Steinmetz, S. K. *Behind closed doors: Violence in the American family*. Garden City, N.Y.: Doubleday (Anchor Press), 1980.

Swart, C., & Berkowitz, L. The effects of a stimulus associated with a victim's pain on later aggression. *Journal of Personality and Social Psychology*, 1976, *33*, 623-631.

Symonds, M. Psychodynamics of aggression in women. *American Journal of Psychoanalysis*, 1976, *36*, 195-203.

Szasz, T. S. *Law, liberty, and psychiatry*. New York: Collier Books, 1968.

Taylor, C. The explanation of purposive behavior. In R. Boyer & F. Cioffi (Eds.), *Explanations in the behavioral sciences*. Cambridge: Cambridge University Press, 1970.

Taylor, S. P. Aggressive behavior and physiological arousal as a function of provocation and the tendency to inhibit aggression. *Journal of Personality*, 1967, *35*, 297-310.

Taylor, S. P., & Pisano, R. Physical aggression as a function of frustration and physical attack. *Journal of Social Psychology*, 1971, *84*, 261-267.

Tedeschi, J. T., Smith, R. B., & Brown, R. C. A reinterpretation of research on aggression. *Psychological Bulletin*, 1974, *81*, 540-562.

Terrace, H. S., Petitto, L. A., Sanders, R. J., & Bever, T. G. Can an ape create a sentence? *Science*, 1979, *206*, 891-206.

Thomas, C. W., Cage, R. J., & Foster, S. C. Public opinion on criminal law and legal sanctions: An examination of two conceptual models. *Journal of Criminal Law and Criminology*, 1976, *67*, 110-116.

Tinbergen, N. Behavior, systematics, and natural selection. In S. Tax (Ed.), *Evolution after Darwin* (Vol. 1, *The evolution of life*). Chicago: University of Chicago Press, 1960.

Toch, H. *Violent men*. Chicago: Aldine, 1969.

Tomkins, S. S. *Affect, imagery, consciousness* (Vol. 1, *The positive affects*). New York: Springer, 1962.

Tomkins, S. S. *Affect, imagery, consciousness* (Vol. 2, *The negative affects*). New York: Springer, 1963.

Tomkins, S. S. Affect as the primary motivational system. In M. B. Arnold (Ed.), *Feelings and emotions: The Loyola symposium*. New York: Academic Press, 1970.

Tomkins, S. S. Script theory: Differential magnification of affects. In H. E. Howe & R. A. Dienstbier (Eds.), *Nebraska Symposium on Motivation 1978* (Vol. 26). Lincoln: University of Nebraska Press, 1979.

Tomkins, S. S. Affect as amplification: Some modifications in theory. In R. Plutchik & H. Kellerman (Eds.), *Emotion: Theory, research, and experience*. New York: Academic Press, 1980.

Tomkins, S. S. The quest for primary motives: Biography and autobiography of an idea. *Journal of Personality and Social Psychology*, 1981, *41*, 306-329. (a)

Tomkins, S. S. The role of facial response in the experience of emotion: A reply to Tourangeau and Ellsworth. *Journal of Personality and Social Psychology*, 1981, *40*, 355-357. (b)

Tourangeau, R., & Ellsworth, P. C. The role of facial response in the experience of emotion. *Journal of Personality and Social Psychology*, 1979, *37*, 1519-1531.

Turner, C. W., Layton, J. F., & Simons, L. S. Naturalistic studies of aggressive behavior: Aggressive stimuli, victim visibility, and horn honking. *Journal of Personality and Social Psychology*, 1975, *31*, 1098-1107.

Turner, C. W., & Simons, L. S. Effects of subject sophistication and evaluation apprehension on aggressive responses to weapons. *Journal of Personality and Social Psychology*, 1974, *30*, 341-348.

Twain, M. A new crime. In M. Twain, *Sketches old and new*. New York: Harper, 1875.

Ueda, T. [A study of anger in Japanese college students through the controlled diary method.] *Journal of Nara Gakugei University*, 1960, *9*, 21-28. (In Japanese with English summary)

Ueda, T. A study of anger in Japanese college students through the controlled diary method, II. *Journal of Nara Gakugei University*, 1962, *10*, 341-348.

van Wulfften Palthe, P. M. Psychiatry and neurology in the tropics. In C. D. de Langen & A. Lichtenstein (Eds.), *A clinical textbook of tropical medicine*. Amsterdam: G. Kolff, 1936.

Veldman, D., & Worchel, P. Defensiveness and self-acceptance in the management of hostility. *Journal of Abnormal and Social Psychology*, 1961, *63*, 319-325.

von Bar, D. L. *A history of continental criminal law*. New York: Augustus M. Kelley, 1968. (Originally published, 1916.)

von Uexküll, J. *Theoretische Biologie* (2 Aufl.). Berlin: Julius Springer, 1928.

Wenger, M. A. Emotions as visceral action: An extension of Lange's theory. In M. L. Reymert (Ed.), *Feelings and emotions: The Mooseheart-Chicago symposium*. New York: McGraw-Hill, 1950.

Wenger, M. A., Jones, F. N., & Jones, M. H. *Physiological psychology*. New York: Holt, 1956.

Westermeyer, J. A comparison of amok and other homicide in Laos. *American Journal of Psychiatry*, 1972, *129*, 703-708.

Westermeyer, J. On the epidemicity of amok violence. *Archives of General Psychiatry*, 1973, *28*, 873-876.

White, L. A. Erotica and aggression: The influence of sexual arousal, positive affect, and negative affect on sexual behavior. *Journal of Personality and Social Psychology*, 1979, *37*, 591-601.

White, P. Limitations on verbal reports of internal events: A refutation of Nisbett and Wilson and of Bem. *Psychological Review*, 1980, *87*, 105-112.

Whitehead, W. E., Drescher, V. M., Heiman, P., & Blackwell, B. Relation of heart rate control to heart beat perception. *Biofeedback and Self-Regulation*, 1977, *2*, 371-392.

Whiting, B., & Edwards, C. P. A cross-cultural analysis of sex differences in the behaviors of children aged three through 11. *Journal of Social Psychology*, 1973, *91*, 171-188.

Wilson, J. R. S. *Emotion and object*. Cambridge: Cambridge University Press, 1972.

Winer, D. Anger and dissociation: A case study of multiple personality. *Journal of Abnormal Psychology*, 1978, *87*, 368-372.

Wittgenstein, L. *Philosophical investigations*. Oxford: Basil Blackwell & Mott, 1953.

Wittgenstein, L. *The blue and brown books*. Oxford: Basil Blackwell & Mott, 1958.

Wolf, S. G. *The stomach*. New York: Oxford University Press, 1965.

Wolfgang, M. E. *Patterns of criminal homicide*. Philadelphia: University of Pennsylvania Press, 1958.

Wolfgang, M. E. Aggression and violence: Crime and social control. In S. Feshbach & A. Fraczek (Eds.), *Aggression and behavior change*. New York: Praeger, 1979.

Wolfgang, M. E., & Ferracuti, F. *The subculture of violence*. New York: Barnes and Noble, 1967.

Woodworth, R. S. *Psychology: A study of mental life*. New York: Holt, 1921.

Worchel, P. Status restoration and the reduction of hostility. *Journal of Abnormal and Social Psychology*, 1960, *63*, 443-445.

Worchel, S. The effect of three types of arbitrary thwarting on the instigation to aggression. *Journal of Personality*, 1974, *42*, 301-318.

Words and Phrases. St. Paul, Minn.: West Publishing Co., 1953 (Vol. 3), 1957 (Vol. 31A).

Zillmann, D. Excitation transfer in communication-mediated aggressive behavior. *Journal of Experimental Social Psychology*, 1971, 7, 419-434.

Zillmann, D. Attribution and misattribution of excitatory reactions. In J. H. Harvey, W. J. Ickes, & R. F. Kidd (Eds.), *New directions in attribution research* (Vol. 2). Hillsdale, N.J.: Erlbaum, 1978.

Zillmann, D. *Hostility and aggression*. Hillsdale, N.J.: Erlbaum, 1979.

Zillmann, D., & Bryant, J. Effect of residual excitation on the emotional response to provocation and delayed aggressive behavior. *Journal of Personality and Social Psychology*, 1974, *30*, 782-791.

Zillmann, D., & Cantor, J. R. Effect of timing of information about mitigating circumstances on emotional responses to provocation and retaliatory behavior. *Journal of Experimental Social Psychology*, 1976, *12*, 38-55.

Zillmann, D., Johnson, R. C., & Day, K. D. Attribution of apparent arousal and proficiency of recovery from sympathetic activation affecting excitation transfer to aggressive behavior. *Journal of Experimental Social Psychology*, 1974, *10*, 503-515.

Zimring, F. E., Eigen, J., & O'Malley, S. Punishing homicide in Philadelphia. *University of Chicago Law Review*, 1976, *43*, 227-252.

Author Index

Subject Index